Environmental Geography and Sustainable Society

About the Editors

Subrata Pan, Assistant Professor of Geography, Department of Geography, Bankura Christian College. Formerly associated with National Atlas and Thematic Mapping Organization, Department of Science and Technology, Government of India and former Lecturer of Geography, Department of Geography, Kalinagar Mahavidyalaya, University of Calcutta, West Bengal. He has more than 17 years of teaching and research experience.

Somnath Mukherjee, Assistant Professor of Geography, Department of Geography, Bankura Christian College. Formerly associated with J.K. College, Purulia, University of Burdwan, West Bengal. He has more than 11 years of teaching and research experience.

Druheen Chakrabortty, Assistant Professor of Geography, Department of Geography, Bankura Christian College. He has more than 7 years of teaching and research experience.

Swarup Ganguly, Department of Geography, Bankura Christian College. He has more than 16 years of teaching and research experience.

ENVIRONMENTAL GEOGRAPHY AND SUSTAINABLE SOCIETY

Edited by
Subrata Pan
Somnath Mukherjee
Druheen Chakrabortty
Swarup Ganguly

CONCEPT PUBLISHING COMPANY PVT. LTD.
NEW DELHI-110059

ISBN-13: 978-93-86682-26-0

First Published 2018

Published and Printed by

Concept
Since 1974

Concept Publishing Company Pvt. Ltd.
A/15-16, Commercial Block, Mohan Garden,
New Delhi-110059 (INDIA)
T: 91 11 25351460, 91 011 25351794
E: publishing@conceptpub.com, *W*: www.conceptpub.com

Cataloging in Publication Data--Courtesy: D.K. Agencies (P) Ltd. <docinfo@dkagencies.com>

Environmental geography and sustainable society / edited by Subrata Pan [and three others].
pages cm
Contributed articles.
Includes bibliographical references and index.
ISBN 9789386682260

1. Environmental geography—India—West Bengal. 2. Environmental geography—India. 3. Sustainable development—India—West Bengal. 4. Sustainable development—India. I. Pan, Subrata, editor.

LCC G143.E58 2018 DDC 333.7095414 23

Dedicated to
The Students of
Department of Geography
Bankura Christian College
and
Our Beloved Parents and Teachers

Foreword

The term "Sustainable Development" first appeared in the Brundtland Report in the year 1987 is defined as the "the development that meets the needs of the present generations without compromising the ability of future generations to meet their own needs". The "Club of Rome" established in the year 1968, advocated for zero growth considering the over-exploitation of nature and natural resources. The causes of over-exploitation of natural resources are known to be many including poverty, population, pollution, inequality in the distribution of wealth, in addition to our way of viewing the nature.

Sustainable development is multidimensional in nature involving the management of natural resources and various social, institutional, technological and cultural aspects. Although, it is generally accepted that our present trends of development should urgently be shifted to the path for achieving sustainable development, initiatives for sustainable development are scattered, scanty and not well promoted. In this circumstance, the volume, "Environmental Geography and Sustainable Society" edited by Dr. Subrata Pan, Dr. Somnath Mukherjee, Mr. Druheen Chakrabortty and Mr. Swarup Ganguly would have significant bearing to the academicians, students as well as to the society.

I believe that the said volume comprising twenty seven articles in six heads certainly add new information that would help promote sustainable development and to build sustainable society.

Dr. Fatik Baran Mandal
Principal
Bankura Christian College
Bankura-722101
West Bengal

Preface

"Environmental Geography and Sustainable Society" attempts to present a synoptic view of the man's activities in changing the face of the earth. This edited volume is designed to provide accurate, orderly and rational description of what is going on in the field of environmental studies. The approach is more geographic in character and the environment is viewed from geographer's point of view. It is also an attempt of bridging the gap between physical as well as human geography. The division in six units has been done to make the volume more attractive and readable to the readers of varied interests.

This volume is succinct, concise and elaborate. The basic concepts are illustrated with findings. We hope the contents and deliberations in this book will definitely provide useful information and methods of study to the interested persons. We know that this study is not sufficient. More introspection needs to be addressed for the understanding of this highly complex issue. Our efforts would be successful if the readers find this report useful in furtherance of research and development in this field. We also expect this to be interdisciplinary. Hence, we have accepted papers from other disciplines too. We believe the analysis and data provided in this volume must benefit not only to the physical and biological scientists, but also to the researchers and scientists in the field of humanities and social science.

We apologise for any errors or omissions and would be grateful if any suggestions or correction is being notified to us from the academic fraternity. We will be privileged if such comments reach to us.

Bankura (W.B.)

Subrata Pan
Executive Editor

Acknowledgements

Any work would not be complete unless collective effort is given. This volume is an example of this collective effort. It got its present shape by the efforts of many distinguished persons who have been really helpful in completing this huge task. At the outset, I like to thank all the contributors who have taken all the pains to write for this volume in such a timely fashion. The help and support of the editors in bringing out this volume needs no mention. At Concept Publishing Company (P) Ltd., New Delhi. I have come across with the person Ashok Kumar Mittal (Managing Director) who really possesses great geographic intellects and he has more geographic wisdom than I actually have. He guided me from the very beginning, from the epistemic cuts in the body of Environmental Geography to the selection of the title of the volume. It is he for whom the present volume has got its present good shape. Along with him, I am really thankful to his entire devoted team of publication.

Finally, I must be thankful to the person—the great scholar and teacher of biological science who has been instrumental in bringing out this volume is Dr. F.B. Mandal our beloved principal sir.

Subrata Pan
Executive Editor

Contents

FORESTRY AND ENVIRONMENT

URBANISATION AND ENVIRONMENT

AGRICULTURE, INDUSTRY AND ENVIRONMENT

List of Contributors

Amrit Kamila, Research Scholar, Dept. of Remote Sensing and GIS, Vidyasagar University, Midnapore.

Arijit Sinhababu, Assistant Professor, Dept of Botany, Bankura Christian College.

ArnabSensgupta, Research Scholar, Dept. of Remote Sensing and GIS, Vidyasagar University, Midnapore.

Arpita Banerjee, Assistant Professor, Dept of Botany, Bankura Christian College.

Ashis Kr. Paul, Professor, Dept. of Geography, Vidyasagar University, Midnapore

Ayanika Sarkar, UGC- JRF, Department of Geography, The University of Burdwan, (ayanika.geo@gmail.com)

Biswajit Das, Junior Research Fellow, Department of Geography, The University of Burdwan, West Bengal, India.

Biswajit Roy Chowdhury, Lecturer in Geography, Vidyasagar College, Kolkata, profbrc@gmail.com

Biswaranjan Mistri, Assistan. Professor, Department of Geography, The University of Burdwan, Golapbab, Barddhaman.

BiswaranjanMistri, Assistant Professor, Department of Geography, The University of Burdwan, (brmistri@gmail.com)

Bumba Khan, Ex-student, Vidyasagar College, Kolkata.

Dillip Kumar Das, Central University of Technology, Free State, 20 President Brand Street, Bloemfontein, South Africa. Email: ddas@cut.ac.za

Donald R. Mawkhlieng, Department of Mathematical Demography and Statistics, International Institute for Population Sciences, Mumbai, 400088. E-mail: mawdonric@gmail.com

Indrani Mukherjee, Department of Geography, Chandrapur College, Chandrapur, Burdwan. E-mail: indranimukherjee662@gmail.com

Jayanta Kumar Maity, Asst. Teacher of Geography, Dudcomra Vidyasagar Vidyapith, Vill. & Post- Patanda, Purba Medinipur. E-mail ID– jayantamaity76@gmail.com

Jill A. Marbaningi· Synod Orphanage Centre, Nongstoin, West Khasi Hills, Meghalaya. 793119, E-mail: jannaveel@yahoo.in

Krishna Biswas, UGC-JRF, Department of Geography, Visva-Bharati, Santiniketan, West Bengal, India.

Kshudiram Chakraborty, Ph.D. Research Scholar, Department of Geography, The University of Burdwan, Golapbab, Barddhaman.

Madhumoy Pal, Assistant teacher, Benda Junior High School, Bankura, West Bengal. E-mail: madhumoypal@gmail.com

Mahua Chatterjee, Assistant Professor, Department of Geography, Lady Brabourne College, Kolkata 700017.

Malavika Sinha· Assistant Professor, Department of Geography, Jogamaya Devi College, Kol. 26. Email: malavikasinha@yahoo.co.in

Manoranjan Chakraborty, Assistant Professor, Department of Botany, Bankura Christian College, Bankura, West Bengal, Pin-722101. e-mail: mrc.bot@gmail.com

Nabendu Sekhar Kar, Assistant Professor of Geography, ShahidMatanginiHazra Government College for Women.

P. Masilamani, Assistant Professor,, Department of Geography,, Bharathidasan University, Tiruchirappalli-620 024.

Partha Nandi· Ex-Student, P.G. Department of Geography, Chandernagore Government College, Chandernagore, Hugli.

Premangshu Chakrabarty, Associate Professor, Department of Geography, Visva-Bharati, Santiniketan, West Bengal , India.

Prithviraj Karak, Assistant Professor, Department of Physiology, Bankura Christian College, Bankura, Pin-722101.

Prof. Sanat Kumar Guchhait, Professor, Post Graduate Dept. of Geography, The University of Burdwan, Barddhaman (W.B.).

Ramamrita Singha Mahapatra, Assistant Teacher, Dubrajpur Sammilani High School, Bankura, *galpolok@gmail.com*

S. Abdul Rahaman, Research Fellow, Department of Geography, Bharathidasan University,, Tiruchirappalli-620 024.

S. Aruchamy,, Professor(Rtd) , Department of Geography,, Bharathidasan University,, Tiruchirappalli-620 024.

Sanjib Chakraborty, Ex-Student, Department of Geography, Bankura Christian College, Bankura, West Bengal.

Sanu Dolui, Ph.D. Research scholar at department of geography, University of Burdwan,Burdwan, westbengal. Sanudolui902@gmail.com

Shrabani Dutta Sinha, Assistant Teacher, DubrajpurSammilani High School, Bankura, *Shrabanidutta61@gmail.com*

Shyamal Dutta, Research Scholar, Post Graduate Dept. of Geography, The University of Burdwan, Barddhaman (W.B.). duttashyamal1987@ gmail.com

Sk Majharul Islamm, Research Scholar, Dept. of Remote Sensing and GIS, Vidyasagar University, Midnapore.

Sk Md. Ismail Al Amin· Research Scholar, Dept. of Botany, Vidyasagar University, Midnapore.

Somnath Rudra, Assistant Professor of Geography, ManbhumMahavidyalaya, Manbazar, Purulia, West Bengal, Email: rudra 347@rediffmail.com

Subodh Chandra Pal, Assistant Professor, Department of Geography, TheUniversity of Burdwan, West Bengal, India.

Subrata Jana, Dept. of Geography, Vidyasagar University, Midnapore.

Sumanta Bid, Research Scholar, Department of Geography, The University of Burdwan.

Susmita Das, Assistant teacher, Gangajalghati Girls Junior High School, Bankura, Westbengal. Email: susmita.das320@gmail.com

Suvradip Halder, Research (Ph.D.) Scholar in Geography, University of Calcutta, Kolkata, West Bengal. suvradip.halder@gmail.com

Introduction

Subrata Pan

The study of environment has always been a recurring theme since its first odyssey as academic discipline. Geography in the ancient age has been defined by Eratosthenes (276 BC) as "the study of the earth as the home of man". This definition has changed a little since then as Hagget (1981) defined it as "the study of the earth's surface as the space within which the human population lives" (Adhikari, 2006). In this long two thousand years, the man-environment relationship has been the focal theme in the discipline. The long standing analysis of these two elements has given birth to three major schools of thought in geography—classical German determinism, post-classical French possibilism and the modern neo-determinism. In the earlier days, people gave more emphasis on natural phenomena than the activities of man; in the intermediate phase it started raising questions on control of nature while in the later stage, the rational man understood the importance of environment in the survival of mankind.

Environmental geography may be said to be the outgrowth of this paradigmatic shift in man-environment relationship. In this way environmental geography has emerged as one of the most important discipline to bridge the long standing gap between the natural sciences and the study of mankind—the economy, society and polity. In geography, it bridges the age-old dichotomy between physical and human branches. The British geographer Mackinder's words in this regard may be remembered, "Geography is the science whose main function is to trace the interaction of man in society and so much of his environment as varies locally". Slowly the environmental geography started occupying the fertile borderlands between physical and human geography (Castree, Demeritt, Liverman and Rhoads, 2009). The scope of geography has also changed from the whole earth in the ancient phase to the earth's surface in modern age. As a consequence, study of 'space' and 'region' has been the focal theme of present day geography. As the environmental geography covers the interdisciplinary fields of research in both physical and human branches, geographers should give special attention to this recently emerging sub-discipline. However, it can be said that geography's public image around the world is partly due to its focus on man-environment interrelations (Castree, Demeritt, Liverman and Rhoads, 2009). Environmental geography should be regarded as a binding discipline to hold the two parts of the discipline together. With the diversified intersection of these two fields of knowledge, this branch can be one of the most diverse and vibrant field of study. It can incorporate the subject matter and methods of both the physical and human geography.

The present volume is designed to represent this multifaceted character of the subject and its vibrant methods of analysis. It aims to show that geographers can better handle the aspects of environment as they are more equipped with spatial analysis tool. Geographers can analyse better the interaction between man and environment in spatial as well as temporal scale. This volume also makes others believe that environment is not only the domain of biological scientists. The interaction between environment, man and its society has always been better studied in geographic arena. One of the major impetus for this book is to rediscover geography in the form of environmental studies as most of the geographers now believe that geography can be revitalized with the help of environment with their own spatial analysis tool.

The present volume consisting of twenty seven deiiberations has been cut into six relevant parts—'Geomorphology and Environment', 'Forestry and Environment', 'Urbanisation and Environment', 'Agriculture, Industry and Environment', 'Water and Environment' and 'Society, Culture, Tourism and Environment'. These six subsections clearly show the fertile borderlands of physical and human geography. However, the dcliberations have been so selected in the volume to maintain symmetry between physical and human aspects. Nevertheless, only twelve chapters in three subsections can be accommodated from physical standpoint. The working definition of environmental geography that we have considered here is *any form of geographic study which incorporates the impact of man's activities on physical or cultural element of the earth's surface.* If the impact is on physical element like geomorphology, hydrology, pedology, forestry and alike those are included in the physical side. If on the other hand, the impact is on any cultural element like agriculture, industry, urbanisation, society, culture and tourism those are included in the human side. These intersections in the body of environmental geography manifest six different ways of man's role in changing the face of the earth. Each and every chapter is independent in thought, substantial in coverage, unique in methodology and as a result readers can start from any part of the book. A short look on the subsections of the book surely reveals a wide ranging aspects and materials in the man-environment relationship. We believe these features of the book will definitely make the volume more lively, interesting and a detailed account in this field. We believe it will be beneficial to both the students, scholars and teaching fraternity working in this area.

References

Adhikari, S. (2015), *Fundamentals of Geographical Thought*, New Delhi: Orient Black Swan.

Singh, S. (1991), *Environmental Geography*, Prayag Pustak Bhavan, Allahabad.

Castree, N., Demeritt, D., Liverman, D. and Rhoads, B. (2009), *A Companion to Environmental Geography*, USA: Wiley Blackwell.

Background

1
Greening Paradigms for Cities in Developing Countries

Dillip Kumar Das

1. Introduction

Cities are the key engines of economic growth, job creation and innovation. Paradoxically they are also major contributors to global warming and environmental problems (Hammer, Kamal-Chaoui, Robert and Plouin, 2011). Thus, the cities are facing daunting socio-economic and environmental challenges. Currently, about 3.5 billion people lives in urban areas and cities and about 70 per cent of the total population of the world are expected to live in cities by 2050 (UNFPA, 2009; UN-Habitat, 2010). Further, more than 500 cities are expected to have more than 1.0 million population and there will be several megacities having population exceeding 20 million. The huge urban population will require enormous amount of resources such as food, water and energy, and infrastructure, and will generate huge quality of wastes as well. Such challenges along with the challenge of climate change and economic down-turn threaten the sustainability of the cities. So, these socio-economic and demographic challenges conjoined with the global recession that occurred in the recent past and the continued concern over challenges of climate change raised questions over the ability of the current models for sustainable economic growth and environmental sustainability of cities. Consequently, a number of countries around the globe have initiated a wide range of policy and strategies to kick-start economic recovery and manage the environment. One such strategy that has been intensively pursued is the green growth strategy to transform the economy to green economy, and the cities remain at the heart of this transition. According to the interim report of OECD (2010a) on the green growth strategy, many countries have incorporated a green growth component in their economic recovery and stimulus packages and created structures to evaluate policies from an economic efficiency, environmental quality, and social equity perspective (OECD, 2010a) because the well-being of cities are intimately tied to the socio-economic and environmental challenges, particularly on the resource (food water and energy), infrastructure and governance nexus. However, while the green growth strategy or green city concept is largely being adopted in the developed countries and cities, the cities in developing world keep similar aspirations to engender green growth strategy and develop as green cities. The challenges in the developing countries however are plentiful. For example, the inadequate public transportation system in cities of South Africa has led to a system depending on privately owned cars or as popularly known as of one man one car system. Similarly, the consumption of huge amount of energy in the public buildings such as university buildings is adding to the already stressed energy supply in the cities of the country. The waste disposal system in Harare, Zimbabwe has resulted to transformation of one of the largest lake in the country—Lake Chivero to one of the most polluted lakes in the country. The apathetic attitude of decision-makers, and municipal authorities and lack of environmental justice and equity and non-inclusion of stakeholders in solid waste management system in Kinshasa, Democratic Republic of Congo (DRC) has made the poor areas of the city inhabitable. Similarly, the poor planning of regional transportation infrastructure in India ensues not only an unsustainable transportation system that is plagued by severe congestion, travel time delays, and traffic crashes but also impacts the economic sustainability of the cities and regions. Thus, such challenges necessitated investigations and evolving of plausible policy interventions in order to realise the aim of greening agenda of cities in developing countries. Therefore, using case studies of cities from countries like South Africa, Zimbabwe, Democratic Republic of Congo and India, the chapter explores how green growth and green cities can be engendered in the cities of developing countries in Africa and Indian subcontinent. In the rest of the sections of this explorative chapter, a discourse on green city concept based on the available literature has been developed. Followed by analysis of different greening paradigms under resource—infrastructure and governance aspects of cities such energy, waste management, and transportation were done by applying systems analysis paradigm to explore how they could contribute to the development of sustainable green cities.

2. Conceptualisation of Green Growth and Green Cities

Although, green growth is a debated term, it is generally defined as a means to create jobs and economic growth while reducing costs and environmental impacts over the long run (Hammer, Kamal-Chaoui, Robert and Plouin, 2011). According to OECD (2011b), green growth implies for fostering economic growth and development while ensuring that natural assets continue to provide the resources and ecosystem services on which the well-being of the world rests. It must be built-upon catalysing of investment, competition and innovation that underpin sustained growth and lead to new economic opportunities. Similarly, urban green growth means fostering of economic growth and development through urban activities that reduce negative environmental externalities, the impact on natural resources and the pressure on ecosystem services (Hammer, Kamal-Chaoui, Robert and Plouin, 2011; OECD 2011b). This leads to an argument that the greening of the traditional urban economy and expanding the green urban sector can generate growth, job creation and increase urban attractiveness, which can be engendered from strong interactions among economic efficiency, equity and environmental objectives at the urban level (OECD, 2011b).

The occurrence of large scale economic activities, consumption of resources such as water and energy, generation of wastes, greenhouse gas (GHG) emissions, requirement of huge infrastructure and services such as transportation and waste management make the cities central to this green growth phenomena (Kennedy, Pincetl, Bunje, 2011). Concerning this scholars have argued that there are significant synergies between environmental and economic objectives in urban areas, and green growth at the local scale can reap significant benefits. Besides, if the challenges of expanding economic opportunities for a growing population, and addressing environmental pressures are left untended, the cities will become unsustainable and may be regarded as opportunities lost (Hammer, Kamal-Chaoui, Robert and Plouin, 2011; OECD, 2011b). So, it is a paradigm that promotes economic development while reducing environmental degradation and preserving natural resources. It offers an opportunity to rethink the conventional economic development model. The traditional efficiency paradigm is giving way to a richer definition of societal progress, where efficiency, equity and environmental sustainability are closely interrelated (Hammer, Kamal-Chaoui, Robert and Plouin, 2011).

Thus, the emergence of green cities occurs with a focus on

reduction of carbon emissions from transportation, public-transportation-oriented urban movement system, compact city planning, reform in energy production, promotion of energy-efficient buildings, creation of area-wide energy management systems, reuse of municipal and industrial wastes, improvement of green urban areas, reduction of heat-island effects etc. (ALMEC Corporation, 2011; Zhou and Williams, 2013). In this context, there are several indicators that are to be met in order to transform or develop a city to a green city. The various relevant indicators include CO_2 emissions, intensity and reduction strategy for CO_2 emissions (under carbon emissions); energy consumption, energy intensity, renewable energy consumption, and clean and efficient energy policies (under energy); residential energy consumption, energy efficient building standards, energy and efficient building initiatives (under buildings); use of non-car transport, size of non-car transport network, green transport and congestion reduction policies (under transportation); water consumption, system leakages, water efficiency and treatment policy, treatment municipal waste production, waste recycling, waste reduction and policies (under water and waste water); and green land-use policies (under land-use); nitrogen dioxide (NO_2), ozone (O_3), particulate matter (< 10 microns), sulphur dioxide (SO_2), and clean air policies (under air) and green action plan, green management and public participation (under governance) (EIU, 2009; Zhou and Williams, 2013). Thus, depending on the potentials and challenges the different cities offer, appropriate policy interventions need to be developed to strengthen the weak links and augment the potentials so that cities can become green and socio-economically and environmentally sustainable.

3. Approach of the Investigation

This book chapter is based on the analysis of five case studies from four developing countries encompassing challenges under resource-infrastructure and governance aspects of cities that include energy, transportation, waste water disposal and resource recovery and solid waste management and engagement of various stakeholders and social solidarities. The case studies include: (1) Sustainable Built Infrastructure for Education Complex Neighbourhoods in South African Cities, focusing on energy efficiency in university educational buildings to transform the buildings to green buildings; (2) Sustainable road transportation system in Kanyakumari district, Tamil Nadu (India), which explored that how sustainability in road transportation can be achieved and how sustainable transportation can impact sustainability of city regions in the country; (3) Re-engineering of public transportation systems for suitable green city in central region of South Africa by considering Bloemfontein city of South Africa; (4) Situating an African city in greening paradigms: case for Harare metropolitan region, Zimbabwe, which investigated the possibility of turning liabilities of urban wastes (specifically waste water) into assets for the goodness of urban citizens; and (5) Exploring environmental justice in solid waste management in Kinshasa in DRC, in which the extent to which environmental injustice is occurring in solid waste management in Kinshasa was evaluated by accounting for the critical factors responsible for state of affairs and examined the relevant theoretical framework(s) and mechanisms that would facilitate the attainment of environmental justice in the city. All the five case study investigations were carried out through thorough critical review of relevant published, unpublished literature and documents. However, both qualitative and quantitative data were collected by using survey research methods and also from the published documents and literature and Applied Systems Analysis (ASA) was considered as a precursor to each of the case study analysis.

4. Greening Paradigms of Green City Development in Developing Countries: Resource Infrastructure and Governance

Energy utilisation and efficiency in the buildings, public transportation, non-car transportation, congestion reduction, shifting to low carbon road emission transportation, waste water treatment, treatment of municipal waste production, waste recycling, waste reduction and public participation (under governance) in the development and implementation of policy intervention measures are some of the major criteria to transform the cities to green cities. Thus, in this section how energy efficiency in buildings—particularly educational complexes, appropriate transportation infrastructure and re-engineering of public transportation, appropriate waste water disposal system and resource recovery from wastes and attaining environmental justice in solid waste management would engender green and sustainable cities are argued and discussed with the aid of case studies as mentioned in the approach section (Section 3).

4.1 Energy Efficiency in Educational Buildings: Green Buildings to Green Cities

Arguments have emerged that how city infrastructure can be re-engineered to enable the city to act as a force for good, and compensate deliberately and positively for the ills of man's interventions in nature (Beck, 2011; Beck *et al.*, 2013). Universities—educational complexes being subsets of the city can lead in these efforts; they can become examples to cities by re-engineering their infrastructure. University infrastructure includes buildings and services of which energy use is important especially in the context of climate change. Thus, it is essential to explore how the interlinkage among the various building related parameters such as appropriate building orientation and form, appropriate thermal mass and insulation, improved efficiencies of electrical and lighting devices, improved natural lighting, and alternative energy systems that is premised and developed upon ASA paradigm can lead to energy efficient solutions with improved building energy usage in the buildings of the universities of South Africa.

In the development of building design, it has been a normal practice for the designers to focus on the building shape and appearance without considering energy and resource consumption. In this method of design development models are created that depict the geometric representation of buildings but do not give an overall understanding of how the design model performs with regards to building aspects that include, efficiency in energy (EE), (Geyer, 2011). However, according to Keeler and Bill (2013) green buildings require an integrated approach to design because every design decision produces a cascade of multiple effects rather than an isolated impact. Successful integrated design requires a necessary understanding of the interrelationship of each material, building system, and the space requirements of buildings. It requires a holistic approach towards the building rather than focus solely on individual parts (Keeler & Burke, 2013). Similarly, green buildings require an interdisciplinary approach which needs to analyse interdependencies of engineering and geometric considerations and optimisation of energy efficiency as energy efficiency is a significant consideration in design of green buildings. So, an approach to design that considers buildings as systems consisting of subsystems that are interdepentent is appropriate to achieve the high performance requirements for green buildings.

In this context, the case study was analysed by considering two buidings in the Central University of Technology, Free State. The first building is of three storeys high and consists of a large Atrium located at its centre; however, the lecture rooms are clustered to the sides of a corridor. The class rooms have large glass windows which remain shut for most of the year. They allow access to daylight but limited ventilation since there are limited openings on the internal walls of the lecture rooms. Lecture rooms use a combination of daylight and artificial light. Similarly, in the one-sided corridor configuration, one side of the corridors has large windows which provide sufficient daylight from the atrium to the corridors but not to the classrooms, because adjacent walls between classrooms and corridors do not have any glazing or openings. A portion of the building has a two-sided corridor with staff offices on either side of the internal walls, which do not have sufficient access to natural lighting, and these spaces are served by artificial illumination, and mechanical ventilation. The second building is an administrative building and also has a large central atrium with transparent roofing, which lights up the entrance lobby. The east and west wings constitute two-sided corridors which have access to natural light from the nearby atrium. There is a lack of natural cross ventilation in the offices of these corridors which are equipped with mechanical ventilation systems.

The evaluation of the two buildings with respect to South Africa Green Star rating revealed that both the buildings score marginally (within first building scoring 13 out of 30 and second building scoring 4 out of 30) and thus significantly fall short of being green. However, a conceptual model based on ASA paradigm and application of System Dynamics (SD) principles suggests that the effect of changing the building form would have a profound effect on the efficiency of the building particularly on the energy use efficiency. The conceptual causal feedback relationships among the various parameters involved in achieving energy efficiency in the buildings indicated that energy consumption is affected by indoor quality and building use, thus energy consumption will increase depending on functions of the buildings. The building orientation and use of natural lights also affect energy consumption depending on functions. These two main prominent parameters have direct impacts on energy consumption. Further, energy consumption also influenced by the building geometry, which is a function of shape and size of the building. It is apparent that the shape and size of the building is decided based on the use of the building apart from its architecture value. Thus, building geometry, building use and energy consumption is interconnected by a feedback mechanism. Further, openings in a building are related to its shape, size and orientation and influence the requirement of lighting (artificial lighting) and ventilation (air-conditioning), which in turn influences indoor quality of the buildings. Besides, indoor quality is also affected by the building materials used in the various elements such as roofs, floors, walls and openings. Thus, there is a clear interlinkage with the various parameters of a building such as orientation, building use, geometry and indoor quality with the energy consumption of a building (Eromobor, *et al.*, 2014)

As observed from the building form of the second building, which consists of a simple rectangular shape with an atrium at the centre performs better particularly with regards to access to daylight. So, rectangular or less complex forms with appropriate orientation, adequacy and location of openings can improve the energy efficiency through proper use of day light and natural ventilation leading to reduction of energy consumption. There are also other consequences in adopting a simpler form such as the effect of building form on the function of space. Adopting the form of a simpler rectangular shape with longitudinal axis facing north improves indoor environmental quality (IEQ) substantially which improves energy consumption (Eromobor, *et al.*, 2014).

So, as argued by Allen & Witzerland (2012) energy demand is met by energy consumption, which in turn causes GHG emissions. Therefore, a reduction in energy consumption in buildings is vital to improve energy efficiency and reduce GHG in the environment and to achieve savings in usage of energy. A saving in energy usage and reduction in GHG is envisaged to contribute to the transformation of cities to green cities.

4.2 Sustainable Transportation for Green City Regions

The emergence of modern means of transportation in the world and most importantly in developing countries like India has a remarkable influence on the socio-economic development of city regions. Transportation enhances the process of economic growth in a region by making needed services available. However, simultaneously the issue of transportation and the environment is ironic in nature since while transportation conveys substantial socio-economic benefits, it is impacting environmental systems at the same time. On one hand transportation activities support increasing mobility demands for passengers and goods. It leads to economic development through the linkage of area of production with area of consumption (Asian Development Bank, 2006). On the other hand, it has resulted in growing levels of motorization and congestion and contributes to environmental problems. The most important impacts of transport on the environment relate to climate change, air quality, noise, and land-use. This has reached a point where transportation is a dominant source of emission of most pollutants and their multiple impacts on the environment. So, it has become an important dimension of the concept of sustainability.

In Indian context, the challenges of Indian road transportation system are multifold. Lack of good motorable roads in many regions in India has been the main hindrance to rapid development. The major roads in India are under huge pressure and in great need of modernization in order to handle the increased requirements of the Indian economy. In addition to maintenance, the expansion of the network and widening of existing roads is becoming increasingly important as they face multiple challenges that include low lane capacity, severe congestions, low speeds, high number of traffic crashes, and environmental damages because of poor fuel efficiency and pollutions (NHDP, 2011; World Health Organization, 2009). Such challenges makes the road transportation system in the city regions in India unsustainable which also contributes to the unsustainability of the cities and regions alike (Pucher, *et al.*, 2005). Thus, there is a need to develop sustainable transportation system that would enable the roads to handle increased traffic, allow for a corresponding increase in the average movement speed on India's roads, reduce crashes and increase both mobility and accessibility while also enabling reductions in contributions to environmental ailments.

Thus, the case study of Kanyakumari district in the Tamil Nadu state in India explored how sustainable road transportation can be achieved and how that would contribute to the sustainability of the city region by using ASA paradigm and SD modelling principles. While developing the ASA paradigm, the city region was considered as system and transportation system was considered as a subsystem that is linked to socio-economic and environmental subsystem. The causal feedback relations among the several of the different subsystems in the city region system revealed that improvement in road network is dependent on the current transportation infrastructure investment, provision or supply of roads *versus* the transportation demand and availability or provision of transportation land by the administrative authorities in the system. All these parameters have a positive relationship with the improvement in road network. The improvement leads to the enhancement in Level of Service (LOS) of the road network. The LOS is affected by the congestion level with respect to capacity of roads and reduction in traffic congestion has a positive effect on LOS thus improving both accessibility and mobility (Rawal, *et al.*, 2015). From environmental point of view, sustainable road transportation is dependent on carbon emission and land severance (wastage). Both the parameters are negatively associated to the sustainable road transportation. Similarly, traffic volume has a bearing on fuel consumption. The positive changes in volume of traffic (like greater public transportation share, modal split, increased non-motorized transportation and pedestrianization, and overall reduction in traffic) can help to reduce the fuel consumption and resultant carbon emission. Similarly, efficient land-use and low wastage of land can help to reduce the land severance in environmental subsystem of the system (Rawal, *et al.*, 2015).

Based on the hypothesis, findings from computational SD model results suggest that a combined policy interventions such as increased road infrastructure investment, change in hierarchies of roads (upgradation of roads) and reduction in the vehicle volume will reduce the road network gap by 40 per cent, which may increase by 136 per cent otherwise by the year 2041. This also will improve the LOS of the road significantly (From LOS E >0.9 to LOS A <0.5 during normal hours and LOS F>1.0 to LOS B<0.72 during peak hours). Thus, as the improvement in road network and upgradation of roads occurs and consequently reduction in congestion level is attained, mobility and accessibility in transportation system will be improved leading to sustainability in road transportation system. Such scenarios will lead to increase in GDP in the city region by 15.48 per cent as well as reduce carbon emission by 24.10 per cent, reduce fuel consumption by 7.3 per cent and wastage of land by 64.10 per cent from the normal case scenario (if no interventions are made). Therefore, investment in road infrastructure, upgradation of road hierarchies and reduction in volume of vehicles will engender sustainable transportation which could consequently contribute to the enhancement in GDP, reduction in fuel consumption and reduction in carbon emissions, thus contributing to the development of sustainable and green city regions (Rawal, *et al.*, 2015).

4.3 Re-Engineering of Public Transportation: Essential Archtype for Greening of Cities

Transportation system being a major component of a city, it brings both positive and negative consequences as discussed in the previous section 4.2. However, public transportation system has the potential to reduce the use of vehicular traffic volume created by individual driven vehicles while providing both accessibility and mobility to people and goods efficiently. Also it is expected to aid in alleviating the environmental pollutions caused by the volume of traffic in the cities. However, like many cities in the developing countries, the South African cities lack adequate public transportation system. From a case study of Bloemfontein city it is found that most people depend on the individual driven cars, which create physical, infrastructural and environmental ailments, making it environmentally unsustainable. Among the various challenges faced in transportation in South Africa, public transportation is the most important concern (Luke & Heyns, 2013). In Bloemfontein, more than 45 per cent people use privately driven cars and the presence of public transportation is marginal. The major reasons of relatively less use of public transportation is the lack of adequate and quality public transportation system in the city and need for the understanding of its contribution to the development of green cities. However, the ASA linked causal feedback relationships among the variables that influence public transportation suggest that land-use and urban activities require transportation needs. The transportation needs calls for development of physical and movement infrastructure. The travel behaviour is influenced by perception of the movement infrastructure, which influence the use of public transportation depending upon its availability adequacy, quality, safety and affordability. The large scale use of public transportation has two major implications such as reduction in the use of privately driven vehicles leading to reduction congestion on the roads and reduction of consumption of fuel as well as reduction of carbon emissions and environmental pollution (Burger, *et al.*, 2014). Thus, if public transportation is used, it will increase safety, reduce fossil fuel consumption, reduce congestion and improve mobility and will be environment friendly, and consequently contribute to the development of sustainable and green cities.

4.4 Enhancing Greening Agenda in Cities through Resource Recovery from Waste

One underlying aspect which is a pre-condition for the well-functioning of the cities is the issue of resources (food, energy, water, nutrients) (*cf.* Kumar *et al.,* 2014). Besides, arguments have emerged that the cities should become regenerative) which while focusing on achieving resource efficiency should ensure that there is no undermining of the ecosystems (Olewiler, 2006; Park *et al.*, 2013).

Thus, using Lake Chivero, in Harare as a case study, this study conceptualised the framework of the energy-water-food-climate change nexus (Kumar *et al.*, 2014) for Harare Metropolitan city region that is sought to propose ways to address the challenges of African cities, in general and the challenges of Harare (the capital of Zimbabwe), in particular. It intends to provide the city with a framework to address the challenges for greening and sustainable development with particular aspects of water supply and distribution, waste disposal, nutrient recovery and food production. Besides, in a city, there is a defined interaction between what the natural environment produces and how human beings harvest, process, consume and deposit their waste in the landscape. For example food is 'imported' into cities and 'exported' in the form of sewage into rivers and seas. With this in mind, it becomes apparent that resources tend to get back into the system by ways or recycling or re-use. This realisation has sparked the recent debate that realises the need to re-use of waste produced by humans and their processes so that the so-called waste then find themselves back into the system as inputs to vital processes of life. In this regard, it is argued that there is a need to view carbon, nitrogen and phosphorus and other materials from the water closet as resources to be recovered than pollutants and waste (Beck, Walker and Thompson 2013).

Harare, with the plethora of its challenges of energy, water, food, and climate change typifies an African city needing attention to arrest these challenges. The rapid population growth and waning infrastructure have ushered a great mismatch between supply and demand of infrastructure and services—housing, water and transport being the dominant needs. Besides, the environmental problems of the city have increased—the range of challenges includes, but not limited to waste management, sewer and water system as well as sanitation and urban agriculture. There is also a problem of industrial and raw sewage effluent. Consequently, one of the major sources of water supply and irrigation, Lake Chivero is polluted because of unrestricted sewage disposal that contains nutrients like Nitrogen (N), Phosphorous (P), and Potassium (K). However, it is argued that the wasted resources of the city such as Lake Chivero can be viewed as significant environment asset for the good of the city.

The water and waste water reticulation systems in Harare is predominantly waterborne and centralised. The sewer system is separated, where the sewage is collected and treated before discharge to water courses. The domestic waste water, along with the industrial waste water that enters the sewerage system with or without pre-treatment after treatment, and storm water and run-off containing nutrients, fertilisers, pesticides eventually enter the Lake Chivero. The Lake has a volume of 2,50,000 mega litres (being 250 × 106 m^3) with an average depth of 9. 3 m. The surface area of the lake is 26 km^2. The catchment of Lake has an area of about 2632 hectares. Besides, a number of small rivers provide the lake with approximately 1,60,000 cubic metres of treated and untreated sewage effluent almost daily. This effluent is the main cause of pollution including eutrophication in the lake and rise of water temperature (Utete and Chikova, 2013). However, the Lake is envisaged to have contained significant amount of nutrients such as N, P, and K which can be recovered. Since, the Lake is an integral part of the Harare urban metabolism and influence the water and waste water system of the city significantly, the protection of the Lake from pollution and recovery of resources from it would contribute to the green growth of the city significantly.

An ASA linked analysis revealed that, the nutrients that enter the lake from the city are a function of the population that is connected to the centralised sewerage and waste water infrastructure although, not all of the nutrients generated by the (sewer-connected) population will reach the lake. However, the quantity that reach the lake is highly significant. The water supply in the city, irrigation, waste water generation and disposal to Lake Chivero, nutrients, food production and food consumption and waste water generated from consumption in the city work in a feedback mechanism. Availability of nutrients in the system allows its production and application in the system for food production. Waste water generation due to water supply and discharging to the lake make it possible higher availability of nutrients in the Lake Chivero. Thus, the lake water, availability of nutrients, its production, its application in the system for food production, food consumption, waste water generation are interconnected through reinforcing mechanisms to produce nutrients in the system. However, on the other hand, the availability of nutrients in the system is balanced by the leakage from lake water through a disruptive feedback mechanism. So, while reinforcing feedback mechanisms enhance the availability and consequent production of nutrients in the system, the disruptive feedback mechanism acts as a reducer. A computation based on ASA model estimated that the Lake already has a sediment of 8,000 tons of N, out of which 5200 tons can be extracted. The extraction of these resources will not only reduce the pollution level of the lake but also assist in production of 35,000 tons of food in the city region. Thus, the waste that are generated in the city if considered as resources and recovered then it would definitely contribute to the environmental and socio-economic well-being of the city and strengthen its green growth agenda.

4.5 Environmental Justice in Solid Waste Management: A Vital Element for Greening Agenda

Solid waste has been observed to be central to polluting the air, water and outbreaks of diseases in many cities in Africa (Wemby, 2002). Although, policy interventions to reduce the menace of solid waste has been long advocated, Environmental Justice in Solid waste management, particularly in African cities are barely visible. The solid waste management challenges have become central to the politics of environmental justice (Agyeman *et al.*, 2003; Dobson, 1998). An unequal society, and undesirable wastes often ending up in the poorest and least powerful communities cause such challenges (Ackerman and Mirza, 2001), although low-income communities may be just as concerned as anyone else about environmental protection.

Besides, two contradictory responses reflecting contrasting theoretical paradigms with regards to waste have emerged. First, some wastes can become assets in local economic development, creating incomes through scavenging, industrial jobs in recycling plants or new businesses using locally available materials. Waste has become a truly enormous industry, and influences economics of cities (Thompson, 1998). Second, wastes are an assault on the community that receives them. Toxic wastes, polluting facilities and industrial by-products for example, often create local health hazards rather than development.

Based on these premise the case study of Kinshasa with the aid of cultural theory supported by ASA paradigm explored how environmental justice in solid waste management can be attained through the constructive engagement of different social solidarities that could assist in reducing the environmental burden and assist in the green growth in the city. Kinshasa is considered as one of the dirtiest cities on the planet. It seems to be emerging alongside two contrasting angles—(1) it portrays an image of a city built respecting urban standards; and (2) it poses an image of a city that is the illustration of pseudo-urbanization, "wild" urbanization with avenues and streets, infrastructures are poorly designed. Moreover, its basic infrastructure for solid waste management is poor and gutters, streets, sidewalks and green spaces that exist, are quickly transformed into dumpsites (Kubanza, 2006 and Tshishimbi, 2006).

Furthermore, most of people in low-income neighbourhoods are living with piles of garbage and refuse despite the initiation of the operation called "Kinshasa-bopeto" (i.e. Kinshasa-cleaned up), in 2005 (Kubanza, 2010; Kubanza, 2006 and Tshishimbi, 2006). Solid waste litters the roads, sometimes piling as high as the plot level, and also causes obstruction of the water drainage system as a significant quantity of garbage is illegally disposed of in the water courses (Kubanza, 2006; Kubanza, 2010 and Tshishimbi, 2006). So, sustainability of Kinshasa is threatened on account of solid waste challenges. Besides, solid waste and related environmental problems with socio-spatial inequalities in the distribution of the waste burdens are seen in the city (Petts, 2001; Petts, 2005; Schubeler, 1996). It is observed that most of the solid wastes generated in Kinshasa are disposed as landfill in the areas available in poor neighbourhoods, although majority of the solid wastes are generated by the rich. Consequently, the urban poor residents are living closer to potential pollution sources thereby making them susceptible to various health hazards. Contrary to this, apparently, the rich urban neighbourhoods enjoy a cleaner environment, better health and sanitation facilities than those who are living in urban poor neighbourhoods. With narrow revenue bases, increased civil conflict and limited technical capacities, the municipal authorities in Kinshasa have been unable to effectively deliver solid waste management services, such as provision of refuse collection and disposal. Besides, stakeholders are not actively involved in the solid waste management process. So, such scenarios result in environmental injustices that in turn challenges the sustainability of the city (Kubanza, 2006; Kubanza, 2010; Misilu *et al.*, 2010; and Tshishimbi, 2006).

So, access to environmental justice for the people in Kinshasa implies a situation whereby people in their homes, neighbourhoods and work places have a right to access a clean, healthy and secure environment. Solution that immediately spring to mind could be social sanctions, such as statutory regulations, that are enforced by the hierarchical actors or governance system in all its authority, without fear or favour, on the marketplace actors or industries. However, good governance and management with stakeholders' engagement perhaps could be the alternative answer to this challenge. However, good governance demands creation of representative, political and administrative systems that allows for the views and priorities of citizens to influence policies and actions as well as discharging of responsibilities by the authorities. In this regard, there exists the other solution that could better suit is—the "egalitarianism" (Thomson, 1998). So, it becomes important to introduce the cultural theory framework aided by ASA paradigm because of their ability to underpin the fundamental socio-cultural nature of the complex problem as well as they can help the poor and vulnerable groups in the Kinshasa to deepen their understanding of their reality.

In this framework, the society can be grouped under four solidarities—individuals (market forces), hierarchy (the authorities-government), egalitarian (social organisations) and fatalist (common individuals). With respect to solid waste management in Kinshasa these four solidarities develop their own storylines independent of each other. Currently in Kinshasa, only two voices—the hierarchical and the individualist enjoy access excluding of the egalitarian—the civil society activist—voice and the elite enjoy a cleaner environment and better sanitation facilities than do those who are living in urban poor neighbourhoods (Kubanza, *et al.*, 2015). Also, there exist clear causal feedback relations among the various factors, which contribute to the current plight of solid waste management. The enormous population, functions in different settlements and economic growth generate high volume of solid waste in the city. However, inappropriate solid waste disposal system on account of lack of appropriate and equitable disposal system leads to dumping of the generated solid wastes in poor suburbs. As a result of the dumping of the materials in the poor suburbs, the quality of environment is degenerated and creates environmental injustice in the city. However, if three of the four social solidarities, i.e. Municipal authorities (hierachist), Private companies (Individualist), and, NGOs/CBOs/CSOs/other community and social organisations (Egalitarian) come together, there is a possibility of participatory governance for solid waste management, which would lead to evolve appropriate solid waste management system and environmental policy. Besides, a locally suitable environmental policy with the assistance of availability of budget (possibly from the contributions from government and private companies), reduction in generation of wastes because of the awareness created by community and social organisations and encouragement for disposal at the source, all stakeholders will share the responsibility of solid waste management and environmental burden equitably. Consequently, most feasible disposal systems will be developed. A feasible disposal system has two consequences (1) it will reduce the waste disposal in the poor suburbs; and (2) it will provide business opportunities to the private companies/businessmen. Further, reduction in the disposal of solid wastes in poor suburbs because of the above mechanism will be able to restrict the misuse or wastage of green and open spaces and makes them available in the suburbs. This process will contribute to enhance the quality of environment, which consequently will augment environmental justice in the city through a reinforcing feedback mechanism among these factors. Therefore, it is envisaged that the participatory governance approach with participation of three important solidarities of the society, i.e. Municipal authorities (hierachist), Private companies (Individualist), and, NGOs/CBOs/CSOs/other community and social organisations (Egalitarian) in collaborative way will bring about an appropriate waste management system with feasible disposal systems, which essentially will augment environmental justice in solid waste management in Kinshasa. Besides, while it will become mutually beneficial to all the three solidarities, i.e., assists in governance and generation of funds for Municipal authorities; creates business for private companies; and aid in advancing the cause of community for community based organisations; it will also save the other solidarity—the fatalist (common people) from the sufferings of a poor environment in Kinshasa. This means that the more the government grants responsiveness (less likely possibility) and participation (also not likely), the more the city will veer environmental justice (Kubanza, *et al.*, 2015).

5. Discussion and Conclusion

During the early twentieth century, while developing or transforming cities, attention was given to induce economic, and social health, resilience in ecosystem of the cities based on the environmental, ecological, and natural resource perturbations. Recent researches have increasingly focused on how urban environments can be not only ecologically sound and socially optimal, but can adapt to a changing global climates as well as the cities can engender economic efficiency. Consequently concepts of green growth, green cities and smart growth have been adopted for development of cities. Also, the nexus among the various vital parameters of the city metabolism—resource (food, water and energy), infrastructure, environment and climate change has been explored to attain sustainability in cities or in other words induce green growth in the cities. However, most of the investigations are confined to the developed countries, although sporadic and loose incorporation of such issues in the planning guidelines or strategies in some developing countries like South Africa can be seen. Therefore, investigations with the aim to explore greening paradigms for cities in developing countries were conducted. The ASA paradigm and the premise of cultural theory which is not far away from what smart growth principles advocate were observed to be suitable for this investigation and were followed. The case studies from the cities of four countries such as South Africa, India, Zimbabwe, and DR Congo across different aspects such as energy, transportation—including public transportation, resource recovery from wastes and environmental justice in solid waste management reveal that resources such as food, energy, water, wastes, infrastructures like transportation and governance have definite nexus and influence greening of cities. For example, design energy efficient buildings based on natural and environmental elements such as natural light, ventilation, orientation and geometry can reduce energy consumption in the educational complexes that can contribute significantly to the environmental well-being and economy of the cities. Appropriate investment in road transportation infrastructure, upgradation of lower hieratical roads to higher hierarchical roads and reduction in vehicular volume will aid in reduction in traffic congestions, improve mobility and accessibility as well as contribute in reducing fossil fuel consumption, and GHG emissions, and enhance the GDP, thus engendering green growth and sustainability in a city region. Moreover, public transportation will reinforce the green growth through reduction in the phenomenon of privately driven vehicles that is prevalent in many developing countries and reduction of GHG. Besides, waste water is still considered as a waste that is disposed to the natural water bodies with or without appropriate treatment engendering environmental pollution, health risks to humans, threatening aquatic life and wastage of precious water resources, although it contains nutrients like N, P, and K. However, the study by considering the Lake Chivero in Harare suggests that waste water generated in the city is in reality a resource from which significant quantity of nutrients can be recovered and utilised in food production. Such a scenario brings rise to use of waste water and recovery of nutrients which has intricate relationships with food production and consumption, thus it reinforces the urban metabolism of resource production and use—food, water and nutrients. Furthermore, the recovery of nutrients will have a positive impact on the reduction of pollutants in the lake that would contribute to the agenda of green growth in the city. Similarly, solid waste is considered as a menace in many cities of developing world. While taking measures to deal with the solid wastes in cities often environmental justice and equity are largely ignored. Although, a large portion of wastes are generated by rich neighbourhoods as seen in Kinshasa, they are disposed of in poor neighbourhoods or water courses subjecting the people in poor neighbourhoods and those who use the contaminated water with appalling sufferings. It is also found that two of four social solidarities such as the hierarchy (decision-makers) and individualist (market forces) have the major voice whereas the other two solidarities—the egalitarian (community organisations) and fatalist (common people) are not engaged in the decision-making or in the development of policy interventions for solid waste management. The result is creation of environmental injustice, environmental pollution and suffering to a large section of the society in the cities. However, from the case study of Kinshasa, it can be advocated that there is a clear interlinkage and feedback relationship among the various aspects such as population, solid waste generation, collection and disposal of solid waste management and among the four social solidities. If the linkages are understood and various solidarities are engaged appropriately in the solid waste management system, it would bring a win-win scenario among all stakeholders. Consequently, there shall be reduction in environmental ailments from the solid waste in the cities and as well as attainment of environmental justice. Consequently, perhaps the strengthening of green growth in cities can be experienced.

Thus, the case studies explored reveal that each of the above mentioned aspects contributes to the green growth agenda of cities or in other words contribute to the development of sustainable green cities. Therefore, all these aspects need to be considered in an integrated manner while developing strategies for development of sustainable green cities in the developing countries.

References

Ackerman, F. and Mirza, S. (2001). Waste in the Inner City: Asset or assault? *Local Environment*, 6(2), 113-120.

Agyeman, J. and Evans, B. (2003). Just sustainability: The emerging discourse of environmental justice in Britain. *The Geographical Journal*, 170(2): 155-164.

Ahmed, R. and Donovan (1992). *Issues of Infrastructural Development: A Synthesis of Literature*.

ALMEC Corporation. (2011). Study of Japanese experiences on sustainable urban development including pollution control and management, resource/energy efficiency and GHG reduction. Available at http://siteresources.worldbank.org/INTURBANDEVELOPMENT/Resources/336387-1270074782769/6925944-1288991290394/Japanese_ Experiences_Sustainable_Urban_Development.pdf.

Allen, S.T.G. and Witzerland, S. (2012). Proceeding of the 29th System Dynamics Conference in climate change actions in the urban context: A tool for Decision makers.

Asian Development Bank (2006). "When do Rural Roads benefit the Poor and How? An In-depth Analysis Based on Case Studies". Asian Development Bank.

Beck, M.B. (2011). Cities as Forces for Good in the Environment: Sustainability in the Water Sector, Warnell School of Forestry and Natural Resources, University of Georgia, Athens, Georgia, (ISBN: 978-1-61584-248-4).

Beck, M.B., R.V. Walker and M. Thompson (2013). Smarter urban metabolism: Earth systems re-engineering. Proceedings of the Institution of Civil Engineers, *Engineering Sustainability*, 166, October 2013, Issue ES5: 229-241.

Burger, E., Das, D., Thomson, M., Beck, M.B. (2014). Re-engineering of public transportation systems for suitable green cities in central region of South Africa, Unpublished Research Report, SA YSSP, 2014.

Chirisa, I., Das, D., Thomson, M., Beck, M.B. (2014). Situating the Africa City in the Applied Systems Analysis and Greening Paradigms: Case for Harare Metropolitan Region, Zimbabwe, Unpublished Research Report, SA YSSP, 2014.

Dobson, A., 1998. *Fairness and Futurity: Essays on Environmental Sustainability and Social Justice*, Choice Reviews Online, 37 (04), pp. 37-2264-37-2264.

Economist Intelligence Unit (EIU). (2009). European Green City Index: Assessing the Environmental Impact of Europe's Major Cities. Munich: Siemens AG. Available at http://www.siemens.com/entry/cc/features/urbanization_development/all/en/pdf/report_en.pdf.

Eromobor, S., Das, D., Thomson, M., Beck, M.B. (2014). Dynamic Modelling of Sustainable Built Infrastructure for Education Complex Neighbourhoods in South African Cities, Unpublished Research Report, SA YSSP, 2014.

Geyer, P. (2012). Systems modelling for sustainable building design. Advanced Engineering Informatics, 26(4), pp. 656-668. Available at: http://linkinghub.elsevier.com/retrieve/pii/S1474034612000444

Hammer Stephen, Kamal-Chaoui Lamia, Robert Alexis and Plouin Marissa (2011). Cities and Green Growth: A Conceptual Framework, OECD Regional Development Working Papers 2011/08, OECD Publishing. http://dx.doi.org/10.1787/5kg0tflmzx34-en

Keeler, M., and Bill, B. (2013). *Fundamentals of Integrated Design for Sustainable Building*. John Wiley & Sons.

Kennedy, C., S. Pincetl, P. Bunje. (2011). "The study of urban metabolism and its applications to urban planning and design." *Urban Pollution* 159: 1965-73.

Kubanza, N.S., 2006. The Resurgences of Endemic' Diseases in the city of Kinshasa, Democratic Republic of Congo, M.Sc. Research Report, Department of Sociology, University of Kinshasa, DRC.

Kubanza, N.S. (2010). Perception and Issues of Solid Waste Management in South Africa: A Case Study of Johannesburg, Masters' Research Report, Department of Development Planning, University of the Witwatersrand, Johannesburg, South Africa.

Kubanza, N.S., Das, D., Thomson, M., Beck, M.B. (2015). Some Happy, Others Sad: Exploring Environmental Justice in Solid Waste Management in Kinshasa, Democratic Republic of Congo, Unpublished Research Report, SA YSSP, 2015.

Kumar, M. Dinesh, Nitin Bassi, A. Narayanamoorthy, M.V.K. Sivamohan (eds.) (2014). *The Water, Energy and Food Security Nexus: Lessons from India for Development*, Routledge Publications, London.

Luke, R., and Heyns, G. (2013). Public transport policy and performance: The results of a South African public opinion poll. *Journal of Transport and Supply Chain Management*, 7(1), 1-8. doi:10.4102/jtscm.v7i1.96.

Misilu, E., C. Shouyu and Z. Li Qin. 2010. Sustainable Urbanisation's Challenge in Democratic Republic of Congo. *Journal of Sustainable Development*, 3 (2), 246-258.

NHDP (2011). "National Highways Development Project Maps, NHDF Project Phases-I, II and III". Ministry of Road Transport and Highways, Government of India. September 2011.

OECD (2010a),—Interim Report of the Green Growth Strategy: Implementing our commitment for a sustainable future, OECD, Paris.

OECD (2011b), Towards Green Growth, Green Growth Strategy Synthesis Report, OECD, Paris.

Olewiler, N. (2006). Environmental sustainability for urban areas: The role of natural capital indicators. *Cities*, 23(3), 184-195.

Park Moonseo, Kim Youngjoo, Lee Hyun-soo, Han Sangwon, Hwang Sungjoo, Choi Min Ji (2013). Modelling the dynamics of urban development project: Focusing on self-sufficient city development—*A Mathematical and Computer Modelling*, 57, 2082-2093.

Petts, J. (2001) Planning for sustainable waste management, in: C. Miller (Ed.) *Planning and Environmental Protection*. Oxford: Hart Publishing.

Petts, J. (2005). Enhancing environmental equity through decision-making: Learning from waste management. *Local Environment*, 10(4), 397-409.

Pucher John, Korattyswaropam Nisha, Mittal, Neha, Ittyerah, Neenu, 2005. Urban transport crisis in India. *Transport Policy*, 12, 185-198.

Rawal, T., Das, D., Thomson, M., Beck, M.B. (2015). Sustainable Road Transportation System in Kanyakumari District, Tamil Nadu (India), Unpublished Research Report, SA YSSP, 2015.

Schubeller, P., K. Wehrle and J. Christen. (1996). Urban Management and Infrastructure. A Conceptual Framework for Municipal Solid Waste Management in Low-Income Countries. UNDP/UNCHS Working Paper No. 9. Habitat/World Bank/SADC Collaborative Programme on Municipal Solid Waste Management in Low-Income Countries. St. Gallen, SKAT.

Thompson, M. (1998). *Waste and Fairness, Social Research*, 65(1), 55-73.

Tshishimbi, E. (2006). Travail des enfants et des jeunes dans la ville de Kinshasa, Galiléo, Kinshasa, DRC.

UNFPA (United Nations Population Fund) (2009). *World Urbanization Prospects*: The 2009 Revision, UNFPA, New York.

UN-Habitat (2010), State of the World's Cities 2010/2011, UN-Habitat, Nairobi.

Utete Beaven and Edmore Happison Chikova. (2013). Gonadal state and condition factor of Oreochromisniloticus (Linnaeus 1758) in a hypereutrophic lake. *Journal of Water Resources and Ocean Science*, 2(6), 165-169.

Wemby, L. (2002). L'Evolution des Modes d'Habitat et des Politiques de L'Urbanisation en République Democratic du Congo, Imprimerie CEDI, Kinshasa, DRC.

World Health Organization (2009). *Global Status Report on Road Safety*.

Zhou Nan and Williams Christopher (2013). An International Review of Eco-City Theory, Indicators, and Case Studies Environmental Energy Technologies Division Lawrence Berkeley National Laboratory, USA.

Geomorphology and Environment

2

Decaying of the Saraswati River in West Bengal

Its Causes and Consequences

Biswajit Das and *Subodh Chandra Pal*

1.0 Introduction

Saraswati is a moribund distributary of the Bhagirathi. This channel was active during the 14th and 15th Century. The Satgaon, the medieval port of Bengal was located on the banks of this river. It takes off from the Hugli River at Tribeni in Hugli District and again discharges into its parent river at Sankrail in Haora District. The river has a length of about 77 km. The Saraswati does not get any upstream flow and its channel remains dry during lean months. It has a small catchment which generates run-off by monsoon rainfall (Rudra, 2012). The Saraswati was the westernmost distributary of the Bhagirathi and once flowed through the Rupnarayan estuary (Rennell, 1788).

1.1 History of the Saraswati River

The Ganges estuary has had a chequered history, with which is connected the rise and decline of the sea ports of Bengal. At Tribeni in Hugli District, Bhagirathi River bifurcated into the Saraswati and the Hugli, *alias* Adi Ganga beside and below Kolkata. The Saraswati was a major maritime river. The ancient course of the Saraswati was described by Rennell (1788) in his "Memoir of a Map of Hindoostan". He wrote "Satgong or Satagong now a inconsiderable village on small creek of the Hugli river, about four miles to the North-West of Hooghly was in 1566 and probably later a large trading city, in which European traders had their factories in Bengal. At that time Satgong was capable of bearing small vessels and I suspect that its then course passing Satgong was by way of Adaumpour, Omptah, and Tamlook and that the river called the Old Ganges was part of its course, and received that name when the circumstances of the change was fresh in the memory of people. The appearance of the country between Satgong and Tamlook countenances such an opinion".

There are evidences that the present Rupnarayan was connected to the Bhagirathi through a branch of Saraswati. At that time, the Saraswati used to flow a course, identified by Rennell (1788) and Fergusson (1863) to the west of its present course. This channel is now nearly wiped out due to sedimentation and expansion of agriculture which made it difficult to identify the old channel on the field. The Saraswati disassociated itself from the Rupnarayan since 700 A.D. and shifted its course eastward to flow along Sankrail, Budge Budge, Uluberia, Falta and Geonkhali causing decline of Tamralipta as a port (Rudra, 1990).

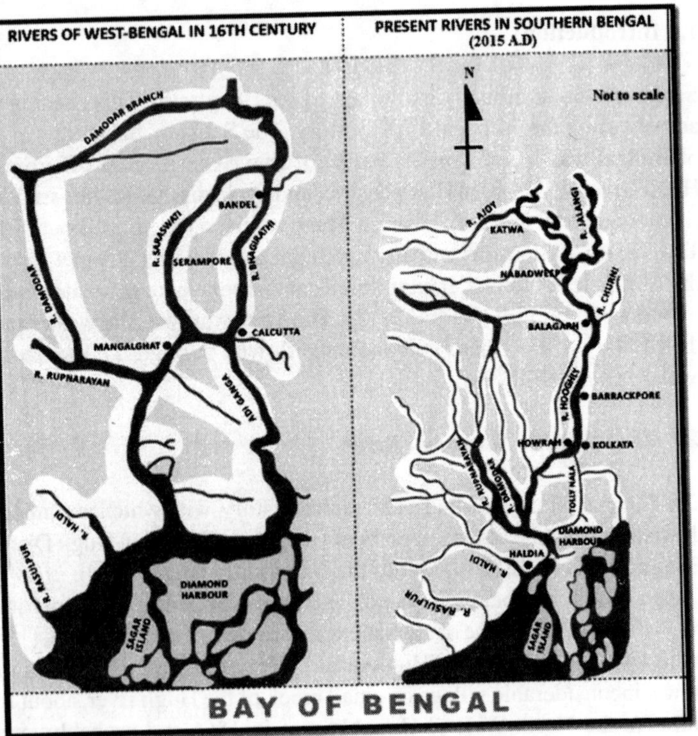

Fig. 2.1: Changes in course of the Saraswati River in West Bengal

Source: Murshidabad.net

The new course of the Saraswati after 8th Century used to flow past Sankrail, a branch evolved due to anthropogenic activities near Kolkata, connected it with the Adi Ganga. At that time, the main course of the Damodar river used to flow into the main Bhagirathi at a few kilometres north of Tribeni near Kalna in 1770 A.D., following a severe flood, the Damodar changed its course and flowed into the Bhagirathi about 50 km south of Kolkata, causing a major change in the Hugli river system. Above the changed confluence point, the Saraswati and the Adi Ganga became extinct and the Hugli flowed along the present course of the Hugli River (*see* Fig. 2.2).

2.0 Materials and Methods

2.1 Objectives

Any work is being conducted with some objectives. This chapter is based on following objectives:

1. To highlight the present condition of the Saraswati River.
2. To find out the reasons responsible for the present condition of the river.
3. To highlight the present form of man-river interaction in day to day life.

2.2 Data Used

Primary and Secondary data are used in this chapter. Secondary data from Census of India, 2011, reports of Irrigation and Waterways Department, Government of West Bengal have been used in this chapter.

2.3 Software Used

Various types of software like Microsoft Word, Paint, Arc GIS (version 9.3) were used to prepare the chapter.

2.4 Methodology

The methods which have been used in this study include both analytical as well as descriptive methods. The study is mainly based on primary data collected from the field by conversation with local people,

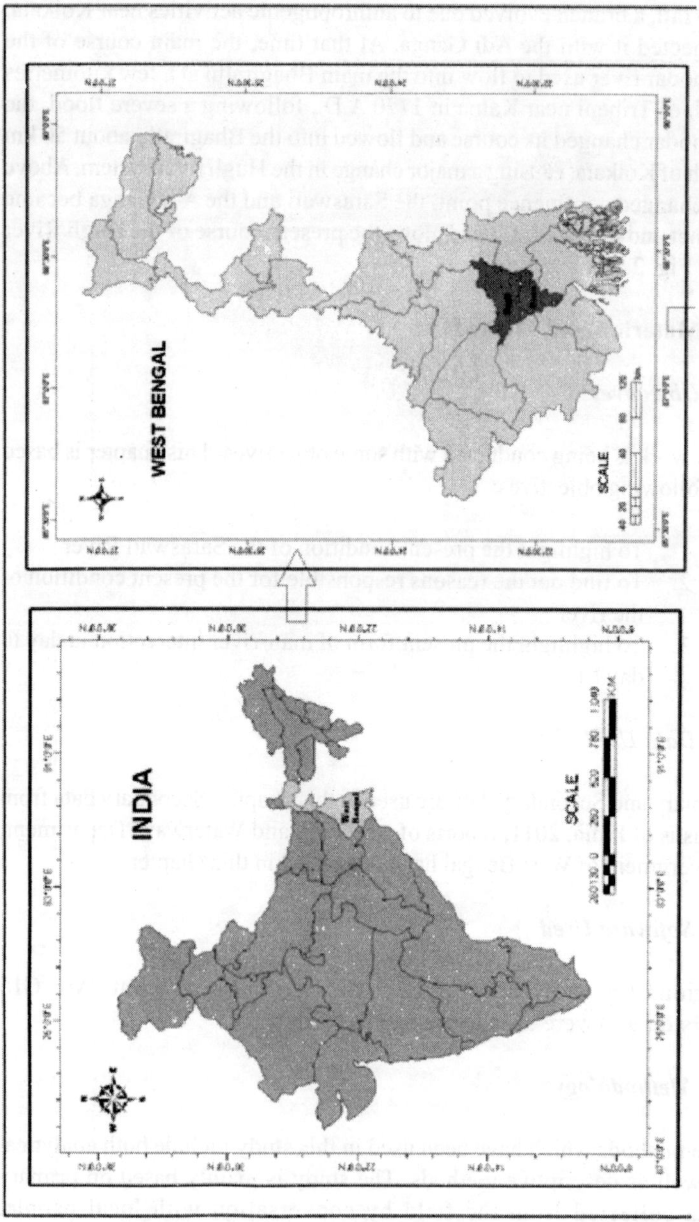
WEST BENGAL
SCALE
INDIA
SCALE

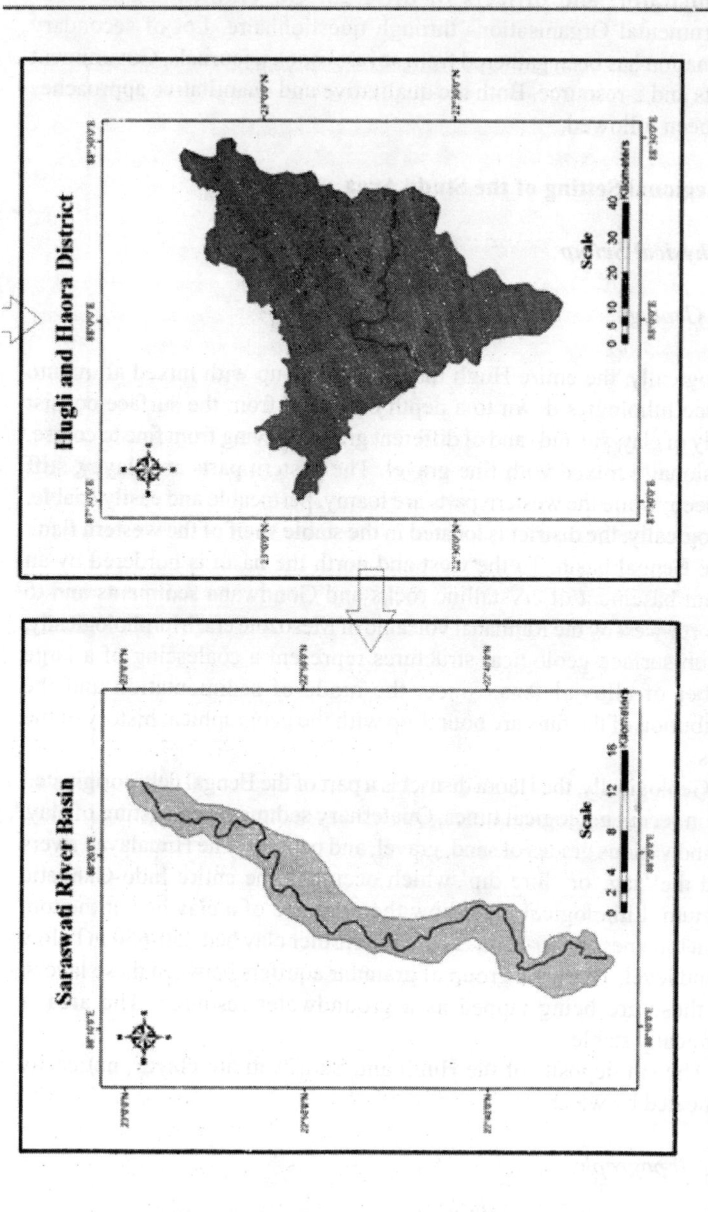

Fig. 2.1: Location Map of the Study Area

Source: NATMO, SOI Toposheet no. : 79B/1, 79B/2, 79B/5, 79B/6.

administrator, and officers of different Governmental and Non-Governmental Organisations through questionnaire. Lot of secondary information has been gathered from several books, journals, Government reports and e-resource. Both the qualitative and quantitative approaches have been followed.

3.0 Regional Setting of the Study Area

3.1 Physical Set up

3.1.1 Geology

Geologically, the entire Hugli district is built-up with mixed alluvium. Surface lithologies down to a depth of 150 m from the surface consist mainly of clay, silt and sand of different grades varying from fine to coarse, occasionally mixed with fine gravel. The eastern parts are clayey, stiff and deep; while the western parts are loamy, permeable and easily friable. Geologically, the district is located in the stable shelf of the western flank of the Bengal basin. To the west and north the basin is bordered by an ancient basement of crystalline rocks and Gondwana sediments and to the north-west by the Rajmahal volcanic of Mesozoic era. Morphologically, the sub-surface geological structures represent a coalescing of a large number of alluvial fans. Since, the mode of sedimentation and the distribution of the fans are bound-up with the geographical history of the rivers.

Geologically, the Haora district is a part of the Bengal delta, originated only in recent geological times, Quaternary sediments consisting of clay, silt, and various grades of sand, gravel, and pebbles. The Himalayan rivers filled the 'sag' or 'fore dip' which occupied the entire Indo-Gangetic alluvium. Lithological logs show the presence of a clay bed at the top, with a thickness of 10-40 m. There is a further clay bed 250-650 m below ground level. There is a group of granular aquifers between these layers, and these are being tapped as a groundwater resource. The area is seismically stable.

The silt deposits of the Hugli and Saraswati are clayey, not easily permeated by water.

3.1.2 Topography

Being a part of the flat plains of the lower Gangetic delta, the topographical homogeneity of the region is remarkable. The region is formed by recent alluvium, only the marked variations are the diversions of the rivers, floodplains and the embankments. The general slope is from north-west to south-east. The average height of the riverside areas varies from 5 to 6 metres above the M.S.L. The characteristic feature of the riverine landscape is the levee formations along all the rivers in between which there are extensive swamps or depressions forming vast sheets of water during the rains.

3.1.3 Drainage

The principal rivers of the Hugli and Haora districts are the Bhagirathi-Hugli, the Damodar and the Rupnarayan and their tributaries and distributaries like the Saraswati, the Kunti, the Behula, the Mundeswari, the Kana Damodar etc. Numerous *khaals* or creeks also intersect the districts. The Sankrail and the Sijberia *khaals* are the lower reaches of the Saraswati and the Kana Damodar respectively.

The Bhagirathi-Hugli is the main westerly channel by which the water of Ganges enters the Bay of Bengal. The lower part of the Hugli river is under the influence of strong tidal forces. The banks are durable and the river therefore carries heavier load and has a fixed regimen, the variation of which, in places, are oscillatory in accordance with the seasonal predominance of the opposing tidal currents.

3.1.4 Climate

The region experiences a hot and humid subtropical climate. The climate consists of three conventional seasons—the hot dry season, the rainy season and the cold dry season. Long summer, profuse rains and high humidity throughout the year are the main characteristics of the region. The hot season begins with strong westerly winds from the middle of the March and continues up to the middle of June. The weather during this time is very hot, sometimes thunderstorm occurs in the afternoon in association with rains with hails. The Kalbaisakhi or the Norwester are often violent and cause sharp drop in temperature.

In the month of June storms and depressions from the Bay of Bengal reaches the region which cause widespread heavy rains. The rains commences in about the middle of June and continues up to September, is the season of heavy rainfall in the region. July and August are the rainiest months. The average annual rainfall of the region varies from 1400 to 1650 mm. 70 per cent of total rainfall occurs during this period.

The post-monsoon season from October to first half of November is fairly pleasant. The cold season last till the end of February, January is the coldest month.

The mean daily temperature varies between 13° Celsius in the winter to 36° Celsius in the summer.

3.1.5 Soil

The entire region is covered with two different types of alluvium—older alluvium and new alluvium, both are of recent geological time. The newer alluvium is mainly composed of sands, silts and clay brought in by the rivers. The surface alluvium formed from the silt deposits of the Bhagirathi-Hugli and its branches like Saraswati, is of sticky clay. Because of the larger accumulation of finer particles particularly silt and clay this soil contains high percentage of Al_2O_3, Fe_2O_3, but low contents of N and CaO. The 0-0.2 m layer is dominantly loamy in texture (53.9%) followed by silty clay (23.3%), silty clay loam (23.1%) and sandy loam (0.71%) in nature. Organic carbon status is usually low to medium, with a range of 1.2 to 7.4 g kg^{-1} (Kundu *et al.*, 2008).

3.1.6 Vegetation

The vegetation of the area is composed almost exclusively of the aquatic plants such as Hydrilla, Utricularia etc. Since, the area entirely consists of low lying swampy land laid out in rice fields. Natural vegetation is not so much present, but man-made orchard fields like mango, *litchi*, banana are abundant in the area.

3.2 Cultural Set up

3.2.1 Demographic Structure

The Saraswati river basin falls in the districts of Hugli and Haora. Major portion of the basin is under the Kolkata Metropolitan Area. The river flows through the eastern part of these districts where population is huge (*see* Table 2.1).

Table 2.1: Demographic Structure of Hugli and Haora Districts

Districts	*Hugli*	*Haora*
Total Population	**55,19,145**	**48,50,029**
Male Population	28,14,653	25,00,819
Female Population	27,04,492	23,49,210
Population Density (persons/km^2)	1753	3306
Average Literacy rate (%)	81.80	83.31
Male Literacy rate (%)	87.03	86.95
Female Literacy rate (%)	76.36	79.43
Sex Ratio	961	939
Rural Population (%)	61.43	36.62
Urban Population (%)	38.57	63.38
Decadal Growth Rate (%)	9.46	13.50

Source: Census of India, 2011.

4.0 Results and Discussion

4.1 Saraswati River and its Uses

At present Saraswati river is able to sustain its existence through a narrow channel from Tribeni to Sankrail and man-river interaction is going on at different dimensions mainly economic, ecologic and aesthetic etc. From the field studies it is revealed that all local inhabitants of all the villages as well as urban settlements through which the river flows are influenced by the channel in both ways—positive and/or negative. All the Blocks through which the river flows are densely populated. Chandernagore, Chinsurah, Tribeni, Shibpur were traditionally prosperous towns. The new townships are emerging in Magra, Singur, Dankuni, and Sankrail.

Passing through the decades, Saraswati has lost its all kind of importance, though some seasonal activities tend to rotate with the life of the river (*see* Fig. 2.1).

Figure 2.1 shows that the river is now being used in different ways. 41.52 per cent of the respondents use the water in agricultural purpose, 20.09 per cent of the respondents use its water in domestic purposes, 7.59 per cent of the respondents use for fishing purposes and 30.80 per cent of the respondents use the river for dumping the waste material. Though the quality of the water is much beyond the utility level, the people uses its tidal water for domestic purposes like washing cloths and dishes, utensils, feed and bath of the cattle etc.

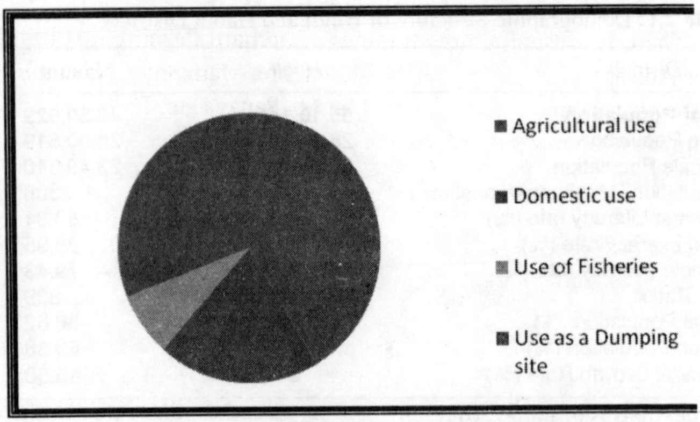

Fig. 2.3: Saraswati River and its Uses

Source: Based on Field Survey by the Authors

Plate 2.1: Vegetables and Orchard farming in the riverside area

Plate 2.2: Adjoining drains polluting the river

There is present a large number of orchard farming just beside the river. Adisaptagram, Bandel, Chandernagore, Mankundu, Nasibpur, Diara are the places famous for Banana, Mango, Papaya etc. The mango orchard designate as an important resource, the floodplain areas is quite profitable for the mango cultivators.

The use of the river channel as a dumping ground is a concern and is not acceptable at all. People started to think the river as a drain, thus all kinds of solid and liquid wastes enter into the river in different ways. The waste materials may be agricultural, urban, domestic, medical, industrial and constructional waste. Almost every type of wastes and wastages from religious places, animal corpses, medical wastes from adjoining nursing homes and plastic products are indiscriminately thrown into the river. Innumerable high and small drains join the river.

4.2 Industries along the River Bank

Various types of industries developed along the river bank from source to mouth. Some poultry farms have developed along the bank side of the river at Chinsurah, Chandernagore. They use the river to dump their garbage. About 13.79 per cent are the poultry farms among all the industries. There are present a number of brick industry, they collect their required soil from the bank side or from the river bed, their percentage is 27.59 per cent. The channel gets widened at Magra, Adisaptagram due to presence of brick industry. Lots of brick industry develops in the Magra, Adisaptagram area due to the availability of clay from the tidal water.

But most illegal production is of indigenous liquor, about 48 per cent are engaged with such kind of production. The polluted water from these production centres mix with the channel and give a big trouble for the inhabitants. The local people of Chinsurah, Chandernagore, Mankundu have complained about the presence of such kind of production. The water of the river transformed into the dirtiest one, it is main source of water and soil pollution. *Gutkha* is also an important industry of the area. In Hugli there are number of *gutkha* industries. The rejected betel nuts (*suparies*) are taken to form the *gutkhas*. These *gutkha* factories also pollute the river water (*see* Fig. 2.4).

Illegal indigenous liquor factories are causing massive pollution over the entire region. Several poor people died every year due to consumption of this liquor (*see* Plates 2.3 and 2.4).

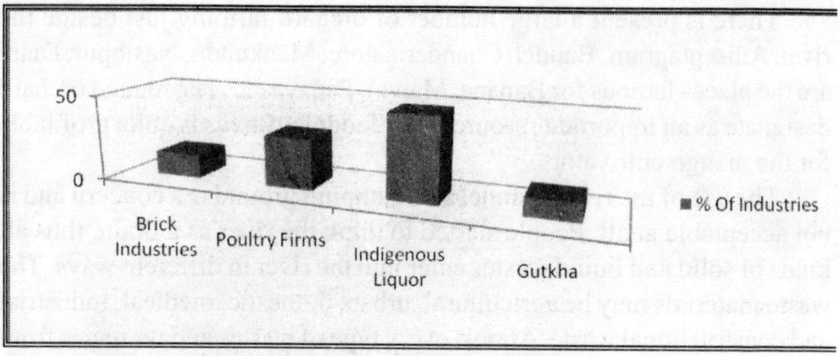

Fig. 2.4: Industries along the Bank of Saraswati River

Source: Based on Field Survey by the Authors

4.3 Decaying of the Saraswati River

4.3.1 Decaying and Change of the Course after the 7th Century

Saraswati was a major distributary of the Bhagirathi-Hugli system. At about 7th Century Saraswati used to flow by meeting all the rivers such as Damodar, Dwarakeswar and Rupnarayan. This tri-junction and the main course of Bhagirathi also followed the path of Saraswati River beside the port of Tamralipta, which was internationally popular for its trading.

Most probably in the 8th Century Saraswati tends to change its course towards east and start to flow along Sankrail. Tamralipta lost its importance. These changes are caused by various factors. Before the 7th Century the main course of the Damodar River used to flow into the main Bhagirathi at a few kilometres north of Tribeni near Kalna, but after the 7th Century Damodar gradually changes its course. Bhagirathi-Hugli River also changes its course in various occasion. After the shifting of the course of the Damodar, Saraswati lost a significant amount of water and it affected the river system.

Major portion of the water of the Bhagirathi-Hugli system used to flow through the Saraswati River, but after the shifting of the Damodar, main flow of the Bhagirathi-Hugli river flows through the Hugli river. Historical evidences shows that the changing of the course of the Damodar and also of the Bhagirathi-Hugli in the 7th Century was resulted by a tectonic movement and as a result of that the channel of the Saraswati was uplifted and for that the flow of the water affected.

Plates 2.3 and 2.4: Liquor Factories Beside the River

Fig. 2.5: Cross profile of the river at Adisaptagram

Source: Google Earth.

Figure 2.5 shows that once the river was very much wide, actually before 18th Century the river was present in the entire low-lying areas of the cross profile but after the 18th Century the river got narrower due to human intervention. Present river have been shown by the arrow in the image. In this cross profile the deepest part is not in the river bed but beside the river bed because there are numerous brick-fields and indigenous liquor factories. They use to store the river water for their industries. These low-lying areas flooded every year in the monsoon season.

4.3.2 Decaying of the River after 1990 A.D.

River Saraswati was a major distributary of the Bhagirathi-Hugli River in the mediaeval period. But after the 7th Century it changes its course and deteriorated through the time, till 1990 A.D. the river flows through a narrow channel, tidal water entered into the channel from Sankrail and Tribeni. Water flow was active till then in a major part of the river, but after 1990 the channel got narrower and choked down and in present tidal water enter the channel but flows merely a couple of km from the source and also from the mouth. Several causes are responsible for the present condition.

4.3.2.1 Causes of Decaying

Decaying of the Saraswati River after 1990 A.D. is caused by both natural and artificial causes.

- *Excessive Siltation*: Siltation is the main natural cause behind the decaying of the river Saraswati. Turbid water of the Hugli River enters into the river and the stagnant condition of the water helps to deposit the excessive silt in the river bed and as a result of this the river got choked up. The head of the river has closed up due to this.
- *Human Encroachment*: After 1990, population of the lower Ganga region increased rapidly. Population Density of the Hugli and Haora districts near the Hugli River are very high. People built their houses illegally in the river bed after choking the river bed. Major portion of the agricultural fields beside the river are actually under the channel area. This can be observed in the field because the steep slopes in the both side of the river are still present in some portion of the river basin.
- *Brick fields along the River*: Numerous brick-fields are present along the river in the source and mouth region. There are almost 15 brick-fields in 8-10 km stretch from Tribeni to Debanandapur and also in the mouth area there are almost 10-12 brick-fields from Sankrail to Domjur. These brick-fields use the silt and clay of the tidal water, for that they cut a channel from the river and divert the river water to a artificial swamp. During the high tide, tidal water flows to the artificial swamp and in the time of low tide, water flows back from the swamp. But the clay and silt remains in the swamp and this clay is used in the brick-fields. Natural flow of the river is affected by these artificial channels and swamps.
- *Illegal Indigenous Liquor Factories*: The main factor behind the polluted water of the river is the production of illegal indigenous liquor (cholai) along the river. For the production of this liquor stagnant polluted water is necessary. For their production they have filled the river with various types of shrubs.

After 1990 this illegal production increased rapidly and as a result of that the water got polluted and also the natural flow of the river got hampered.

4.3.2.2 Impact of Decaying

There are several consequences of decaying of the river Saraswati. Decaying condition of the Saraswati river affect the area immensely. Major impacts of the decaying of the river are—

- *Identity Crisis:* After the decaying of Saraswati River it almost become extinct. The river got narrower, flow hampered. Now-a-days people do not recognise the river because once a big river now filled with shrubs and in some parts people started living in the riverside after filling-up the river as well as they are using that river bed for cultivation purposes.
- *Water Scarcity*: Water level in the river is very low during the summer season and in some parts the river completely dried-up during the summer. Farmers of the adjoining villages dependent on the water of the river for irrigation, but this situation create lots of problems for the farmers.
- *Waterlogging*: Waterlogging is a major problem after the deterioration of the river. Natural flow of the river gets obstructed by various factors and this led to the waterlogging condition in some parts of the river. This condition helps to grow in the various types of shrubs, insects, mosquitoes etc.
- *Water Pollution*: Water in the maximum parts of the river are very much polluted and it is not in a condition to be used in any work. The colour of the water is completely dark. Numerous drains from the adjoining cities join the river and it worsens the situation.
- *Flood Condition*: Flood condition occurs in the monsoon season over a major part of the river. The river channel is narrow and shallow, in the rainy season when huge amount of water came to the channel from adjoining areas, overflow occurs. In every year various parts of Tribeni, Adisaptagram, Chinsurah, Chandernagore, Begampur, Domjur and Sankrail gets flooded.

4.4 Revival Policies, Programmes and People Movements

The protection of natural resources is the core concept of sustainable development, where socio-economic development must be accompanied by environmental protection. Once a vibrant water body, river Saraswati had decayed due to both natural and human factors. In this context, the attempt to revive the river is therefore a significant case as it is a important natural resource.

4.4.1 Activities Involved with the Revival Project

The Irrigation and Waterways (I & W) Department of the Government of West Bengal aims to revive the river into an effective drainage channel with a proper hydraulic design. The I & W Department has started the scheme of IKSKS (Illsura-Kedarmati-Suakhal-Kunti-Saraswati Drainage System) and merge with other systems like Ghia-Kunti river basin and Ganga Flood Control Commission to control the flood condition and to revive all the rivers which are near to decay.

Saraswati Nadi Bachao Andolan (SNBA) led by the Saraswati Nadi Bachao Committee (SNBC) was a movement for the revival of the river. SNBA confronts agencies and opposes practices responsible for the decay of Saraswati River. SNBC is clearly devoted to this purpose and it emerged as a body in 1998 to co-ordinate the movement into a unified effort. The movement is particularly strong in Domjur and Sankrail where participates in big way.

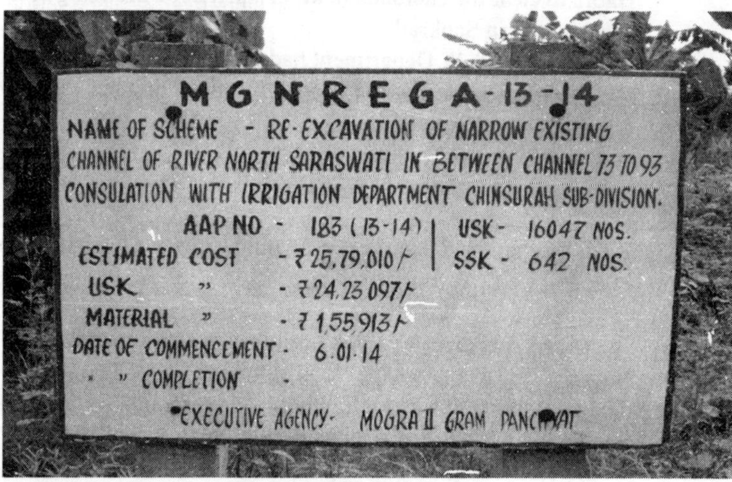

Plate 2.5: Initiatives for the revival of the river

4.4.2 Government and SNBC Initiatives

A number of steps have been taken for the revival of river Saraswati—

- SNBC publishes literature from time to time to increase consciousness among the people about the consequences of deterioration of the river channel and appeals to the people along with well documented articles on the socio-economic, cultural and historical significance of the river.
- SNBC organises convention and deputation to enlist support from various sections of the society like local intellectuals, social activists and working class.
- SNBC is continuously negotiating with the Government agencies to clear encroachment and for the dredging of the channel.
- Irrigation and Waterways Department of West Bengal and the Ganga Flood Control Commission has taken up the matter and decided to work together along with SNBC. Funds had been allocated for the dredging of the channel, but the project did not implemented due to various causes.
- SNBC took the matter of revival of the river Saraswati to the Kolkata High Court in March 2006, which on its verdict on December 2006 told the district administration of Hugli and Haora to clear the encroachment. In April 2008 dredging of the river started in Sankrail.
- In 2011, the I & W Department had taken the project to restart the dredging work, but the project did not implemented after 4 years.

4.4.3 Prospects after the Revival of the River

Once revived, it is believed that the river would cater to a host of socio-economic needs—

- Improved drainage facilities in both the districts may enable both the districts to escape flood situation.
- The availability of water throughout the year might significantly encourage agriculture. Alongside this, many small fishermen would earn living by catching fishes.
- The river would help develop waterways, provides small traders with opportunities for cheaper transport.

- A river accommodates a huge reservoir of biodiversity, specially endangered species. Saraswati River accommodates some endangered species like turtle, varieties of snakes etc.
- The revival of river Saraswati may help both reduce pollution and maintain the ecological balance of the areas.
- If the river is revived then it may be able to avoid the malfunctioning of acute drainage congestion, which is responsible for the massive waterlogging and disruption of normal life.
- Health problems of the riverside people may improve if the river is revived.

The revival of the Saraswati River thus promises the growth of many sections of the local economy and also improves the environmental condition of the area.

5.0 Conclusion

At the end of the study it is clear that though the interrelationship between man and thc river is being demolished but the picture of the future may change in the expected direction if the Irrigation and Waterways Department of West Bengal, Ganga Flood Control Commission, Saraswati Nadi Bachao Committee and other organisations keep their promises. It is pleasure by knowing that an environment of consciousness being developed in the local people, although the awareness is not strong everywhere.

Protecting or reviving the river has broader socio-cultural dimensions, if the river gets revived it would accommodate innumerable possibilities with the potential to generate employment for many people. Some projects were taken for the revival of the river but they were not implemented properly. Lots of things need to be done in the future for successful revival of the river and it needs to be done in holistic way. Hope that the river based prosperity in the area may re-emerge if the essence of the life of the river Saraswati would restored.

Acknowledgements

We would like to thank the local people of the study area for their co-operation. We are very much thankful to the officers of the Irrigation and Waterways Department of Hugli and Haora districts for their help. We are expressing our gratitude to the members of the Saraswati Nadi Bachao Committee for their help and co-operation during the work. The first author is thankful to his friends Basanta Mandal, Sadhan Malik for their help and suggestions during the work.

References

Bagchi, K., (1944), *The Ganges Delta*. Calcutta University, pp. 1-157.

Bandhyopadhyay, B., (2007), *Chandernagore-er Sankhipta Itihas*. Chandernagore Pouro Nigam, pp. 2-4.

Census of India (2011), *West Bengal*, Vol. I, www.censusindia.gov.in

Majumdar, S.C., (1942), *Rivers of Bengal Delta*. Calcutta University, pp. 1-85.

Mukherjee, R.K., (1938), *The Changing Face of Bengal*. Calcutta University, pp. 158-190.

O'Malley, L.S.S., and Chakraborty, M.M., (1910), *Bengal District Gazetteers, Hooghly and Howrah Districts*, Bengal Secretariat Book Depot.

Ray, H.P., (2006), The Archaeology of Bengal: Trading Networks, Cultural Identities. *Journal of the Economic and Social History of the Orient*, Vol. 49, No.1, pp. 69-89, BRILL, http:/www.jstor.org/stable/25165129, (accessed April 09, 2015).

Rudra, K., (2010), *Banglar Nadikatha*. Sahitya Samsad, pp. 20-35, 41-49.

Rudra, K., (2012), *Rivers of West Bengal—A Status Report*. West Bengal Pollution Control Board, pp. 70-72.

Seth, H., (1963), *Sankshipta Chandernagore Parichoy*. Chandernagore Pustakagar, p. 265.

3

Changing Channel Morphology of River Bhagirathi at Purbasthali Block, Burdwan District, West Bengal

A Contemporary Perspective

Indrani Mukherjee

Introduction

The nature of deltaic rivers is to shift their course constantly, varying from one bank to another, popularly known as 'reach points' or 'meander belt', over centuries and even over decades. River channel shifting is a part of nature's design in forming delta lands. The height of the river plain rises with the sedimentation carried by the river flow. Gradually, the delta becomes moribund and river flows towards more low-lying areas. The same process is then repeated and new channels are formed. The left-out part becomes ox-bow lake, *bil*, marshes etc. These features are nothing but the salient evidence of frequently changing river courses (Bagchi, K. and Mukherjee, K.N., 1978).

About Study Area

Purbasthali lies close on the Tropic of Cancer. Purbasthali is a large block with 186 villages in Burdwan district of West Bengal. It is 120 km north from Kolkata. The block is bounded by the rivers almost in all directions, i.e., the Brahmani on the northwest, Khari, one of many offshoots of the Damodar on the west, Banka, the principal tributary of Khari (*Gazetteers, Burdwan*) on the south-west and Jalangi on the east respectively between the geographical co-ordinates from 88° 19′ 45″ to 88° 22′ E longitude 23°26′ to 23°26′45″N latitude. Purbasthali is located on the agriculturally rich alluvial plain in the east-central part of deltaic Bengal. Temperatures in this region vary from 17-18 °C in winter to 30-32 °C in summer. Topographic configuration is the typical monotonously low dipping Gangetic plain of West Bengal with an average height of 14 m above mean sea level. During monsoon river gets flooded, with the water level within the wetland getting higher and under heavy rains the enclosed islands get submerged. The area is extremely rich in alluvial soil content.

Location of Study Area

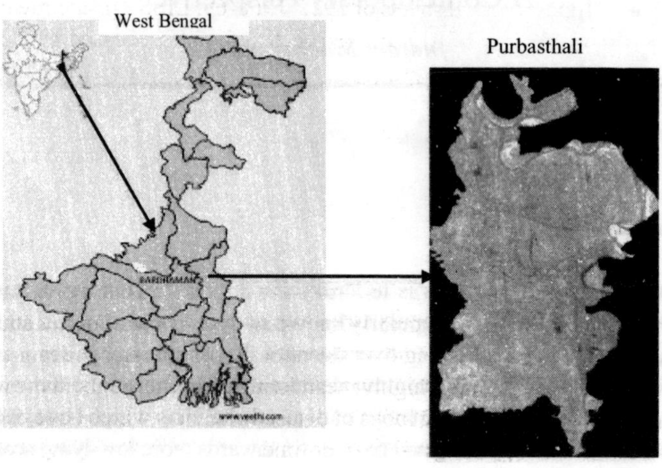

Objectives of the Study

The main objectives of the study are following:

- To find out the morphological changes of the river Bhagirathi in the study area.
- To identify the areas with most oscillating channel pattern of the river Bhagirathi.
- To find out the possible causes of such dynamic character of the channel.

Methodology

Morphometric measures

- SI = meandering length/straight length
- Meander cut off: For the study of the cut-offs an angle is taken between the meander curves. The angle is said to be "θ". The "θ" value when reaches 5° or less and the distance between two tangents are 1 km or less the meander reaches the breaking point (Basu, S.R., 2005).

Channel Change

- Topographical sheets of 1927, 1968-69, LISS-III satellite image of 2008 and 2015 are geo-rectified and processed to identify the nature of channel oscillation and major areas of change.

Morphological Changes of the River Bhagirathi

Change in Terms of Total Length, Number of Loops and Number of Cut-offs within the Study Area

The Bhagirathi is the principal perennial stream of the study area. It enters into the study area in the north-western part, just few kilometres south of Katwa town. The total length of the river within the study area is about 69.9 km. The river takes a highly meandering course throughout the whole study area and leaves long loops of disused channels which have become ox-bow lakes, *bils* and swamps over time.

The Bhagirathi, in its upper reaches (the reach upward the Nabadwip town) is at present a comparatively insignificant stream, but surrounding country gives evidence of the vast size which it attained when it formed the main bed of the Ganges (*Gazetteers*, Nadia, April 1978). Alterations are continually taking place, loops being formed, cut through and reformed throughout the whole stretch of the Bhagirathi in its seaward course. So the traces of old channels in the form of semi-circular *bils* or lakes are frequent along the banks (*see* Table 3.1).

Table 3.1 depicts some important morphological aspects of the river Bhagirathi in the study area. The total length of the river Bhagirathi (within the study area) was 73.97 km during 1927, which reduced to 70.47 km in 1968-69 and now it is 69.89 km. However, the number of cut-offs has increased from five in 1927 to nine in 2008. These morphological aspects

Table 3.1: Some Aspects of Fluvial Morphology

Morphological Properties (within study area)	*Bhagirathi*		
	1927	1968-69	2015
Actual length of river	73.97	70.47	69.89
Number of meander loops	9	10	8
Number of cut-offs	5	6	9

Source: Raw Data obtained from Topographical Sheets No. 79 A/2, 79 A/3, 79 A/6, 79 A/7 and 79A.
Survey of India, LISS-III image of November 2008 and 2015, and compiled by researcher.

reveal that the river Bhagirathi is in very dynamic condition and having a tendency to shortening its course by straightening the channel.

Sinuosity Index of the River Bhagirathi within the Study Area

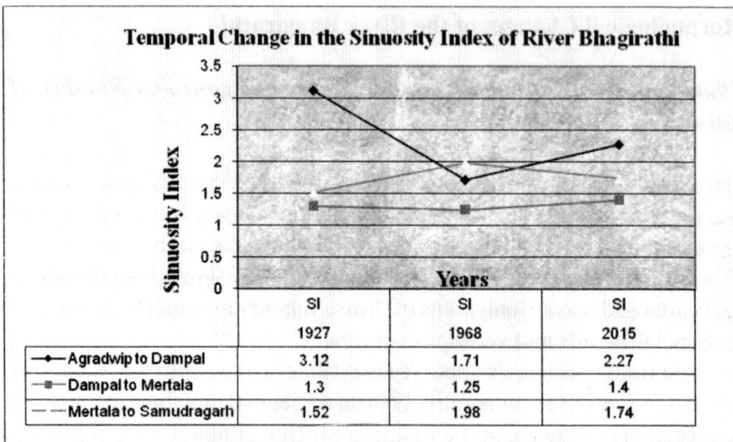

Fig. 3.1: Temporal Change in the Sinuosity Index of River Bhagirathi

From Fig. 3.1 the sinuosity index of the river Bhagirathi at some particular stretches clearly depicts that the river has a winding course, due to flat gradient on which it flows and also due to the amount of sediment it is carrying. In these parts sinuosity ranges from 1.25 to 3.12. In 1927 the river in the Agradwip to Dampal stretch was flowing through a very winding or torturous course, the index was 3.12, due to which Agradwip loop (Fig. 3.2) now became a cut-off namely *Chara Ganga*.

The sinuosity index is still very high (2.27) in this area. In Mertala to Samudragarh stretch the river is flowing through a meandering course, index ranging from 1.52 to 1.98. The loop near the Nabadwip became very acute in 1970 to 1980 period, during the 1985 monsoon (year got from the respondents during door-to-door survey) the river by-passed the loop which now became an ox-bow lake namely *Chupi bil.*

The channel deposition sometimes enhances the intensity of erosion in certain portions. In the study area, formation of mid-channel bars (near the village Nawapara, Kamalnagar, Charkasthasali) and several point bars have become the sites of cultivation. In course of time, these will be stabilised making the existing channel narrower and enhances the energy level of the fluvial system. The immediate impact is severe erosion few kilometres downstream in the villages like Mertala and Majida, where the flow vectors would naturally be accelerated.

Formation of Cut-offs or *Bil*s

The cut-offs or the *bils* are nothing but the former river courses, left-out as a part of dynamic fluvial condition. These cut-offs are mainly formed due to loose texture of the soil and the variation in the amount of discharge in the rivers. Continuous extension of the meander bends when reaches at the breaking point, the river by-passed the meander loop with ultimate formation of cut-offs. The formation of cut-offs have led to the sudden increase in gradient because of the straitening of the channel and the increasing the hazard of river bank erosion (Basu, S.R., 1972).

For the study of the cut-offs an angle is taken between the meander curves. The angle is said to be "θ". The value of "θ" is defined to be the angle made between two tangents in the outward direction and the tangents being drawn from such two points on the curvature of the meanders so that the angle between the tangents just shifts from inward to outwards direction. The "θ" value when reaches 5° or less and the distance between two tangents is 1 km or less the meander reaches the breaking point. It was observed that at Purbasthali-Mayapur reach the angle made between two tangents was 4°-5° and the distance was 0.75 km which reached at the breaking point and cut-off had occurred namely Chupi bil (Basu, S.R., 1972). In 1927, the loop near Agradwip was reached near the breaking point where the angle remained 5° and distance was 1.4 km (Fig. 3.2). This loop became a cut-off namely Chara Ganga about 1950s. With this idea, the author tried to find out the possibility of the formation of the cut-offs which will occur in near future in the study area.

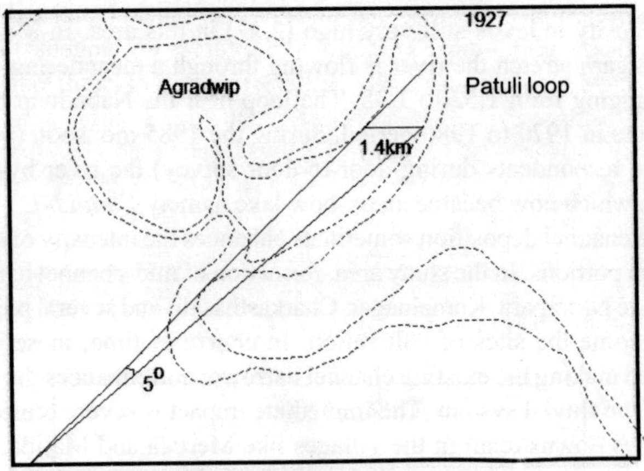

Fig. 3.2: Formating of cut-offs or *Bils*

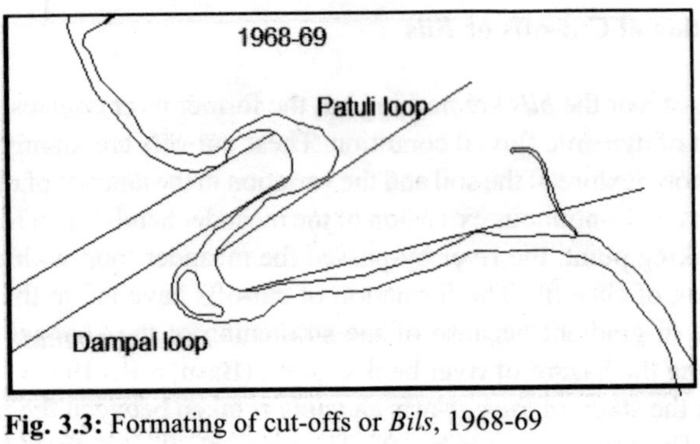

Fig. 3.3: Formating of cut-offs or *Bils*, 1968-69

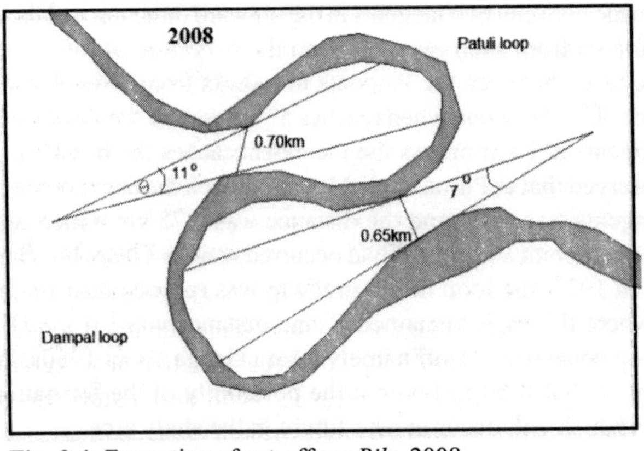

Fig. 3.4: Formating of cut-offs or *Bils*, 2008

It is seen from the study of the meander curves near Patuli and Dampal that during the year 1968-69 for both of the curves the tangents remained parallel and divergent respectively. In 2008, the angle of Patuli loop became 11° with distance 0.70 km and Dampal loop with 7° angle and distance 0.65 km. From the study of these meanders it can be assumed that both of the loops have changed in between the year 1968-69 and 2008, but they have not yet reached up to the breaking point, so, they will not form a cut-off in very near future. The tangents remained parallel in case of other loops like Per Media and Samudragarh, so, there have no chance of cut-off formation in near future (Fig. 3.5).

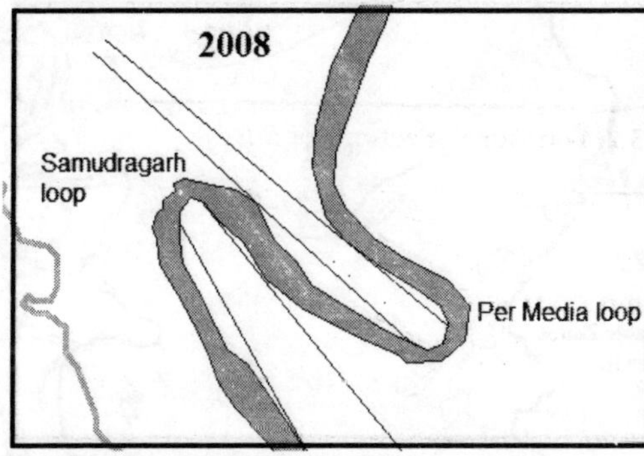

Fig. 3.5: Parallel tangents in 2008

Channel Shifting of the River Bhagirathi in the Purbasthali

Changes during the Period of Rennell (1779) and 1927

Comparing the maps of 1779 and 1927 (Fig. 3.2), it is observed that during the time of Rennell (1779), the northern course of the river Bhagirathi comprising of two meandering bends was situated in the middle part of Agradwip in between the 23°30′N to 23°35′N latitude and 88° 15′E to 88° 20′E longitude (Fig. 3.2). The concave part of one meander belt was covering the villages namely Santoshpur, Mamudpur, Patuli, while another bend was covering the villages such as Jhaudanga, Sarisa of Purbasthali-II block. The river took a sharp bend at the northern part of the village Majida, then it moved southwards (following the 88° 20′E longitude) up to the northern part of the village Sajiara. It is interesting to note that in 1927, another new loop became active near Agradwip (left side of 1779 course) and the meander bend near Patuli was stretched

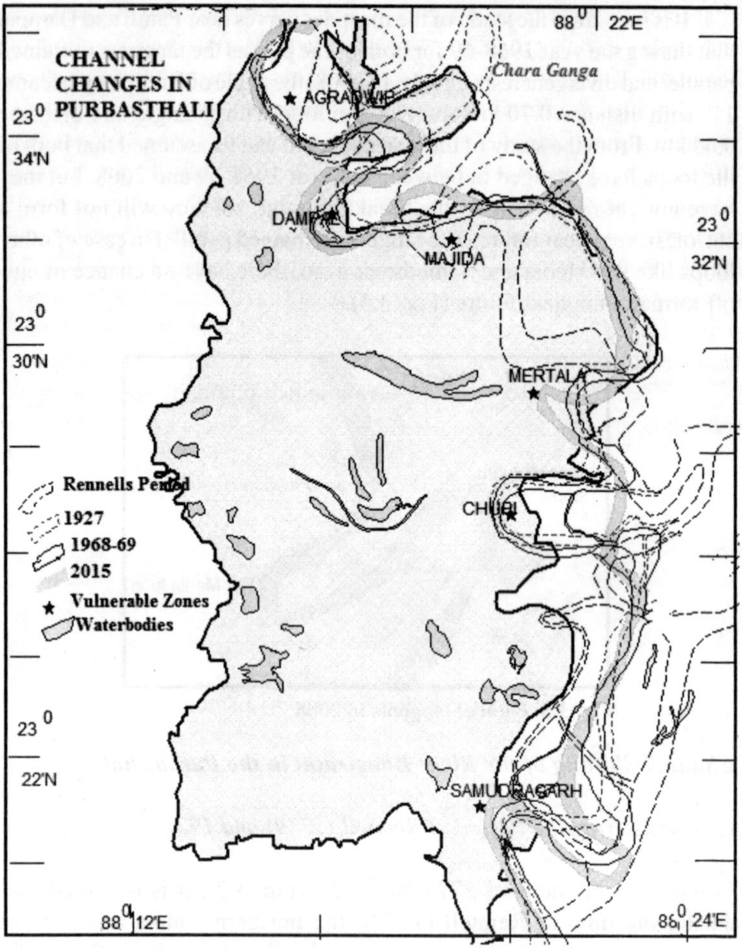

Fig. 3.6: Channel shifting of River Purbasthali

Source: SOI topo sheets of English and Metric scale of the year 1927 and 1968 and Georectified Google earth image of 2015, LISS-III image of 2008, November, and prepared by researcher.

more in northwestwards. The small meander bend, few kilometre downstream of Patuli, started to move westwards in this period, eroding the right bank near the villages like Dampal, Narayanpur. The southward moving straight part (Fig. 3.6) became left-out part namely Kamakshya

Khal in due course of time and river was shifted eastward. There were four meander bends in between the village Mertala and junction of Bhagirathi-Jalangi in 1779, of which eastward moving meander belts near the village Mertala and Char Kasthasali became ox-bow lakes namely Sujanpur Bil and Mara Ganga. Another two bends became active and shifted about 1 to 3 kilometre westward eroding the villages such as Gopipur, lower part of Mertala, Sankarpur, Purbasthali of Purbasthali-II block. In the downstream part of Bhagirathi-Jalangi junction, considerable change occurred near the town of Nabadwip. The active channel in the western part of Nabadwip became inactive and three bends were developed near the town of Nabadwip and the villages of Bankar Dhopadi and Jaluidanga. The creation of Nawapara bil was only remarkable change in the river Jalangi and rest of the river remained relatively stable with its numerous bends.

Changes during the Period of 1927 and 1968-69

From the maps of 1927 and 1968-69 (Fig. 3.6), it is clearly observed that since the Rennell's period, a considerable change has been occurring near the Agradwip. The active loop during the period 1927 became palaeochannel namely Chara Ganga and the main flow shifted towards the western part (Purbasthali side). The meander bend near Patuli was reactivated and consequent erosion occurred at Dampal, Patuli, Jhaudanga. The meander bends became narrower at the downstream part of Bhagirathi-Jalangi junction, half a kilometre downstream from the junction point, the intensity of erosion increased at the eastern bank of Bhagirathi (western bank was more erosion prone in 1927) near the villages like Maheshganj, Char Maijdia. On the other hand, the river shifted to the western bank and there was loss of a considerable amount of land of the villages namely Per Media, Gadhkhali, south-eastern part of Nabadwip town of Nabadwip block and Jaluidanga, Nasaratpur of Purbasthali block. The meander bend near the villages Per Media and Bankar Dhopadi became narrower and shifted more eastward.

Changes during the Period of 1968-69 and 2015

Closing of the meander loop and formation of an ox-bow lake, few kilometre upstream of Nabadwip is the most interesting geomorphic feature which has been evolved in this area during last 40 years (1969 to 2009). The rate of bank erosion has increased to alarming condition in some places. Most recently, the erosion near Agradwip side has decreased but it has increased to the Char Bishnupur side of Katwa block.

Causes of River Bank Erosion in the Purbasthali

The changing river courses are interrelated with the river bank erosion. The river bank erosion is a dynamic natural process in the deltaic landscape. The river is a living reality that needs space. The bank erosion varies significantly along river channels. This spatial variability in erosion rates is controlled by some factors like longitudinal and vertical variation of grain size, moisture content, organic content, bank vegetation, channel curvature, bank angle and related variations in shear stress applied on a given bank.

The river Bhagirathi has a natural tendency to shape its course according to the varying discharges received from Farakka barrage and its western tributaries. In order to tackle the continuous excess volume of water during the monsoon period, the river increases its length by meandering. When the curvature of the river loop reaches at a breaking point the river course is by-passed through the process of cut-off. Thus, the tendency of the river to straighten its course ultimately increase its gradient, increase in gradient also increase the velocity of the flowing water and the process of erosion become severe endangering the nearby settlements (Basu, S.R., 1972).

A close observation of the bank material along the channel of Bhagirathi depicts clearly the gradual fining of bank material upwards. Here the cohesive clay layer (about 1m) overlie non-cohesive micaceous sandy layer. This type of vertical stratification is mainly responsible for severe bank erosion through undercutting of bottom layer during the monsoon months with heavy discharge. Long crack develops and bank collapses into the river along this line.

Repeated wetting and drying can contribute to cracking which will in turn reduces shear strength of bank materials and increases its vulnerability to erosion. During the time of bankful discharge, a huge amount of water enters into the side of bank. Returning water pressure at the post-monsoon period also causes erosion.

The discharge of the river plays very significant role in bank erosion. Water flowing in the channel exerts a drag force on the river banks which lead to the detachment of surface partials. Fast moving water current during the rising stage of discharge removes unconsolidated sediment from the base of bank which ultimately collapses. The Ganga being a meandering channel, erosion of the bank is a common feature.

Conclusion

The discussion in the preceding reveals that the river Bhagirathi has an oscillating course since the past. On the basis of the records available and observations made, the river Bhagirathi is flowing in a highly meandering channel throughout the whole study area. From the Fig. 3.6 it is clear that in most of the stretches the river Bhagirathi is following a meandering course since Rennells time to 2015. Concave banks of the river are the maximum erosion prone zones which have been observed during the field study and from the maps of the Bhagirathi floodplain. Continuous shifting of the river course threatens the railway lines and roads, settlement, schools, agricultural lands etc. The life of people in the area is highly insecure and uncertain. Bank erosion affects people, irrespective of farm sizes. Riverbank erosion causes setback for village agriculture. Along with homestead settlements, it erodes farmland, infrastructure and the communication system. The big farmers are the worst affected, followed by medium farmers, and marginal groups. The affected people lose their assets and are forced to draw on savings and often fall into further debt. Most of the environment-induced refugees turn mainly into labourers or rickshaw pullers. A large proportion of the victims remain unemployed due to lack of work opportunities. Moreover, women head many of these families. The female-headed households displaced by riverbank erosion and residing on embankments are the most deprived group. Fortunately, now-a-days, social workers are focusing on these problems and also suggesting strategies of survival to these people

References

Bagchi, K. and Mukherjee, K.N. (1978). *Diagnostic Survey of Deltaic West Bengal*. Calcutta: The Project from Geography Department, Calcutta University.

Basu, S.R. and Chakravorty, S.C. (1972). Some considerations over the decay of the Bhagirathi drainage system. In K.G. Bagchi (Ed.), *The Bhagirathi-Hooghly Basin* (pp. 59-77). Calcutta: R.D. Press.

Bhattacharya, K. (1959): *Bangladesher Nad-Nadi o Parikalpana*. Bidyadae Pvt. Ltd., Calcutta.

Fergusson, J. (1912). On Recent Changes in the Delta of the Ganges. In Kumud Ranjan Biswas (compiled), *Rivers of Bengal*, Vol. I (pp. 183-227). Kolkata: Government of West Bengal.

Garrett, G.H.E. (1910, 2001). *Bengal District Gazetteers, Nadia*. Calcutta: Bengal Secratariat Book Depot.

Goudie, A. (Ed.) (1981). *Geomorphological Techniques*, George Allen & Unwin, London.

Gregory, K.J. (Ed.) (1977). *River Channel Changes*. Chichester: John Wiley & Sons.

Hirst, F.C. (1915). Report on the Nadia Rivers. In Kumud Ranjan Biswas (compiled), *Rivers of Bengal,* Vol. III, Parts-I and II. Kolkata: Government of West Bengal.

Hunter, W.W. (1877). *A Statistical Account of Bengal*, Vol. II. London: Trubner & Co.

Inglis, W.A. (1909). The Canals and Flood Banks of Bengal. In Kumud Ranjan Biswas (compiled), *Rivers of Bengal*, Vol. V, Part-II (pp. 47-54). Kolkata: Government of West Bengal.

Peterson, J.C.K., 1997. *Bengal District Gazetteers Burdwan, West Bengal District Gazetteers*, Higher Education Department Government of West Bengal, Bikash Bhavan, Calcutta.

4

Assessment of Ecology of Lateritic Tract of Rarh Bengal and its Anthropogenic Modification in Ajay-Damodar Interfluve of Barddhaman District, West Bengal

Shyamal Dutta and *Sanat Kumar Guchhait*

1. Introduction

Lateritic region of West Bengal covers more than one-third of the area of the state and is comprised of parts of the Central and Western Districts, i.e. Birbhum, Barddhaman, Bankura, Puruliya and Paschim Medinipur. All of these districts belong to Rarh Bengal (Pradhan, *et al.*, 2012; Bagchi, K., Mukherjee, K.N., 1979). As a part of Rarh Bengal, Barddhaman is an important district among the western plateau districts of West Bengal. Considering the drainage and physiographical parameters the said region belongs to Ajay Damodar Interfluve which is a part of Bengal Sedimentary Basin. This interfluve region is characterized by active tectonic actions with number of active sub-surface faults in different directions (Bagchi and Mukherjee, 1979; Singh, *et al.*, 1998; Nath, *et al.*, 2014). So, this region is very much significant in terms of its geological formation as well as topographic expression. Topographic variation in relation to geological formation has a strong resemblance with edhaphic and floristic composition of the region. The lateritic concentration in the west-central part is mainly due to the effect of varied geological formation in different time span which is further associated with high concentration of tropical dry deciduous forest (mainly *sal* forest) in the region of Pandebswar, Durgapur-Faridpur, Kanksa-Panagar, Aushgram and Galsi. Administratively, the entire Protected Forest region under Barddhaman Forest Division is situated in and around the lateritic tract of Barddhaman District. Considering the level and degree of development in case of agriculture, industrial, mining as well as urbanization Barddhaman District is much ahead among the other districts of Rarh Bengal and is placed more advanced position in all-over West Bengal. But with the pace of developemnt during last three to four decades the natural resources like soil and forest has lost its glory and continuously degraded either in quantity or quality. Present study concerns critical assesment of structure-topography relationship and its impact on bio-climate and soil charateristics in the central part of Barddhaman District, as well as drastic change of components of natural environment due to massive anthropogenic actions for the last four decades.

2. Methods and Database

2.1 Study Area

The focused central part of Barddhaman District is occupying an area of 4910 sq.km. including the surrounding area under study. This area is located in the middle portion if the shape of the whole district is assumed as a hammer like shape. The study area is bounded by the Ajay River in the north, girdled by Damodar River on the south while the Kunur River flows through the middle part from west to east direction. Taking a square shape area comprising the part of Southern Birbhum and northern Bankura District the study is carried out for multi-temporal satellite image interpretation, but major emphasis is given of the central part of Barddhaman District (*see* Fig. 4.1).

The study area lies in the east-central part of the 'Rarh Bengal' (Bagchi and Mukherjee, 1979) and is divided into four distinct geomorphic units through contour lines. On the basis of Pedo-geomorphological classification (Singh *et al.*, 1998), the western part of the region lies under the "Old Fluvial or Deltaic Plains", whereas eastern part lies on the "Young Fluvial Plains". Geologically, the area is characterized by Quaternary sediments on the east and by Gondwana Super Group with some lateritic patches on the western part (GSI, 2001). Elevation of the region ranges from 2 to 154 m (as per SRTM data, 2013), where a major portion of land comes under Plateau Fringe (*see* Figs. 4.2a and 4.2b).

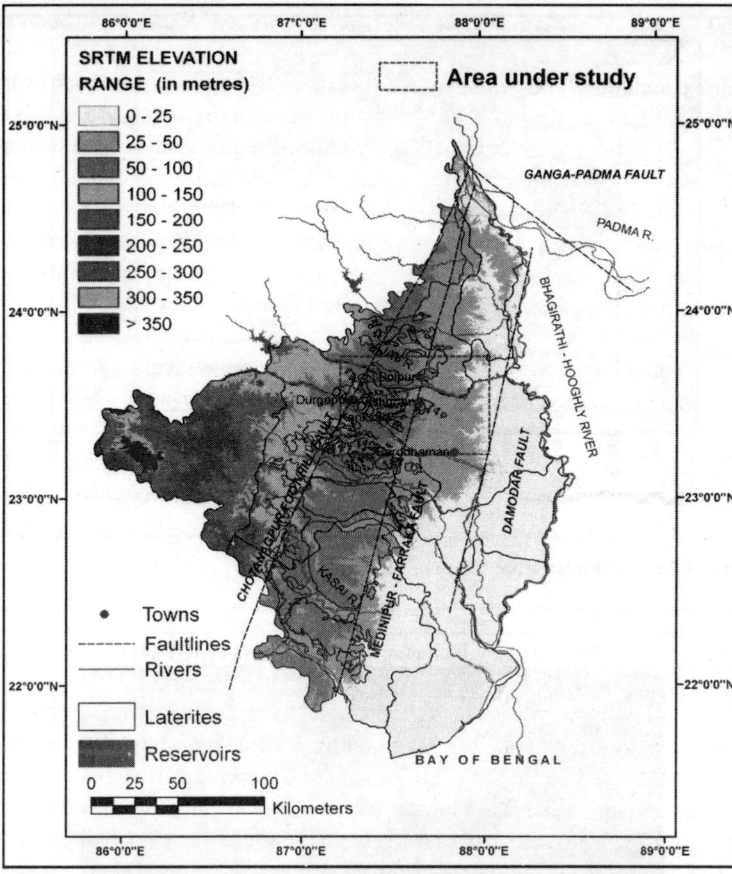

Fig. 4.1: Physiographic diversity, location of Laterites and Locational Specifities of Study Area under Rarh Bengal

2.2. Spatial Mapping

Present lateritic interfluve region of Ajay-Damodar River under Barddhaman district has been investigated to examine the influences of Quaternary neotectonic activities on surface topography and Pedo-geomorphology of the said region by applying an integrated study on fluvial geomorphology and digital topography analysis using topographic maps (1:50,000), ASTER DEM (30m.) and STRM DEM (30 m) and multi-spectral imagery (LISS IV and Landsat 5). To a mass spatial

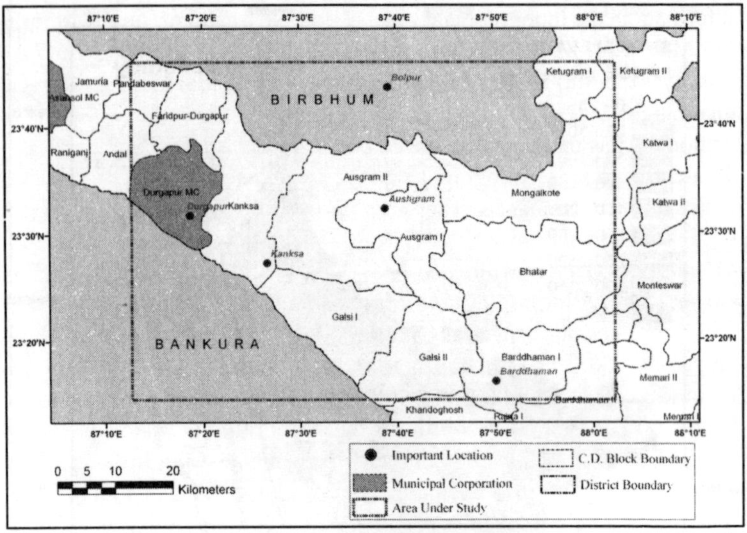

Fig. 4.2a. Administrative set up of Study Area

Fig. 4.2b. SFCC of Ajay-Damodar Interfluve shows red patches which indicates the remnants forest cover in Barddhaman District

information, the topographical sheets (1:50,000 scale) of Survey of India (73 M/3, M/4, M/6, M/7, M/10, M/11, M/14, M/15), GSI (Geological Survey of India) district resource maps of Barddhaman, geological quadrangle map of Barddhaman (73 M), and district planning maps of National Atlas of Thematic Mapping Organization (NATMO) are used. To identify major physiographic features of southern West Bengal, seven Landsat ETM+ (Enhanced Thematic Mapper Plus) post-monsoon images of 2000-2001 (path/row: 138/43, 138/44, 138/45, 139/43, 139/44, 139/45 and 140/44) are downloaded from the website of GLCF (Global Land Cover Facility: http://glcf.umd.edu/data/landsat/). The Landsat ETM+ sensor has six multispectral bands (1, 2, 3, 4, 5, and 7) with spectral range of 0.450-2.350 μm and spatial resolution of 30 m, including two thermal bands (6.1 and 6.2) with 60 m resolution and one panchromatic band of 15 m spatial resolution. These georeferenced bands (UTM WGS84) of each scene are integrated in one image using Erdas Imagine 9.1 software. Finally, seven images are joined using mosaic tool of Erdas Imagine 9.1 to get total coverage of southern West Bengal. The ASTER (Advanced Space Borne Thermal Emission and Reflection Radiometer) elevation data with 30 m resolution (GCS WGS84) of 2011 is downloaded from the website of the Earth Explorer (http://earthexplorer.usgs.gov/) and it is also processed through Erdas, using AOI and subset tools. All unrectified raster and vector data are projected in UTM (Universal Transverse Mercator) assigning datum of WGS84 (World Geodetic Survey, 1984) using the project raster tool of ArcGIS 9.3 software to overlap these data accurately. The contours of elevation are generated using ASTER data and the spatial analyst tool of ArcGIS with an interval of 50 m. To identify and plot the region of laterites we have applied NDVI (Normalized Difference Vegetation Index) and Iron Oxide Index using the processed FCC image. Niyogi *et al.* (1970), Bagchi and Mukherjee (1983), Biswas (1987), Singh *et al.* (1998), and Sarkar *et al.* (2005) have investigated the composition of soil series and radiometric dating of laterite which are used to recognize soil-geomorphic units of lateritic *Rarh* region. Though the present area under study totally belongs to central part of Rarh Bengal, and then spatial mapping is done after subsetting the area of interest (AOI) from whole Rarh Bengal to give more focus at district level. To analyze bio-climatic features forest cover mapping has been done using the previous-mentioned SOI topographical maps. In this purpose protected forest boundary of Barddhaman forest division has been used to generate the vector occupied by the green belt. Physical and chemical properties of block level soil samples have been derived from different district level published reports. Population and urbanization history of whole district has been analysed from *District Gazetteers and District Census Handbook* (1971-2011).

3. Results and Analysis

Laterite tract of West Bengal though primarily a geo-genic feature, but its formation is no more a reflection of geological influence, rather a definite type of climatic process that leads to form a specific type of lithology. This lithology also respond to distinct form of pedo-ecology that inherently welcomes a particular type of bio-ecology where diversity of flora and fauna are distinct in nature. Following section crops up all this facets of laterite tract.

3.1. Physiographic Framework of Study Area

As a part of Rarh Bengal, Barddhaman is an important district among the western plateau districts of West Bengal. Considering the drainage and Physiographical position, the district belongs to Ajay Damodar Interfluve which is a part of Bengal Sedimentary Basin. This interfluve region is characterized by active tectonic actions with number of active sub-surface faults in different direction (Bagchi and Mukherjee, 1979; Singh *et al.*, 1998; Nath *et al.*, 2014). On the basis of 156 m. contour, the Rarh tract is again sub-divided into plateau proper and plateau fringe (Bagchi and Mukherjee, 1979). Western part of the present study area belongs to this broad plateau fringe region, whereas the eastern part of the study area belongs to piedmont and moribund delta respectively towards east (Bagchi and Mukherjee, 1979). General slope of this region is from NNW to SSE (*see* Figs. 4.3a and 4.3b).

As reflected from SRTM DEM (30 m.) of present study region, area west of the Chotonagpur Foothill Fault (CFF) has maximum elevation above 80 metres whereas the eastern part of the Medinipur-Farrkka Faults (MFF) have an average elavtion below 50 metres. The exact region between these two faults has an average elevation between 50-80 metres with continuous rolling topographic undulation that mainly reflects as a micro-fringe region in Barddhaman District. So, there is an inmportant affect of tree fauts on topography of said region. These faults were reactivated by the stress of neotectonic activities during the early Pleistocene epoch (Singh *et al.*, 1998), which are Chhotanagpur Foothill Fault (CFF) in the western part, Medinipur Farakka Fault (MFF) in the

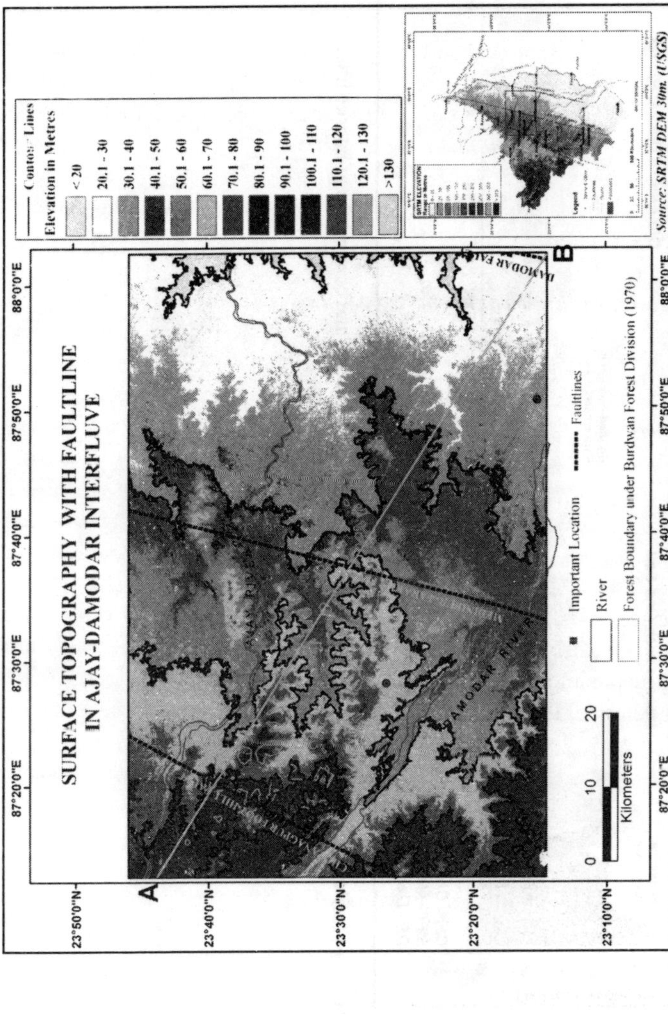

Fig. 4.3a: A Surface Topography of Ajay-Damodar Interfluve of Barddhaman District along with Fault-line and Protected Forest Boundary

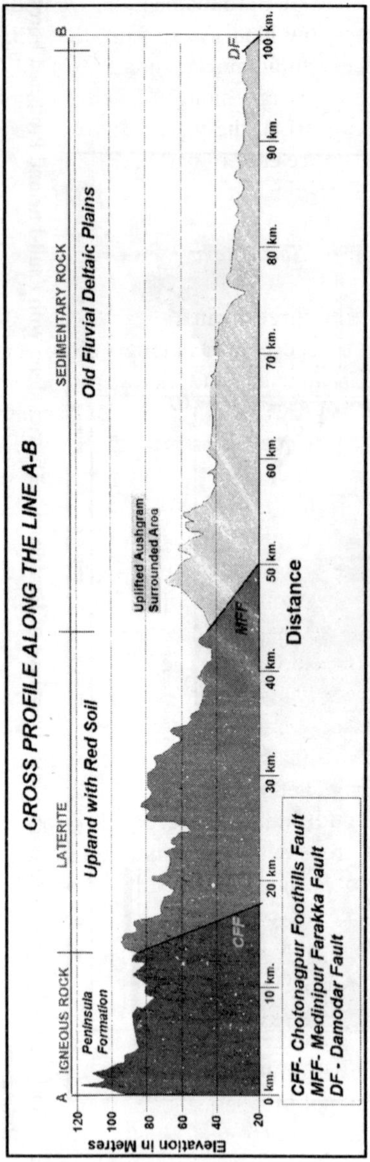

Fig. 4.3b: Cross-profile along NNW-SSE direction with its geological formation and occurrence of laterite tract

middle of the Ajay-Damodar Interfluve of Barddhaman and Damodar Fault (DF) in the eastern sedimentary low land. As a result, the entire ADI region was divided into four geotectonic blocks in the NWW-SEE direction and figured up a step-like landscape along the entire region (Fig. 4.3b). According to Nath *et al.* (2014), the western part of CFF comes under the 'Indian Shield' and entire eastern part is under 'Bogra Shelf' or western Foreland Shelf of Bengal Basin.

3.2. Geological Formation and Laterite Soil Characteristics

Geologically, this region experiences three formations—Gonwana, Tertiary and Quaternary succesively. It exposes as Quaternary sediments on the east and by Gondwana Super Group with some lateritic patches on the western and west-central part (GSI, 2001) (Fig. 4.4); it is also overlaid by Vindhyan Alluvium (Agricultural Finance Corporation Ltd., 2013). Gondwana formation includes Supra-Panchet formation with coarse grained ferrugiouns sandstone and red siltstone mainly around the Durgapur urban area, Panchet formation with sandstone and red-green clay manily in Faridpur-Andal area, Raniganj Formation with sandstone, coal and shale, granite gneiss of Proterozoic formation (GSI, 2001). Quaternary formation includes Laterite, newer and alluvium which constitute the maximum portion of the study area. This whole are is a small part of Bengal basin more specifically under Rarh Bengal of Bengal Basin. The major peninsular river system of Damodar, Ajay, Mayurakshi, Brahmani, Kasai and Subarnarekha etc. is the chief carrier of ferruginous coarse sediments into the shallow-marine shelf zone of Bengal Basin since the Paleogene, forming later a north-south undulating secondary lateritic upland due to prolong lateritization processes and minimal upliftment (Niyogi *et al.*, 1970). This shelf zone of Bengal Basin is still tectonically active and since the Late Eocene, tectonic upliftment and subsidence initiated marine transgression and regression to this region, developing different fluvio-deltaic sedimentary units wherein the ferruginous profiles (*in situ* and *ex situ* laterites) are of the oldest formations of Bengal Basin. Laterite in this region is maily *ex situ* in character.

An emblematic north-south lateritic belt of West Bengal [geographically recognized as *Rarh* Bengal by Bagchi and Mukherjee (1983)], with the ferruginous gravels and kaolinite deposits (from Rajmahal Hills to Subarnarekha Basin) borders this province to make the transitional diagnostic landforms and distinct sedimentation pattern in between the Archean-Gondwana Formation at west and recent Quaternary alluvium

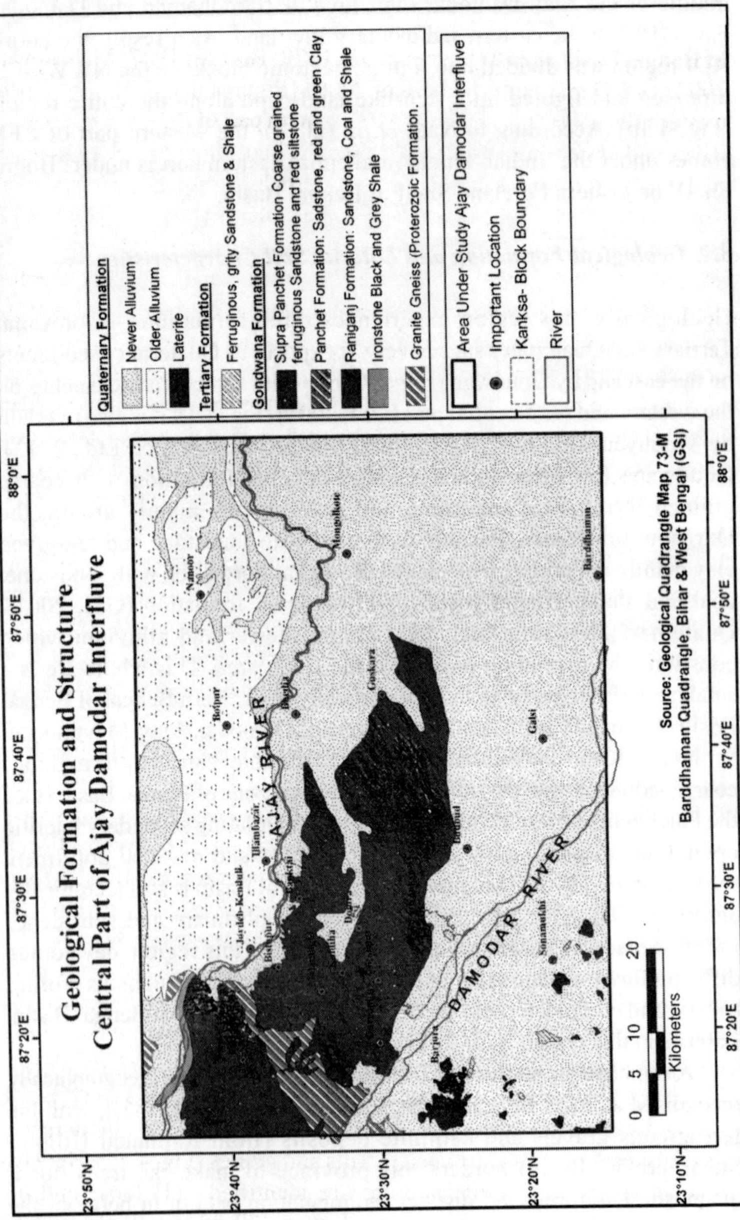

Fig. 4.4: Geological Formation and Lithological composition of Central part of Barddhaman District

of Bengal Basin at east (Niyogi *et al.*, 1970; Biswas, 1987; Mahadevan, 2002; Das Gupta and Mukherjee, 2006) (Figures 4.1, 4.2). The north-western Bengal Basin, in between the western part of Bhagirathi-Hooghly River and eastern part of Chotanagpur Plateau, shows all the variations of lateritic terrain, consisting of western hilly upland, intermediate degradational plain and eastern older deltaic plain (Mukhopadhyay, 1972; Biswas, 1987). On the intermediate degradational plain (dissected by rills and gullies), a great variety of laterites (*i.e.* primary and secondary laterites) is observed, showing the sub-surface horizons of hard duricrust, mottled zone and pallid kaolinitic zone. The general belief is that the high-level or primary laterites were formed due to *in situ* chemical weathering of basalt plateau in the monsoon wet-dry climate, and the low-level or secondary laterites are formed by denudation and transport of primary laterites and cementation of accumulated detritus. The laterites of West Bengal are investigated by Morgan and McIntire (1959), Hunday and Banerjee (1967), Niyogi *et al.* (1970), Sengupta (1972), Goswami (1981), Biswas (1987), Vaidyanadhan and Ghosh (1993), Das and Bandyopadhyay (1995), Singh *et al.* (1998), Ghosh and Ghosh (2003), Chatterjee (2008), and Mukhopadhyay and Pal (2009). They have provided significant geological and geomorphological explanations of lateritic landforms which carry distinct palaeogeographic individuality of this north-western marginal part of the Bengal Basin.

Present study area is under the low level laterite zone. The low-level laterites separate the lithological formations of Archean, Gondwana and Paleogene gravels from the Sijua and Chuchura Formations (Quaternary alluvium) deposited over the shelf of Bengal Basin between Pliocene and Pleistocene (Das, 1972). The secondary laterites specifically found as the interfluves in Illambazar, Bolpur, Kanksa, Ausgram, Bankura, and Bishnupur though the variations of horizons are still observed. The presence of a sub-surface layer of kaolinitic clay reddened from above by ferrocolloids (Biswas, 1987) and of rounded pebbles of different rocks, gravelly appearance of crust and the general absence of conventional horizons of laterite signify a detrital origin (*ex situ*) in *Rarh* Bengal.

In the forest tract of Durgapur, Kanksa, Galsi, Augram I and II blocks of Barddhaman district (Ajay-Damodar interfluve), the hardcrust of gravelly laterite is partly eroded by rills and gullies (Fig. 4.4b). Here two distinct layers of pisolitic nodules are identified—(1) loose and less compacted gravelly iron concreted zone (70-80 cm thick) and (2) compacted and hard layer composed of regularly spaced nodules cemented by red clayey matrix being oxblood in colour (Singh *et al.*, 1998; Biswas, 2002).

Different types of soil are encountered in different topographical, biological and hydrological as well as geological condition within the Barddhaman district. In the west coarse gritty soil blended with rock fragments is formed from the weathering of pegmatite, quartz veins and conglomeratic sandstones, as well as sandy soil in a discontinuous patches. This soil is of reddish colour, medium to coarse in texture, acidic in reaction, low in nitrogen, calcium, phosphate and other plant nutrients. Water holding capacity of this soil increases with depth as well as with the increase of clay portions. Towards the east alluvial soil attains an enormous thickness in the low level plains to the east. This alluvial soil is formed of alluvium brought down by the Ajay, Damodar, Bhagirathi and numerous other rivers. These soils are sandy, well drained and slightly acidic in nature. The soil of the lateritic region is characterised by nutrient-poor acidic (pH 5-6.4) sandy loam, clay loam to sandy clay loam with varying levels of sand (48.3-85%), silt (2-28.3%), clay (10.1-29.1%) and organic carbon (0.21-9.89%) (Bhattacharya, *et al.*, 1998; Bhattacharyya *et al.*, 2001; Sarkar *et al.*, 2006, Ghosh and Maji, 2011) (*see* Table 4.1).

3.3. Bio-Climatic Features

Barddhaman experiences a climate which is transitional between CWg3 and AW1 types, where 'C' stands for "warm temperate rainy climates with mild winter", 'W' for "dry winter not compensated for by total rain in the rest of the year",'g3' for "eastern Ganges type of temperature trend and 'AW1' for "tropical savannah climates". The climate of the area is of tropical monsoon type with three seasons, *viz.* winter season from about the middle of November to mid-February. Pre-monsoon or dry summer is from mid-February to mid-June which is intervened by tropical cyclones and hailstorms. From middle of June to mid-October is the wet summer or monsoon when there is appreciable rainfall. The tropic of cancer has overpassed almost the central part of the Barddhaman district (23^{0}30′ North Latitude). As a result the climate of this district is tropical; weather is hot and humid as monsoon climate is. Relative humidity is oppressively high all the year round especially from the middle of May to mid-October. The eastern part of the district the weather is comfortable in winter, but in the western part the temperature considerably goes down. No great difference has been observed in the temperature in different seasons in the Bhagirathi delta. But in the Asansol-Durgapur belt, there is marked

Table 4.1: Block level Physical and Chemical properties of Soil in Laterite tract of Barddhaman District

Block	*Predominant type*	*% to Total Area*	*Other Type*	*% to Total Area*	*Organic Carbon*	*Average P_2O_5*	*Average K_2O*	*pH*	*E.C.*
Barddhaman I & II	Clay Loam	46	Clay, Loam, Sandy Loam	54	N	L	L	A	N
Kanksa	Sandy Loam	55	Loam, Clay Loam and Lateritic	45	L	L	M	A	N
Ausgram I	Clay Loam	40	Loam, Sandy Loam, Clay	60	L	M	M	AN	N
Ausgram II	Sandy Loam	35	Clay, Clay Loam, Loam	65	LM	N	M	AN	N
Bhatar	Clay Loam, Sandy	60	Clay and Loam	40	L	N	M	A	N
Galsi I	Clay	50	Clay Loam, Loam and Sandy Loam	50	M	M	M	A	N
Galsi II	Clay	50	Clay Loam, Loam and Sandy Loam	50	M	M	M	A	N
Ketugram I	Clay Loam	50	Loam and Sandy	50	L	M	M	N	N
Ketugram II	Clay Loam	60	Loam and Sandy	40	L	M	M	N	N
MongolKote	Clay Loam	48	Sandy Loam and Loam	52	L	M	M	A	N
Faridpur-Durgapur	Lateritic	48	Sandy Loam and Loam	52	L	A	VL	A	N
Andal	Lateritic	65	Sandy Loam	35	VL	L	L	A	N
N=NORMAL, M=MEDIUM, L=LOW, VL= VERY LOW; SOIL REACTION (pH): A= Acidic									

Source: Block Level Landuse Categories, 1991.

difference between the winter and the summer temperatures. Block level statistics (Table 4.2) of rainfall shows notable seasonal variation in rainfall, whereas the rainfall decreases in the block situated in the west of said area.

Table 4.2: Block level Normal Rainfall in Laterite tract of Barddhaman District

Block	*Rainfall in mm*			
	Pre-Monsoon	*Monsoon*	*Post-Monsoon*	*Annual Total*
Kanksa	224.1	907.9	14.8	1146.8
Aushgram I	301.7	1138.7	0	1440.4
Aushgram II	375.6	1252.8	41.2	1669
Faridpur	215.1	1190.5	22.5	1428.1
Katoya I	278	925	61	1124
Mangolkote	275	716	102	1093
Bhatar	468.9	1574	109.98	2153.56

Source: Agriculture Development Office of Blocks.

This area is identified as "Tropical Wet-Dry Savanna Morphogenetic Region" where the dominant pedogeomorphic processes are mod-max chemical weathering mainly in wet season, moderate physical weathering, mod-max mass wasting, max fluvial erosion, mod-max fluvial processes (rain-splash, sheet wash, rill and gully erosion), and Laterisation (Chorley, Schumm and Sugden, 1984).

In the District, most of the Western part is barren and a small part of it is still covered with *Sal* (*Shorea robusta*). The natural vegetation is thus *Sal*-forests which are mostly confined to the western uplands of Asansol Subdivision and are mostly protected. The eastern part of the district on the other hand is fertile alluvial plain mostly covered with crop fields. In the Blocks (administrative units) of Kanksa and Aushgram large tracts of land are still covered with *Sal* trees (*see* Fig. 4.5).

The Durgapur forests are continued in the Birbhum district beyond the Ajay river while the forest area in the Asansol subdivision forms a part of the forest area of Dumka District of Jharkhand. The Forest cover of the district, as a whole, have an area of about 277 km^2 which is about 3.94 per cent of the total area of the district (*Source*: SFR, 2011). In the Blocks (administrative units) of Kanksa and Aushgram I and II, large tracts of land are still covered with *sal* trees. The Ajay River flows past unhindered forming the border in the north. Two rivulets, Kunur and Tumuni, Khari flow through the area and join the Ajay River (Khari join Damodar River). In case of Barddhaman district, the State Forest Report (2011) shows that

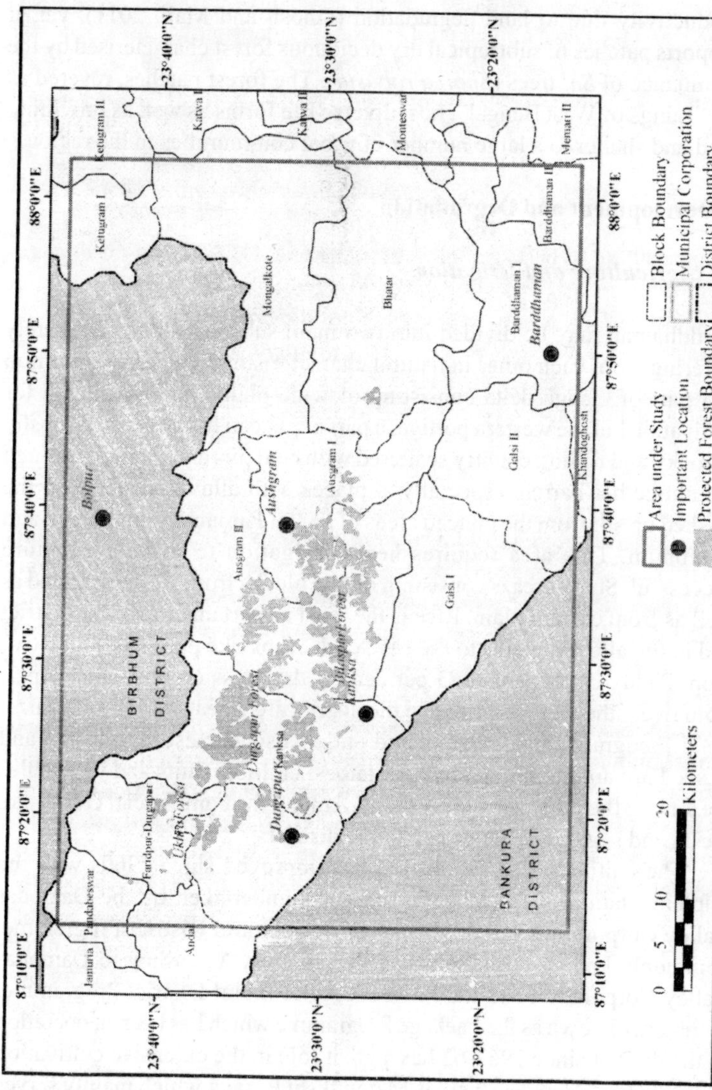

Fig. 4.5: Protected Forest Boundary of Burdwan Forest Division is only residues in Laterite tract in Barddhaman District

the district has only 225 sq. km., i.e. 3.2 per cent of forest coverage of the total geographic area which includes very dense, moderately dense and open forest cover. This region faces the immediate challenge of decreasing productivity due to land degradation (Ghosh and Maji, 2011), yet, it supports patches of subtropical dry deciduous forest characterised by the dominance of *Sal* trees (*Shorea robusta*). The forest patches, revered as the "Lungs of West Bengal", host diverse life forms as well as providing food and shelter to a large number of tribal communities in the region.

4. Development and Degradation

4.1 Agriculture and Irrigation

Barddhaman may be divided into two main sub-tracts, one completely differing from each other in natural characteristics. The eastern portion is a part of Ganga delta consisting of wide plains highly suitable for cultivation but the western portion, a part of plateau fringe consists mostly of rocky and rolling country scattered with coal pits and factories though not altogether barren, especially at places with alluvial deposits of the washed up silt from the plateau areas of Santal Parganas, Singhbhum and Manbhum. This area requires heavy irrigation to make agriculture successful. Study area is consisting of few blocks from western upland as well as from eastern plain. Rice is the most important crop of the district and in the alluvial plains to the east, cash crops like potato is a lucrative crop. Paddy covers about 83 per cent of the gross cropped area. Apart from rice, other cereals grown in the district are wheat, barley and maize. Total foodgrains include gram and pulses also. Rapeseed, mustard and linseed are among the oilseeds. Potatoes, chillies, fruits and vegetables are among the other subsidiary crops. Among the commercial crops jute, mesta and sugarcane are grown in the district.

The cultivation in the district has improved since 1960s with the implementation of the irrigation projects undertaken by the Damodar Valley Corporation and the Intensive Agricultural District Programme, commonly known as the Package Programme. According to Damodar Valley Corporation and the Intensive Agricultural District Programme, commonly known as the Package Programme which has been in operation in the district since 1962-63 has a great role in the extensive cultivation of the district. Besides, there is Mayurakshi Project which mainly serves the Birbhum district, also irrigates a vast tract of arable land of Ketugram Police Station of Barddhaman district. Apart from these, several small and minor irrigation schemes were implemented in the district in recent years.

Effect of developmental activities have changed the land-use pattern of the central blocks to a great extent within the last two or three decades. Forest cover is decreased massively with the advent of population increase and agro-irrigational development as well as industrial expansion mainly around Durgapur region. Forest cover remains only in some patches in the block of Pandebswar, Kanksa, Aushgram I and II blocks as protected forest cover, which constitutes the total forest cover of whole district. Built-up area and agricultural land has been increased at cost of forest land significantly. Though forest cover is still increased as a effect of social forestry programme mainly in Aushgram Block but it is very incompatible with the total area of the district (*see* Tables 4.3, 4.4 and Figs. 4.6a and 4.6b).

Table 4.3: Block level Landuse categories in 1991

Block Name	*Total Area (hec.) 1991*	*Forest (%)*	*Irrigated Area (% to NSA)*	*Net Sown Area (%)*	*Cultivable Waste-land (%)*	*Area not Available for Cultivation (%)*
Andal	3581	0.00	9.83	53.53	20.83	25.64
Pandebswar	7092	0.00	5.42	56.84	14.03	29.13
Durgapur-Faridpur	14109	6.01	7.39	74.34	8.29	11.36
Kanksa	27726	25.91	34.77	50.19	4.82	19.08
Aushgram I & II	63505	4.90	60.63	79.11	3.97	12.03
Bhatar	41212	0.00	89.26	81.06	1.73	1.52
Galsi I & II	38647	0.00	75.08	98.48	0.00	22.91
Barddhaman I & II	39049	0.00	85.46	76.41	0.68	17.21
Mongalkote	36709	0.00	63.59	80.67	4.67	14.67
Ketugram	35419	0.00	81.97	79.70	4.71	15.59

Source: District Statistical Handbook, Barddhaman District, 1991.

4.2 Population Change and Urbanization

It has become increasingly clear that human population have modified natural environment to a great extent. Thereby, the relationship between population and environment has experienced complex transformation that is still not well understood. Population size increased inherently linked to the environment as a result of individual or group resource consumption in the form of use and abuse of resources. As a result population growth and their increasing resource creating activities has degraded air, water, forest and land. At the same time population increase in the newly emerged urban centers in term of census towns (CTs) doubled the pressure on

Table 4.4: Block level Landuse categories in 2001

Block	Total Area (in hec.) 2001	Forest (%)	Net Sown Area (%)	Irrigated Land (% to NSA)	Cultivable Wasteland (%)	Area not available for Cultivation (%)
Ondal	3931.62	0.36	53.02	8.26	20.50	26.11
Pandabeswar	3642.29	1.00	55.67	34.78	9.36	33.97
Faridpur Durgapur	14125.94	8.98	68.52	8.58	4.86	17.64
Kanksa	26631.61	23.43	51.20	37.58	7.82	17.56
Ausgram - II	36045.14	19.14	56.18	45.98	6.23	18.45
Ausgram - I	22233.55	6.32	78.97	77.46	2.32	12.39
Bhatar	41501.18	1.37	80.83	88.52	1.74	16.05
Galsi - I	25279.81	4.22	74.31	71.56	0.77	20.70
Galsi - II	21909.17	0.09	94.84	99.91	0.58	4.48
Burdwan - I	25041.23	0.40	84.25	90.76	0.00	15.35
Burdwan - II	18957.23	0.38	80.42	82.90	0.42	18.78
Mangolkote	36544.21	0.01	80.84	72.01	4.40	14.74
Ketugram - I	19397.55	0.00	81.39	91.31	5.27	13.34
Ketugram - II	16002.94	0.00	83.61	87.84	2.40	13.99

Source: District Statistical Handbook, Barddhaman District, 2001.

existing resources in same time span. But as priority, general population dynamics and urbanization pattern is to be understood since nineteen century and two decades before. After publishing the general census in 1872, an approximate population record has been made as 14,86,400 populations which decreased from previous decades as a effect of terrible epidemic of fever between 1862-72. In 1881, it was found that the population had still decreased further to 13,94,220. This decrease was entirely due to the mortality from the fever which after 1873 made no further westerly progress in Barddhaman (*District Gazetteer*, 1997). During the next decade population remained practically stationary, the total number of persons recorded in 1891 being 13,91,880. In the west, Kanksa, Aushgram region still showed large decrease which was undoubtedly due to the after effects of the epidemic. On the other hand, the increase in the Asansol area, 28.9 per cent was phenomenal, the development of the railway works at Asansol consequent on the opening of the Bengal-Nagpur Railway and the increasing activity in the coal and iron fields having attracted a large immigrant population from parts of Chotanagpur Plateau, Bankura, Bihar (*District Gazetteer*, 1997).

During the next decade conditions were generally favourable and the district in consequence made a rapid recovery in population. In 1901, the growth of the population in the Asansol P.S. is phenomenal; it was 30 per cent since 1891 and by 130 per cent since 1872. Nearly one-third of

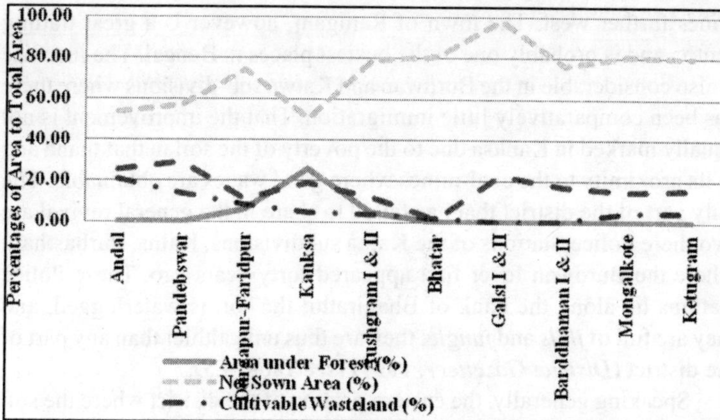

Fig. 4.6a

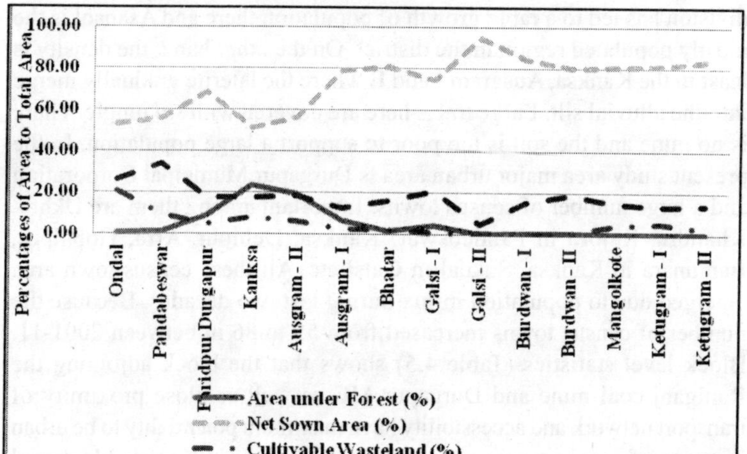

Fig. 4.6b

Fig. 4.6 a and b: Uneven block level distribution of land-uses in Barddhaman District

Source: District Statistical Handbook, Barddhaman District, 2001.

the present inhabitants were born in other districts, and of the district-born many have doubtless migrated from other areas (*District Gazetteer*, 1997). Raniganj shows an increase of 12 per cent since 1891, which is somehow surprising in view of the fact that its coal mine are nearly worked out, and that the people find more remunerative employment in the new mines further west. The town of Raniganj, however is a great trading centre, and is probably one of the busiest places in Bengal. The increase is also considerable in the Burdwan and Katwa sub-divisions where there has been comparatively little immigration. That the improvement is not equally marked in Kanksa due to the poverty of the soil in that thana and to its proximity to the coal-mines where good wages are obtainable. The only part of the district that has failed to share in the general revival are two there Police Stations of the Kalna subdivisions, Kalna, Purbasthali, where the Burdwan fever first appeared forty years ago. These Police stations lie along the bank of Bhagirathi; the soil is waterlogged, and they are full of *jhils* and *jungle*; they are thus unhealthier than any part of the district (*District Gazetteer*, 1997) (*see* Table 4.5).

Speaking generally, the eastern portion of the district where the soil is alluvial is much more thickly populated than the western which rests on the laterite, but the development of the coal mines in the Asansol sub-division has led to a rapid growth of population there and Asansol is the mostly populated region in the district. On the other hand, the density is least in the Kanksa, Ausgram I and II where the laterite gradually merge into the alluvial silt. Large tracts here are covered with *sal* jungle. There is no mine and the soil is too poor to support a large population. In the present study area major urban area is Durgapur Municipal Corporation and a large number of census towns. Important among them are Ukhra, Khandra, Kajora in Pandebswar; Kanksa, Debipur, Arra, Gopalpur, Bamunara in Kanksa, Sukdal in Galsi etc. All these census town area emerged due to population influx during last two decades. Because the number of census towns increased from 55 to 86 in between 2001-11. Block level statistics (Table 4.5) shows that the block adjoining the Raniganj coal mine and Durgapur MC as well as close proximity of transport network and accessibility have maximum potentiality to be urban in terms of census towns e.g., Kanksa, Gopalpur in Kanksa block and Ukhra, Kajora in case of Andal.

5. Conclusion

Discussion so far embarks the panoramic importance of laterite and in-depth analysis of degradation of laterite tract of central Barddhaman. Geogenic origin of laterite of West Bengal as well as India under the influence of alternate hot and humid climate have formed a pristine natural set-up that is endowed with natural forest with medicinal plants, different types of leaves, fruits, flowers, barks, roots those are traditionally used

Table 4.5: Decadal population Dynamics and Urbanization Scenario in Central Barddhaman District

Sl. No.	*C.D. Block*	*Total Area (sq. km.)*	*Year- 2001*				*Year-2011*			
			Total Population 2001	*Population Densiy 2001*	*Number of Urban Centres (CT) 2001*	*% of Urban population*	*Total Population 2011*	*Population Densiy 2011*	*% of Urban population*	*Number of Urban Centres (CT) 2011*
1.	*Galsi-I*	257.4	174123	676	1	6.77	187588	729	12.33	3
2.	*Andal*	84.9	168853	1989	13	75.47	186915	2,202	80.95	14
3.	*Faridpur-Durgapur*	156	105532	676	3	15.74	115924	743	26.36	6
4.	*Pandabeswar*	97.8	146541	1498	12	74.27	161891	1,655	83.50	14
5.	*Kanksa*	278.4	151276	543	3	20.36	178125	640	41.84	7
6.	*Burdwan-I*	250.4	179828	718	NIL	NIL	215943	862	18.57	4
7.	*Burdwan-II*	189.6	138897	733	NIL	NIL	152939	807	4.15	1
8.	*Ausgram-I*	222.3	106850	481	NIL	NIL	119363	537	NIL	0
9.	*Ausgram-II*	360.5	136263	378	NIL	NIL	150896	419	NIL	0
10.	*Bhatar*	415	236478	570	NIL	NIL	263064	634	NIL	0
11.	*Galsi-II*	219.1	133977	611	NIL	NIL	147177	672	NIL	0
12.	*Mongalkote*	365.4	233958	640	NIL	NIL	263240	720	NIL	0
13.	*Ketugram-I*	194	145859	752	NIL	NIL	165408	853	NIL	0
14.	*Ketugram-II*	160	107054	669	NIL	NIL	118567	741	NIL	0

Source: District Census Handbook, Barddhaman District, 1951-2011.

by the tribals generations after generation. Such a intensive man-forest interaction has led to form deep ecological awareness, affection to natural elements (tribals never cut green trees rather collect dried up branches, rarely kills forest animals) and unitedness with nature.

Such a gamut of man-nature interaction has been degraded massively within the last seventy one year, with the massive modification of natural ecology by anthropogenic activity and mining. Establishment of railways, massive industrialization before independence have degraded the surface and sub-surface geo-ecology as well as rapid clearing of natural forest. Post-independence period is responsible for dam construction, alignment of canals, massive industrialization in Durgapur area and extension of agriculture in irrigated tract. All those have massively degraded the bio-geo-ecology of almost entire Ajay-Damodar Interfluve within remnants in Durgapur Forest Region (Kanksa-Aushgram Area). But this forest area is now experiencing massive degradation due to loss of forest, excavation of laterite (locally named *Murrum*) as well as rapid crowding of population around Durgapur Industrial Region leading to rapid sub-urbanization. It would not be a surprise if the remnants of Kanksa-Aushgram Forest are lost due to spillover urbanization.

References

Agricultural Finance Corporation Ltd., 2013. Comprehensive District Agriculture Plan for Burdwan District, pp. 5-45. Eastern Regional Office, Kolkata: Government of West Bengal.

Bagchi, K., Mukherjee, K.N., 1979. *Diagnostic Survey of Rarh Bengal*, Part I, Morphology, Drainage and Flood: 1978, (first ed.) Calcutta: Department of Geography, University of Calcutta, pp. 8-27.

Bagchi, K., Mukherjee, K.N., 1983. Diagnostic Survey of Rarh Bengal (Part II). Calcutta: University of Calcutta, pp. 23-29.

Bhattacharya, K., J.K. Datta, and G.N. Chattopadhyay. 1998. Improvement of edaphic cyanobacterial population through liming in red and lateritic rice soils of West Bengal. *Folia Microbiologica*, 43: 667-71.

Bhattacharyya, P., R. Pal, A. Chakraborty, and K. Chakrabarti. 2001. Microbial biomass and activity in a laterite soil amended with municipal solid waste compost. *Journal of Agronomy and Crop Science*, 187: 207-11.

Biswas, A., 1987. Laterites and lateritoids of Bengal. In: Datye, V.S., Diddee, J., Jog, S.R., Patil, C., (eds.) *Exploration in the Tropics*. Pune: Prof. K. R. Dikshit Felicitation Committee, 157-167.

Biswas, A. (2002): Laterites and lateritoids of Rarh Bengal. In: *Arabinda Smaranika* edited by Roy, R. (Pratiti, Chuchura), 157-167.

Census of India (1991), *Bardhaman, District Census Handbook* (Primary Census Abstract) Directorate of Census Abstract, Government of West Bengal.

Census of India (2001), *Barddhaman, District Census Handbook* (Primary Census Abstract) Directorate of Census Abstract, Government of West Bengal.

Census of India (2011), *Barddhaman, District Census Handbook* (Primary Census Abstract) Directorate of Census Abstract, Government of West Bengal.

Chatterjee, N., 2008. Laterite terrains of the Chotanagpur Plateau fringe region (case study of the Mayurakshi Basin, eastern India). *Indian Journal of Landscape System and Ecological Studies*, 31(1): 115-130.

Chorley, R.J., Schumn, S.A., Sugden, D.E., 1984. *Geomorphology*. London: Methuen, 320-324.

Das, S., 1972. Sedimentation in the Ajay-Damodar Basin. In: Bagchi, K.G., (ed). *The Bhagirathi-Hooghly Basin: Proceedings of the Interdisciplinary Symposium*. Calcutta: University of Calcutta, 9-17.

Das, K., Bandyopadhyay, S., 1995. Badland development over laterite duricrusts. In: Jog, S.R., (ed). *Indian Geomorphology*, Volume I: *Erosional Landforms and Processes*. New Delhi: Rawat Publications, 31-41.

Das Gupta, A.B., Mukherjee, B., 2006. *Geology of N.W. Bengal Basin*. Bangalore: Geological Society of India, 1-154.

District Gazetteer of Burdwan (1997) by J.C.K. Peterson: Biswas, K.R. (ed.), Government of West Bengal, Calcutta.

Geological Survey of India, GSI, 2001. *District Resource Map*: Barddhaman. Government of India, Kolkata.

Ghosh, S., Ghosh, S., 2003. Land degradation due to indiscriminate "Murrum" extraction near Durgapur Town, West Bengal. In: Jha, V.C., (ed.). *Land Degradation and Desertification*. Jaipur: Rawat Publications, 255-267.

Ghosh, S., and T. Maji. 2011. Pedo-geomorphic analysis of soil loss in the lateritic region of Rampurhat I block of Birbhum district, West Bengal, and Shikaripara block of Dumka district, Jharkhand. *International Journal of Environmental Sciences*, 1: 1734-51.

Goswami, A.B., 1981. Hydrogeology of the lateritic terrain of Bankura and Midnapore districts, West Bengal. In: *Proceedings of the International Seminar on Lateritisation Processes*, Trivandum, India, 407-410.

Hunday, A., Banerjee, S., 1967. Geology and Mineral Resources of West Bengal. *Memoirs of the Geological Survey of India*, Volume 97. Delhi: Government of India.

Mahadevan, T.M., 2002. *Geology of Bihar and Jharkhand*. Bangalore: Geological Society of India, 1-563.

Morgan, J.P., McIntire, W.G., 1959. Quaternary Geology of the Bengal Basin, East Pakistan and India. *Geological Society of America Bulletin*, 70(3): 319-342.

Mukhopadhyay, S.C., 1972. Tectonic landforms of the south-western fringe area of the Bhagirathi-Hooghly Basin. In: Bagchi, K.G., (ed.). *The Bhagirathi-Hooghly Basin: Proceedings of the Interdisciplinary Symposium.* Calcutta: University of Calcutta, 39-48.

Mukhopadhyay, S., Pal, S., 2009. Granulometry of soil, climatic panorama and spatio-temporal dynamics of soil erosion of Santiniketan Badland—A parametric statistical approach. *Indian Journal of Landscape System and Ecological Studies*, 31: 185-192.

Nath, S.K., Adhikari, M.D., Maiti, S.K., Devaraj, N., Srivastava, N., Mohapatra, L.D., 2014. Earthquake scenario in West Bengal with emphasis on seismic hazard microzonation of the city of Kolkata, India. *Natural Hazards and Earth System Sciences,* 14, 2549-2575.

Niyogi, D., Mallick, S. and Sarkar, S.K. (1970): A preliminary study of laterites of West Bengal, India. In: *Selected Papers Physical Geography* (Vol. 1) 21st International Geographical Congress edited by Chatterjee, S.P. and Das Gupta, S.P., Calcutta: National Committee for Geography, 443-449.

Sarkar, M., A. Banerjee, and P.P. Pramanick, 2006. Kinetics and mechanism of fluoride removal using laterite. *Industrial and Engineering Chemistry Research*, 45: 5920-7.

Sengupta, S., 1972. Geological framework of the Bhagirathi-Hooghly Basin. In: Bagchi, K.G., (ed.). *The Bhagirathi-Hooghly Basin: Proceedings of the Interdisciplinary Symposium*. Calcutta: University of Calcutta, 3-8.

Singh, L.P., Parkash, B., Singhvi, A.K., 1998. Evolution of the Lower Gangetic Plain landforms and soils in West Bengal, India. *Catena*, 33(2): 75-104.

State Forest Report (2011) West Bengal, Directorate of Forest, Government of West Bengal, Kolkata.

SRTM DEM (30 m.), 2013. United State Geological Survey (USGS).Http:// earthexplorer.usgs.gov/.

Vaidyanadhan, R., Ghosh, R.N., 1993. Quaternary of the East Coast of India. *Current Science*, 64(11-12): 804-815.

5

Vulnerability of Flood in Kamla-Balan River Basin

A Case Study of Darbhanga District, Bihar

Suvradip Halder

Introduction

A flood is an unusual high stage of a river due to run off from rainfall and/or melting of snow in quantities too great to be confined in the normal water surface elevations of the river or streams, as the result of unusual meteorological combination. Flood is considered as a climatic as well as geo-hydrological hazard, but it has anthropogenic origin too. Flood is a result of influence of man on environment. Flood in most of the cases is a quasi-natural hazard which becomes disaster especially in the developing countries like India which is the second most flood affected country in the World. Bihar is India's most flood-prone state, with 76 per cent of the population in the north Bihar living under the recurring threat of flood devastation. 19 out of total 38 districts have been affected by flood in Bihar. The districts are Supaul, Darbhanga, Bhagalpur, West Champaran, Muzaffarpur, Sitamarhi, Khagaria, Sheohar, Madhubani, East Champaran, Araria, Saharsa, Samastipur, Madhepura, Kisanganj, Katihar, Begusarai, Purnea and Vaishali. Flood is like an environmental demon or peril for the people of Mithilanchal or North Bihar. North Bihar is the poorest and the most hazardous region in the country for its poor socio-economic development due to flood. The devastating river basins of North Bihar are Mahananda, Kosi, Kamala-Balan, Bagmati, Budhi Gandak and Gandak from east to the west.

Objectives

- To establish flood as an environmental blight in Madhubani district.
- To find out flood prone zones.
- To show the block-wise damage due to flood.
- To find out the causes of flood.
- To depict the impacts of flood on development.
- To assess the existing flood controlling measures.
- To suggest better specific, curative and preventive measures.

Data Sources and Methodology

(a) Sources of Data

(1) *Primary Data*: By household survey: Interviews on the basis of Questionnaire to collect socio-economic data as well as people's perception on flood situation.

(2) *Secondary Data*: Map of Kamla-Balan river basin, information on relief, drainage, climate, embankments etc., sedimentation, embankments and water level from Flood Control Department, Patna, Jhanjharpur—I and II, F.M.I.S., Patna. Information and data regarding damage and relief measures from Disaster Management Department, Patna, Madhubani and Darbhanga. Demographic data from Census of India, Patna. Satellite imageries taken by Landsat ETM. Ground water data from CGWB, Patna. Data of rainfall, river discharge and gauge from CWC, Patna.

(b) Methodology

(1) *Pre-Field*: Gathering knowledge regarding the study area, characteristics and effects of Kamla-Balan river from some Government Project Reports, different books, journals, thesis and internet.

(2) *Field*: Household survey: Interviews on the basis of Questionnaire to know people's perception on flood situation and status of development. Collection of data on river discharge, water level, sedimentation, embankments, flood damage, relief, population, sex-ratio, literacy rates, number of bank, post offices, school, rainfall etc. from different authorities. Taking photographs.

(3) *Post Field*: Processing, tabulation, sorting and analysis of data, information and literature through cause-effect discussions, preparation of location map, graphical diagrams and suggesting better management techniques.

Study Area

Among the six river systems of Mithilanchal I have selected Kamla-Balan river basin which covers parts of mainly Madhubani (63 % of the study area) and Darbhanga (31%), Saharsa (3%) and Samastipur (3%) districts within 25°30′N to 27°30′N latitude and 85°30′E to 86° 30′E longitude. The river Kamla-Balan drains a total basin area of 7232 sq km. Out of this 4488 sq. km. lies in Bihar in India and the rest 2744 sq km which is the upper reach lies in Nepal. This river is a tributary of Karhe river which is a tributary of Kosi river. Kamla-Balan meets Karhe at Manarwa Khaira which is at the border area of Darbhanga and Samastipur district. As my Study Area I have selected the part of Kamla-Balan river basin which lies in Darbhanga district only comprising 14 C.D. Blocks, *viz.*, Keotiranway, Darbhanga, Bahadurpur, Baheri, Manigachi, Tardih, Ghanshyampur, Kiratpur, Gorabauram, Alinagar, Biraul, Benipur, Kusheshwar Sthan and Kusheshwar Sthan East (*see* Figs. 5.1 to 5.5).

Total area of my study area is 1391 sq km. Kamla river gets its source from Mahabharatal range near Sindhuliagarhi at an altitude of 1200 m in Nepal. The total length of the river Kamla-Balan is 328 km of which 208 km is in Nepal and the remaining 120 km is in India. River Kamla and Balan entres India at Jainagar and Ladania respectively. Balan meets Kamla at Pipraghat in Babubarhi block in Madhubani district. The Tributaries of Kamla-Balan are Balan, Trishula, Dhori and Soni. Paleo channels of Kamla are Pyatghat Kamla, Sakri Kamla, Jiwach Kamla and Old Kamla (*see* Fig. 5.3).

The main land-uses of the study area are vegetation (natural vegetation, planted vegetation and agricultural crops together), built-up area (settlement and transportation lines), water bodies (rivers, lakes and wetlands) and sand deposits.

Furious Scenario of Flood (*see* Figs. 5.7 to 5.12)—The study area experienced massive floods in 20 different years (1974, 1975, 1976, 1978, 1979, 1982, 1985,1986,1987, 1988, 1989, 1992, 1995, 1998, 2000, 2002, 2004, 2007, 2009 and 2011) in the history of last 40 years. Normally flood occurs in July, August and September over here. But in some years it was extended up to November too, e.g., 1987, 2007. Actually, the effect of flood becomes most fatal during August and September. As per the vulnerable flood occurred in 2007, block-wise average

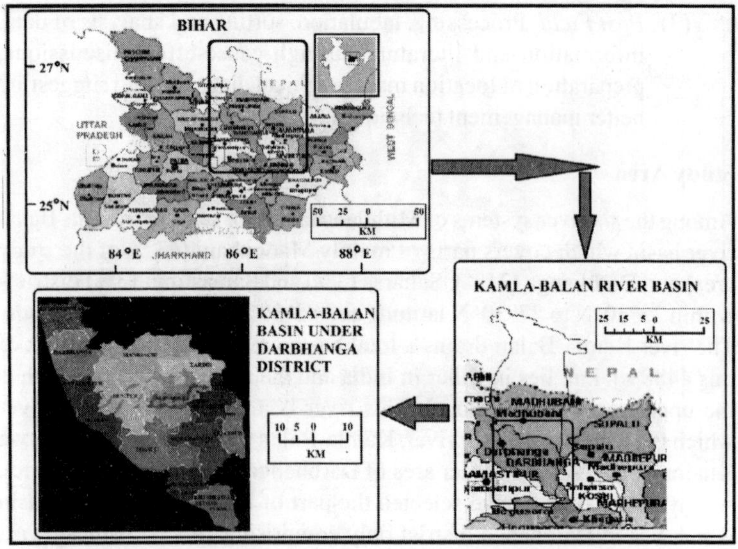

Fig. 5.1: Location of Study Area

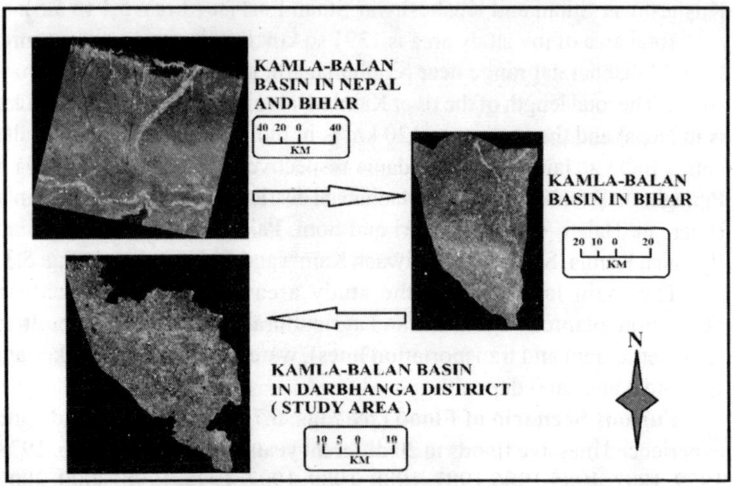

Fig. 5.2: Location of Study Area as Satellite Imagery

Source: Landsat ETM Data, Dated—2nd February, 2015

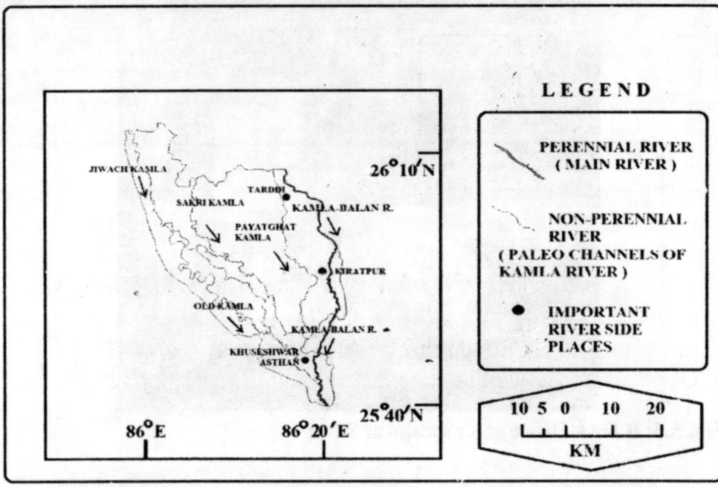

Fig 5.3: Drainage Map of Study Area

Source: Based on Landsat ETM Data of 2nd February, 2015.

Fig. 5.4: Kamla Barrage at Jainagar

Fig. 5.5: B.D.O. Office at Kusheshwar Sthan

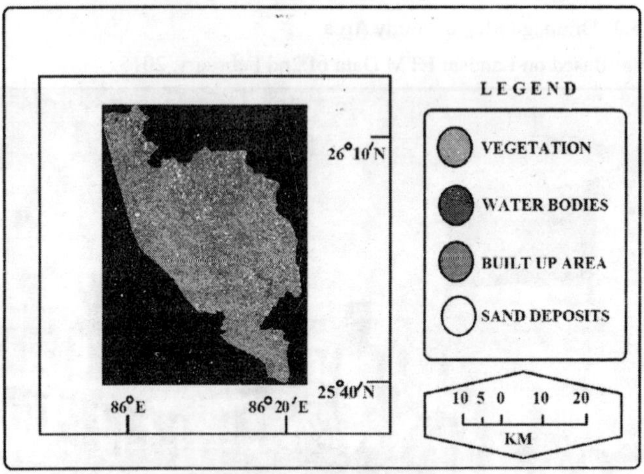

Fig. 5.6: Land Use and Land Cover of Study Area

frequency, percentage of area affected by flood and number of houses damaged as it is near the main river and have very less slope. But western and north-western parts of the study area are more affected as per the crops damaged by flood as these parts produce more crops than the other parts. Maximum vulnerable flood was in 1987 during last 30 years.

During last 10 years most devastating flood was in 2007. A significant flood affected part is almost at the south-eastern part of the study area (Kusheshwar Sthan and Kusheshwar Sthan Purbi block) as this area gets

Fig. 5.7: Flood in Study Area

Fig. 5.8: Flood Affected People

innundated for almost 5-6 months after flood. Biraul suffers from maximum crop damage and Alinagar experiences flood in maximum area (almost 70% of total block area). As per Central Water Commission, Jhanjharpur Danger Level of Kamla-Balan is 50 m at Jhanjharpur and 67.75 m at Jainagar. In 2007, maximum water level became 53.3 m at Jhanjharpur and 69.35 m at Jainagar.

The average height of flood water stagnant in the study area is almost 1-3 m above the mean height of the land. The road bridge connecting Kusheshwar Sthan with other parts of Darbhanga district on Kamla-Balan river at Katwara was washed away by heavy discharge of the river during flood in 2007. Normally, almost 100 per cent crops are damaged

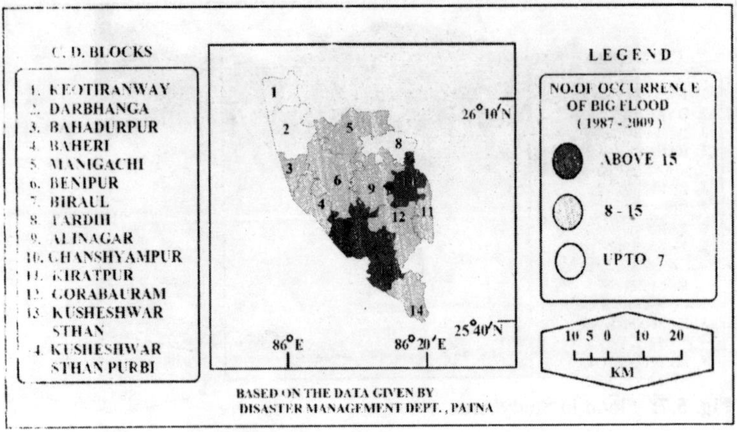

Fig. 5.9: Frequency of Flood (Block-Wise)

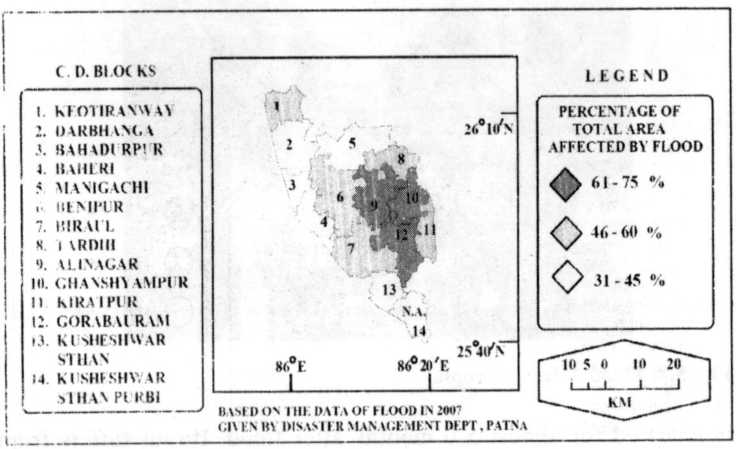

Fig. 5.10: Block-wise Area Affected by Flood

by flood as per the local people. Some dangerous diseases like Malaria, Jaundice, Cholera, Heavy Fever etc. break out as after effects of floods over here. Due to flood, the area is covered by a layer of deposit of sand hampering the fertility of soil.

Causes of Flood (*see* Fig. 5.13)

- Heavy Rainfall in Nepal as well as in Study Area.

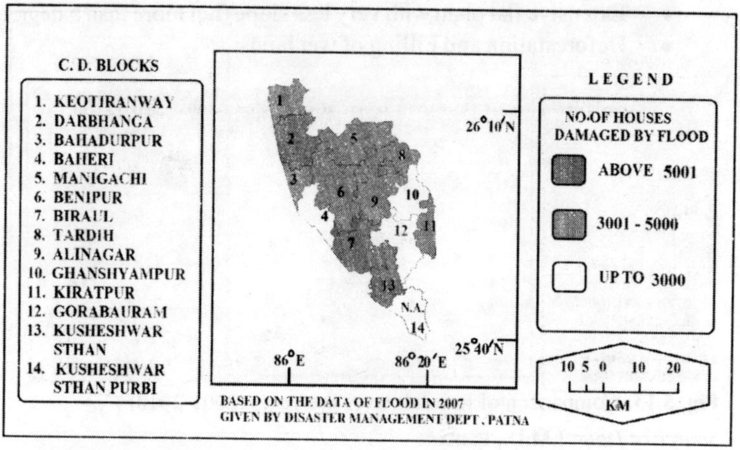

Fig. 5.11: Damage of Houses by Flood (Block-Wise)

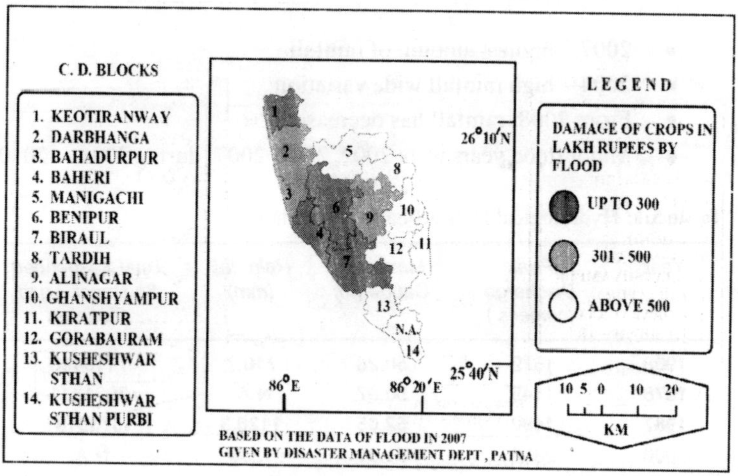

Fig. 5.12: Damage of Crops by Floods (Block-Wise)

- Huge Sediment load in the river (mostly sand and silt).
- Huge Discharge and water level (gauge) in the river.
- Shallow Ground Water level with good recharge.
- Breaching of embankment (by river itself and by people also).
- Human encroachment in the river course mainly for agricultural and residential purposes.

- Extensive flat plain with very less slope (not more than 5 degree).
- Deforestation and Filling of wet lands.

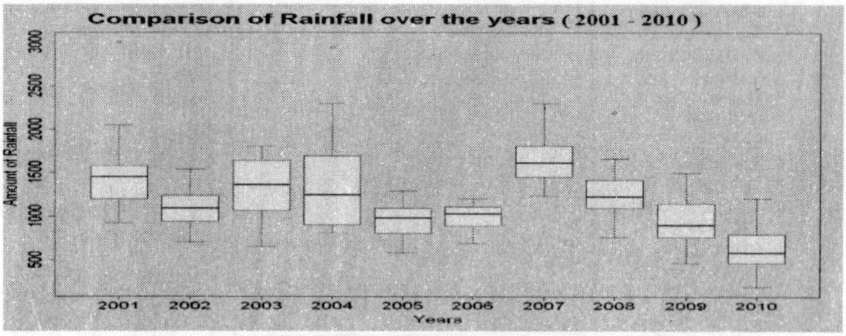

Fig. 5.13: Comparison of Rainfall Over the Years (2001-2010)
Source of Data: I.M.D., Patna.

Observations from the Box Plot ....

- 2007—highest amount of rainfall
- 2004—high rainfall wide variation
- From 2008, rainfall has decreased.
- Major flood years were 2002, 2004, 2007 (during 2001—2010)

Table 5.1: Hydrological Data at Jhanjharpur Station

Year	*Peak Discharge (cumecs)*	*Maximum Gauge (m)*	*Rain fall (mm)*	*Total Suspended Sediment Load (Tonnes)*
1968	1679	50.28	710.7	7110446
1978	1145	50.97	N.A.	3921341
1987	**1480**	**52.65**	**1126.3**	**13733181**
2000	2356	51.91	1239	N.A.
2009	4337	51.71	874.7	N.A.

Source: F.M.I.S., Patna and Flood Control Department, Patna and Jhanjharpur-I, Central Water Commission, Patna.

Table 5.1 shows that in 1987 flood was most vulnerable.

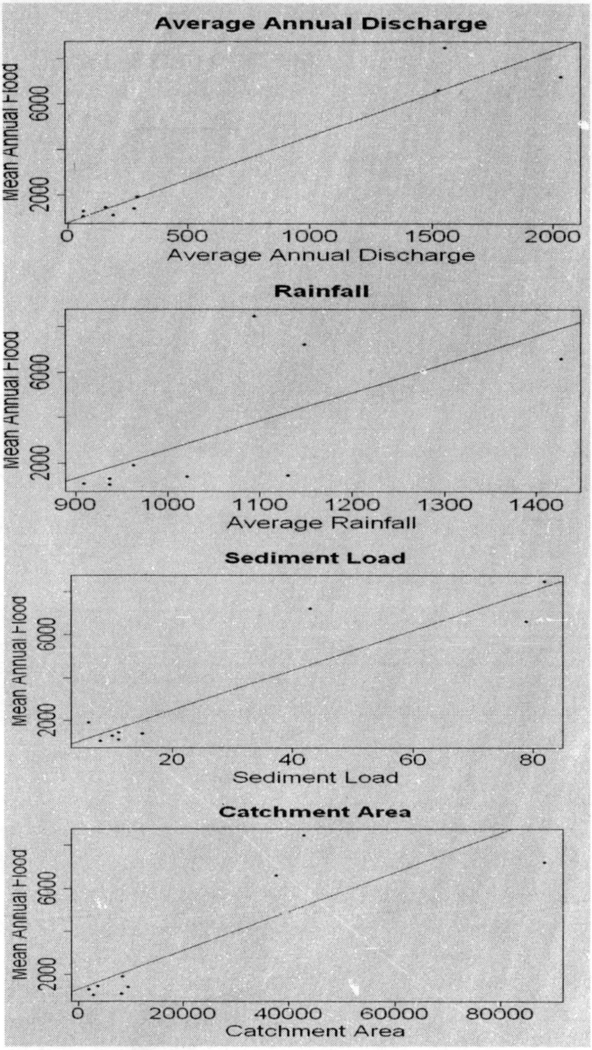

Fig. 5.14: Relation of Mean Annual Flood Discharge with Some Important Factors

Source of Data: I.M.D., Patna; CWC, Patna; Flood Control Department, Patna.

Fig. 5.14 shows that high discharge, huge sediment load and broad catchment area are the reasons for flood.

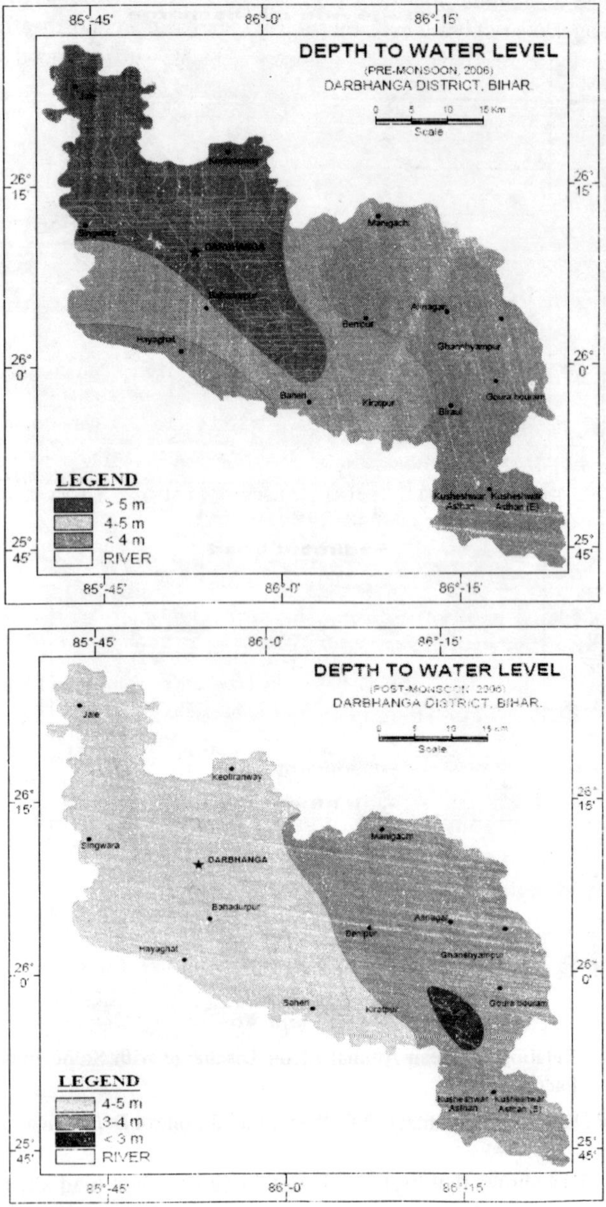

Fig. 5.15: Depth of Water Level in Darbhanga District, Bihar
Source: C.G.W.B., Patna.

Fig. 5.15 shows that the eastern, south-eastern and southern parts of Darbhanga district lying in Kamla-Balan river basin are mostly affected by flood as these areas have shallow ground water table with very good recharge.

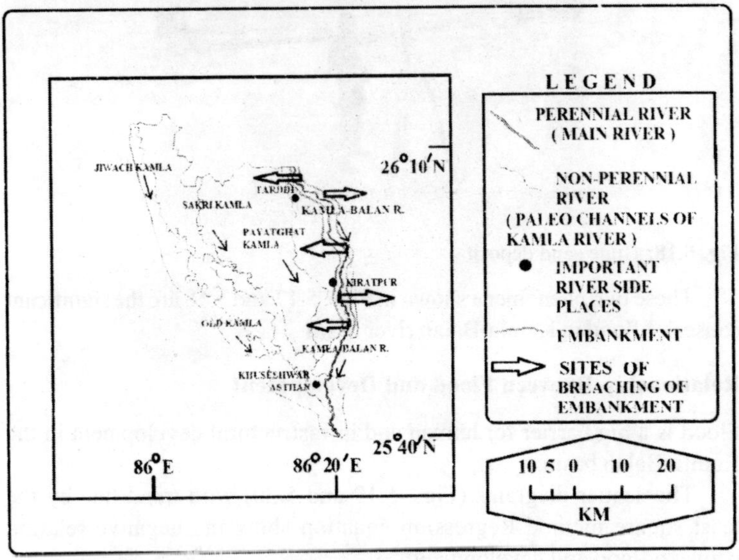

Fig. 5.16: Sites of Breaching of Embankment
Source of Data: Flood Control Department, Jhanjharpur.

Embankment at both sides of the river is breached due to river itself (during heavy discharge and rainfall) and due to man also when local inhabitants cut some portion of it to pass the overflown water of river. Breaching of embankment causes huge and vulnerable flood within a very short notice of time (*see* Fig. 5.16).

Fig. 5.17: Human Encroachment within River

Fig. 5.18: Huge sand deposit

These two phenomena shown in Figs. 5.17 and 5.18 are the significant causes of flood in Kamla-Balan river basin.

Relationship Between Flood and Development

Flood is a big barrier for human and infrastructural development in the Kamla-Balan basin.

The scatter diagrams (Figs. 5.19 and 5.20) with trend line by the least square method Regression equation show the negative relation between flood and development.

Table 6.2: Demographic Status of Darbhanga District in the Study Area

Name of the District	*Block-Wise Average Total Infrastructure*	*Block-Wise Average Population Density*	*Block-Wise Average % of Total Workers*	*Block-Wise Average Sex-Ratio*	*Block-Wise Average Literacy Rate*
Darbhanga	19.5	1051	32.5	923.66	35.45

Source: Census of India, 2011.

Table 6.2 shows that Darbhanga district in my study area has less than 50 per cent literacy rate on an average. It is due to lack of schools and colleges over there due to flood causing low human development.

Control of Flood

Existing Flood Mitigation Processes

- Construction of right and left embankment of Kamla-Balan river

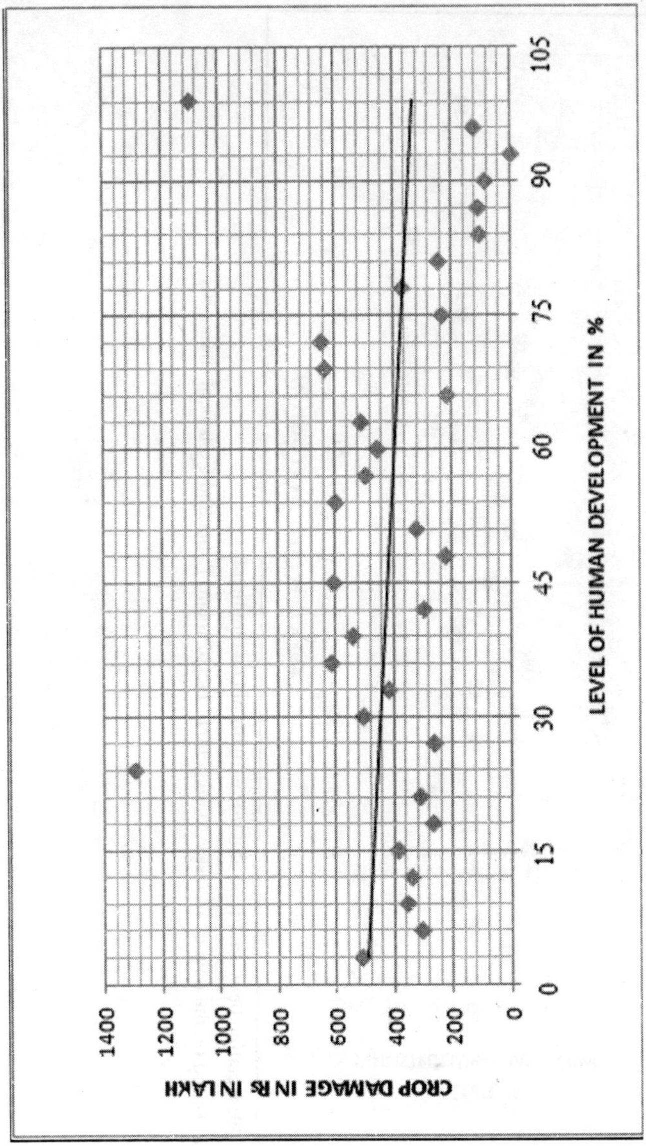

Fig. 5.19: Relation between Flood and Human Development

Source: Based on the data of Disaster Management Department, Patna and Census of India, 2011

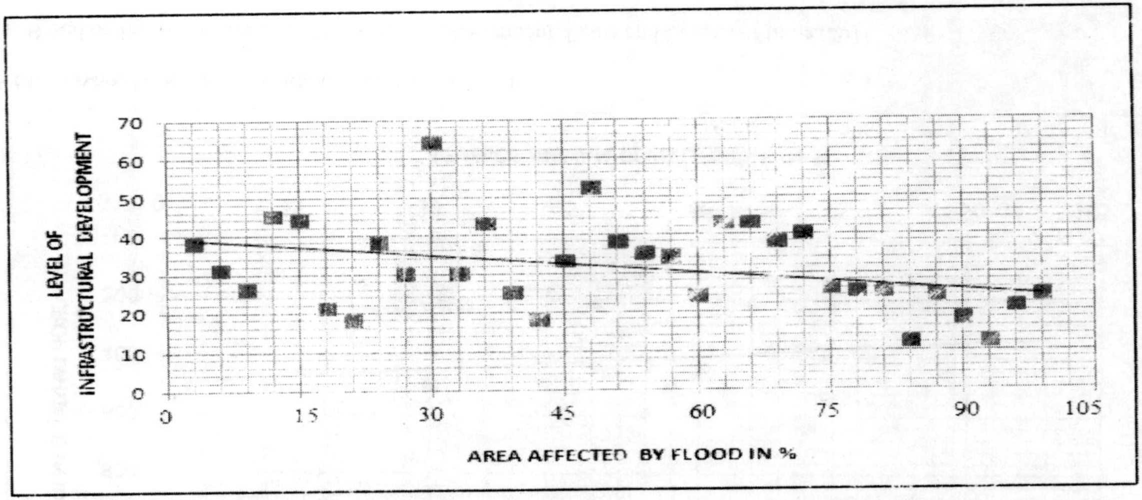

Fig. 5.20: Relation between Flood and Infrastructural Development

Source: Based on the data of Disaster Management Department, Patna and Census of India, 2011.

during 1952-53 (Left Embankment up to 94 km and Right Embankment up to 91.5 km away from Jainagar).

- Distribution of relief materials.
- Merging of road with rail bridge at Jhanjharpur. This is the one and only bridge in the world where train and bus move through the same track, i.e., rail line is located on the road.
- Construction of barrage at Kamla river at Jainagar during 1952-53.
- Construction of concrete houses on elevated walls or pillars.
- River Bank Repairing.
- There is an N.G.O. named as *'Sakhi'* (Head Office is at Jhanjharpur town) which helps the flood affected people a lot in rehabilitation, distribution of relief materials, rescue work etc. (*see* Figs. 5.21 and 5.22).

Fig. 5.21: Officers visiting Flooded Areas

Fig. 5.22: Embankment of Kamla-Balan River

Relief Materials Distributed in 2009

- Rice—1 Qt./Family
- Dal—70 Kg./Family
- Chura—100 Gm/Head
- Money—Rs. 200/Person, Rs. 2250/Family
- To The Affected Farmer—Rs. 4000/Ha
- To Reconstruct Kutcha House—Rs. 1500/Family, Rs. 2500/Family, Rs. 5000/Family
- To Construct Pucca House—Rs. 25000/Family (Mukhya Mantri Avas Yojana)
- Others—Gur, Bread, Polythene, Rehabilitation by Making a Lot of Tents etc.

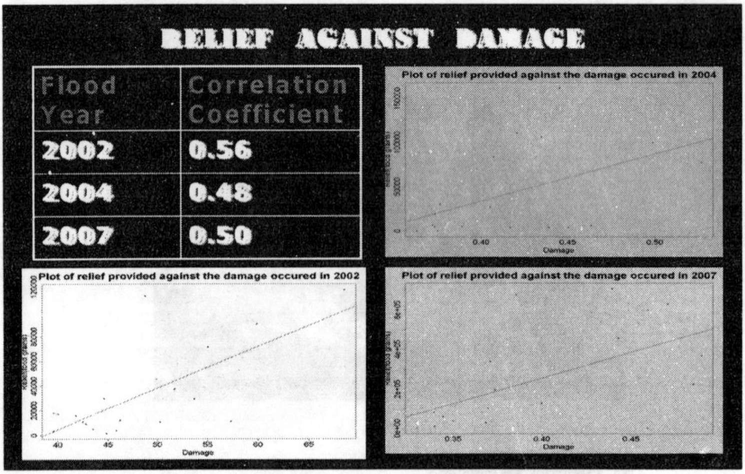

Fig. 5.23: Relief Against Damage

Source: Calculated by the Author.

The above calculation (*see* Fig. 5.23) shows that the average Coefficient of Correlation (r) in the years 2002, 2004, and 2007 between damage by flood and relief measures is 0.5. That means the efficiency of relief measures is half to the requirement for the damage due to flood in the study area. It means existing flood mitigation is significantly insufficient to the flood affected people in Kamla-Balan river basin.

Human Adjustment

- The people of the study area have adjusted with the disproportion of relief measures to the magnitude of flood.

- On one hand many of the local people definitely suffer from the flood hazard, but some others specially the poors take the opportunity to grab the relief materials.
- Some families have their own boats.
- Many poor people till now are unable to make their houses like the former ones which were abolished by the flood of 2009.
- Affected people take shelter in the school buildings during flood. So, then school education ceases for a long time.
- Distressed people cultivate within the portion between two embankments near the river course after the rainy season for well availability of river water for irrigation purpose.
- In some areas the people with middle to high income have built their concrete houses on elevated walls or pillars.

Findings

- There is a significant imbalance or disparity in Development in the various blocks of my study area due to Flood.
- Eastern and south-eastern parts of the study area are mostly affected as per Flood frequency, percentage of area affected by flood and number of houses damaged as it is near the main river and have very less slope.
- Southern and south-eastern parts have comparatively less population, less crop production and less development as these parts are mostly affected by flood and inundated for a long period (5-6 months) after flood.
- But western and north-western parts of the study area are more affected as per the crops damaged by flood as these parts produce more crops than the other parts.
- Not only geo-climatic extremities but also human interference and encroachment are responsible for flood.
- Efficiency of existing flood mitigation is almost half with respect to the requirement.
- Damage of crops in money due to flood is more significant than the damage of any other aspects.
- Transport is badly affected due to flood, specially roads and rail lines cannot be constructed due to flood.
- The nature of the flood is of low intensity but high extent over my study area.
- Number of roads, rail lines, schools, health centres etc. cannot be increased due to innundation for a long period after.

- The people have adjusted with flood with respect to its positive as well as adverse effects as the blessing or curse of the God.
- Block-wise almost 50 per cent area is affected by flood on an average.

Proposals for Flood Management

- To modify Kamla barrage and to make more new plans associated with this barrage and to extend this project to control floods in the middle and lower Kamla-Balan valley region.
- To find out whether middle course in Kamla-Balan river is absent or not as it is an important factor to find out more reasons and management of flood in the study area.
- To follow proper Water Resource Management in Kamla river as well as in its tributaries and distributaries.
- To study on paleochannels and water passes of Kamla-Balan river.
- To construct another barrage at the point of entry of Balan river in India near Ladania in Madhubani district.
- To complete the construction of embankment up to 104 km at the left and 96.5 km at the right bank of the Kamla-Balan river.
- To nourish and repair embankments regularly.
- To distribute sufficient and adequate relief measures properly.
- To set up more rainfall, discharge and gauge recording stations in the middle and lower Kamla-Balan basin.
- To stop human encroachment in the river valley specially within the course.
- To dredge the main river properly and its old courses.
- To dig few new canals from main river as well as from the reservoir at Kamla barrage southward to diverge huge water and to improve drainage system.
- To arrange full rehabilitation of people before the flood attack as information regarding the amount of water released at Jainagar barrage comes to the Block Office about 7 to 8 hours before to minimize the flood affect.
- To maintain and not to disturb the natural drainage system.
- To use Geoinformatics (Remote Sensing and G.I.S.) for Flood inundation mapping and Flood plain zoning.
- To arrange Flood Insurance and International cooperation.

- To base on Ecological approach more (Biomatting, Afforestation, building small reservoirs in low-lying areas, making wetland park, to stop constructional activities in flood plains etc.).
- To forecast the flood before sufficient time and to increase mass consciousness.
- To build Flood Monitoring System.
- To keep and store the data regarding flood and relevant all aspects and parameters scientifically to study, research and analyse the causes, consequences and control of flood.

Acknowledgements

I am grateful to my Supervisor Dr. Nandini Chatterjee, Associate Professor, Department of Geography, Taki Government College, West Bengal State University, West Bengal; Officers and clerks of Disaster Management Department, Patna and Darbhanga; Engineers and clerks of Flood Control Department, Patna, Jhanjharpur I and II, F.M.I.S., Patna, Census of India, Patna, C.W.C. and C.G.W.B., Patna, I.M.D., Patna and obviously to the local people of different places of my study area who have helped me in my works in different ways. I am also thankful to Department of Geography, Bankura Christian College to give me a chance to present my paper over here.

References

Basu, R. and Bhaduri, S. (2007): *Contemporary Issues and Techniques in Geography*, Progressive Publishers, Kolkata.

Central Ground Water Board (2009): *Ground Water Information Booklet*, Madhubani District, Bihar State, CGWB Pub., Patna.

Disaster Management Department, Government of Bihar (2004): *Situation Report: Bihar Floods* –27.7.04.

Mishra, D. Kumar (2008): "Bihar Floods: The Inevitable Has Happened", *Economic & Political Weekly*, 6 September.

Sinha, R. and Jain, V. (1998): Flood hazards of north Bihar rivers, Indo-Gangetic plains. In: Kale, V.S. (Ed.) *Flood Studies in India, Memoir Geological Society of India*, 41, pp. 27-52.

Ward, R. (1978): *Floods—A Geographical Perspective*, MacMillan Press, London.

Raghunath, H.M. (2000): *Hydrology: Principles, Analysis and Design*, New Age International (P) Limited, Publishers, New Delhi.

Kale, V.S. (1997): Flood studies in India: A brief review. *Journal of the Geological Society of India*, 49, pp. 359-370.

Mayer, L. and Nash, D. (Ed.) (1987): *Catastrophic Flooding*, Allen & Unwin, Boston.

Verma, Binoy Nath (Ed.) (1998): *Flood Devastation and Agricultural Development in Eastern India*, B.R. Publishing Corporation, Delhi.

Sinha, Dr. V.N.P., Nazim, Dr. M. and Ahmed, Dr. P. Firoz (2013): *Bihar—Land, People and Economy*, Rajesh Publications, New Delhi.

Ahmed, Enayat (1965): *Bihar—A Physical, Economic and Regional Geography*, Ranchi University, Ranchi.

Forestry and Environment

6

Forest Cover Mapping of Chilika Watershed

Sk Majharul Islam, Amrit Kamila, Arnab Sengupta, Sk Md. Ismail Al Amin, Subrata Jana and *Ashis Kr. Paul*

Introduction

Forest is the very important part of the world's biosphere. They play a crucial role to control global climate, climate change, global and local ecology and conservation of soil and water. Forest also acts as solar energy and carbon sink. A single hectare of forest land absorbs 10-20 tons of carbon dioxide per year using photosynthesis process and converts the carbon to lignin, cellulose, starch and woody biomass (Wikipedia, 2015a). Forest is the supplier of woods, and other non-timber forest products such as *kendu* leaves, *sal* leaves, edible fruits, honey, resin, glue, *harida*, tamarind, *kanda-khai, mahua* flower, *mahua* seed, *sal* seed, *char* seed, cashew, rubber, rope-grass and *karra* leaves for medicinal purpose. Forest serves the forest dependents with foods, health needs, shelter, energy, and as a source of income. Woods energy is only energy source in the rural areas of the developing countries (SOFO, 2014). The Forest dependent people build their home using forest products. Forest products support 18 per cent of world's population (SOFO, 2014). Population pressure and overuse of forest make the deforestation and World's forest cover is shrinking at every moment. World's largest densest Amazon Rain forest is reducing 21,000-4500 sq. km. per year (Wikipedia, 2015b; Tucker *et al.,* 2000). Bi-annual State of Forest Report of Forest Survey of India SFR, 2011 shows decrease of 367 sq. km. forest area from previous report SFR, 2009. In spite of decrease of forest cover at National Level,

SFR, 2011 shows, Odisha State forest cover has increased by 48 sq. km., though good quality of forest decreased. Very Dense Forest Cover (forest canopy density more than 70%) decreased by 13 sq. km. and Moderately Dense Forest Cover (forest canopy density less than 70% and greater than 40%) decreased 28 sq. km. (SFR, 2009 ; SFR, 2011).

Chilika watershed is situated at East Coast of India, 450 km south-east of the Kolkata (Fig. 6.1). This watershed is situated at western side of Mahanadi Delta. This watershed is part of four districts which are Puri, Khurda, Ganjam, Nayagarh. Area of Chilika watershed is about 5240 sq. km. Chilika Lagoon is in the southern part of this basin with 1165 sq. km. water spread area. Chilika watershed has rich forest resource which takes part to maintain Chilika lagoon environment. This forest is

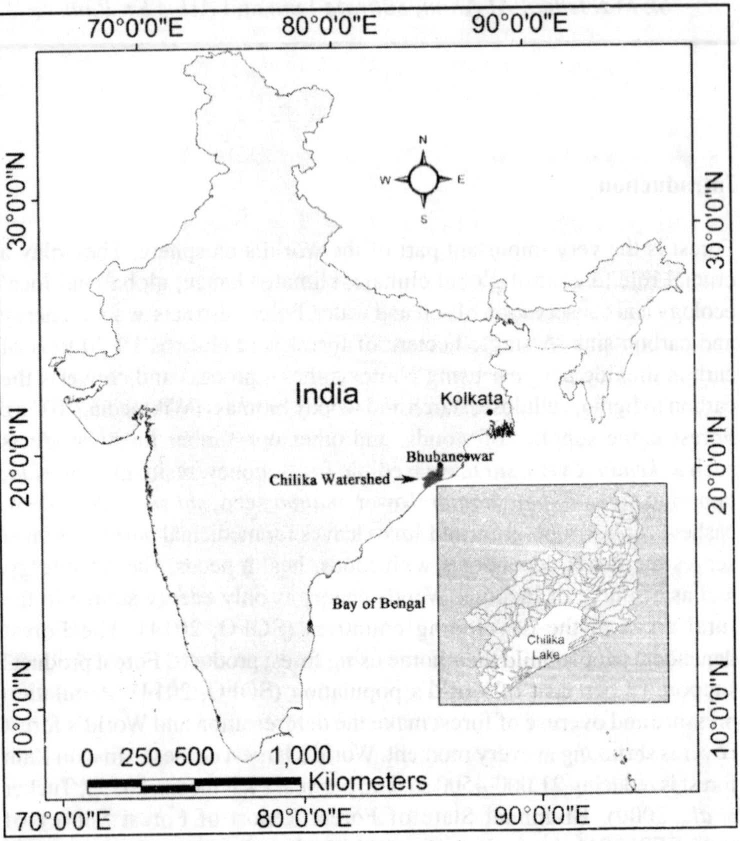

Fig. 6.1: Location Map of the Chilika Watershed

also decreasing gradually for agricultural land and settlement area extension. Cyclone also plays important role to forest destruction. After devastating Cyclone Phailin, 2013; Hudhud, 2014; Odisha Super Cyclone, 1999 forest cover of coastal area has wiped out. Decreasing rate of Chilika lagoon fishing fisherman and fish labour also diverted their profession to illegal felling which is causing more degradation of forested area. Deforestation affected Chilika lagoon by high rate of siltation and surface run-off from the Chilika basin.

Amount of forest cover area is an important characteristic of environmental richness. Manual method of forest cover measurement and mapping is very laborious and time consuming, and less reliable than remote sensing measurement using multispectral and hyperspectral images. In the absence of full coverage of hyperspectral image partly coverage hyperspectral images are being mapped such as forest type. Moderate spatial resolution multispectral images of 4 decade are used to map forest cover and change dynamics.

Material and Method

At first review of the existing literature of the forest cover mapping have done (Gao, 1996; Thenkabail *et al.,* 2000; Wang *et al.,* 2008; Rao *et al.,* 1987; Barrett *et al.,* 2000; Sahoo *et al.,* 2015; Beltran *et al.,* 2001; Moran *et al.,* 1997; Tucker, 1979; Rouse *et al.,* 1974 and Löw *et al.,* 2014). Then study of forest types and cover and phenology of this watershed region are studied from various writing and State of Forest Report, Odisha, makes a brief draft of this work, such as data to be used and process to be followed to draw a useful conclusion of forest cover mapping in cost-effective way. For the forest area and canopy density measurement, lots of literature supports Normalize Difference Vegetation Index (NDVI) is good method to follow for this work (Rouse, *et al.,* 1974; Pettorelli, *et al.,* 2005). After consulting many literatures and available series of satellite image interpretation, it is found that last half of November is the best time to complete this work using freely available Landsat imageries. In rainy season (June-September) maximum green cover of this watershed is seen, but sky is fully or partly covered by cloud, remote sensing using optical spectrum is unfavourable in this time. In October field is filled with paddy, continuous paddy field misidentified as forest because of nearly same spectral reflection in multispectral image. Available hyperspectral image classification (Fig. 6.3) and literature review shows this area is mainly covered by deciduous trees. In the winter, spring and summer season deciduous forest canopy decreases, specially leafless season of March and April.

Landsat Satellite sensor images (MSS, TM, ETM+) and Hyperion hyperspectral images of this watershed are also downloaded from USGS website then radiometric, geometric and atmospheric corrections are applied using ENVI 5.1 software. Among them four good quality images are chosen to perform the work. Only about 20 per cent area coverage of hyperion image is available for download so forest cover mapping is completed with moderate spatial resolution multispectral TM and MSS image. November, 1972 MSS image, November, 1989 TM image, November, 2004 TM image and November, 2011 TM image are selected for the analysis. Survey of India (SoI) toposheet is consulted for collateral data. Toposheets of 1929, 1972, and 2005 are used for this study. Forest cover boundary of 1929 is digitized and area is calculated using SoI 1929 toposheet and ArcGIS 10.1 software. Ground survey of the study area is proceeding with canopy density measurement with Lehmann Densiometer and sampling position collected from Garmin GPS map 76csx (horizontal accuracy under 30 metres). Ground survey of canopy density is measured in some selected relatively accessible forest patches in the dense forest, open forest and scrub area identified in 1:50,000 SoI Toposheet of 2005.

At first with processed image NDVI is applied and then the index values are tallied with ground canopy density measurement results (Fig. 6.2). NDVI value ranges between +1 to –1, normally high index value associated with high chlorophyll healthy dense vegetation and negative value denotes absence of vegetation. Canopy density more than 70 per cent is very dense forest, Canopy density more than 40 per cent, but less than 70 per cent is moderately dense forest and canopy density more than 10 per cent but less than 40 per cent is open forest (Table 6.1) (SFR, 2011). Canopy density of forest more than 40 per cent is called good quality forest in terms of ecological significance. Open forests are poor quality of forest. Using ENVI Decision Tree Classification with NDVI threshold value forests are divided only into dense forest and open forest classes. Overall accuracy of this method is 82 per cent. Accuracy is higher in the dense forest part and lower in open forest. Relatively coarse resolution MSS image is only used to demarcate forest area. No canopy density difference is applied with this method. Unavailability of *in situ* canopy density data NDVI threshold value of dense and open forest of 2011 is applied to 2004 and 1989 image.

Table 6.1: Forest Cover Types

Forest Survey of India Forest Cover Types	
Forest cover	*Canopy density range*
Very Dense Forest (VDF)	> 70 per cent
Moderately Dense Forest (MDF)	40-70 per cent
Open Forest (OF)	10-40 per cent
Non-forest cover	*Crown density range*
Scrub	<10 per cent

Source: SFR, 2011.

Flow Diagram of Multispectral Image Classification Methodology

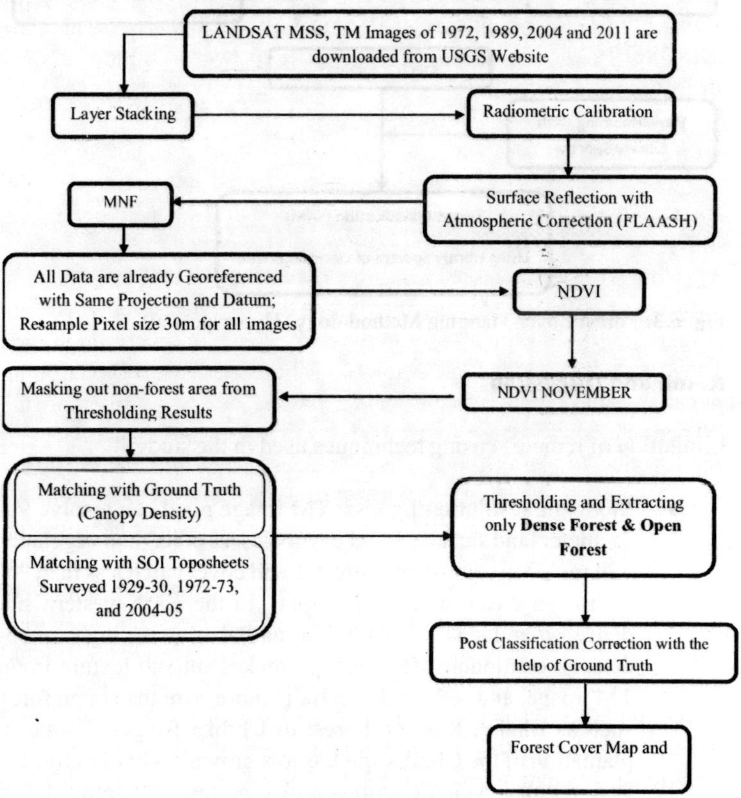

Fig. 6.2: Forest Cover Mapping Methodology (Multispectral)

Flow Diagram of Hyperspectral Image Classification Methodology

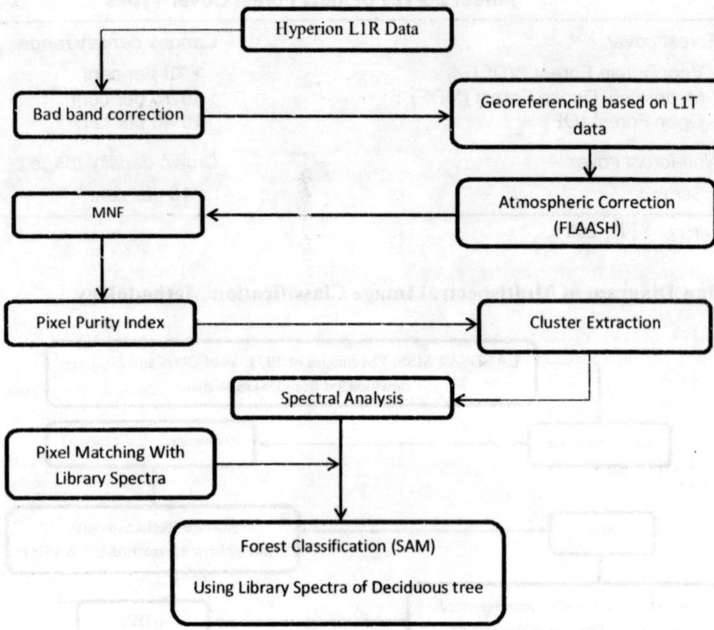

Fig. 6.3: Forest Cover Mapping Methodology (Hyperspectral)

Result and Discussion

Limitation of remote sensing techniques used in the study:

- Moderate resolution Landsat TM image pixel can resolve 900 sq. meter land surface. Land cover classes other than vegetation will mixed in semi-dense forest. Land cover patch less than 900 sq. m can create mixture in signal. In the north-western side dense *sal* and teak forests of Tamna Paharh have high canopy density, continuous trees canopy makes smooth texture in the TM image, and reflected spectra is more pure than open forest such as Bhaleri Reserve Forest of Chilika fringes. Casuarina plantation of the Chilika spit has low crown cover of individual tree, regular cyclonic storms and sand and salt spray during summer months and illegal felling degraded the casuarina forest. Using this method with moderate spatial resolution TM image casuarina forest shows more ground reflectance than canopy reflectance so this method is unable to map the spit plantation except partly mapped in 1989 image.

- Plants having less chlorophyll in their canopy show low index value and mixed with other land cover classes. *Sal*, teak, cashew tree have high chlorophyll content in their canopy so they display high NDVI value but Casuarina plantation of the Chilika spit has low NDVI value and it is difficult to discriminate from other land cover classes.
- Variation in spectral reflectance characteristics in different phenological stages of forest is very important (Reed, *et al.*, 1994). Trees without leaf and with leaf can create two different signatures in two different seasons. As Hyperspectral image classification showing spectral curve match with deciduous trees in this watershed region in spring leafless situation of deciduous trees may cause low NDVI value evenly in dense forest.
- Presence of continuous bushy vegetation and continuous agricultural land can cause problems for inclusion as forest land because of same spectral response as tree canopy. Reed (*Phragmites karka*) covered the North eastern part of Chilika lagoon has also misclassified as forest for its spectral response, smooth texture and wide extent.

Effect of climatic condition on vegetation health is also reflected in some satellite image, which is to be analysed carefully (Nemani, *et al.*, 2003; Roerick, *et al.*, 2003; Zhou, *et al.*, 2003; Yu, *et al.*, 2003; Wang, *et al.*, 2003). Among weather components rainfall is very important to maintain forest health. Annual average rainfall in this watershed is about 1202 mm (CDA). The majority of the rainfall occurs in June to October during the South-West monsoon spell. In 1987, rainfall in the basin is very low Landsat TM image of the December, 1987 shows very low NDVI value all-over the basin and total areal coverage also decreased. When results are compared with 2011 result, this result shows, 1987 forest cover is less than 2011 forest area. After a normal rain year 1989 November image showing the actual scenario. November, 2000 image also showing low NDVI value after very low rainfall in the monsoon months (*see* Figs. 6.4 and 6.5).

Forest cover of Chilika Watershed in 1930 is about 1340 sq. km. of about 5240 sq. km. geographical area (Fig. 6.4). Forest cover reduced in the first time of satellite based multispectral measurement in 1972

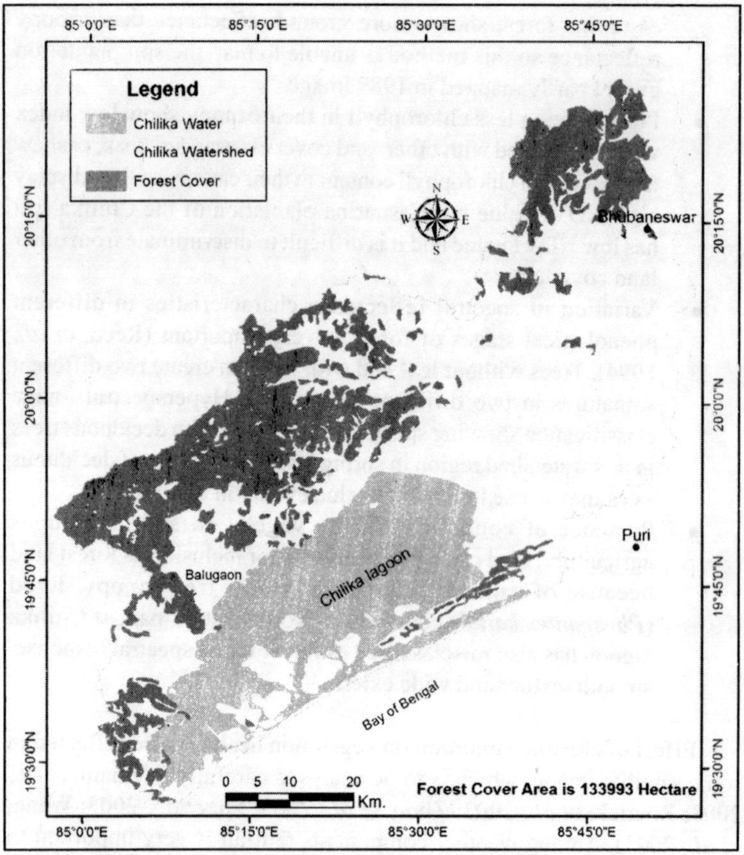

Fig. 6.4: Forest Cover Map of Chilika Watershed, 1930

with Landsat 1 MSS sensor is about 856 sq. km. (Fig. 6.5). Measurement using Landsat 5 TM in 1989 forest cover area further decreases to 610.3935 sq. km. with Open Forest 374.56 sq. km. and Dense Forest 235.82 sq. km. (Fig. 6.6). In 2004 measurement Forest area is 572.81 sq. km. with Open Forest 338.79 sq. km. and Dense Forest 234.01 sq. km. (Fig. 6.7). In the last measurement in 2011 forest cover decreases further and forest quality also degraded in the major part of the forested area. Very Dense Forest and Moderately Dense forest become Open Forest and barren land all-over the forest area of the Chilika basin. Forest cover is about 568.44 sq. km. with Open Forest 390.10 sq. km. and Dense Forest 178.343 sq. km. (Fig. 6.8).

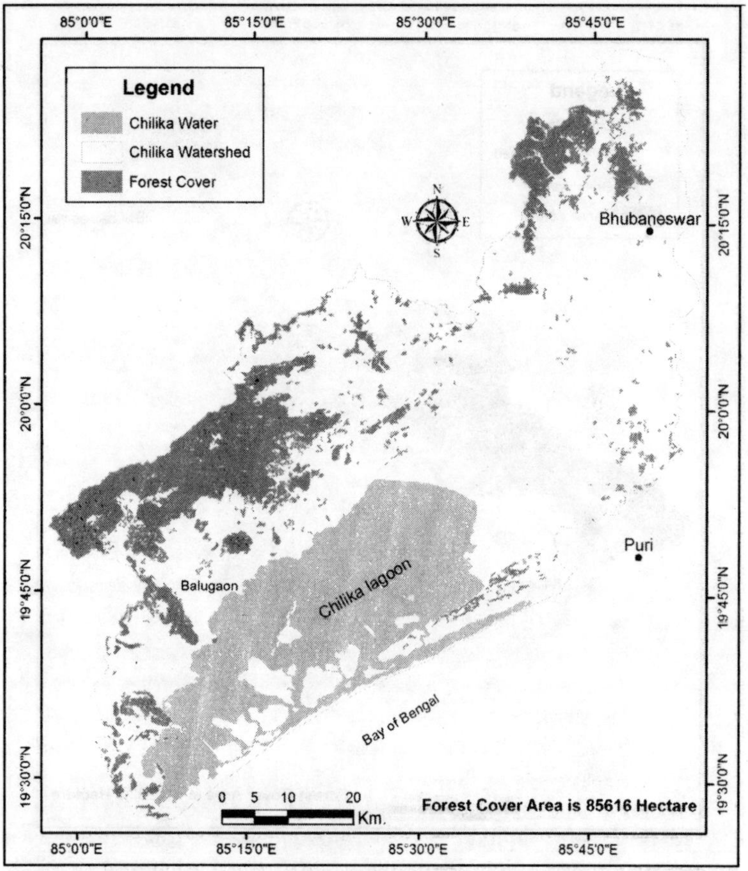

Fig. 6.5: Forest Cover Map of Chilika Watershed, 1972

The forest area has decreased mainly in the forest fringes. Badamal, Baharmal, Tamna, Bankar, Katuala, Rajin, Dhanai, Arang, Patia and Sulia Reserve forest had densest forest cover of *sal*, teak and bamboo which are decreased. Chulijhinka, Jharan, Sandhimul, Champagarh, Bhataparha Protected Forest had dense canopy cover which is also degraded. Smaller patches of forest cover near Chilika fringes is seen on Jhinkaridi, Bhaleri Reserve Forest, Solari Protected Forest, which is mainly dominated by degraded Open Forest. Karakhol and Talakhol Reserve Forest is dominated by planted species of cashew, teak, eucalyptus, acacia. Ghantashiila Reserve Forest at Chilika southern fringe had dense forest cover in 1930,

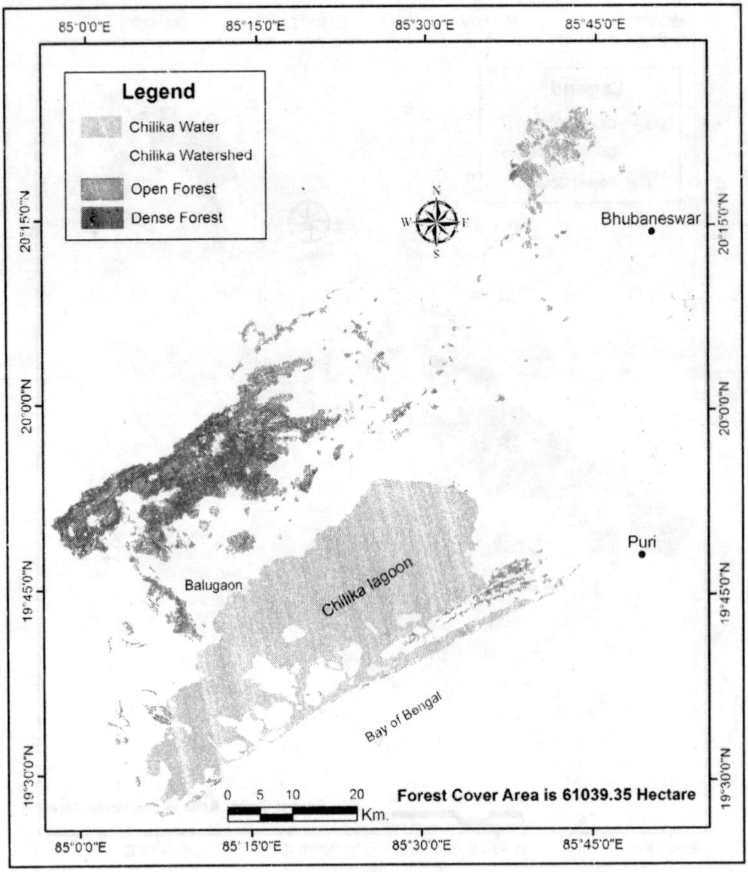

Fig. 6.6: Forest Cover Map of Chilika Watershed, 1989

but from 1989 image dense cover is wiped out replacing some dense scrubs. Barakuda and Samala Island had forest cover but now they are covered with scrub. Mainly hilly area of this watershed is covered by forest, but recent alluvium plain is mainly forestless. Some plantation by forest department is increasing the green cover area. Eucalyptus, teak, cashew, acasia, mango, and mixed plantation is seen in the western and northern side of lagoon watershed. Casuarina is planted throughout the Chilika spit, though health of forest is very poor.

Illegal felling of trees for commercial purpose in the dense *sal* and teak forest of this watershed affected highly to the landless forest

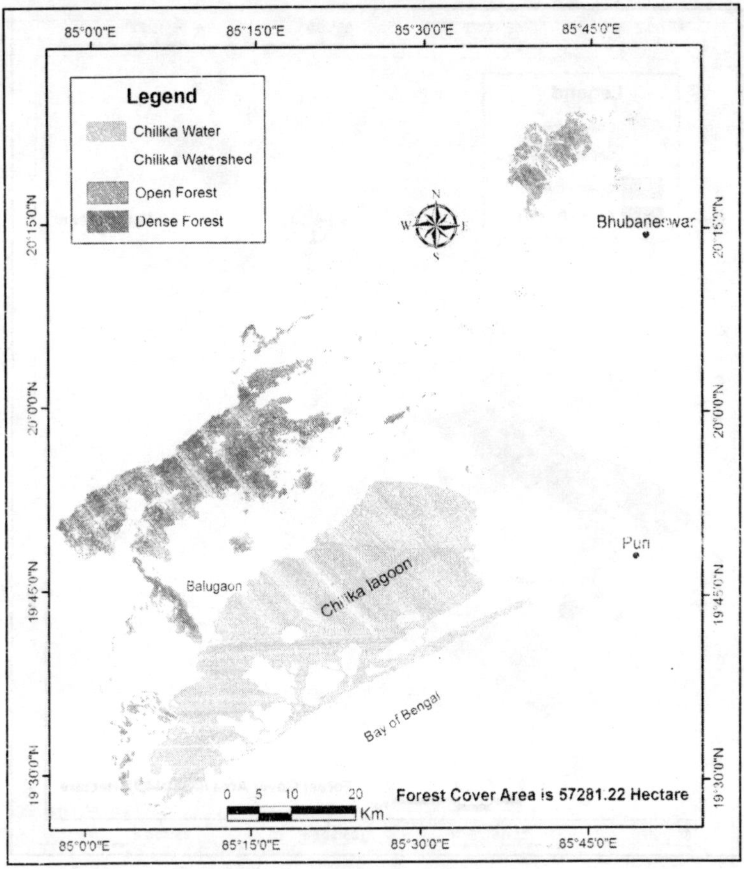

Fig. 6.7: Forest Cover Map of Chilika Watershed, 2004

dependent tribal and local people's food security that mainly depends on Non-Timber Forest Products (NTFP). Dense Mixed Forest supplies *mahua* flower, *mahua* seed, *sal* seed, *tulsi*, *kendu* leaf, *sal* leaf, wild potato, honey, glue, resin, fruits, roots etc. Large scale forest destruction affects the NTFP productivity which directly affects their livelihood. As deforestation affected forest dependents livelihood then they engaged more and more destruction and removal of forest to fulfil their livelihood support which continues like poverty cycle.

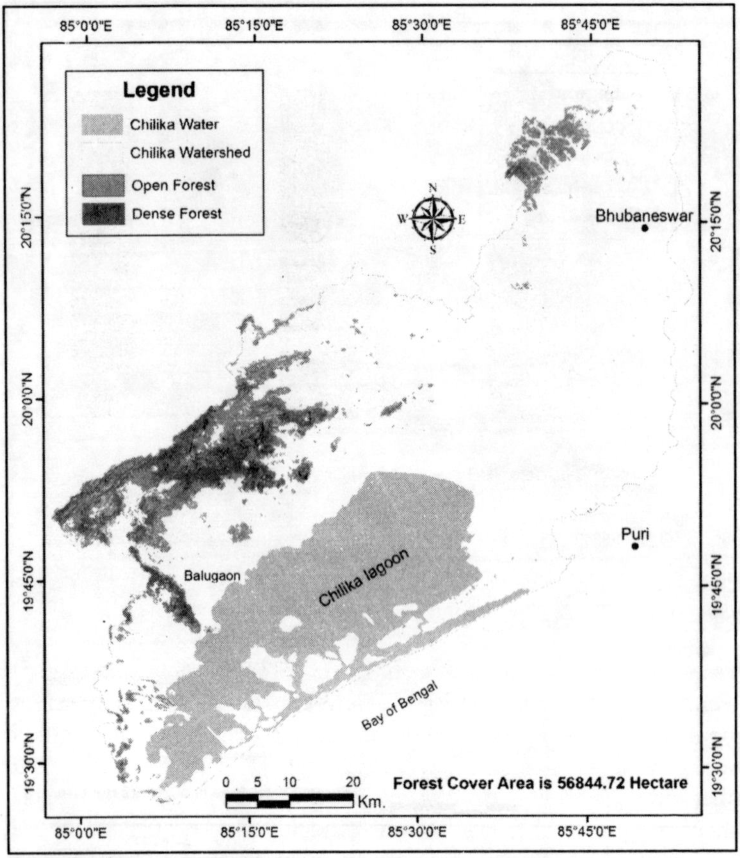

Fig. 6.8: Forest Cover Map of Chilika Watershed, 2011

Conclusion

Forest has important role to control regional ecology, environment and economy. For environmental balance, significant forested area is required, but only 11 per cent of watershed area is covered by forest which was 26 per cent in 1930. This study shows that Total forest cover is decreasing gradually in this watershed region and densest forest cover is degraded thereby becoming less productive Open Forest (Fig. 6.9). Government of Odisha has taken initiative to increase the green cover, by plantation of casew, acacia, bamboo, eucalyptus, teak and casuarina. Impact of large scale deforestation, forest dependent society becomes

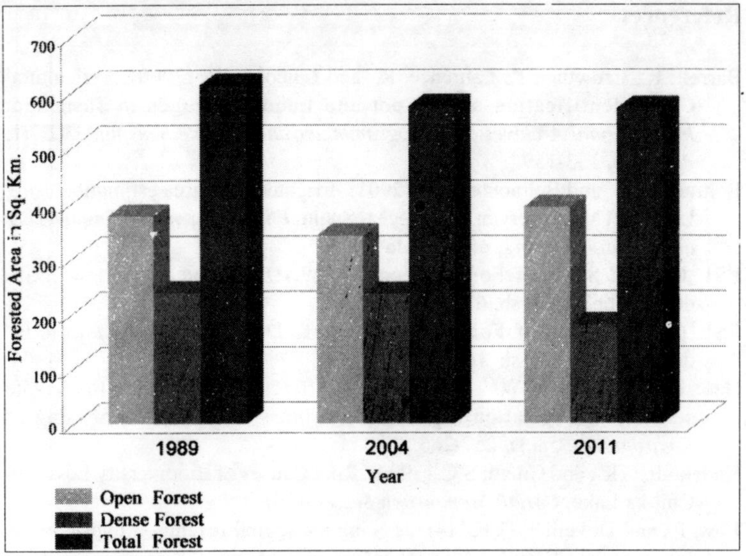

Fig. 6.9: Forest covers decreasing

Source: Calculated by the Authors.

poorer for the unavailability of sufficient NTFP for maintaining their livelihood. With the increasing of world population, forest dependent population also increased thereby creating pressure and competition among them. Another side forest cover and NTFP are decreasing and other side Forest dependent population is increasing. This creates situation more critical. Incomeless unemployed forest dependent are engaged in illegal felling of woody trees. In the lagoon fringe region forest dependent pupils are diverted to lagoon fishing which cause competition among fishermen and resource pressure of lagoon. Forest cleared lands remain barren and some are converted to agricultural land. Barren field and agriculture field has greater soil erosion than forested land. Land erosion is directly affected the lagoon ecology. High silt supply from deforested and agricultural land enters the lagoon through the Rajua Nala, Mangaljodi nala, Kusumi nala, Sulia nala, Tarimi, Kantabania, Kansari, Janjira River and swallowed the lagoon. Organic and inorganic nutrient materials from lagoon watershed create lagoon eutrofication (Kodekodi, *et al.,* 1999; Shankar, 1992).

References

Barrett, R., Crowther, P., Laurence, R., and Lincolne, R. (2000). Agricultural Crop Identification using Spot and Landsat Images in Tasmania. *International Archives of Photogrammetry and Remote Sensing, 33*(B7/1; PART 7), 133-139.

Beltran, C.M., and Belmonte, A.C. (2001). Irrigated crop area estimation using Landsat TM imagery in La Mancha, Spain. *Photogrammetric Engineering and Remote Sensing, 67*(10), 1177-1184.

FSI, (2009). State of Forest Report-2009, Dehradun, www.fsi.nic.in/details.php?pgID=sb_61

FSI, (2011). State of Forest Report-2011, Dehradun, www.fsi.nic.in/details.php?pgID=sb_16

Gao, B.C. (1996). NDWI—a normalized difference water index for remote sensing of vegetation liquid water from space. *Remote Sensing of Environment, 58*(3), 257-266.

Kadekodi, G.K., and Gulati, S.C. (1999). Root Causes of Biodiversity Losses in Chilika Lake. *CMDR Monograph Series*, (26).

Löw, F., and Duveiller, G. (2014). defining the spatial resolution requirements for crop identification using optical remote sensing. *Remote Sensing, 6*(9), 9034-9063.

Moran, M.S., Inoue, Y., and Barnes, E.M. (1997). Opportunities and limitations for image-based remote sensing in precision crop management. *Remote Sensing of Environment, 61*(3), 319-346.

Nemani, R.R., Keeling, C.D., Hashimoto, H., Jolly, W.M., Piper, S.C., Tucker, C.J., and Running, S.W. (2003). Climate-driven increases in global terrestrial net primary production from 1982 to 1999. *Science, 300*(5625), 1560-1563.

Pettorelli, N. 2005. Using the satellite-derived NDVI to assess ecological responses to environmental change. *Science Direct*, Elsevier.

Pettorelli, N., Vik, J.O., Mysterud, A., Gaillard, J.M., Tucker, C.J., and Stenseth, N.C. (2005). Using the satellite-derived NDVI to assess ecological responses to environmental change. *Trends in Ecology and Evolution, 20*(9), 503-510.

Rao, P.N., and Rao, V.R. (1987). Rice crop identification and area estimation using remotely-sensed data from Indian cropping patterns. *International Journal of Remote Sensing, 8*(4), 639-650.

Reed, B.C., Brown, J.F., Vander Zee, D., Loveland, T.R., Merchant, J.W., and Ohlen, D.O. (1994). Measuring phenological variability from satellite imagery. *Journal of Vegetation Science, 5*(5), 703-714.

Roerink, G.J., Menenti, M., Soepboer, W., and Su, Z. (2003). Assessment of climate impact on vegetation dynamics by using remote sensing. *Physics and Chemistry of the Earth, Parts A/B/C, 28*(1), 103-109.

Rouse, J.W., Jr., Haas, R.H., Schell, J.A., Deering, D.W. (1974). Monitoring Vegetation Systems in the Great Plains with Erts. *Third Earth Resources Technology Satellite-1 Symposium—Volume I: Technical Presentations.*

NASA SP-351, compiled and edited by Stanley C. Freden, Enrico P. Mercanti, and Margaret A. Becker, NASA, Washington, DC., p. 309.

Sahoo, R.N., Ray, S.S., and Manjunath, K.R. (2015). Hyperspectral remote sensing of agriculture. *Current Science*, *108*(5), 848.

Shankar, U. (1992). *Chilika: A Lake in Limbo, Down to Earth*, 7 (31 August), 25-32.

State of Forest Report, Forest Survey of India-2011, http://www.fsi.nic.in/cover_2011/chapter2.pdf

State of World's Forests 2014 (SOFO)—Food and Agriculture Organization, United Nations, www.fao.org/3/a-i3710e.pdf

Thenkabail, P.S., Smith, R.B. and Pauw, E.D. (2000). Hyperspectral vegetation indices and their relationships with agricultural crop characteristics. *Remote Sensing Environment*, 71, 158-182.

Tucker, C.J. (1979). Red and photographic infrared linear combinations for monitoring vegetation. *Remote Sensing of Environment*, *8*(2), 127-150.

Tucker, C.J., and Townshend, J.R. (2000). Strategies for monitoring tropical deforestation using satellite data. *International Journal of Remote Sensing*, *21*(6-7), 1461-1471.

Wang, F.M., Huang, J.F. and Wang, X.Z. (2008). Identification of optimal Hyperspectral bands for estimation of rice biophysical parameters. *Journal of Integrated Plant Biology*, 50(3), 291-299.

Wang, J., Rich, P.M., and Price, K.P. (2003). Temporal responses of NDVI to precipitation and temperature in the central Great Plains, USA. *International Journal of Remote Sensing*, *24*(11), 2345-2364.

Wikipedia, 2015a. Carbon sink, https://en.wikipedia.org/wiki/Carbon_sink

Wikipedia, 2015b. Deforestation of the Amazon rainforest, https://en.wikipedia.org/wiki/Deforestation_of_the_Amazon_rainforest#cite_note-22

Yu, F., Price, K.P., Ellis, J., and Shi, P. (2003). Response of seasonal vegetation development to climatic variations in eastern central Asia. *Remote Sensing of Environment*, *87*(1), 42-54.

Zhao, T., and Schwartz, M.D. (2003). Examining the onset of spring in Wisconsin. *Climate Research*, *24*(1), 59-70.

Zhou, L., Kaufmann, R.K., Tian, Y., Myneni, R.B., and Tucker, C.J. (2003). Relation between interannual variations in satellite measures of northern forest greenness and climate between 1982 and 1999. *Journal of Geophysical Research: Atmospheres (1984-2012)*, *108*(D1), ACL-3.

7

To Live and Let Live

Human Being and Elephant Conflict

Sumanta Bid and *Malavika Sinha*

The democratic civil society is trying to restore the peace and harmony. The basic objective of Society is *to live and let live*. This idiom expresses the idea of allowing *each other* to live their lives within favourable habitat or niche (micro-habit). The habitat, immediate milieu of living organism may be tiny like a rock pool or may be long like a vast forest track. Inter -and intra-specific competition for the survival is a nature's law. Human-elephant conflict is an example for the growing competition between people and wildlife for space and livelihood throughout Africa and Asia (Di Fonzo, 2007). The Asian elephant is categorised as an 'endangered' species in the Red List of the World Conservation Union (IUCN, 2008: www.iucnredlist.org) and it is classified with the Convention for International Trade of Endangered Species under Appendix I (Perera, 2009).

Sources of Information and Methodology

This chapter is based on the literature review. Basic information collected from Forest Divisional Reports of Bankura, Purulia and Midnapore 2011. The proposed work is executed in a holistic and environmentalist approach. Basic observation is empirical.

Study Area

The study area lies in forested fringe of the *Rarh* plain of West Bengal

(Charts 7.1 and 7.2). The area covers the part of districts Puruliya, Bankura and West Midnapore of 27,222 sq. km. (Fig. 7.2). The geographical extension of the area is 21°36' N to 23°42' N and 85°49' E to 88°15' E.

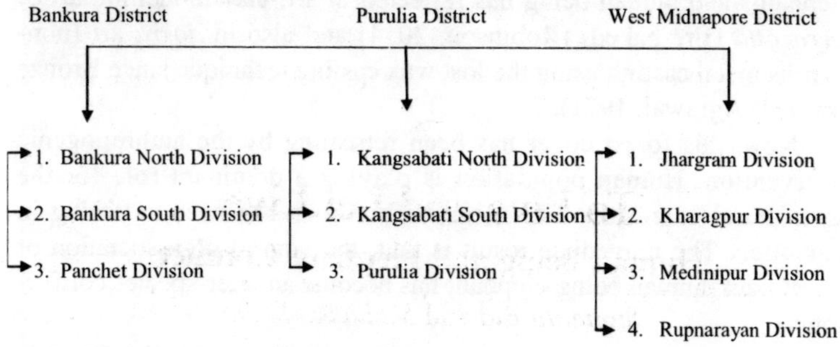

Fig. 7.1 : Forested fringe of the Rarh plain of West Bengal

Niche of Elephant

The availability of food and secure shelter are prime need of each living organism of earth. The food habit and shelter of animal depends on climatic adaptation. This adaptation (for food and habitat) has changed through time. The Elephants are classified as mega herbivores and elephant consumes up to 150 kg (330 lb) of plant matter per day. They are categorised as feeders, and both grazers and browsers. Therefore, availability of food is a major determinant of carrying capacity of elephants in a given area. Elephant is the animal of undulating plateau (Chotanagpur plateau) and the topography varies from 120 m to 320 m. The area is characterized by dry and wet sub-humid tropical climate with the regime of south-west monsoon. According to Köppen, the tract lies in '*Aw*' type of climate (Spate, 1954). The availability of surface water is one of the prime criteria for elephants. The forest type is Tropical Dry Deciduous Forests as per Champion and Sheth's revised classification. The dominant flora consists of *Shorea robusta,* and *Burtea frondosa*. About 45 per cent of the total forest consists of pure *sal,* about 15 per cent of mixed *sal* including open scrubs, and about 40 per cent of the area is under plantation (Anon 2010, Anon 2010-2011, Anon 2013a, Anon 2013b). These thrice combinations—climate, vegetation and topography—lead to concentrate the elephant in these zone since neolithic era. The archaeological remnants of Gandeshwari river basin area and ancient non-ferrous metal melting *dokra* artisan of Bankura, Purulia and Midnapur have cleared the habitat history of elephant of study area (Sinha S., 2015).

This study area is also the land of Acheulian culture. The evidences of palaeolithic tools are observed in this area. That facts reveal that here human habitation of this zone is very ancient. The association of the forest, elephants and human being has reflected in art; clay modelling art of *terracotta* (fire baked) (Robinson, 2014) and also in *dokra* art (non-ferrous metal casting using the lost wax casting technique since Bronze era (D.P. Agrawal, 1971).

Now, this forest cover has been retreating by the anthropogenic intervention. Human population is playing a dominant role for the agricultural extension. The mega herbivorous has been suffering in starvation. The immediate result is that, the land of co-association of forest track-human being-elephant has become an inter-species conflict zone.

Niche Route of Elephant

Migratory movements reflect an animal's need to eat, breed, avoid predators and find a tolerable physiological environment. These movements are revealing the animal's evolutionary history, during which natural selection has resulted in behaviours and changing environments. The migration behaviour of elephant (seasonal) is an ideal metric for understanding organismal responses to changing environments over space and time (e.g., climate change and land-use change). The Asian elephant follows strict migration routes that are determined by the monsoon season. The eldest elephant of the Asian elephant herd is responsible for remembering the migration route. This Asian elephant migration takes place between the wet and dry seasons and problems arose when farms were built along the migratory routes of the Asian elephant herds, as the Asian elephants caused a great deal of destruction to the newly founded farmland. The age group composition of migratory elephant from Dalma (WLS) to south West Bengal is very much diversified within a particular herd (Fig. 7.1).

The human-elephant conflict has become a dominant fact after 1990. Before 1990 elephant migratory track confined within Dalma Wild Life Sanctuary (WLS) to eroded plateau of Purulia. Though the elephant migration (seasonal or diurnal) track lies within reserve forest area but due to the changes in forest composition (change in woody forest species), change of forest layers (forest shrub and grass land) and due to decay of forest density, the scarcity of food of mega herbivorous has become acute.

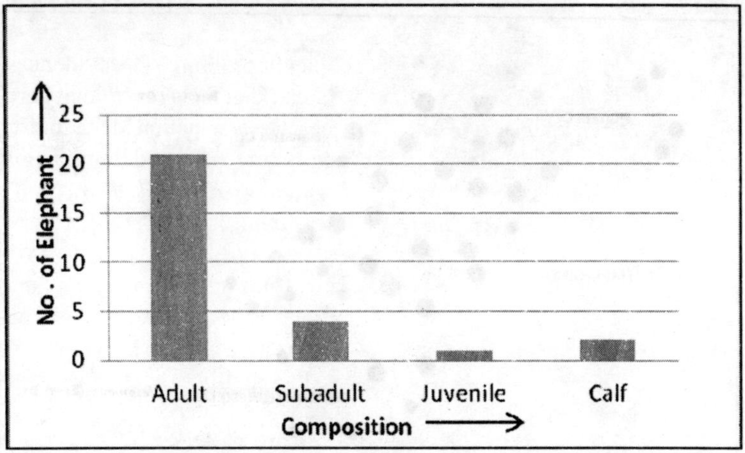

Fig. 7.2: Composition of Migratory Elephant in South West Bengal

Source: A.K. Singh, 2013.

This acute starvation of elephant leads to migration and immediate result is inter-species conflict. These inter-species conflict zone lies in Sonamukhi Block, Borjora Block, Gangajalghati Block, Baliatore area of Bankura District, Garbetha I and II Blocks, Chandrakona I Block, and Bankadaha forest track area of Midnapore (Fig. 7.3).

The Usual Route of Migration of Elephant

Jharkhand (Dalma Hill) → Jhargram Division → Midnapur Division → Rupnarayan Division → Panchet Division → Bankura North Division → Panchet Division → Rupnarayan Division → Midnapur Division → Kharagpur Division → Jhargram Division → Jharkhand.

Route in Details

Entry: Dalma hills of Jharkhand ↔ Kankrajhore ↔ Bhulaveda ↔ Barigahti ↔ Silda ↔ Malaboti ↔ Sijuaghat (cross Kangsabati River) ↔ Lalgarh ↔ Goaltore ↔ Hoomgarh ↔ Gorbeta ↔ Dhadka ↔ Shayamnagar ↔ Bankadaha ↔ Prakashghat ↔ Patrasayar ↔ Sonamukhi ↔ Brindabanpur ↔ Barjora.

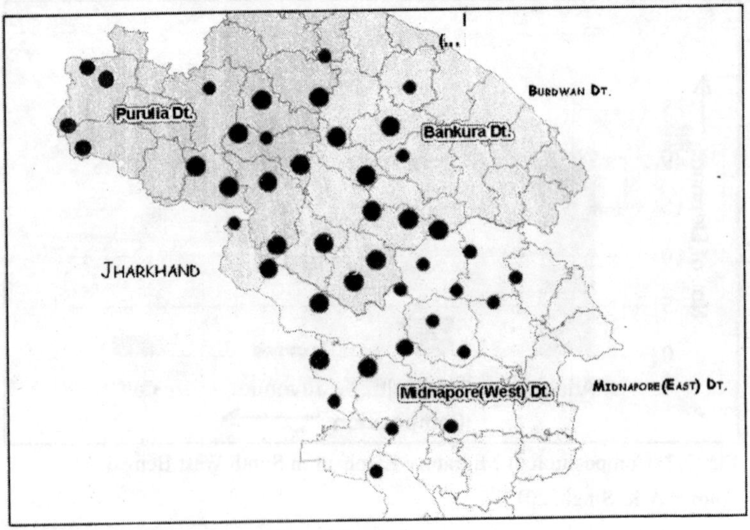

Fig. 7.3: Man-elephant Conflict of Study Area.

Inter-species Conflict

According to Mr. S. Das, Divisional Forest Officer, Bankura (North), elephants used to leave Bankura in January, but for the past few decades herds have been staying till May or June. Mr. Das explains that in Bankura the forest cover is sporadic. Elephants remain inside the forest in the day and raid villages at night. On one such night on 2013, January 19, a herd ravaged hectares of potato fields and scores of huts in Dadhimukha village (Borjora Block, Bankura District). The people showed around 20 houses, two flour mills and a vast expanse of potato, cabbage and cauliflower fields destroyed by elephants. Elephants pulled down the wall of Vishwanath Mandal's flour mill and ate nearly 600 kg. of wheat flour. In 2013, rogue elephants killed six people in Barjora range.

Result of Inter Species Conflict

The immediate result of inter species conflict occur in terms of both loss of lives (*Homo sapiens* and *Elephas maximus indicus*) and economic loss too (Fig. 7.4) (Anon, 2011-12).

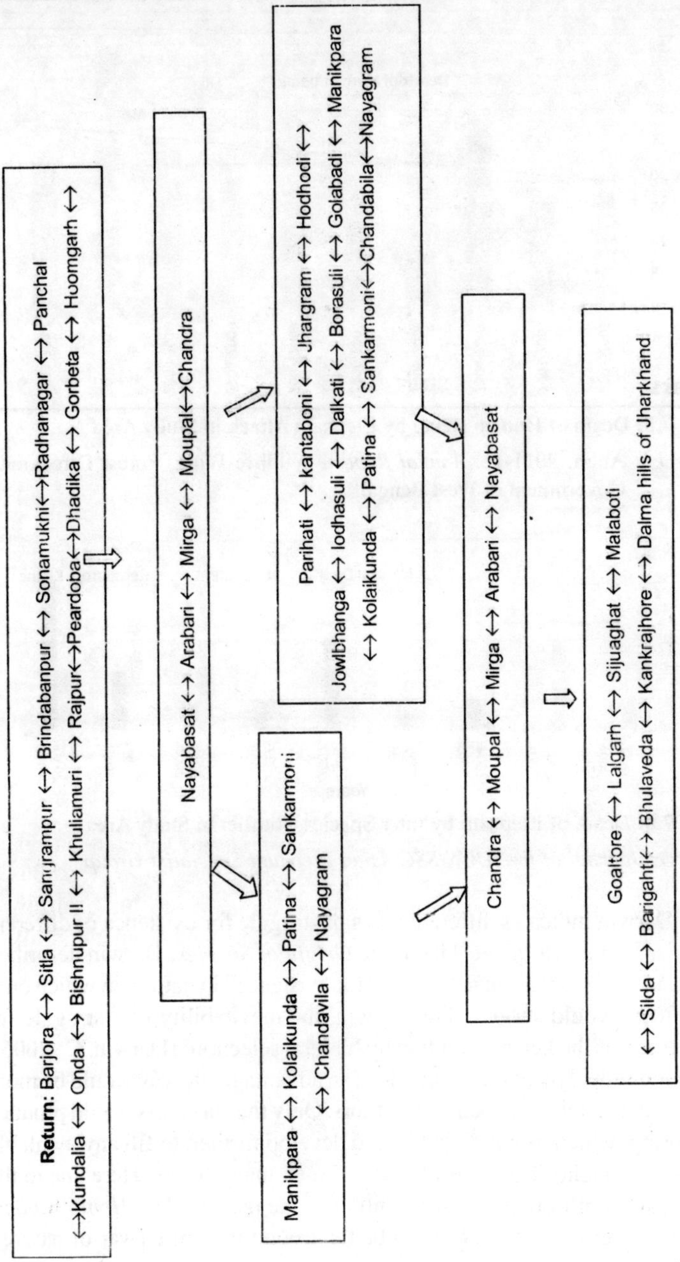

Fig. 7.3: Entry and Exit Route Detail

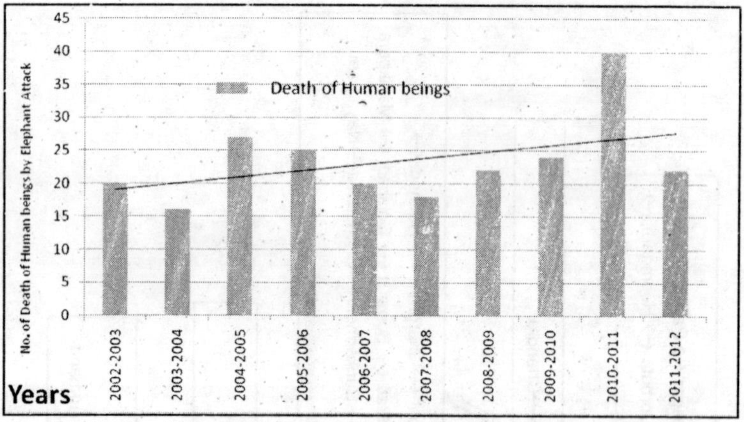

Fig. 7.5: Death of Human Being by Elephant Attack in Study Area

Source: Anon, 2011-12. *Annual Report*, Wildlife Wing, Forest Directorate, Government of West Bengal.

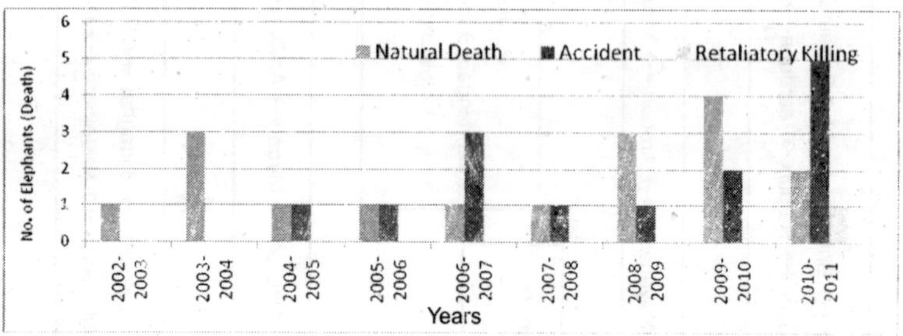

Fig. 7.6: Death of Elephant by Inter Species Conflict in Study Area

Source: *Journal of the IUCN/SSC Asian Elephant Specialist Group.*

Darwin indicates different ways of struggle for existence of different species in the natural world. On the *Origin of Species*, Darwin described that there was a continual "struggle for existence" in nature, in which only the fittest would survive. For Darwin, the inevitability of a struggle for survival was the key to evolution by 'natural selection' (Darwin, C., 2006). Any individual plants and animals in an advantageous way would be more likely to triumph over their competitors. Only the survivors would produce offspring, which might diversify and develop further, to fill any available ecological niche. The "war of nature" took many forms. Here due to the aggressive anthropogenic intervention of the natures' law *Homo sapiens* conflict over the space creates a battle ground in nature (war of nature).

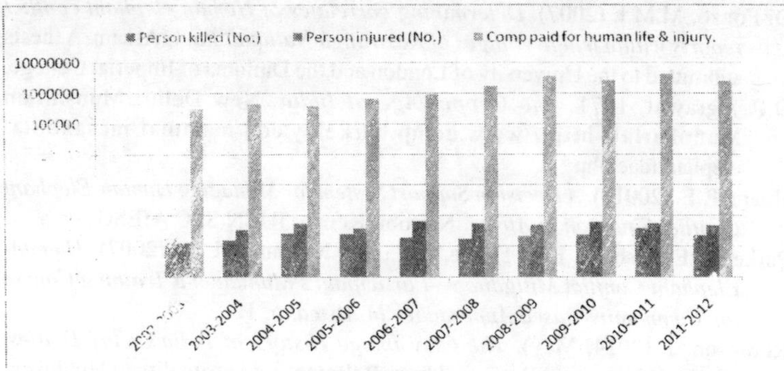

Fig. 7.7: Payment of Ex-gratia Relief for elephant depredation in Study Area

Source: Anon, 2013, Elephant Problem in Purulia. *Divisional Report of Purulia division.*

The "war of nature" is mainly for ecological niche (habitat, food, shelter) and the anthropogenic intervention violates the nature's law. The Darwinian concepts of natural selection and nature's law for survival have been facing a crucial situation.

References

Anon, 2010. *A Paradigm Shift in the Elephant Depredation in South Bengal*. Divisional Report of Bankura (North) Division.

Anon, 2010-11, *State Forest Report*. Forest Department, Government of West Bengal.

Anon, 2013a. *Elephant Depredation Problem in Paschim Medinipur.* Divisional Report of Rupnarayan Division.

Anon, 2013b. *Elephant Problem in Purulia*. Divisional Report of Purulia division.

Anon, 2013d. Data of PCCF, WL & CWLW Office.

Bist, S.S. (2002). An overview of elephant conservation in India, *The Indian Forester*, 128, Dehradun, pp. 121-136.

B.M. A. Oswin Perera (2009). The Human-Elephant Conflict: A Review of Current Status and Mitigation Methods, *Gajah: Journal of the IUCN/SSC Asian Elephant Specialist Group,* 30, pp. 41-52.

Bhattacharya, B.K., *et al.*, (1985). *West Bengal District Gazetteers*: Puruliya, pp. 2-22.

Chatterjee, A.B.; Gupta, A.; Mukhopadhyay, K.L.; and Mukhopadhyay, P.K., (ed.) (1970). *West Bengal,* KLM Firma, Calcutta.

Darwin, C., 2006, *On the Origin of Species*, (Dover Thrift Editions) Paperback: 336 pages.

Di Fonzo, M.M.I. (2007). *Determining correlates of Human-elephant conflict reports within fringe villages of Kaziranga National Park,* Assam. A thesis submitted to the University of London and the Diploma of Imperial College.

D.P. Agrawal, 1971. *The Copper Age of India*. New Delhi: Munshiram Manoharlal, http://www.ucmp.berkeley.edu/mammal/mesaxonia/elephantidae.php

Hoare, R.E. (2001b). *A Decision Support System for Managing Human-Elephant Conflict Situation in Africa.* Nairobi, Kenya: IUCN/SSC AfESG.

Parker, G.E., Osborn, F.V., Hoare, R.E., and Niskanen, L.S., (2007). *Human-Elephant Conflict Mitigation—Participant's Manual of a Training Course for Community-Based Approaches in Africa,* p. 12.

Robinson, J. (2014, May). *The Clay Image History of India's Clay Deities.* (Oxford University) Retrieved from Religion and Spirituality of Hinduism, About. Com: http://hinduism.about.com/od/artculture/a/clayimage.htm

Singh, Anil kumar, Rina Singh and Sushanta Chowdhury (2002). Human-Elephant Conflicts in Changed Landscapes of South-west Bengal. *Indian Forester,* Vol. 128, No. 10, pp. 1119-1132.

Singh, A.K., (2006). *Ecological Investigation of Human-Elephant Conflicts in South-West Bengal,* thesis Ph.D., Saurashtra University, pp. 62 and 69.

Sinha, S., Sinha, M. and Chakraborty, D., 2015, *International Journal of History and Cultural Studies (IJHCS)* ISSN Print:24547646, www.arcjournals.org

Spate, O.H.K., and Farmer, B.H., (1954). *India and Pakistan—A Regional Geography,* Methuen & Co. Ltd., London.

8

Impact of Global Warming and Climate Change on Plant Disease Development

Manoranjan Chakraborty

Global warming is one of the most burning global environmental issues. Global warming is the biggest threat to mankind, changing temperature can induce severe plant disease epidemics which threaten food security if they affect vegetables, staple crops and can damage landscapes if they affect amenity species. Accelerated temperature change affects components of complex biological interactions differentially, often causing changes in crop yield and quality directly or indirectly, through diseases. Plant diseases are one of the important factors which have a direct impact on global agricultural productivity and increase in temperature will further aggravate the situation.

Global warming will directly influence infection, reproduction, dispersal and other critical stages in the life cycle of a pathogen. The impact will be different for different pathogen groups, such as root-infecting *vs.* shoot-infecting pathogens and biotrophs *vs.* necrotrophs. Other major impacts on diseases will be through changes in host physiology and host-pathogen interactions. *Pachymetra* root rot caused by *Pachymetra chaunorhiza* is favoured by temperatures above 24°C. An increase in temperature would increase the proportion of the year suitable for the fungus to infect roots and would therefore allow a greater number of generations in a season. The severity of the disease also depends to a large extent on soil moisture levels. Increased summer rainfall would favour *Pachymetra* root rot.

Changes in temperature and precipitation regimes due to climate change may alter the growth stage, development rate and pathogenicity of infectious agents, and the physiology and resistance of the host plant. A change in temperature could directly affect the spread of infectious diseases and their survival between seasons. There are indications of increased aggressiveness at higher temperatures of stripe rust isolates (*Puccinia striiformis*), suggesting that rust fungi can adapt to and benefit from higher temperatures. Climate change is also reported to cause a shift in the geographical distribution of host pathogens. A change in temperature may favour the development of different dormant pathogens, which could induce an epidemic. Increase in temperature with sufficient soil moisture may increase evapotranspiration resulting in humid microclimate in crops and may lead to incidence of diseases favoured under these conditions. Diseases such as common bunt (*Tilletia caries*) and karnal bunt (*Tilletia indica*) in wheat can be of importance under changing climatic conditions in regions with low productivity if proper seed treatment is not followed in this crop. In India, in the last decade the disease scenario of chickpea and pigeon pea has changed drastically; dry root rot (*Rhizoctonia bataticola*) of chickpea and *Phytophthora* blight (*Phytophthora drechsleri* f. sp. *cajani*) of pigeon pea have emerged as a potential threat to the production of these pulses. Higher risk of dry root rot has been reported in *Fusarium* wilt chickpea-resistant varieties in those years when the temperature exceeds 33°C. In North America, needle blight (*Dothistroma septosporum*) is reported to be spreading northwards with increasing temperature and precipitation increase or decrease in disease severity and spread (Gautam *et al.*, 2013). In India, wheat, rice and potato are important crops. Analysis of the last 30 years historical weather data from different locations of Punjab has indicated that significant changes have occurred in the weather causing early warming in February. Such climatic changes will influence wheat crop, which is of importance in the region. On the other hand, the importance of leaf rust, foliar blights *Fusarium* head blight and stem rust may increase in Punjab in the future due to elevated temperature (Gautam *et al.*, 2013).

A change in temperature may favour the development of different inactive pathogens, which could induce an epidemic. Temperature is one of the most important factors affecting the occurrence of bacterial diseases such as *Ralstonia solanacearum, Acidovorax avenae* and *Burkholderia glumea*. As the temperature increases, the duration of winter and the rate of growth and reproduction of pathogens may be modified (Ladanyi and Horvath, 2010). *Acidovorax avenae* sub sp. *avenae* has emerged as a disease of upland rice in Southern Europe during periods of high temperatures and *Burkholderia gladioli* has emerged as a serious pathogen of orchids in Thailand. *B. glumea* is emerging as a problem on rice in the Southern United States and the pathogen has become much more prevalent in Southern South Korea during periods of high temperatures. One possible explanation of the increase in these bacteria is global warming. A common trait among them is an optimum growth temperature of 32-36 °C; most grow well up to 41°C. An increase in extreme weather conditions, including extended heat waves, storms such as hurricanes appear to favour these high temperature bacteria. Similarly, the incidence of vector-borne diseases will be altered. Climate can substantially influence the development and distribution of vectors. Changes may result in geographical distribution, increased overwintering, changes in population growth rates, increases in the number of generations, extension of the development season, changes in crop-pest synchrony of phenology, changes in interspecific interactions and increased risk of invasion by migrant pests. Research has shown that host plants such as wheat and oats become more susceptible to rust diseases with increased temperature. Earlier onset of warm temperatures could result in an earlier threat from late blight with the potential for more severe epidemics and increases in the number of fungicide applications needed for control. The effects of elevated temperature on plants will tend to vary greatly throughout the year. During colder parts of the year, warming may relieve plant stress, whereas during hotter parts of the year it may increase stress. A striking example of the potential effect on the yield of crop plants in response to elevated temperature, rice yield in the Philippines was estimated to decline 10 per cent for each 1 °C increase in the minimum temperature during the dry season (Rayees *et al.*, 2013).

Elevated temperature is thus likely to affect most plant pathosystems, included those that are already troublesome or out of control undercurrent climate conditions. As an example, take Sudden Oak death, caused by the *Phytophthora ramorum*. *P. ramorum* inoculated branch cuttings of coast live oaks (*Quercus agrifolia*) developed larger lesions in spring, a result interpreted to suggest a role of synchronicity between host cambium activity and pathogen colonization rate. Such co-occurrences between host phenology and pathogen sporulation are likely to be affected by climate shifts (Marco Pautasso *et al.,* 2012). At the same time, climate change may modify the pattern of susceptibility to *P. ramorum* in ecosystems not currently affected but at risk due to the presence of potentially sporulating hosts (e.g. plantations of Japanese larch, *Larix kaempferi*), from the Appalachians to the Mediterranean, from New Zealand to Japan.

The nature and magnitude of climate change will influence changes in geographical distribution of many pathogens. Using three temperature change scenarios and a 20 per cent increase in rainfall, Brasier and Scott (1994) predicted that global warming will make the oak decline pathogen, *Phytophthora cinnamomi,* more severe in regions of Europe where it is currently present and spread it northward and eastward. Of the two poplar rusts, *Melampsora allipopulina* is more thermophilic than *M. laricipopulina.* Fast growing poplar clones are now grown in much of northern Europe. These clones are generally more susceptible to the thermophilic *M. allipopulina* and this pathogen appears only sporadically due to temperature limitations. A change to warmer climate has serious implications for a large area in northern Europe where poplar growing is being encouraged as an alternative to producing agricultural surpluses (Chakraborty *et al.*, 1998).

Elevated temperature and CO_2 concentration are also posing higher threat perception of late blight (*Phytophthora infestans*) disease of potato and important diseases of rice, namely blast (*Pyricularia oryzae*) and sheath blight (*Rhizoctonia solani*). Some workers suggest that elevated CO_2 concentration and climate change may accelerate plant pathogen evolution, which can affect virulence. In soybean, elevated concentration of CO_2 and O_3 altered the expression of three soybean diseases, namely downy mildew (*Peronospora manshurica*), brown spots (*Septoria glycines*) and sudden death syndrome (*Fusarium virguliforme*) and plant response to the diseases varied considerably.

In contrast, high levels of CO_2 alone or in combination with high concentration of O_3, increased the severity of *Septoria* leaf spots. The workers concluded that high levels of CO_2 and O_3 induced changes in the soybean canopy density and leaf age, which likely contributed to disease expression modification. In addition to high disease incidence and severity due to changes in host, reproduction of the pathogens has also been reported to increase at high CO_2 levels in barley powdery mildew and anthracnose (*Colletotrichum gloeosporioides*). Elevated levels of CO_2 can directly affect the growth of pathogens. For example, the growth of the germ tube, appressorium and conidium of *C. gloeosporioides* fungi is slower at high concentrations of CO_2 (700 ppm). Germination rates of conidia on leaves were lower at CO_2 concentrations of 700 ppm than those observed at 350 ppm. However, once the pathogen infects the plant, the fungus quickly develops and achieves sporulation. In contrast, the rate of germination sporulation was greater at high concentrations of CO_2.

Temperature can also affect disease resistance in plants, thus affecting the incidence and severity of the diseases. Temperature sensitivity to resistance has been reported for leaf rust (*Puccinia recondita*) in wheat, broomrape (*Orobanche cumana*) in sunflower, black shank (*Phytophthora nicotianae*) in tobacco and bacterial blight (*Xanthomonas oryzae* pv. *oryzae*) in rice.

Furthermore, many economically important plant-infecting viruses are transmitted by soil living organisms, such as plasmodiophorids, fungi and nematodes. The diseases caused by these viruses are especially difficult to control, because the vectors cannot be controlled by chemicals and they may form resting spores containing infectious virus. Increased soil moisture and temperature in temperate regions, including northern Europe, are expected to increase the activities of zoospores and nematodes that transmit viruses. *Potato mop-top virus* (PMTV) and *Beet necrotic yellow vein virus* (BNYVV) are transmitted by the plasmodiophorids *Spongospora subterranea* and *Polymyxa betae*, respectively.

Many pathosystems, and it seems the cereal rusts in particular, are affected by temperature. At times about half of the wheat cultivars on the UK Recommended List (e.g. HGCA, 2003) showed differential resistance expression when tested against isolates of brown rust (leaf rust) (caused by *Puccinia triticina*), either effective at 10 °C and not at 25 °C or *vice versa.* The effect was not necessarily attributable simply to resistance gene expression response to temperature as isolates too showed differential temperature responses independent of resistance responses. These differential responses to disease expression at different temperatures were also found against other rusts such as stripe rust and oat stem rust. In wheat stem rust the classical temperature sensitivity of the *Sr6* gene was extensively reported by some workers. In rice, for example, some resistance genes, such as *Xa7* effective against some *Xanthomonas oryzae* pv. *oryzae* races, are more effective at high temperatures than low, whereas other resistance genes are less effective.

The implications of climate change for crop pests and diseases cannot easily be summarized; even specific predictions will be difficult because of the complex multi-trophic relationships between many microbial organisms including pathogens, their vectors and their respective host plants. Changing disease scenario due to climate change has highlighted the need for better agricultural practices and use of eco-friendly methods in disease management for sustainable crop production. In the changing climate and shift in seasons, choice of crop management practices based on the prevailing situation is important. In such scenarios, weather-based disease monitoring, inoculum monitoring, especially for soil-borne diseases and rapid diagnostics would play a significant role. Integrated disease management strategies should be developed to decrease dependence on fungicides. In addition, monitoring and early warning systems for forecasting disease epidemics should be developed for important host-pathogens which have a direct bearing on the earnings of the farmers and food security at large.

References

Brasier, C.M. and Scott, J.K. (1994). European oak decline and global warming: A theoretical assessment with special reference to the activity of *Phytophthora cinnamomi. EPPO Bulletin*, **24**: 221-232.

Chakraborty, S., Murray, G. M., Magareyc, P.A., Yonow, T. D., O'Brien, R.G. Cmft, E., B.J., Barb :tti. M.J., Sivasithamparam, K., Dudzinski, M.J., Sutherst, R.W., Amhc, C. and Emmett. R.W. (1998). Potential impact of climate change on plant diseases of economic significance to Australia. *Australasian Plant Pathology*, **27**: 15-35.

Gautam, H.R., Bhardwaj, M.L. and Kumar, R. (2013). Climate change and its impact on plant diseases. *Current Science,* **105 (12)**: 1685-1691.

Ladanyi, M., and Horvath, L. (2010). A review of the potential climate change impact on insect populations—general and agricultural aspects. *Appl. Ecol. Environ. Res.*, **8**: 143-152.

Marco Pautasso, M., Döring, T.F., Garbelotto, M., Pellis, L. and Jeger, M.J. (2012). Impacts of climate change on plant diseases—opinions and trends. *Eur. J. Plant Pathol.,* DOI 10.1007/s10658-012-9936-1.

Rayees, A., Ahanger, R.A., Tauseef, A., Bhat, S.A., Imtiyaz, A., Wani, S.A. Ganai, S., Khan, O.A., Junaid, J. and Tariq A., Bhat, T.A. (2013). Impact of Climate Change on Plant Diseases. *Int. J. Modern Plant and Anim. Sci.*, **1(3)**: 105-115.

9

Selection of Some Disease Resistant Tree Legume for New Plantation Programme

Arijit Sinhababu and *Arpita Banerjee*

Introduction

In nature, plants growing in fields are exposed to several pathogenic organisms that cause diseases. Development of disease may be considered one of the biotic stresses that can affect plant's normal growth and development and in extreme cases, can kill the host plant. Fungi are an important group of organisms that are pathogenic to plants. Infection of the host plant by the causal organism may occur at different stages of development and also different parts of a plant.

Generally. seeds, which are dried at low moisture content and stored at a low temperature, are free from fungal attacks. The fungi normally attack seeds during storage when the seed moisture content is in equilibrium with relative humidity greater than 65 per cent (Harrington, 1973). Seeds are susceptible to micro-organisms and lose their viability (Delouche, 1974) under tropical conditions. In poor storage conditions seeds were found to carry various micro-organisms, adversely affecting seed quality and viability (Heppery and Sinclair, 1982; Terkony *et al.*, 1983). Mohanan and Sharma (1988), Sharma and Bhardwaj (1988), Chalermponge (1990) reported several diseases of seeds and seedlings of *Acacia* species. A number of mycoflora like *Rhizopus*, *Erysiphae*, *Verticillum*, *Penicillium* and *Thermomyces* were associated with tree seeds such as *Acacia*, *Albizia* and *Cassia* causing germination failure of such species (Bedell, 1998).

Disease occurrence varies according to the climatic conditions under which the plant was grown. Seed treatments with antipathogenic agents and fungicides have proved useful in storing seeds against post-damage and loss of viability. Singh and Khan (1999), Singh and Mehrotra (1999) isolated some seed borne fungi of forest tree like *Acacia*, *Albizia*, *Bauhinia* and studied their control using fungicides like Bavistin, Blitox and Dithane M-45. A number of workers (Mamatha *et al.*, 2000; Gupta *et al.*, 2001; Singh *et al.*, 2001) have tried to find out the suitable control measure for several fungal species under *in vivo* and *in vitro* conditions. Although plants lack an immune system, they are often found to be surprisingly resistant to diseases caused by fungi. Plants produce a large, diverse array of organic compounds, like phenolics, alkaloids and other secondary metabolites that appear to have no direct function in growth and development, but serve as defense compounds against herbivores and pathogen (Taiz and Zeiger, 2002). It is an established fact that many secondary metabolites of plants, particularly phenolics impart a great role in conferring resistance in plants against different pathogens (Deverall and Dann, 1995; Rathna Kumar and Balasubramanian, 2001).

Before undertaking afforestation programme pathological study of the selected plants is essential, since incidence of pathogen frequently occurs through seeds as well as seedlings. In the present investigation with local trees, plants were first screened under field condition for occurrence of pathological diseases and the responsible organisms. Disease occurrence and causal organism was confirmed through Koch's postulation experiment. Next, pathogenic fungi were tested against fungicides for their sensitivity. Finally, seedlings of the selected plants were analysed for accumulation of phenolic substances as defense compound in response to pathogenic infection to specific fungi. This will give an insight of relative resistance of these fuelwood plants against fungal diseases.

Materials and Methods

In the present investigation, four tree species [*Bauhinia variegata* Linn., *Cassia fistula* Linn., *Delonixregia* (Hook.) Raf. And *Peltophorum pterocarpum* (DC.) K. Heyne] of the family *Leguminosae* (*Fabaceae*) were used and seedlings (20 days old) were taken as experimental plant materials to assess responses to pathogenic attack.

All the plant samples in this research were taken from Bankura district which is the western most district of West Bengal. Bankura lies between 22° 38″ and 23° 38′ North latitude and between 86° 36′ and 87° 46′ East longitudes. The soil is mainly dry lateritic type and having the pH ranges from 5.5 to 6.5 at different regions of the district.

(A) Identification of Plant Pathogens Responsible for Diseases

Seeds, leaves and stem lesions with infections were collected from in and around Bankura, surface sterilized with 0.1 per cent $HgCl_2$ for 2-3 minutes (Halloin, 1975), washed three times with sterile water and dried with sterilized blotting paper before plating on to malt-agar medium. Infected portions were cut into small pieces and 3-4 such pieces were inoculated on ME-plate. The inoculated petridishes were incubated at 28 ± 2°C in BOD incubator for 3-5 days. The incubated dishes were examined for occurrence of any fungal or bacterial colonies. The colonies appeared on these plates were counted and characterized. One set of fungi appeared after incubation was preserved on malt-agar slants for further studies.

Composition of Malt-extract agar medium was:

Malt extract	–	5 g
Agar	–	4 g
Water up to	–	250 ml
pH adjusted to	–	6.9

Staining Procedure

For general microscopic observation of the isolates, lactophenol cotton blue stain was used for staining. A few mycelia portion of each isolate was taken separately on clean slides. A few drops of lactophenol cotton blue were added on the mycelia. The preparation was fixed by gentle heat and the stain was allowed to react for 2-3 minutes at room temperature, washed thoroughly with lactophenol and finally mounted in lactophenol after proper teasing and examined under microscope. The nature of hyphae, reproductive structure and resting spores were noted.

The staining reagent was composed of Lactophenol and cotton blue in the following proportions:

Solution A

Lactic acid	–	1 part
Phenol	–	1 part

Glycerine – 1 part
Distilled water – 1 part

Solution B

Cotton blue (0.05%-0.1%)

Solution A and Solution B were Mixed in Equal Volume.

Identification of the fungal culture was done by microscopic observation of the stained cultures following the standard literature (Funder, 1968; Bilgrami *et al.*, 1979).

(B) Confirmation of Causal Agent for Diseases in Seeds or Seedlings by Reinoculation (Koch's postulation)

For pathological study healthy seeds of four fast growing tree species *viz.*, *B. variegata*, *C. fistula*, were taken as plant material. After germination they were placed on sand beds to generate seedlings. Then 20 days old seedlings were taken as plant samples. Koch postulation experiments were performed using cultures isolated from the infected plant parts. This was done using conidia of freshly grown isolates against seedlings of their specific hosts (the plant species from which they were originally isolated). For this purpose, 20 days old seedlings were taken.

To infect, seedlings were first rubbed mildly with sterilized sand and then applied with conidia at different inoculums density [low (100 conidia ml^{-1}), medium (600-1200 conidia ml^{-1}) and high (3000 or more conidia ml^{-1})] of all the fungal isolates. One control set was maintained. Five seedlings were inoculated for each treatment. After 15 days of treatment seedlings were observed carefully for the development of any symptoms comparable to their mother host. Very mild symptoms appeared on the leaves and stem treated with high inoculums density. Next, infected seedlings (leaves and stem) were cut into pieces, thoroughly surface sterilized with 0.1 per cent $HgCl_2$ for 2-3 minutes, washed three times with sterile water and dried with sterilized blotting paper before plating on to malt-agar medium (with same composition). The inoculated petridishes were incubated at 28 ± 2°C in BOD incubator for 3-5 days. Seeds were also mixed with isolated pathogens similarly under aseptic condition. After 15 days only monocultures were obtained in most cases.

(C) Effect of Fungicides on Isolated Fungal Pathogens

The fungi, which were isolated in earlier step, were then tested for their growth responses in presence of two common systemic fungicides *viz.*, Blitox and Dithane M 45. Different concentrations (50-1000 μg ml^{-1}) of these fungicides were mixed with malt-agar medium and each fungus was tested for their ability for growth in presence of fungicides. The inoculated petridishes were incubated at 28 ± 2 °C in BOD incubator for 3-5 days.

(D) Assessment of Defense against Pathogens

Assessment of the plant defense against pathogen was done by analyzing the accumulation of free phenols by the seedlings infected with specific pathogens. Seedlings of 20 days were first rubbed mildly with sterilized sand and then applied with conidia of pathogens producing leaf diseases (leaf curl and spot) at medium inoculum density. One control set was also maintained. Five seedlings were inoculated for each species. After 7 days of treatment leaves of the seedlings were analysed for total free phenol content.

The extraction and estimation of the total free phenol content was done according to the method of Bray and Thorpe (1954). The leaf samples (50 mg) were homogenized in 5 ml 80 per cent ethanol and kept at 65 °C in a water bath for 5 minutes. The mixture was centrifuged at 5000 rpm for 10 minutes. The supernatant was taken in a beaker, 4 ml of distilled water was added and the mixture was kept on a hot water bath. After complete evaporation of alcohol, the aqueous phase was mixed with 4 ml of ether in a separating funnel and shaken thoroughly for 10 minutes. After a rest for a while the upper ether layer was taken and mixed with 3 ml hot distilled water and kept in open air until the ether was evaporated. One ml of this aqueous extract was taken and to this 3 ml of 5 per cent Na_2CO_3 (w/v) and 1 ml of Folin phenol reagent were added and the mixture was kept in a boiling water bath for 1 minutes. Absorbance of the blue colour developed was measured at 650 nm. Content of phenol was calculated by comparing the absorbance with a standard curve prepared from catechol (Sigma Chemical Co., USA). The content of free phenol was expressed as mg g^{-1} fresh weight.

Results and Discussion

Infected seeds and leaves of the selected plants produced different fungal colonies, in ME plates, which are enlisted in Table 9.1. In infected seeds of *Bauhinia variegata*, fungal species like *Verticillium* and *erysiphae* were found. For leaf curl and leaf spot diseases, infected leaf produced colonies of *Phytophthora* sp. In case of *Cassia fistula*, seeds were infected with *Penicillium* sp. While *Erysiphae* sp. and *Taphrina* sp. were found to be associated with leaf curl diseases and other two fungal species like *Alternaria* sp. and *Curvularia* sp. responsible for leaf spot diseases. In case of *Delonixregia,* seed infection was due to *Penicillium* sp. and leaf curl disease was due to *Phytophthora* sp. and one other unknown fungal species. *Peltophorum pterocarpum* seed were infected by *Thermomyces* sp. and *Penicillium* sp. while in case of leaf spot disease the fungal colonies produced on culture medium was very much similar to *Curvularia* sp. and *Alternaria* sp.

Table 9.1: Fungal Pathogens Causing Diseases of Four Tree Legumes

Plant Species	*Infected Plant Parts*	*Name of the Pathogens*
Bauhinia variegata	Seed	*Verticillium* sp., *Erysiphae* sp.
	Leaf curl	*Phytophthora* sp., *Curvularia* sp.
	Leaf Spot	*Phytophthora* sp.
Cassia fistula	Seed	*Penicillium* sp.
	Leaf curl	*Erysiphae* sp., *Taphrina* sp.
	Leaf spot	*Alternaria* sp., *Curvularia* sp.
Delonixregia	Seed	*Penicillium* sp.
	Leaf spot	*Phytophthora* sp., *Curvularia* sp.
Peltophorum pterocarpum	Seed	*Thermomyces* sp., *Penicillium* sp.
	Leaf spot	*Curvularia* sp., *Alternaria* sp.

Source: Authors' Observation.

After re-inoculation of the pathogens (fresh conidia) in seed or young seedlings (20 days old) of the respective plants followed by inoculation into malt agar medium, fungal colonies produced in ME-plates were found to be less in number compared to earlier (Table 9.2) for each plant species. Thus only *Verticillium* species was observed in case of seed infection of *B. variegata* after Koch's postulation. While for leaf infection of young seedlings of this species single colony of *Phytophthora* sp. could be isolated. After Koch's postulation experiment, infected seeds of *Cassia fistula* showed only *Penicillium* species thus confirming this fungus as the casual organism of seed infection. Similarly, *Alternaria* sp. and *Erysiphae* sp. caused leaf spot and leaf curl diseases, respectively. Newly infected seeds of *Delonixregia* produced colonies of *Penicillium* sp. and infected leaf part showed the presence of *Phytophthora* sp. in ME medium. In case of seed of *Peltophorum pterocarpum* monoculture of *Penicillium* sp. was isolated, while infected leaves produced colonies of *Curvularia* sp. only. Here also *Alternaria* and some other unknown fungi, which are found earlier, were totally absent in reisolated plates.

Table 9.2: Organisms Isolated after Koch's Postulation Experiments

Plant Species	*Seed infection*	*Leaf spot*	*Leaf curl*
Bauhinia variegata	*Verticillium* sp.	*Phytophthora* sp.	*Phytophthora* sp.
Cassia fistula	*Penicillium* sp.	*Alternaria* sp.	*Erysiphae* sp.
Delonixregia	*Penicillium* sp.	*Phytophthora* sp.	—
Peltophorum pterocarpum	*Penicillium* sp.	*Curvularia* sp.	—

Source: Authors' Observation.

Chemicals are commonly, successfully and economically used to control seed and seedling diseases of tree legumes (Mamatha *et al.*, 2000; Singh *et al.*, 2001). The fungi, which were re-isolated, were then tested for their sensitivity to two common systemic fungicides (Blitox and Dithane M-45). It was observed that (Table 9.3) the growth of the fungi responsible for seed infection (*viz.*, species of *Penicillium* and *Verticillium*) was not affected by lower concentration of both the fungicides (50-500 μg ml^{-1}), but at higher concentration (1000 μg ml^{-1}) colonies of those organisms were not formed at all in ME culture medium. In case of fungal species causing leaf diseases (either leaf spot or leaf curl) in all the tree legumes, 200 μg ml^{-1} concentration and above inhibited growth as no colony appeared in these concentrations.

Table 9.3: Fungicide Tolerance Level of the Isolated Pathogens (After Koch's Postulation against Blitox and Dithane M-45).

	Blitox (μg ml^{-1})						*Dithane M 45 (μg ml^{-1})*					
	0	50	100	200	500	1000	0	50	100	200	500	1000
Seed												
Penicillium sp.	+	+	+	+	+	–	+	+	+	+	+	–
Verticillium sp.	+	+	+	+	+	–	+	+	+	+	+	–
Leaf Curl/Spot												
Curvularia sp.	+	+	+	+	–	–	+	+	+	+	–	–
Phytophthora sp.	+	+	+	–	–	–	+	+	+	+	–	–
Alternaria sp.	+	+	+	+	–	–	+	+	+	+	–	–
Erysiphae sp.	+	+	+	+	–	–	+	+	+	–	–	–

Source: Authors' Observation.

When seedlings (20 days old) of the fast growing fuelwood yielding plants were inoculated with pathogens responsible for leaf diseases phenol content increased in leaves of all species (Fig. 9.1). However, such increase

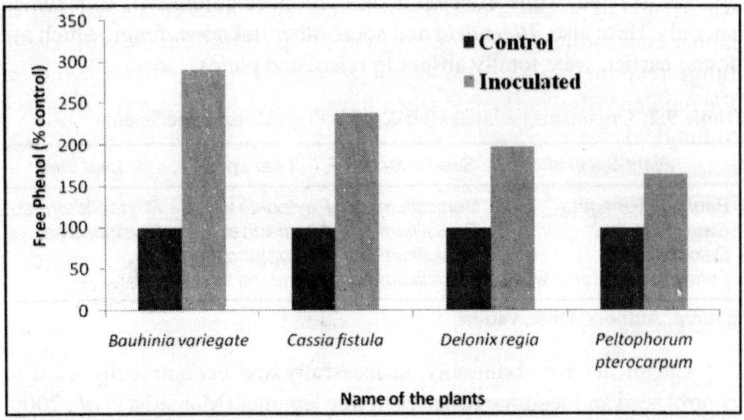

Fig. 9.1: Free Phenol Contents of Investigated Plants under Inoculated Condition (By Pathogen Responsible for Leaf Infection)

Source: Authors' Observation.

was highest in *B. variegata* seedlings followed by *C. fistula*, while *P. pterocarpum* seedlings showed lowest amount of phenol among all species.

For any plantation programme, the selected plants should be assessed first for their susceptibility to the pathogens prevalent in the locality of plantation. In afforestation programme, large quantities of seeds of forest trees are being collected and used for raising seedlings in nurseries. Depending on moisture content seed can carry a number of pathogenic organisms and unhealthy seeds have the potential of introducing dangerous diseases to new plantation areas. Mostly fungi as compared to bacteria, viruses or nematodes cause large number of plant diseases that occur more commonly in seeds.

Several workers reported about different types of fungi responsible for seed and seedling diseases. In the present investigation, causal organism of seed infection was *Penicillium* (for *C. fistula*, *D. regia* and *P. pterocarpum*) and *Verticillium* species (for *B. variegata*) and the causal organism of leaf curl was *Phytophthora* (for *B. variegata*) and *Erysiphae* species (for *C. fistula*). For leaf spot infection, the causal organism was confirmed to be *Phytophthora* species for both *B. variegata* and *D. regia*. While *Alternaria* and *Curvularia* species were confirmed to be the causal organisms for the leaf spot diseases of *C. fistula* and *P. pterocarpum* respectively.

In the present study, it was observed that the fungi responsible for seed infection of these trees *viz.*, *Penicillium* and *Verticillium* species were found to be less sensitive since their growth was inhibited only at higher concentration (1000 μg ml^{-1}) in ME medium. On the other hand, fungi responsible for leaf diseases *viz.*, *Alternaria*, *Curvularia*, *Phytophthora* and *Erysiphae* species were found to be far more sensitive to fungicides as they can be controlled at 200 μg ml^{-1} concentration for both fungicides. There are variable reports on the effectiveness of the fungicides to control fungal diseases. In the present study, both the fungicides affected the growth of the test fungi (responsible for leaf diseases) remarkably at 200 μg ml^{-1} concentration. Limited work has been done on control of foliage diseases of tree legumes. Tree pathologists have generally minimized the importance of foliar diseases as they rarely affect timber production, usually, the most valuable forest product. However, if the tree legume is grown as a source of forage and green manure, then the effect of foliar diseases is very important.

When seedlings were inoculated with the pathogens responsible for specific leaf diseases, phenol content increased in leaves of all species. It is an established fact that many secondary metabolites of plants particularly phenolics impart a great role in conferring inducible resistance to the plant against different pathogens. However, such increase was highest in *B. variegata* seedlings followed by *C. fistula* and *D. regia*. This intrinsic character of the plant may be inducible in nature, which helps plants to overcome the unfavourable condition. Thus, *B. variegata* and *C. fistula* are possibly more resistant to diseases at seedling stage.

References

Bedell, P.E. (1998). *Seed Science and Technology* (Indian Forestry Species). Allied Publishers, India, pp. 346-354.

Bilgrami, K.S., Jamaluddin and Rizwi, M.A. (1979). *Fungi of India*. Part-I. Today and Tomorrow Printers and Publishers, New Delhi, pp. 110-205.

Bray, H.G. and Thorpe, W.V. (1954). Analysis of phenolic compounds of interest in metabolism. In: *Methods of Biochemical Analysis* (Ed. Glick, D.). Vol. I. Inter Science Publication, New York, pp. 27-52.

Chalermpongse, A. (1990). Introduction to forest pathology in Thailand. In: *Proceedings of the IUFRO Workshop—Pests and Diseases of Forest Plantations* (Ed. Hitacharen, C., MacDicken, K.G., Ivory, M.H. and Nair, K.S.S.). Regional office for Asia and the Pacific, FOA, Bangkok, pp. 107-113.

Delouche, L.C. (1974). Maintaining seed quality, production, marketing and use. *T.V.A. Muscle Shoal Alobama, Bull.*, 4: 69-70.

Deverall, B.J. and Dann, E.K. (1995). Induced resistance in legumes. In: *Induced*

Resistance to Disease in Plants (Ed. Hammerschmidt, R. and Kuc, J.). The Netherlands: Academic Publishers, pp. 1-30.

Funder, S. (1968). The identification of fungi by microscopic examination. In: *Practical Mycology Manual for Identification of Fungi*. Third edition. Hafner Publishing Company Inc., New York and Kingston-upon Thames, pp. 39-101.

Gupta, S., Sharma, S., Gupta, A. and Chand, L. (2001). Biochemical studies of major storage proteins from the seeds of pigeonpea [*Cajanuscajan* (L.) Millsp.]. *Physiol. Mol. Biol. Plants*, 7(2): 167-174.

Harrington, J.F. (1973). Problems of seed storage. In: *Seed Ecology* (Ed. Heydecker, W.). Butter worths, London, pp. 251-263.

Heppery, R.R. and Sinclair, J.B. (1982). Quality losses in Phomopsis infected soyabean seeds. *Phytopath.*, 68: 1684.

Mamatha, T., Lokesh, S. and Rai, V.R. (2000). Impact of seed mycoflora of forest tree seeds on seed quality and their management. *Seed Research*, 28(1): 59-67.

Mohanan, C. and Sharma, J.K. (1988). Diseases of exotic acacias in India. *Journal of Tropical Forestry*, 4: 357-361.

Rathna Kumar, A.L. and Balasubramanian, P. (2001). Induction of phenols as a phytoalexin response in groundnut rust resistance. In: *Stress and Environmental Plant Physiology* (Ed. Bora, K.K., Singh, K. and Kumar, A.). Pointer Publishers, Jaipur, India, pp. 322-328.

Sharma, R.C. and Bhardwaj, L.N. (1988). Forestry nursery diseases and their management. In: *Advances in Forestry in India* (Ed. Ram Prakash). Vol. II. Dehra Dun, India, International Book Distributors, pp. 91-118.

Singh, D., Maheshwari, V.K. and Gupta, A. (2001). Fungicidal control of Cercospora leaf spot in seed crop of Okra [*Abelmoschus esculentus* (L.) Moench.]. *Seed Research*, 29(2): 254-256.

Singh, P. and Khan, S.N. (1999). Assessment of seed-borne fungi of some forest trees and their management. *Indian J. Forestry*, 22(3): 281-284.

Singh, P. and Mehrotra, M.D. (1999). Seed-borne fungi of some forest trees and their control. *Indian J. Forestry*, 22(4): 320-324.

Taiz, L. and Zeiger, E. (2002). Stress physiology. In: *Plant Physiology*. Third Edition. Sinauer Associates Inc. Publishers, Sunderland, Massachusetts, pp. 591-632.

Terkony, D.M., Egli, D.B., Stuckey, R.E. and Alles, J.B. (1983). Relationship between weather and soyabean seed infected by Phomopsis. *Phytopath.*, 73: 914-918.

Urbanisation and Environment

10

Urban Expansion and Change of Landuse of Baidyabati Municipality: 1977-2015

Partha Nandi and *Nabendu Sekhar Kar*

Introduction

Expansion of urban area is mainly caused by increase in population in *situ* and migration from rural areas. Such population increase affects urban areas in terms of infrastructure, environment, water supply and other vital resources. Landuse and Land cover (LULC) are two separate terminologies which are often used interchangeably (Bhatta, 2014). Land cover refers to the physical characteristics of earth surface, i.e. distribution of vegetation, water, soil and other physical features of the land. While land-use refers to the way in which land is used by humans at their habitat, usually related with the functional role of land for economic activities (Rawat & Kumar, 2015). Land use—Land cover changes are directly or indirectly depended on population growth. As the population of an area increases, the demand for land increases. As a result built-up area expands, while other land covers, such as a bare land, vegetation and landuse like agricultural land shrinks. At present remote sensing has become an important and powerful tool for LULC study. With the help of remote sensing it is possible to identify urban expansion trends as well as overall land-use and land cover change. Remote Sensing has the capacity of capturing such changes at various scales with useful results. Present work seeks to study urban expansion trends with census data and to utilize remotely sensed data and images to analyse the land-use and land cover change to find out trends of urban expansion of Baidyabati Municipal area during 1977 to 2015. The problems faced by the residents of newly formed built-up areas and future demographic and urban growth trends are also investigated.

Study Area

Baidyabati is one of the oldest municipality of Hooghly district established in the year 1869 comprising 22 wards (http://www.hooghlydistrict.info/baidyabati-municipality-details-hooghly-district.html). It extends between 22°47′N to 22°79′N latitudes and 88°19′E 88°32′E longitudes, situated at the right bank of the River Hugly 30 km N of Kolkata. The Baidyabati Municipal area is surrounded by Champdani municipal area on the North-East, Serampore Municipal area on the South-East, Bighati Gram Panchayat area on the North-West and Pearapore Gram Panchayat area on the South-West (*see* Fig. 10.1).

Objectives

The objectives of the study are:

- To analyse the trend of urban expansion of Baidyabati Municipal area during 1977-2015.
- To monitor urban landuse and land cover (LULC) change by producing a series of landuse maps of Baidyabati Municipal area at different imaging year in order to detect changes between 1977-2015.
- To point out the problems faced by the residents of recent expanded areas.
- To predict future population and urban area growth trend of Baidyabati.

Data Source

Primary data and information were gathered from ground truth verification (GTV) by Global Positioning System (GPS), oral interviews and household questionnaire survey. Freely available satellite images are downloaded from archives of USGS and Bhuvan platform to analyse the changes of landuse. Secondary data was obtained by reviewing past

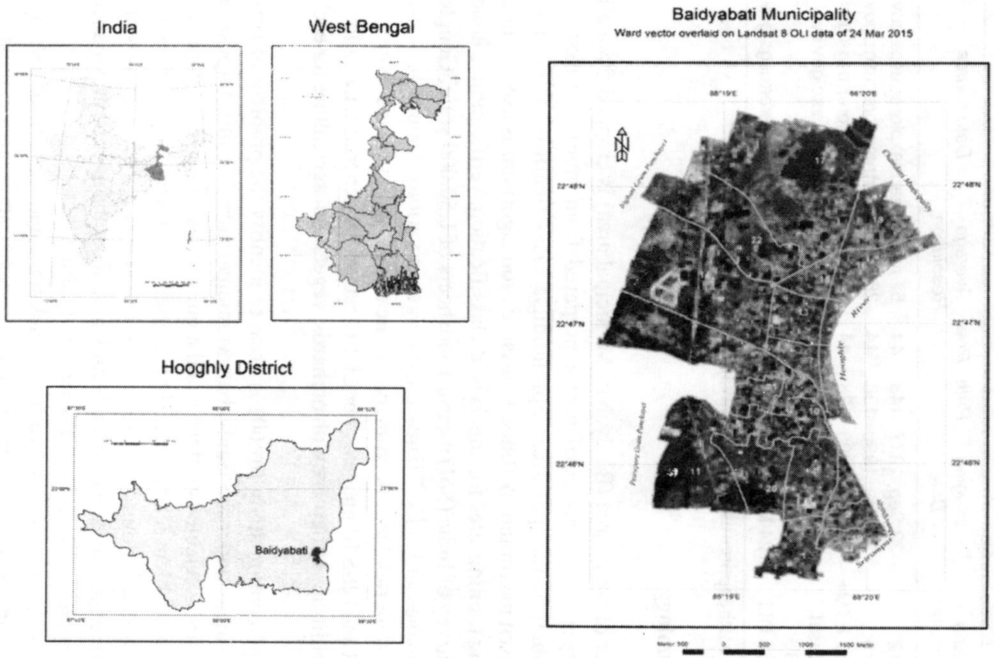

Fig. 10.1: Location of Baidyabati Municipality in Hooghiy District of West Bengal, India. Baidyabati Municipality is located 30 km N of Kolkata and comprises 22 wards

literatures, various reports published by Government and Non-government sectors, Census of India etc. (Table 10.1).

Table 10.1: Details of the images used for LULC classification of Baidyabati Municipalty during 1977-2015

Data Particulars	Imaging Date	Path	Row	Average Resolution	Data source
Landsat 2	22 Sep, 1977	148	44	57 m	earthexplorer.usgs.gov
Landsat 5	14 Nov, 1990	138	44	28.5 m	earthexplorer.usgs.gov
Landsat 7 ETM+	17 Nov, 2000	138	44	14.25 m	earthexplorer.usgs.gov
Resourcesat 1 LISS 3	25 Nov, 2011	108	05	24 m	bhuvan3.nrsc.gov.in
Landsat 8 OLI	24 Mar, 2015	138	44	30 m	earthexplorer.usgs.gov

Source: earthexporer.usgs.gov&bhuvan3.nrsc.gov.in

Methodology

A subset of study area (Baidyabati Municipal area) is cropped from all the imageries by municipal vector prepared from municipal map of Baidyabati Municipal area. For landuse classification of the data supervised maximum likelihood classification algorithm is used. While selecting training sites for supervised classification, verification is done from Survey of India (SoI) metric Toposheets of 1:50,000 scale, Google Earth images and GTV. Thereafter, changes in various landuse and land cover categories have been mapped, measured and analysed from the Landsat and LISS III images. Four LULC classes are generated, i.e. fallow/ water, built-up, settlement with orchards, vegetation/ agriculture for each images.

A perception study (n=60) is done to identify the problem of new built-up areas under the Baidyabati Municipal area. For this purpose, a sample site is selected randomly and a questionnaire survey is done. To detect the problem related to civic facilities and amenities responses are ranked with a 7-Point Scale following Likert Scale. The responses are given weightage of their respective rank to find out the relative importance of the problem affecting the responders (Table 10.2).

All major operations like layer stacking, import-export of satellite data, subset creation, supervised image classification, area calculation and accuracy assessment are done with PCI Geomatica 9.1 software. Microsoft Excel 2007 is used for statistical analysis.

Table 10.2: An example is given for the methodology applied to rank the perception of respondents in the new-built-up area of Baidyabati Municipality. (a) Rank given by the respondents to most severe to least severe problems in a 7 point scale. (b) Weightage given for the ranks and (c) final table (a x b) showing relative importance of the problems affecting the responders (n=60).

a	*Rank*	*Drinking Water*	*Road*	*Street light*	*Waste Disposal*	*Cleanness*	*Sewage*	*Drainage*
	1	9	0	0	0	5	0	1
	2	0	2	0	3	2	0	8
	3	2	1	0	2	2	4	4
	4	1	8	1	4	0	0	1
	5	2	3	1	2	5	2	0
	6	1	1	7	2	0	4	0
	7	0	0	6	2	1	5	1

b	*Rank*	*Drinking Water*	*Road*	*Street light*	*Waste Disposal*	*Clean-ness*	*Sewage*	*Drainage*
	1	7	7	7	7	7	7	7
	2	6	6	6	6	6	6	6
	3	5	5	5	5	5	5	5
	4	4	4	4	4	4	4	4
	5	3	3	3	3	3	3	3
	6	2	2	2	2	2	2	2
	7	1	1	1	1	1	1	1

c	*Rank*	*Drinking Water*	*Road*	*Street light*	*Waste Disposal*	*Cleanness*	*Sewage*	*Drainage*
	1	**63**	0	0	0	**35**	0	7
	2	0	12	0	**18**	12	0	**48**
	3	10	5	0	10	10	**20**	20
	4	4	**32**	4	16	0	0	4
	5	6	9	3	6	15	6	0
	6	2	2	**14**	4	0	8	0
	7	0	0	6	2	1	5	1
	Total	**85**	**60**	**27**	**56**	**73**	**39**	**80**

Source: Primary Survey by the Authors.

Limitations

The spatial resolutions of downloaded freely available satellite data is considered poor in case of urban land-use study. For this reason in some cases two classes of LULC are clubbed in a single class. The images are pertaining to different seasons which introduce some errors in LULC identification.

Results and Discussion

Demography

The places along the western bank of River Hugli are the oldest agglomeration of urban settlements of Bengal, was populated by European settlements way back in the 15th century (Toynbee, 2006). Major colonial and post-colonial industrialization took place in this region, which have made this area economically viable and attracted migrants from rural areas. As a result of industrial development along river Hugli, with recent development of tertiary activities, huge increase in urban population is observed here. The places situated on the western bank of river Hugli such as Rishra, Sreerampore, Baidyabati, Bhadreswar, Chandannagar, Chinsura, Bandel, Bansberia, Tribeni etc. are among the oldest municipalities of West Bengal (Sarkar, 1998) (*see* Table 10.3).

Trend of population increase is a good indicator to analyzing the urban growth pattern of an area. Census figures between 1901 and 2011 show that there is steady increase of population in the Baidyabti Municipal area except in between 1911 to 1921 and 1941-1951 following general population growth trend of Bengal (Sarkar, 1998). A massive increase of 78.08 per cent was observed in the decade just after independence (1951-1961) primarily related with the prosperity of the Hugly Industrial Region.

In the last four decades average decadal growth is found to be high due to good facilities offered by the region or various favourable urban amenities as well as the industrialization. The trend of urbanization here is basically attributed to rural urban migration with natural increase. In the Baidyabti Municipal area migration of huge amount of neighbouring people is noted. The post-independence rapid growth of population leads to unplanned urbanization in this area. At present the population numbers

Table 10.3: Trend of Population growth during 1901-2011 in Baidyabati

Year	*Total Population*	*Population Density Persons / km-²)*	*Decadal Growth Rate (%)*
1901	17174	1254	—
1911	20516	1498	19.46
1921	16471	1202	–19.72
1931	18486	1349	12.23
1941	25825	1885	39.70
1951	24883	1816	–3.65
1961	44312	3234	78.08
1971	54130	3951	22.16
1981	70573	5151	30.38
1991	90081	6575	27.64
2001	108229	7900	20.15
2011	121110	8840	11.90

Source: Census of India, 2011.

are increasing at a decreasing rate, but the rate is still very high (11.90% in 2011).

Landcover/Landuse

Geomorphologically, the area under Baidyabati Municipality can be divided into two sections: (i) elevated river bank of Hugly on the eastern portion; and (ii) low back swamps of the western portion.

Major urban concentration is seen on the eastern portion along the River Hugly whereas on the western section urban built-up is sporadic and most of urban settlement is concentrated with agricultural fields in pockets.

The LULC derived from the MXL classification during 1977-2015 shows that during 1977 to 2011, the urban built-up area coverage was quite unchanging (around 500 ha) mainly concentrating on the eastern part of the municipal area. But a massive growth of 26.56 per cent of built-up area is recorded between 2011 (537.4975 ha) and 2015 (901.3325 ha) in the wards 4, 8, 11, 14, 17, 20 and 22. Ground truth verification also discloses the same. The lands converted to built-up areas are mostly fallow/water bodies (back swamp of River Hugly) and vegetation/agricultural fields. A net decline of 14.52 per cent, 13.87 per cent of vegetation/agriculture and fallow/water is recorded during 2011 to 2015 respectively. From ground truth verification it is also found that ~80 per cent of the families surveyed arrived here during this period and the new built-up have created massive change of the area. It is also noted that the area is occupied mainly by the Bihari-Muslim migrants and most of the cases the occupancy is found illegal.

Table 10.4: LULC areas (ha) pertaining to different image year used in the study to detect changes in urban built-up during 1977-2015

	Year-wise area in ha	*1977*	*1990*	*2000*	*2011*	*2015*
Landuse Classes	Fallow/Water	399.275	423.6025	341.5375	368.1875	178.2725
	Built-up	504.545	505.9525	517.9875	537.4975	901.3325
	Settlement with Orchards	231.625	207.6325	221.1675	194.0675	219.0425
	Vegetation/Agriculture	234.555	232.8125	289.3075	270.2475	71.3525
	Total	**1370**	**1370**	**1370**	**1370**	**1370**

Source: Prepared by the Authors.

Problem Faced by the Residents of New Built-up Areas

The process of urbanization or expansion at a rapid rate has created many problems in this region. The major expansion is seen towards West and North-West of Baidyabati Municipal area by conversion and filling of wetlands and agricultural fields into built-up.

A questionnaire survey is done here to find out/enlist major problems faced by the residents, ranked based on the perceptions of the residents. Here two main challenges are prominent; these are non-availability of drinking water and problems related to drainage. In this area residents depend on only one municipal tap serving nearly a large area. The drainage system in this area is unplanned due to illegal occupations and constructions. So, the lack of adequate drinking water and sanitation facilities leads to health issues such as diarrhea due to drinking of unsafe water. Wetlands are naturally lowlands, so waterlogging is common even in driest seasons, which often leads to diseases like malaria and dengue. The most of these water related challenges are suffered by the poor of this region (Fig. 10.2).

Cleanliness is also another major challenge which is faced by the local people of this area. The area is used as waste dumping and sewage outlet of Baidyabati Township. This affects the health of the residents and environ of the area. This area is heavily polluted and the surface water of the DVC canal flowing through the area is unfit for household use. The situation turns worse in rainy season (Fig. 10.3).

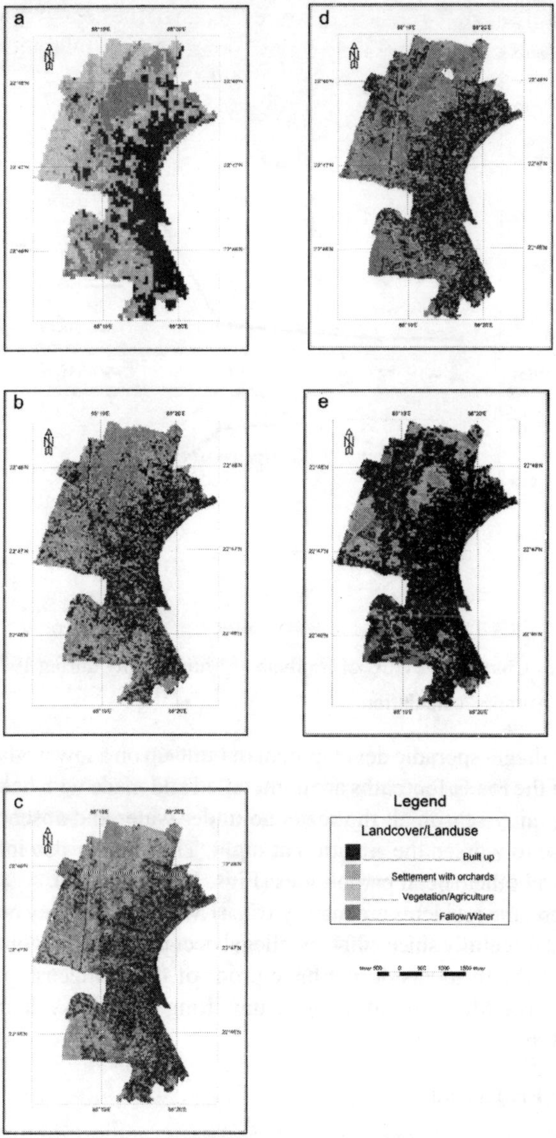

Fig. 10.2: LULC maps of Baidyabati Municipality generated by supervised MXL classification showing growth of urban built-up during 1977-2015. (a) Landsat 2 MSS of 22 Sep., 1977, (b) Landsat 5 TM of 14 Nov., 1990, (c) Landsat 7 ETM+ of 17 Nov., 2000, (d) LISS III of 25 Nov., 2011, (e) Landsat 8 OLI of 24 Mar, 2015

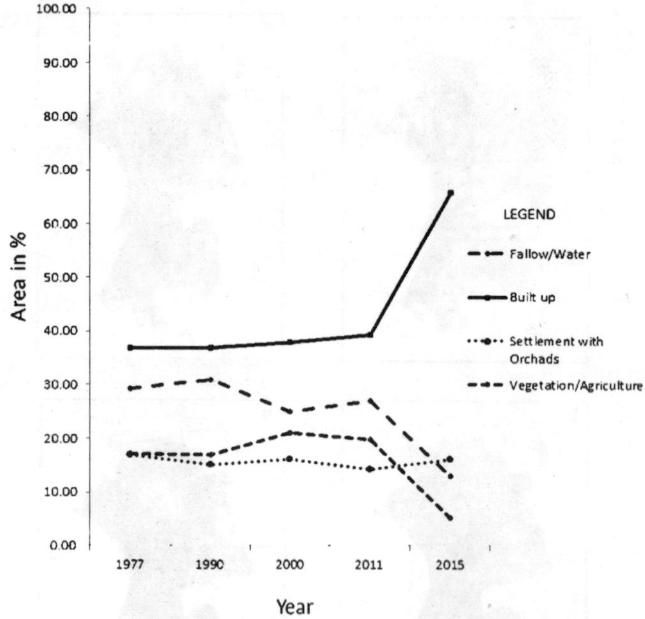

Total area: 1370 ha

Fig. 10.3: Change of LULC of Baidyabati Municipality during 1977-2015
Source: Authors' calculation.

As illegal sporadic development of built-up on a low wetland is seen, most of the roads/footpaths are unmetalled and made with heaps of mud. During rainy season all the roads go under water and absence of street light use to worsen the situation at night. This area is also infamous for crime and other social pathologies (Figs. 10.4 and 10.5).

Here, the residents are mainly Bihari Muslims and they occupied the wetland forcefully since 2004 and illegal occupancy is still going on. Even many of the residents do not have proof of their citizenship. For these reasons, the Municipality is quite unwilling to address their problems (Fig. 10.6).

Future Projection

From the population figure from Census of India and built-up area figure derived from the study future projection of population as well as the increase of built-up area is measured for 2021. It is found that if the present rate of growth continues population projection of Baidyabati will

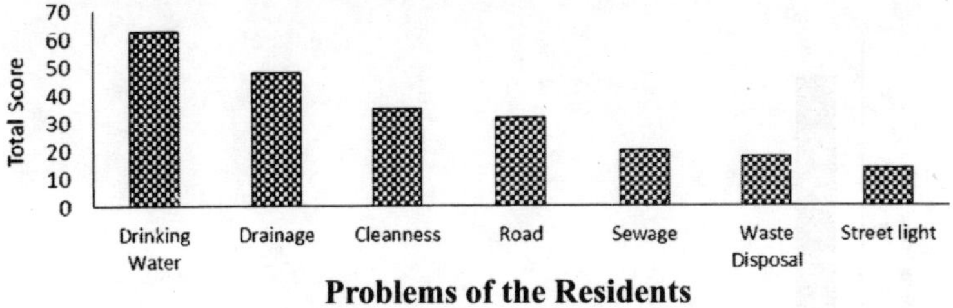

Fig. 10.4: Problem faced by the residents of new built-up areas of Baidyabati Municipality ranked on the basis of their perception (n = 60)

Source: Primary Survey.

Fig. 10.5: Major problems faced by the residents of new built-up areas of Baidyabati Municipality. (a) Unsafe drinking water, (b) waterlogging, (c) absence of waste disposal and proper sanitation facilities, and (d) dreadful condition of roads.

be 1,35,513 with 71.432 per cent of built-up. So, a net 5.63 per cent increase of built-up is projected.

Following the present trend it can be assumed that in future agricultural land and open space will decrease by the rapid growth of urban built-up. So, in future a crunch of open space is likely to be happen which will severely affect the urban environment. To control this unplanned urbanization, the government authorities specially the

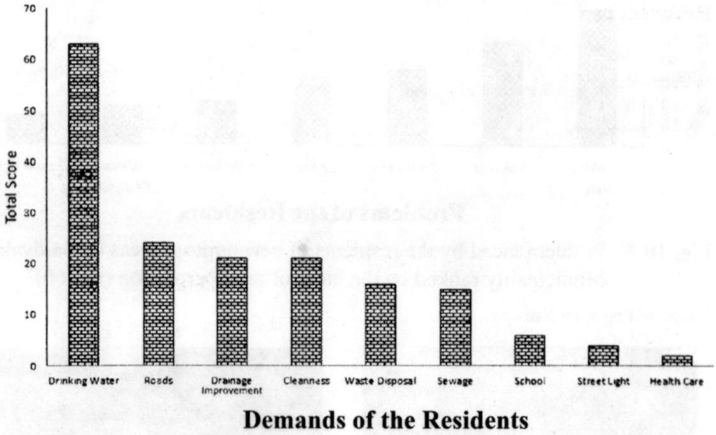

Fig. 10.6: Demands of the residents of new built-up areas of Baidyabati Municipality ranked on the basis of their perception (n = 60)

Source: Primary Survey.

Municipality should take initiative to formulate proper urban planning to manage this kind of probable situation.

Conclusion

Baidyabati Municipal area is one of the main commercial and administrative area of Hooghly district. This study demonstrates the utilization of remote sensing and geographic information system in analyzing the urban expansion includes the mapping and to identify the urban LULC change. The extent of urbanization is seen in the study area as one of the important potential threat to environment in terms of sustainable development.

It is very essential to identify the possibilities for most advantageous use of different landuse and landcover for the selected area, formulation and implementation of landuse planning scheme to meet the rising demands for urban habitants and their welfare. The information about LULC also helps to monitor the demands of growing population associated with the dynamics of landuse change. This is very important for the urban planning authorities to implement a proper plan for Baidyabati and for doing this, information generated from remote sensing sources only are not sufficient. This study may provide reliable inputs for urban planners who are planning for future development and obviously to provide basic amenities such as drinking water, sanitation, cleanness, sewage, roads electricity etc. in this municipality of Hooghly district.

References

Bhatta, B., 2014, *Remote Sensing and GIS* (Second Edition), Oxford University Press, ISBN 10: 0-19-807239-2.

CoI: Census of India (2013): West Bengal 2011 Primary Census Abstract, Census of India, Hooghly District, West Bengal Circle [CD-ROM]. Kolkata.

Rawat, J.S. and Kumar, M., 2015, Monitoring landuse/cover change using remote sensing and GIS techniques: A case study of Hawalbagh Block, District Almora, Uttarakhand, India, *The Egyptian Journal of Remote Sensing and Space Sciences*, 2-7.

Sarkar, A., 1998. *Urban System Urban Growth and Urbanization in the 20th Century West Bengal*, New Academic Publishers, Delhi, ISBN:81-86772-03-0.

Toynbee, G, 2006. *Administration of Hooghly District with Some Account of the Early English, Portuguese, Dutch and Danish Settlements from* 1795 to 1845 (2nd Edition), Bengal Secretariat Press, Kolkata.

11

Does Urban Slums of Selected States in India differ in Housing Conditions, Basic Amenities with Context to Ownership, Physical Location and Notification Status?

Donald R. Mawkhlieng and *Jill A. Marbaningi*

The pattern of human settlement is dynamic over time and taking new shape where urban areas are becoming not just dominant human's choice for settlement, but in fact the power house for development throughout the World. The towns and cities round the world are becoming the centres of wealth and prosperity for the nations. People from different corners within or outside a country migrate to the towns and cities where they perceive as ideal platform to fulfill aspirations realizing dreams and having a promising career. In the race for having better life with a decent standard of living, urban centres around the globe attracted people with golden opportunity for generating wealth and this led to progress and advancement of the urban centres throughout the World. The increasing inflow and growth of population in urban centres which has resulted from growing Industrialization and other forms of development has created an ever increasing level of urbanization. The unprecedented pace of urbanization has brought a historic change in the history of human civilization where for the first time the urban population has outnumbered the rural population. This has developed an overcrowding settlement and pressure for space in urban centres. According to the States of the World's cities 2012/2013, Prosperity of cities, UN Habitat Report, more than half of world is now urban and it is expected by the middle of this century, out of ten people living in the planet, seven will be living in the urban areas. Interestingly around 82 per cent of the world's population is concentrated in the developing countries and out of every 10 urban residents in the world, around seven people are living in developing countries. India is one of the six major developing nations which have a high contribution to the world's population and India's urban centres like Mumbai, Delhi etc. added a significant population to the World's urban population. Urban population in India therefore plays a major role in determining the global figure of population scenario as India being one of the leading giant of population statistics is accounted for the reason that half of the world's urban population now lives in Asia. India's urban population being one of the fastest growing population on the other hand is hugely comprising of the urban cities population, in the recent decades migration from small villages across the country into the cities driven by the search for better way of life have led to lack of space, overcrowding, excess requirement of facilities, degradation of environment among others. The urban pull have resulted in negative consequences such as shortage and compact housing space, critical inadequacies in hygienic conditions and public utilities which are the characteristics of urban slums. Slum areas are those areas which have the highest concentration of people under the worst shelter, physical and environmental conditions. As per UN Habitat Report, a slum is characterized by lack of durable housing, insufficient living area, and lack of access to clean water, inadequate sanitation and insecure tenure. Under Indian Central Government Act, Section-3 of the Slum Area Improvement and Clearance Act, 1956, slums have been defined as mainly those residential areas where dwellings are in any respect unfit for human habitation by reasons of dilapidation, overcrowding, faulty arrangements and designs of such buildings, narrowness or faulty arrangement of streets, lack of ventilation, light, sanitation facilities or any combination of these factors which are detrimental to safety, health and morals. Census of India have specifically categorised slums into three types: All notified areas in a town or city notified as "Slum" by State, Union territories Administration or Local Government under any Act including a "Slums Act" may be considered as Notified Slums. All areas recognized as "Slum" by State, Union territories Administration or Local Government, Housing and Slum Boards, which may have not been formally notified as slum under an Act may be considered as Recognized Slums. A compact area of at least 300 population or about 60-70 households or poorly built congested tenements, in unhygienic environment usually with inadequate infrastructure and lacking in proper sanitary and drinking water facilities. Such areas should be identified personally by the Charge Officer and also inspected by an officer nominated by Directorate of Census Operations. This fact must be duly recorded in the charge register. Such areas may be considered as Identified Slums. The NSSO, for the purpose of survey in 1976-77 defined slum as declared and undeclared slums. The declared slums were areas which have been formally declared as slum by the respective municipalities, corporations, local bodies or the development authorities. The undeclared slums were defined as "an aereal unit having twenty five or more *katcha* structures mostly of temporary nature, or inhabited by persons with practically no private latrine and inadequate public latrine and water. For the purpose of the survey in 1993 and 2002, NSSO adopted the definition of slums as "A slum is a compact settlement with a collection of poorly built tenements, mostly of temporary nature, crowded together usually with inadequate sanitary and drinking water facilities in unhygienic conditions. Such an area, for the purpose of this survey, was considered as if at least 20 households lived in that area. Slums are the picture of the living conditions of urban poor, where majority of the people are engaged in low economic activities under informal sector. According to the Global Report on Human Settlements 2003, slums have the most intolerable of urban housing conditions, which frequently include: insecurity of tenure; lack of basic services, especially water and sanitation; inadequate and sometimes unsafe building structures; overcrowding; and location on hazardous land. In addition, slum areas have high concentration of poverty and of social and economic deprivation, which may include broken families, unemployment and economic, physical and social exclusion. Slum dwellers have limited access to credit and formal job markets due to stigmatization, discrimination and geographic isolation. Slums are often recipients of the city's nuisances, including industrial effluent and noxious waste, and the only land accessible to slum dwellers is often fragile, dangerous or polluted-land that no one else wants. People in slum areas suffer inordinately from water-borne diseases such as typhoid and cholera, as well as more opportunistic ones that accompany HIV/AIDS. Slum women—and the children they support—are the greatest victims of all. Census India have identified 1743 slums reported towns in 2001 with 4,35,56,155 households and population of 22,31,11,858 and 2613 slums reported towns in 2011 with 6,27,92,741 households and 29,18,38,124 population. There were 1,01,50,719 households and 5,23,71,589 slum population in 2001 and 1,39,20,191 households with 6,54,94,604 slum population in 2011. The context of selecting Urban slums of India has several reasons and one of the many reasons is that though slums are known to be of backward and poor strata of the society, however, they are the active agents of development of the country (Bandyopadhyaya, Abir; Agrawal, Vandana). Study also suggest that slums are the first stopping point for immigrants—they provide the low cost and only affordable housing that will enable the immigrants to save for their eventual absorption into urban society. As the place of residence for low-income employees, slums keep the wheels of the city turning in many different ways. The majority of slum dwellers in developing country cities earn their living from informal sector activities located either within or outside slum areas, and many informal entrepreneurs operating from slums have clienteles extending to the rest of the city. Most slum dwellers are people struggling to make an honest living, within the context of extensive urban poverty and formal unemployment. Slums are also places in which the vibrant mixing of different cultures frequently results in new forms of artistic expression. Out of unhealthy, crowded and often dangerous environments can emerge cultural movements and levels of solidarity unknown in the suburbs of the rich. Against all odds, slum dwellers have developed economically rational and innovative shelter solutions for themselves. However, these few positive attributes do not in any way justify the continued existence of slums and should not be an excuse for the slow progress towards the goal of adequate shelter for all (*Global Study on Human Settlements,* 2003).

Research on Housing basic amenities has gained recognition in many fields of research. The reason may be credited to be due the linkages it has with other dimensions of research be it social research, environmental research, health research etc. Many studies have used housing conditions and household amenities to examine the aspects of health status, quality of life, poverty and social development, however few existing literatures were found in India which have linkage between housing conditions and basic amenities with poverty, social development and quality of life. In this review, we try to understand the need of household basic amenities related to health, poverty, and the pattern and variation of availability of basic amenities in India.

They believed that health promoting factors such as housing conditions, household amenities etc. could contribute to health improvement among the population and sometimes even more significantly than health services began in the 19th century when the European experience mortality decline. Deploring living and working conditions which is congested, unsanitary and unliveable resulted in sickness and higher death rates; this is evident from the cholera epidemic in 1831 in England. It was later realized that such sickness and high death rates can be prevented (Dubos, 1968). Slowly, the mortality reduction surfaces after prevention of Tuberculosis, typhoid, fever, dysentery, diarrhea etc. through rising standard of living conditions, hygienic and safe water, waste disposal, personal hygiene etc. (Mckeown and Lowe). WHO document on 'Housing and Health' suggested 11 principles relating to housing needs and health action (WHO, 1987). These principles highlight the role of adequate housing in control of communicable diseases and health promotion. In many studies, housing condition emerged as a significant predictor of general and mental health status (Navaro *et al.*, 2010, Adarkwa & Oppong, 2007). Some studies have well related the housing condition to poverty which broadens the concept of housing condition as an indicator for social development (Townsend, 1979). Individuals, families and groups in the population can be said to be in poverty when they lack the resources to obtain the types of diet, participate in the activities, and have the living conditions and amenities which are customary, or at least widely encouraged or approved, in the societies to which they belong Zainal, N.R., Kaur, G., Ahmad, N.A., and Khalili, J.M., (2012) have enlightened the issue of considering housing condition as a social economic indicator of urban poverty from the empirical evidence of the relationship between housing conditions and quality of life. Basic Amenities were taken as one of the six important indicators for many points of time in constructing the Social development index of the country (Kaustav Banerjee, *Social Development Index*, 2010). Household amenities is an indicator of socio-economic position in industrialised and non-industrialised countries (Galobardes, B., Shaw, M., Lawlor, D.A., Lynch, J.W., and Smith, G.D., 2006).

The Government of India has been developing facilitatory approach towards providing adequate housing right from the beginning of the five year plans. Though, there has been a development in this regard, but statistics shows that it is still far from achieving greater heights. The growth rate of population for India in the last decade which was 17.64 per cent wherein rural and urban areas which was 12.18 per cent and 31.80 per cent respectively, the growth rate for the number of households for the country was 28.5 per cent where for rural areas 21.7 per cent and urban areas 41.07 per cent, but there are many which are houseless or does not have access to proper living conditions. The growth rate of houseless Louseholds especially in Urban is remarkably higher which is around 36.7 per cent and this is a strong indication that the country's National Housing and Habitat Policy 2007 which stress on providing affordable houses for all with special emphasis on economically weaker section of the society is far from achieving the desired target. Most of India's slum-dwellers do not have access to basic amenities such as clean drinking water, electricity, housing, and sanitation (NUHM, 2008). A resurgence of malaria, dengue and tuberculosis indicates that much of the poor health emanates from a lack of basic amenities such as sanitation, clean water and housing, coupled with a lack of awareness about the need to take precautionary measures against preventable and infectious diseases. There is a need for policy to identify the vulnerable urban poor population and provide awareness and more research should be done on the factors that prevent them from availing the services provided to them (Gupta, Mitra A., 2002).

Basic Amenities Scenario in India based on 2001-2011 Censuses

***Drinking water*:** As regards amenities available with the households, 87 per cent of households are using Tap, Tube well, Hand pump and Covered well as the main source of drinking water while 43.5 per cent use tap water. Only 47 per cent of households have source of water within the premises while 36 per cent of households have to fetch water from a source located within 500 m in rural areas/100 m in urban areas and 17 per cent still fetch drinking water from a source located more than 500 m away in rural areas or 100 m in urban area. When more than 50 per cent of the households does not have water source within the premises is matter of concern and more than one-third of the household does not have any availability of water in the vicinity is also a major concern.

***Lighting*:** As far as main source of lighting is concerned, 67 per cent households use electricity which shows an increase of 11 point over 2001. The rural-urban gap has reduced by 7 percentage points from 44 per cent in 2001 to 37 per cent. Around 31 per cent households use kerosene as lighting which cause local and indoor air pollution—a nasty mix of particulates, carbon mono-oxide and carcinogenic gases (World Health Organisation). Smoke from kerosene lamps is responsible for respiratory infections, lung and throat cancers, serious eye infections, cataracts as well as low birth weights. Acute respiratory infections like influenza and pneumonia kill nearly 2 million children in developing nations each year, more than the annual number of all deaths at all ages from all causes in the European Union.

Bathing facility: 58 per cent of the households have bathing facility within the premises, showing an increase of 22 points over 2001.

Latrine Facility: 47 per cent of the households have latrine facility within premises with 36 per cent households have water closet and 9 per cent households have pit latrine. There is 11 points decline in households having no latrine from 64 per cent to 53 per cent in 2011. A high percentage of household with no toilet facilities encourage open defecation which is a major cause for high morbidity in India. 61 per cent households have Kitchen facility with 55 per cent within premises and 6 per cent outside premises.

More than two-third of the population in India belongs to rural areas and the study shows that basic household amenities in such areas are still way behind the standard. The statistical figure says that around 82 per cent of the rural households do not have access to basic amenities which are surprisingly disappointing. *The National Sample Survey Office (NSSO) Study on Housing Conditions and Amenities in India*, 2008-09, reveals that just 18 per cent households in rural India have access to basic amenities such as drinking water and electricity. Further, the social groups—STs (75%), SCs (76%) and OBCs (69%)—in rural areas don't have sanitation facility in their households. **Bathroom facility was not available to nearly 64 per cent of the rural households**. In urban areas, only 22 per cent of the households were deprived of bathrooms. Further, nearly 65 per cent rural households had no latrine facility as against 11 per cent for their urban counterparts. The Government Survey highlights that only 30 per cent of rural population had access to safe drinking water and 55 per cent depend on tube well or hand pumps to meet their drinking water requirements. In fact, 15 per cent of rural people were still looking for dependable source of water. According to *World Bank Report* released on the eve of *first ever UN World Toilet day which was on 19th November, 2013* stated that more than 2.5 billion people worldwide lack access to toilets, one billion people practice open defecation and 600 million in India openly defecate. Further, the report says that 53 per cent of the household in India use open defecation, diseases like diarrhoea, which *UNICEF* says kills 1,000 Indian children aged under five every day. Poor sanitation and the illnesses it causes cost the Indian economy 12 billion rupees (255 million dollars) a year, according to the health ministry. Furthermore, the study of Economic impacts of inadequate sanitation in India found that estimates of the economic impacts of inadequate sanitation in India amounts to Rs. 244 trillion (US$53.8 billion) a year which is equivalent of 6.4 per cent of India's GDP in 2006. Although, there is no proper clear cut definition given for classification of households into 'good', 'livable' and 'dilapidated' from the census report "Tables on Census Houses, Household Amenities and Assets 2001" majority of the census houses are good and livable condition that is 97 per cent of the census houses in India whereas only 3 per cent are in dilapidated condition.

Many studies have linked the living conditions with health status with context to India and were successful in showing that there is a definite contribution of housing conditions and sanitary facilities in health improvement (Nayar, K.K., 1997). Srinivasan and Mohanty, 2008 reveals that there is a strong relationship between basic amenities and housing conditions on Children's growth and malnutrition. Some studies have been able to bring out the existence of inequity across states and among different size and class of urban settlements in India (Kundu, Amitabh; Bagchi, Soumen and Kundu, Debolina, 1999). The deprivation of some sections of the society in attaining proper basic amenities in India is a clear indication that more needs to be done to lift up the standard of living of certain backward Caste and Religions. Interestingly, study also shows that deprivation of basic amenities is higher in urban areas than rural areas which suggest that more in-depth studies on urban settlements may bring a positive impact in the growth and development of the country. The importance of basic amenities and housing conditions is not limited to health, but extends to other dimensions such as policy-making and as an indicator for understanding the developmental status of the Country. For example Guruswamy and Abraham in 2006 suggested that there is a need to include basic amenities and housing conditions in redefining the poverty line of the country. Social conditions, health (Srinivasan, K. and Mohanty, S.K., 2004) conditions and Household environmental conditions are the outcome factors of the poor economic conditions in the slums and due to unhygienic environmental conditions, the slum dwellers are at constant risk of adverse health hazards (Sajjad, 2014). However, very few or no study have probed the variation in slums across India taking the background characteristics of the physical location and ownership status of the slums, therefore, study on urban slum conditions gain more importance in understanding the insights of deprived urban slums on basic amenities in this respect.

Objectives

1. To study the Housing Conditions pertaining to the physical location, ownership status and notification status of urban slums in selected states of India.
2. To examine the basic amenities with respect to ownership, physical location status and notification status of the urban slums in selected states of India.
3. To examine the effects of ownership status, physical location and notification status of urban slums on availability of latrine facility, drainage, drinking water, electricity and household structure.

Data Source and Methodology

The National Sample Survey Organisation (NSSO) conducted all India Survey on urban slums in the 69th round from July to December 2012. The slums sample were taken using the random sampling technique from the urban blocks of the whole country. It is the fifth survey done for collecting information from slums in India. The survey captured many slums characteristics such as proportions of slums without electricity, drainage facility available, major source of drinking water, latrine facility, household structure etc. and information were taken relating to slums which are notified and not notified. Total sample surveyed is 881 throughout the country. In this paper, an attempt was made to merge those states with few samples so as to avoid misleading results and these states were clubbed into "others". The independent variables considered in this study were merged together so as to avoid small sample size complication and to bring out conclusive outcomes. For examples ownership of the slum land were merged into three categories out of the five categories in the questionnaire, where 'private' ownership is one of the three category and "railway and local bodies" are group together as the second category, while 'others' and 'not known' as the third category. Similarly, the six categories of "Physical location of the slum" was represented into three categories where slums located in health risk areas such as *nullah*/drain, railway lines, river bed and hilly terrain are clubbed as one category, park and open space as the second category and others as the third category. Descriptive statistical analysis such as cross tabulations were used to obtain the percentage distributions of different indicators for basic amenities and household conditions with respect to the ownership status, physical location and notification status of urban slums in India and multivariate analysis was used to obtain the effects of physical location and ownership status of urban slums on availability of latrine facility, drainage, drinking water, electricity and household structure. Cross tabulations and multinomial logistic and binary logistic regression analysis have been carried out to measure the association between the dependent variables such as latrine facility, available of drainage facility, drinking water, electricity and household structure of urban slums against the independent variables such as ownership status, physical location and notification status of the urban slums.

The multinomial logistic regression model has been used to analyse and identify the effects of ownership status, physical location and notification status on the availability of drainage facility, drinking water and household structure. The response variables such as latrine facility, availability of drainage facility, drinking water for the analysis has been categorised into three mutually exclusive exhaustive categories, however binary logistic regression was used for availability of electricity which was categorised into two categories where either HH or SL or none is taken as zero. Also for notification status, not notified is taken as zero.

Results and Findings

In Table 11.1, we notice that most of the households in urban slums have comparatively high percentage of *pucca* households than semi-*pucca* or *katcha* Households. In Andhra Pradesh, *pucca* houses have the highest percentage that is 83 per cent whereas in Bihar and Odisha percentage of *pucca* Households in urban slums is only 14 per cent and 26 per cent respectively. Semi-*pucca* households has the highest percentage in Odisha with 52 per cent followed by semi-*pucca* with 26 per cent and *katcha* 22 per cent. The percentage distribution of semi-*pucca* houses in Rajasthan is very low that is only 2 per cent. The percentage of *katcha* households in Bihar has the highest percentage with 57 per cent followed by semi *pucca* which is 29 per cent and *katcha* 14 per cent. In all, around 62 per cent of the total slums households are *pucca* houses, 26 per cent are semi-*pucca* and only 12 per cent are *katcha* houses. The above figures may suggest that the urban slums household conditions relating to household structure did have an improvement over time in some states, but others are not so fortunate as they are still being deprived of proper housing structure. This also indicates the variation among the selected states of India with respect to household structure.

Table 11.1: Percentage Distribution of Type of Household Structure in Urban Slums by State

States	*Pucca HH*	*Semi-Pucca HH*	*Katcha HH*
Punjab	65	18	18
Rajasthan	73	2	24
Uttar Pradesh	70	14	16
Bihar	14	29	57
West Bengal	67	27	6
Jharkhand	32	47	21
Odisha	26	52	22
Chhattisgarh	44	40	16
Madhya Pradesh	57	41	3
Gujarat	58	32	11
Maharashtra	69	25	6
Andhra Pradesh	83	11	6
Karnataka	67	28	5
Tamil Nadu	52	29	19
Others	54	30	16
Total	**62**	**26**	**12**

Source: India-Urban Slums Survey, NSS 69th Round.

From Table 11.2, we observed that among the Private Ownership of the urban slums, around 70 per cent are *pucca* houses, 19 per cent are semi-*pucca* houses and 11 per cent are *katcha* ones. Among Railway and local bodies, around 57 per cent are *pucca* households, 31 per cent are semi-*pucca* houses whereas others and not known have around 55 per cent of *pucca* households and 32 per cent of semi-*pucca* houses. Among the Ownership status of the slum land, the percentage distribution of *katcha* houses are relatively the same.

From Table 11.3, we notice that based on the Physical location of the slum, higher percentage of *pucca* houses occur in all the categories. Among the urban slums located along *nullah*/drain/railway line/river bed/hilly terrain, 59 per cent are *pucca* houses, 30 per cent semi-*pucca* houses and 11 per cent *katcha* houses. Among urban slums located in the Park/open space, around 60 per cent are *pucca* houses, 25 per cent are semi-*pucca* houses and 15 per cent are *katcha* ones. Among the urban slums located in the other category around 70 per cent are *pucca* houses, 20 per cent are semi-*pucca* houses and 10 per cent are *katcha* houses.

From Table 11.4, the percentage distribution of *pucca* houses among the not notified slums in urban slums of India is 48 per cent and semi-*pucca* it is 34 per cent whereas *katcha* houses contribute about 19 per cent of the total households. Among the notified urban slums, 76 per cent are *pucca* houses, 19 per cent are semi-*pucca* houses and only 5 per cent

Table 11.2: Percentage Distribution of Type of Household Structure in Urban Slums by Ownership Status of the Slum Land

Ownership Status of the Slums	*Pucca HH*	*Semi-Pucca HH*	*Katcha HH*
Private	70	19	11
Railway and local bodies	57	31	12
Other and not known	55	32	12
Total	**62**	**26**	**12**

Source: India-Urban Slums Survey, NSS 69th Round.

Table 11.3: Percentage Distribution of Type of Household Structure in Urban Slums by Physical Location of the Slum

Physical location of the Slum	*Pucca HH*	*Semi-Pucca HH*	*Katcha HH*
Along nullah/drain/railway line/river bed/hilly terrain	59	30	11
Park/open space	60	25	15
Others	70	20	10
Total	**62**	**26**	**12**

Source: India-Urban Slums Survey, NSS 69th Round.

Table 11.4: Percentage Distribution of Type of Household Structure in Urban Slums by Notification Status of the Slum

Notification status of the Slum	*Pucca HH*	*Semi-Pucca HH*	*Katcha HH*
Not notified	48	34	19
Notified	76	19	5
Total	**62**	**26**	**12**

Source: India-Urban Slums Survey, NSS 69th Round.

are *katcha* houses. The figures from Table 11.4 shows that the notified slums are doing better than the not notified ones with respect to household structure of the surveyed households.

From Table 11.5, we see that the percentage distribution of public/community/shared latrine in Maharashtra is highest with 58 per cent followed by no latrine which is 24 per cent and own latrine which is 17 per cent. Interestingly, Jharkhand has very high percentage of urban slums with no latrine that is 95 per cent, only 5 per cent of the residents in the urban slums have access to own latrine. There is no public/community/shared latrine used by the urban slums residents in Jharkhand. More than half of the urban slums residents in states like Odisha, Chhattisgarh and Gujarat do not have access to any latrine facilities. In Punjab, Karnataka and Andhra Pradesh, more than 50 per cent of the urban slums residents have their own

Table 11.5: Percentage Distribution of availability of Latrine Facility in Urban Slums by State

States	*Public/Community/ Shared Latrine*	*Own Latrine*	*No Latrine*
Punjab	12	53	35
Rajasthan	12	39	49
Uttar Pradesh	32	34	34
Bihar	5	5	90
West Bengal	45	27	27
Jharkhand	0	5	95
Odisha	4	15	81
Chhattisgarh	20	20	60
Madhya Pradesh	9	46	45
Gujarat	18	26	56
Maharashtra	58	17	24
Andhra Pradesh	14	64	22
Karnataka	17	62	22
Tamil Nadu	44	23	34
Others	44	34	22
Total	**30**	**34**	**36**

Source: India-Urban Slums Survey, NSS 69th Round.

household latrine. The figures gives a clear indication that still a high degree of urban slums residents go for open defecation as there are no latrine facilities available to them which may be a serious issue to be concern.

From Table 11.6, out of the total private households in the urban slums, 40 per cent of them have their own latrine facility, whereas 31 per cent have public/community/shared latrine facility and only 29 per cent have no latrine facility available to them. However, in the land where the ownership is categorised as "not known and other", 42 per cent of the residents in the urban slums do not have any latrine facility and 31 per cent have access to public/community/shared latrine facility and only 26 per cent have own latrine. Among the household owned by railway or local bodies, around 41 per cent of the residents does not have latrine facility and only 31 per cent have own latrine and only 28 per cent have public/community/shared latrine.

From Table 11.7, out of the total slums located along *nullah*/drain/ railway line/river bed/hilly terrain, 38 per cent of them have no latrine facility followed by 36 per cent of having own latrine and 27 per cent having public/community/shared latrine facility. Out of all the slums located in the park/open space about 43 per cent have no access to latrine facility whereas 33 per cent of the slums residents have access to public/ community/shared latrine facility and only 24 per cent have own latrine

Table 11.6: Percentage Distribution of Availability of Latrine Facility in Urban Slums by Ownership Status of the Slum Land

Ownership Status of the Slums	*Public/Community /Shared Latrine*	*Own Latrine*	*No Latrine*
Private	31	40	29
Railway & local bodies	28	31	41
Other & not known	32	26	42
Total	**30**	**34**	**36**

Source: India: Urban Slums Survey, NSS 69th Round.

Table 11.7: Percentage Distribution of Availability of Latrine Facility in Urban Slums by Physical Location of the Slum

Physical Location of the Slum	*Public/Community/ Shared Latrine*	*Own Latrine*	*No Latrine*
Along *nullah*/drain/railway line/river bed/hilly terrain	27	36	38
Park/open space	33	24	43
Others	34	38	28
Total	**30**	**34**	**36**

Source: India: Urban Slums Survey, NSS 69th Round.

facility. Out of all the urban slums located in those areas which are categorises as others, around 38 per cent are having their own latrine facility and 34 per cent, public/community/shared latrine facility and only 28 per cent with no latrine facility.

From Table 11.8, Percentage Distribution of Availability of Latrine Facility in Urban Slums by Notification status of the Slum, about half of the urban slums have no access to any latrine facility followed by public/ community/shared latrine facility which is 27 per cent and those who were having own latrine facility contributes only 23 per cent. However, out of all the urban slums which are notified 45 per cent are having their own latrine facility followed by public/community/shared latrine facility which is 33 per cent and no latrine which is 22 per cent.

From Table 11.9, Percentage Distribution of Availability of Drinking Water in Urban Slums by State, we notice that most of the urban slums have tap as the major source of drinking water which is followed by tube well/borehole/well and others. In Karnataka, around 88 per cent of the slums are having tap as major source of the drinking water, followed by tube well/borehole/well which is 8 per cent and other source of drinking water contribute only 3 per cent. On the other hand, in Jharkhand, only 11

Table 11.8: Percentage Distribution of Availability of Latrine Facility in Urban Slums by Notification Status of the Slum

Notification status of the Slum	Public/Community/Shared Latrine	Own Latrine	No Latrine
Not notified	27	23	50
Notified	33	45	22
Total	**30**	**34**	**36**

Source: India: Urban Slums Survey, NSS 69th Round.

Table 11.9: Percentage Distribution of availability of Drinking Water in Urban Slums by State

States	Tap	Tube well/ Borehole/Well	Others
Punjab	59	41	0
Rajasthan	83	15	2
Uttar Pradesh	39	50	11
Bihar	14	81	5
West Bengal	68	28	3
Jharkhand	11	74	16
Odisha	30	63	7
Chhattisgarh	76	24	0
Madhya Pradesh	57	36	7
Gujarat	77	16	7
Maharashtra	81	14	5
Andhra Pradesh	83	12	5
Karnataka	88	8	3
Tamil Nadu	85	2	13
Others	77	13	10
Total	**71**	**23**	**6**

Source: India: Urban Slums Survey, NSS 69th Round.

per cent of the households in the urban slums have tap as the source of drinking water while tube well/borehole/well have the highest percentage with 74 per cent and other source of drinking water with only 16 per cent. In Bihar, 81 per cent of the tube well/borehole/well contribute as the major source of drinking water for the households in the urban slums. Only 14 per cent of the household have tap as the major source of drinking water and around 5 per cent as the other source of drinking water. In Tamil Nadu only about 2 per cent of the household in the urban slums have tube well/ borehole/well as the major source of drinking water whereas tap contributes 85 per cent as the source of drinking water and around 13 per cent of the drinking water are from other sources. In Jharkhand, out of the total source of drinking water, 16 per cent are from other sources whereas 74 per cent of the drinking water are from tube well/borehole/well as the major source and 11 per cent as tap as the source of drinking water.

From Table 11.10: Percentage Distribution of Availability of Drinking Water in Urban Slums by Ownership status of the Slum Land, tap constitute 72 per cent as the source of drinking water for the Private owned urban slums, followed by tube well/borehole/well with 23 per cent and other sources with only 5 per cent. Among the urban slums owned by railway and local bodies, 71 per cent of the sources of drinking water is from tap followed by tube well/borehole/well which is 22 per cent and other sources 7 per cent. Among the ownership of the slums which are classified as "other and not known", 65 per cent are having tap as the major source of drinking water, 29 per cent as tube well/borehole/well and 6 per cent others as the major source of drinking water.

From Table 11.11: Percentage Distribution of Availability of Drinking Water in Urban Slums by Physical Location of the Slum, 70 per cent of the slums located along *nullah*/drain/railway line/river bed/hilly terrain are having tap as the source of drinking water and 25 per cent are having tube well/borehole/well and 6 per cent are having others as the source of drinking water. In the park/open space, 66 per cent of the households are

Table 11.10: Percentage Distribution of Availability of Drinking Water in Urban Slums by Ownership Status of the Slum Land

Ownership Status of the Slums	*Tap*	*Tube well/ Borehole/Well*	*Others*
Private	72	23	5
Railway & local bodies	71	22	7
Other & not known	65	29	6
Total	**71**	**23**	**6**

Source: India: Urban Slums Survey, NSS 69th Round.

Table 11.11: Percentage Distribution of Availability of Drinking Water in Urban Slums by Physical Location of the Slum

Physical Location of the Slum	*Tap*	*Tube well/ Borehole/Well*	*Others*
Along *nullah*/drain/railway line/river bed/hilly terrain	70	25	6
Park/open space	66	25	9
Others	77	18	5
Total	**71**	**23**	**6**

Source: India: Urban Slums Survey, NSS 69th Round.

having tap as source of drinking water, 25 per cent as tube well/borehole/well and 9 per cent others as the source of drinking water. Among the physical location classified as others, 77 per cent are having tap as the source of drinking water followed by tube well/borehole/well with 18 per cent and other sources with only 5 per cent.

From Table 11.12: Percentage Distribution of Availability of Drinking Water in Urban Slums by Notification status of the Slum, among the not notified slums, around 64 per cent of the total households are having tap as the source of drinking water and 28 per cent of the drinking water are from tube well/borehole/well and only 8 per cent are from other sources. Among the notified urban slums, about 78 per cent of the housenolds are having tap as the major source of drinking water followed by tube well/borehole/well which constitute around 18 per cent and other sources about only 5 per cent.

Most of the households in urban slum comprises of tap as the major source of drinking water which was followed by tube well/borehole/well and other sources. This suggest that there is an improvement in drinking water facility across the state and not much variation is seen from different categories of physical location, ownership status of the urban slums as well as the notification status of the slum.

From Table 11.13: Percentage Distribution of availability of electricity in Urban Slums by State, we observed that most of the urban slums have high percentage of availability of electricity both in Household and Street lights except in some states. This shows that slums areas across the state is more or less equip to the daily need of lights in their everyday uses, maybe the fact of being located in the urban centres in the country could have been contributed to be less deprived of many of the basic needs in general and availability of electricity in general across all urban slums. In Bihar, around 86 per cent of the households in urban slums either have only household or only Street lights or none of them, whereas 14 per cent of the urban slum in Bihar have electricity available both in Household and Street

Table 11.12: Percentage Distribution of Availability of Drinking Water in Urban Slums by Notification Status of the Slum

Notification status of the Slum	*Tap*	*Tube well/ Borehole/Well*	*Others*
Not notified	64	28	8
Notified	78	18	5
Total	**71**	**23**	**6**

Source: India-Urban Slums Survy, NSS 69th Round.

Table 11.13: Percentage Distribution of availability of electricity in Urban Slums by State

State	*Either HH or SL or None*	*HH & SL*
Punjab	53	47
Rajasthan	29	71
Uttar Pradesh	57	43
Bihar	86	14
West Bengal	20	80
Jharkhand	68	32
Odisha	46	54
Chhattisgarh	8	92
Madhya Pradesh	23	77
Gujarat	26	74
Maharashtra	19	81
Andhra Pradesh	4	96
Karnataka	12	88
Tamil Nadu	16	84
Others	40	60
Total	**25**	**75**

Source: India: Urban Slums Survey, NSS 69th Round.

light. Jharkhand also shows poor availability of electricity, where about 68 per cent are having electricity in either Household only or Street light or none of them and 32 per cent of the households in urban slums were having electricity both in Household and street light. Andhra Pradesh is doing well in electricity availability as 96 per cent of the households in urban slums have access to electricity both in the household and street lights.

From Table 11.14: Percentage Distribution of Availability of electricity in Urban Slums by Ownership status of the Slum Land, both the private owned slums and slums owned by railway and local bodies have relatively equal percentage of electricity availability that 24 per cent of electricity are available only either in Household or street light or none of them. 76 per cent of the electricity available to urban slums in both households and street lights. Among the other and not known category of the ownership status of the urban slum, 35 per cent are either available only in Household or Street light or none of them whereas 65 per cent are available both in household and street light level.

From Table 11.15: Percentage Distribution of Availability of electricity in Urban Slums by Physical Location of the Slum, among the slums located along *nullah*/drain/railway line/river bed/hilly terrain, only 24 per cent are having electricity either in Household or street light or having no electricity available to them, whereas 76 per cent of the households in urban slums were having electricity both in the Household and street light. Among the

Table 11.14: Percentage Distribution of Availability of Electricity in Urban Slums by Ownership Status of the Slum Land

Ownership Status of the Slums	*Either HH or SL or None*	*HH & SL*
Private	24	76
Railway & local bodies	24	76
Other & not known	35	65
Total	**25**	**75**

Source: India: Urban Slums Survey, NSS 69th Round.

Table 11.15: Percentage Distribution of Availability of Electricity in Urban Slums by Physical Location of the Slum

Physical Location of the Slum	*Either HH or SL or None*	*HH & SL*
Along *nullah*/drain/railway line/river bed/hilly terrain	24	76
Park/open space	36	64
Others	20	80
Total	**25**	**75**

Source: India: Urban Slums Survey, NSS 69th Round.

slums located in the park/open space, only 36 per cent of the households in the urban slums are having electricity either in Household or street light or having no electricity available to them, whereas 64 per cent of the households are having electricity both in household and street lights. Among the physical location categorise as others, 20 per cent are having electricity in either Household or street lights or none of them and 80 per cent are having electricity both in the household and street light.

From Table 11.16: Percentage Distribution of Availability of electricity in Urban Slums by Notification status of the Slum, among the not notified slums, 63 per cent have electricity available to them both in household and street light. However, 86 per cent of the total notified slums are having electricity available to the both on Household and street light.

From Table 11.17, we observed that the slums owned by railway and local bodies are less likely to have public/community/shared latrine facility (RRR .65, $p < .05$) compared to no latrine. The RRR is lower among railway and local bodies to have public/community/shared latrine as compared to slums owned by private. In terms of Physical location, the slums located in areas specified as others are more likely to have public/community/shared latrine facility (RRR 1.6, $p<0.05$) compared to no latrine. The RRR is higher among others to have public/community/shared latrine as compared to slums located along *nullah* or railway line or river

Table 11.16: Percentage Distribution of Availability of Electricity in Urban Slums by Notification Status of the Slum

Notification status of the Slum	*Either HH or SL or None*	*HH & SL*
Not notified	37	63
Notified	14	86
Total	**25**	**75**

Source: India: Urban Slums Survey, NSS 69th Round.

Table 11.17: Relative Risk Ratio (RRR) from Multinomial Logistic Regression for Determinants of availability of Latrine Facility in Urban Slums of India

Latrine Facility	*RRR*	*[Conf. interval]*	
Public/community/shared latrine			
Ownership Status			
Railway & local bodies	0.6569175**	.4520749	.9545777
Others & not known	0.7719512	.4627806	1.28767
Physical Location			
Park/open space	1.181032	.7710553	1.808996
Others	1.601476**	1.061349	2.416477
Notification			
Notified	0.768609***	1.961527	3.907769
Own latrine			
Ownership Status			
Railway & local bodies	0.5414431***	.3752195	.7813042
Others & not known	0.4739105***	.2759868	.813775
Physical Location			
Park/Open Space	0.6591094*	.4177675	1.039873
Others	1.261331	.8412758	1.891124
Notification status			
Notified	4.180171***	2.96653	5.890325

Ref. category: No latrine, Level of significance: *P<0.1, **P<0.05, ***P<0.01.

Source: Calculated by the Authors.

bed or hilly terrain. Again the slums which are notified are less likely to have public/community/shared latrine (RRR .76, p<0.01) compared to no latrine, the RRR in this case is lower among notified slums as compared to not notified ones. The slums owned by railway and local bodies are less likely to have own latrine facility (RRR .54, p< .01) compared to no latrine. The RRR is lower among railway and local bodies to have own latrine as compared to slums owned by private. The slums owned by others and not known are less likely to have own latrine facility (RRR .47, p< .01) compared to no latrine. The RRR is lower among others and not known to have own latrine as compared to slums owned by private. In terms of Physical location, the slums located in park or open space are less likely to have own latrine facility (RRR .65, p<0.1) compared to no latrine. The RRR is lower among slums located in park or open space to have own latrine as compared to slums located along *nullah* or railway line or river bed or hilly terrain. Lastly, the slums which are notified are more likely to have own latrine (RRR 4.18, p<0.01) compared to no latrine, the RRR in this case is higher among notified slums as compared to not notified ones.

From Table 11.18, we noticed that the slums owned by railway and local bodies are less likely to have covered and underground drainage facility (RRR .43, p<.01) compared to no drainage. The RRR is lower among railway and local bodies to have covered and underground drainage facility as compared to slums owned by private. The slums owned by category specified as others and not known are less likely to have covered and underground drainage facility (RRR .44, p< .05) compared to no drainage. The RRR is lower among category specified as others and not known to have covered and underground drainage facility as compared to slums owned by private. In terms of Physical location, the slums located in areas specified as others are more likely to have covered and underground drainage facility (RRR 1.9, p<0.05) compared to no drainage. The RRR is higher among others to have covered and underground

Table 11.18: Relative Risk Ratio (RRR) from Multinomial Logistic Regression for Determinants of Drainage Facility in Urban Slums of India

Drainage Type	*RRR*	*[95% Conf. Interval]*	
Covered & underground drainage			
Ownership Status			
Railway & local bodies	0.433793***	0.270414	0.695885
Others & not known	0.4491946**	0.234189	0.861593
Physical location			
Park/open space	1.226593	0.719473	2.091156
Others	1.966598**	1.166106	3.316601
Notification			
Notified	6.547105***	4.150275	10.32813
Open drainage			
Ownership Status			
Railway & local bodies	0.7453092	0.515223	1.078147
Others & not known	0.5314269**	0.320699	0.880622
Physical location			
Park/open space	0.5921831**	0.389185	0.901064
Others	1.347367	0.887564	2.045373
Notification			
Notified	5.230815***	3.661847	7.47203

Ref. category: No Drainage, Level of significance: *P<0.1, **P<0.05, ***P<0.01.

Source: Calculated by the Authors.

drainage latrine as compared to slums located along *nullah* or railway line or river bed or hilly terrain. Again the slums which are notified are more likely to have covered and underground drainage facility (RRR 6.54, p<0.01) compared to no drainage, the RRR in this case is higher among notified slums as compared to not notified ones. Furthermore, the slums owned by category specified as others and not known are less likely to have open drainage facility (RRR .53, p<.05) compared to no drainage. The RRR is lower among category specified as others and not known to have open drainage facility as compared to slums owned by private. In terms of Physical location, the slums located in park or open space areas are less likely to have open drainage facility (RRR .59, p<0.05) compared to no drainage. The RRR is lower among areas such as park or open space to have open drainage facility as compared to slums located along *nullah* or railway line or river bed or hilly terrain. Again the slums which are notified are more likely to have open drainage facility (RRR 6.54, p<0.01) compared to no drainage, the RRR in this case is higher among notified slums as compared to not notified ones.

From Table 11.19, we see that the slums which are notified are more likely to have tap as the major source of drinking water (RRR 1.88, p<0.05)

Table 11.19: Relative Risk Ratio (RRR) from Multinomial Logistic Regression for Determinants of Drinking Water Facility in Urban Slums of India

Drinking water	*RRR*	*[95% Conf.*	*Interval]*
Tap			
Ownership Status			
Railway & local bodies	0.753003	0.407996	1.389752
Others & not known	0.902433	0.362971	2.243662
Physical Location			
Park/open space	0.661772	0.337259	1.298532
Others	1.08236	0.539215	2.172606
Notification			
Notified	1.88479**	1.064961	3.33575
Tube well bore			
Ownership Status			
Railway & local bodies	0.68048	0.350714	1.320314
Others & not known	1.161091	0.444846	3.030559
Physical Location			
Park/open space	0.657944	0.317698	1.362584
Others	0.720172	0.336673	1.540511
Notification			
Notified	1.016661	0.547593	1.887532

Ref. category: others, Level of significance: *P<0.1, **P<0.05, ***P<0.01.
Source: Calculated by the Authors.

compared to other source of drinking water, the RRR in this case is higher among notified slums as compared to not notified ones.

From Table 11.20, we noticed that the slums owned by category specified as others and not known are less likely to have electricity available to them as compared to slums owned by the private (OR .65, p<0.1). The slums located in the park or open space again are less likely to have electricity available to them as compared to the slum located along the *nullah* or railway line or river bed or hilly terrain (OR .64, p<0.05). However, the slums which are notified are more likely to have electricity as compared to the not notified slums (OR 3.5, p<0.01).

Table 11.20: Odds Ratio from Binary Logistic Regression for Determinants of Electric Facility in Urban Slums of India

Availability of electricity	*Odds Ratio*	*[95% Conf. interval]*	
Ownership Status			
Railway & local bodies	1.063241	0.746015	1.515361
Others & not known	0.653227*	0.408044	1.045728
Physical Location			
Park/open space	0.649490**	0.438169	0.962728
Others	0 .216555	0.813393	1.819548
Notification Status			
Notified	3.53532***	2.523449	4.95296

Ref. category: either HH or SL or none, Level of significance: *P<0.1, **P<0.05, **P<0.01

Source: Calculated by the Authors.

From Table 11.21, we see that the majority of the households in the slums owned by railway and local bodies are less likely to have *pucca* household structure (RRR .65, p< 0.1) compared to *katcha* household structure. The RRR is lower among households owned by railway and local bodies as compared to slums owned by private. Again the majority of the households in the notified slums are more likely to have *pucca* household structure as compared to *katcha* houses (RRR 6.2, p<0.01), the RRR in this case is higher by among notified slums than the not notified slums. Also most of the households in the notified slums are more like to have semi-*pucca* houses than *katcha* houses (RRR 2.1, p<0.01). The RRR is higher in notified slums as compared to the not notified ones.

Conclusion

The analysis has shown that the ownership status of the urban slums, physical location of the slums and the notification status of the slums does have an effect on the availability of latrine facility, drainage, and

Table 11.21: Relative Risk Ratio (RRR) from Multinomial Logistic Regression for Determinants of Household Structure in Urban Slums of India

Type of HH Structure	*RRR*	*[95% Conf.]*	
Pucca			
Ownership Status			
Railway & local bodies	0.656559*	0.404516	1.065643
Others & not known	0.734867	0.370846	1.456211
Physical location			
Park/open space	0.910064	0.527569	1.569874
Others	1.209578	0.701249	2.08639
Notification			
Notified	6.2031**	3.713543	10.36172
Semi-pucca			
Ownership Status			
Railway & local bodies	1.228315	0.725289	2.080214
Others & not known	1.400262	0.678226	2.890976
Physical location			
Park/open space	0.700277	0.38955	1.258858
Others	0.75948	0.418901	1.376961
Notification			
Notified	2.1923***	1.261859	3.808992

Ref. category: *katcha,* Level of significance: *P<0.1, **P<0.05, ***P<0.01.

Source: Calculated by the Authors.

drinking water, electricity and household structures. Slums that are owned privately are seen to have better conditions in most of the cases than those slums owned by railway or local bodies and others. Private owned slums are more likely to have access to own latrine and public or community or shared latrine than those owned by the railway or local bodies. They are found to have more access to covered underground and open drainage than those slums owned by railway or local bodies. Private owned slums have better access to electricity and *pucca* household structure than those slums owned by owners which are categorised as others and not known. In the other hand, the slums which are located in the areas specified as others have more likely to have access to public or community or shared latrine facility and own latrine facility. They are also found to be more likely accessible to covered and underground drainage system than those slums located along the *nullah* or railway line or river bed or hilly terrain. However slums located along *nullah* or railway line or river bed or hilly terrain have more access to electricty and open drainage than the slums situated in the park or open space. We observed there is a strong effect that notification status of the urban on our different dependent variables. Therefore, we can conclude that there is clear indication that there exist a variation between the notified and not notified urban slums of India where in most of the cases the notified slums are doing better than the not notified ones.

Policy Implications

From the above findings, we can draw to a point the attention that the not notified slums are lacking most of the basic amenities and housing conditions, the slums which are owned by the railway and local bodies and others needs further assistance to bring-up for better basic amenities such as drinking water, latrine facility, drainage and electricity. Still there are many urban slums in India that does not have any latrine facilities available to them, which suggest that the practices of open defecation are still at large, this require urgent attention from the government.

References

Anand, A., and Bansal, T., Spatial Distribution and Availability of Basic Amenities: *An Analysis Across States and Size Class of Urban Centres in India-2011.*

Census of India, 2001. *Primary Census Abstract:* Office of the Registrar General and Census Commissioner. Ministry of Home Affairs, Government of India.

Census of India 2011. *Primary Census Abstract:* Office of the Registrar General and Census Commissioner. Ministry of Home Affairs, Government of India.

Chandrasekhar, S., and Montgomery, M. (2010). *Broadening Poverty Definitions in India: Basic Needs in Urban Housing* (No. 27). IIED.

Chakrabarty, N., and Bhattacharjee, D. (2013). Basic Household Amenities and its Interrelationship with Public Health Facilities: a Quantitative Study on Assam. *Indian Journal of Public Health Research and Development*, *4*(4), 213-217.

Das, B., and Mistri, A. (2013). Household Quality of Living in Indian States: Analysis of 2011 Census. *Environment and Urbanization Asia*, *4*(1), 151-171.

Edelman, B., and Mitra, A. (2006). Slum Dwellers' Access to Basic Amenities: The Role of Political Contact, Its Determinants and Adverse Effects. *Review of Urban and Regional Development Studies*, *18*(1), 25-40.

Ellaway, A., and Macintyre, S. (1998). Does housing tenure predict health in the UK because it exposes people to different levels of housing related hazards in the home or its surroundings? *Health and Place*, *4*(2), 141-150.

Galobardes, B., Shaw, M., Lawlor, D.A., Lynch, J.W., and Smith, G.D. (2006). Indicators of socio-economic position (part 1). *Journal of Epidemiology and Community Health*, *60*(1), 7-12.

Goli, S., Arokiasamy, P., and Chattopadhyaya, A. (2011). Living and health conditions of selected cities in India: Setting priorities for the National Urban Health Mission. *Cities*, *28*(5), 461-469.

Gupta, I., and Mitra, A. (2001). Basic amenities and health in urban India. *The National Medical Journal of India*, *15*, 26-31.

Guruswamy, M., and Abraham, R.J. (2006). Redefining poverty: a new poverty line for a new India. *Economic & Political Weekly*, 2534-2541.

Karn, S.K., Shikura, S., and Harada, H. (2003). Living environment and health of urban poor: a study in Mumbai. *Economic & Political Weekly*, 3575-3586.

Khan, J.H., Ahmed, N., and Hassan, T. (2013). Dimensions of housing and household amenities and assets in Madhya Pradesh. *Asian Journal of Research in Social Sciences and Humanities*, *3*(6), 179-194.

Khan, J.H., and Hassan, T. (2013). Patterns of Availability of Housing and Household Amenities in Odisha. *Journal of Business Management and Social Sciences Research*, *2*(4), 58-67.

Kundu, A., Bagchi, S., and Kundu, D. (1999). Regional distribution of infrastructure and basic amenities in urban India: issues concerning empowerment of local bodies. *Economic & Political Weekly*, 1893-1906.

Mahadeva, M. (2006). Reforms in housing sector in India: impact on housing development and housing amenities. *Habitat International*, *30*(3), 412-433.

Nayar, K.R. (1997). Housing Amenities and Health Improvement: Some Findings. *Economic & Political Weekly*, 1275-1279.

NSSO, 2003. *Condition of Urban Slums 2002: Salient Features*. NSS 58th round. Ministry of Statistics and Programme Implementation. Government of India. Report. 486:58/0.21/1.

Reddy, V.R. (2001). Declining social consumption in India. *Economic & Political Weekly*, 2750-2751.

Sajjad, H. (2014). Living Standards and Health Problems of Lesser Fortunate Slum Dwellers: Evidence from an Indian City. *International Journal of Environmental Protection and Policy*, *2*(2), 54-63.

Shah, F., and JaiswaT.R. (2002). The Status of Housing and Related Amenities in Rajasthan. *Indian Journal of Regional Science*, *34*, 71.

Shaw, A. (2008). *Basic Amenities in Urban India*, 47(1), 159-189.

Srinivasan, K., and Mohanty, S.K. (2008). Household Deprivation and Its Linkages with Reproductive Health Utilisation. *Economic & Political Weekly*, 67-76.

Thomson, H., Petticrew, M., and Douglas, M. (2003). Health impact assessment of housing improvements: incorporating research evidence. *Journal of Epidemiology and Community Health*, *57*(1), 11-16.

Zainal, N.R., Kaur, G., Ahmad, N.A., and Khalili, J.M. (2012). Housing Conditions and Quality of Life of the Urban Poor in Malaysia. *Procedia—Social and Behavioural Sciences*, *50*, 827-838.

12

Study of Urban-Ecology of a New Town

A Social Area Analysis Approach

Sanu Dolui

Introduction

As a town grows there is tendency of different functions to occupy different area within the town so that housing, industry and commercial activities became dominant function in different parts of the town. These dissimilarities in functional zones are readily recognizable. Invention of modern society was associated with basic change in economic and social relationship, change in range and intensity of social activity in the city, give us the option to choose from different social and economic activities. Diversity and differentiation of function and activity, give rise to complex social order and which alter the traditional city structure or city-periphery relationship. Social area analysis may be the best procedure to study complex social pattern of city. Social area analysis help us to differentiate social areas of a city which have similar kind of social, economic, cultural and demographic characteristics of the resident. Such a homogeneity in certain area of a city gives the area a unique identity which separates it from the surrounding areas.

Conceptual Background

It is human inhabitable nature to compete for limited space and for access to the most preferable location for residence and business activities. Initial phase of social area study, social areas have been identified through the classical models, these models are concentric zone model (Burgess, 1925), sector model (Hoyt, 1939) and multiple nuclei model (Harris and Ullman, 1945). The progress started from the traditional ecological theory. But main shortcomings of classical ecological theory of social area were the dependence on very few variables and lack of theoretical base to support the use of selected variable, but with invention of social area analysis method was initially developed by American Sociologist Shevky and Williams (1949) as a method for classification census tracts of Los Angeles, and later modified by Shevky and Bell in 1955 as a model of social change sought to overcome these deficiencies of classical model by using a multivariate classification procedure from a larger sets of variable that represent the social, economic and demographic characteristics of census tracts in a city. Social area generally "contains persons having the same level of living, the same way of life and the same ethnic background and we hypothesize that persons living in a particular type of social area would systematically differ with respect to characteristic attitude and behaviours from persons living in another type of social area" (Shevky and Bell: 20). From these arguments are derived the three basic constructs of increasing scale by: Social rank (or economic status), Urbanization (or family status) and Segregation (or ethnic status).

Study Area

The study area Memari is a town and a municipality in the Bardhamansader south sub-division of Burdwan district in the Indian state of West Bengal. The town was formed in 1991 before in the Memari municipality, the area is under AMADPUR GRAM PANCHAYAT, it is small town consists of 16 wards and total area is 8.85 sq. km. Usually, the Memari town is grow based on market or bazar based economy, the town act as a services centre to the surrounding rural hinterland. Latitudinal extension 23° 10′ N to 23° 12′N and the longitudinal extension 88° 5′E to 88° 7′E.

Research Design

Research design stand for an advance planning of the method to be adopted for collecting the relevant data and the techniques to be used in their analysis, keeping in view the objective of research. Here for the present study we can divide the whole work into following parts:

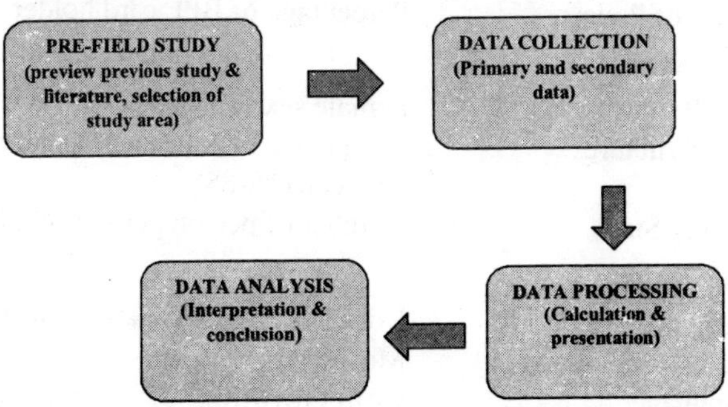

Objective of the Study

The principal objective of the present work is to study the social and spatial structure of a newly developed town, Special emphasis is on social area analysis approach to study the man-environment relationship in a rational way.

Sub-Objective

1. Study city's social structure by its demographic, economic, social and ethnic characteristics.
2. Try to sketch urban social zones based on similar socio-economic and living status.
3. To observe the zones of newly developed town and try to find out factor of this zoning.

Social Area Analysis of Memari Municipality

Here we selected 16 variables for social area analysis of Memari town, after analysing secondary data of Memari municipality thoroughly (2011 Census data).

Dimension or Parameter for Social Area Analysis

Dimension	**Selected Variable Selected**
Socio-Economic Status	
1. Occupation	Population engaged in non-agriculture activities.
2. No. of Earning Member	Single earning family
3. Income	More than 10,000+ per month per household.
4. Education	Female population engaged in higher education
5. Workforce	Percentage of women in workforce
6. Level of Poverty	Percentage of BPL card holder
Family Status	
1. Sex-Ratio	Female sex-ratio
2. Age Structure	Percentage of male and female population between (18-65)
3. Family Size	Number of person per household
Ethnic Status	
1. Religion	Concentration of ward-wise Hindu and Muslim population
2. Language	Concentration of Bengali and Arbi speaking people

3. Caste — Percentage of ward-wise S.C. and S.T. population.

Source of Data and Sample Selection: Mainly this study is based on primary data from household survey and also some data should be taken as basis of selection of sample and choice of variable (*see* Table 12.1 and Figs. 12.2-12.5).

Explanation: Here we represent socio-economic, family status and ethnic status of Memari Municipality by P.C.A. mapping and also co-relate all these variable by composite Z score to find out co-relation between those variable, in the diagram (positive, negative co-relation) we can see ward number and its co-relation value, Ward nos. 11, 12, 7, 4 have highly positive correlation between socio-economic, family and ethnic status, ward nos. 8, 15 correlation is moderately positive, ward nos. 1, 2, 3 correlation slightly negative, ward nos. 9, 10, 13, 14, 16 the correlation is highly native that indicates distance from the city centre effects the co-relation between those variables. Generally education, sex-ratio, percentage of population engaged in non-agriculture activity, literacy rate, economic opportunity are higher near the city centre so result is positive near to it. In the margin of city or peri-urban area some ethnic patches, minority people, slum dweller are living and their socio-economic, living status is much lower as compared to city centre (Fig. 12.1).

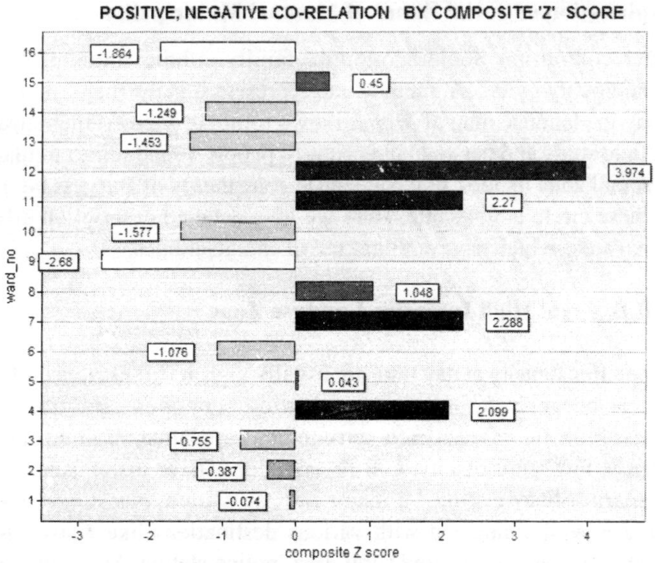

Fig. 12.1: Positive, Negative Co-Relation by Composite 'Z' Score

Source: Computed by Author.

Table 12.1: Sample Household Selection.

Ward No.	Total Household	Percentage of Household Surveyed	Actual No. of Household Sample Survey	Adjusted Household Survey
1.	1008	5	50.40	50
2.	613	5	30.65	31
3.	631	5	31.55	32
4.	557	5	27.85	28
5.	421	5	21.05	21
6.	322	5	16.10	16
7.	693	5	34.65	35
8.	599	5	29.95	30
9.	497	5	24.85	25
10.	810	5	40.50	40
11.	558	5	27.90	28
12.	590	5	29.50	30
13.	559	5	27.95	28
14.	718	5	35.90	36
15.	483	5	24.15	24
16.	926	5	46.30	46
				Σ 500

Source: Primary data of household survey (2013) and Secondary data of Memari Municipality Census (2011).

Explanation of Social Zones of Memari Municipality

After computing Socio-economic, family, ethnic status of Memari Municipality by P.C.A. method and represent it in the maps, thoroughly study the landuse map of Memari town (*Source:* Memari municipality), on field study and personal interview of people, found some circular type of social zone its look like concentric zone theory of Burgess but radius of these circle is not same. Here we give detailed description different social areas which have similar kind of characteristics.

C.B.D. Area: High Intensive Landuse Zone

Population density at day time are usually high at C.B.D. area of the city, this is because the city centre provide economic opportunity and accessibility therefore attracts surrounding population. Position of C.B.D. Area is in Centre of city, C.B.D. area consists of major land-use like Memari railway station—a major railway station, bus stand—this bus stand is well connected with various destinations like Katwa, Kalna, Bardhaman and associated rural area, police station. Municipal office,

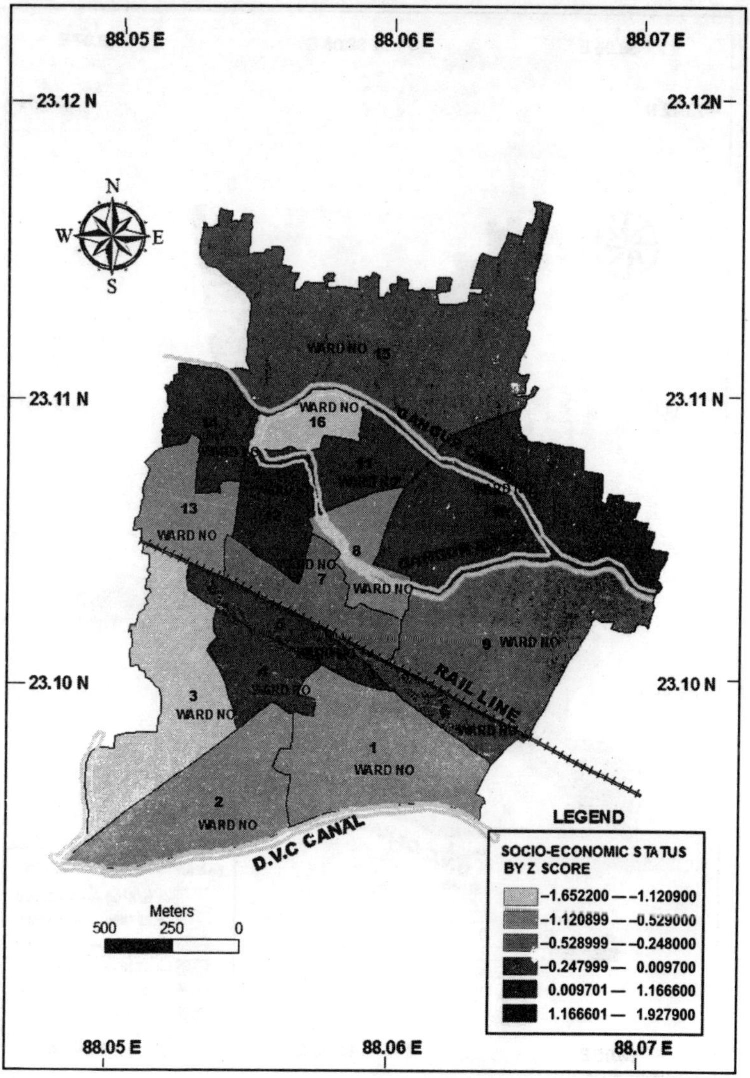

Fig. 12.2: Socio-Economic Status of Memari Municipality

Data source: Primary Household survey of 2013, Memari municipality.

location of different banks (State Bank of India, Union Bank of India, Reserve Bank India, Maharashtra Bank, Allahabad Bank). Main market occupied both side of railway stations, bazaar, cinema hall, municipal

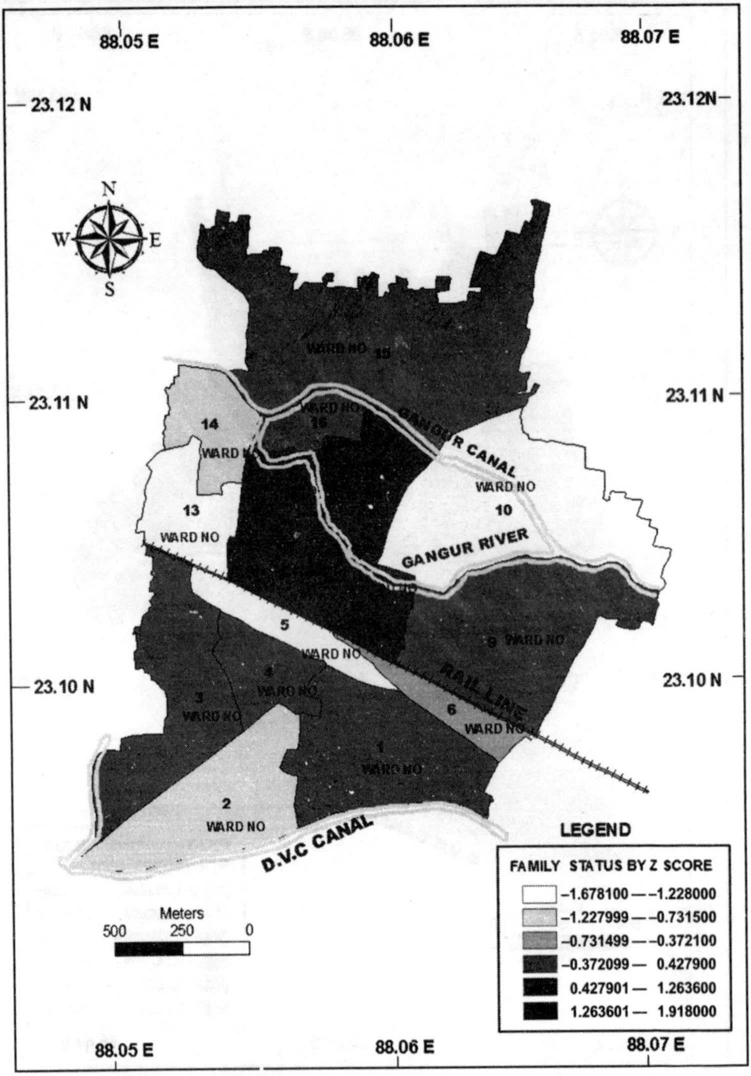

Fig. 12.3: Family Status of Memari Municipality

Data source: Primary household survey of 2013, Memari municipality.

office, head post office, petrol pump, residential complex, hotels, marriage hall, major road and transport network is the major landuse of C.B.D. area. So, one can easily identify this is the heart of the city.

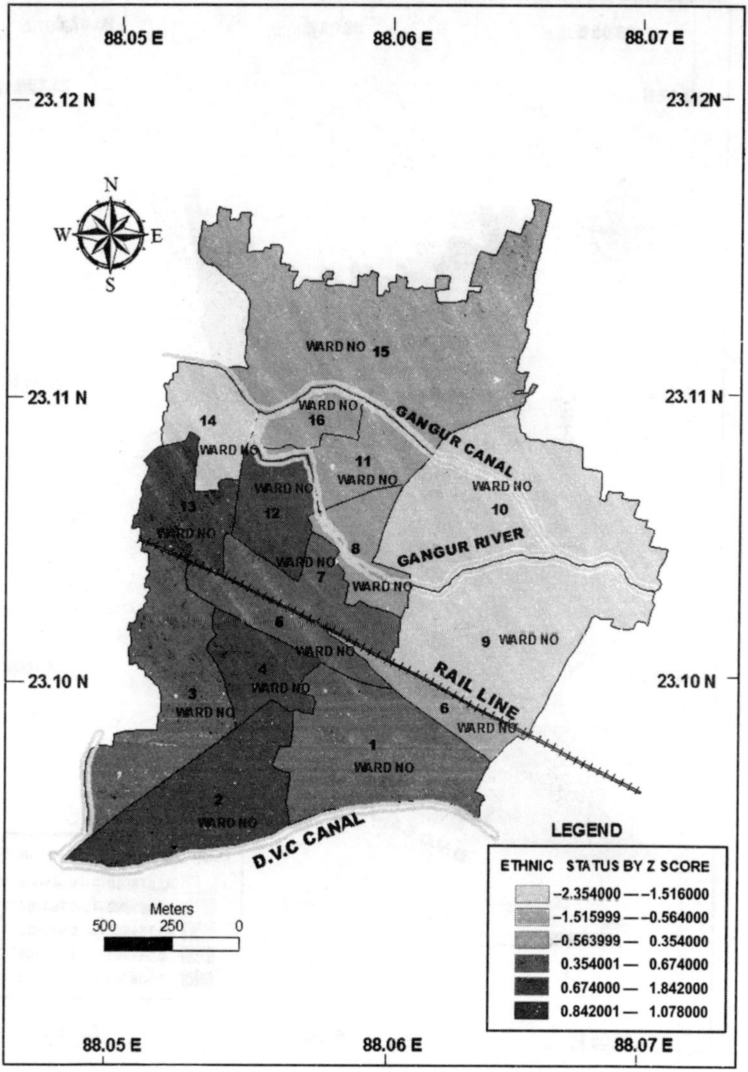

Fig. 12.4: Ethinic Status of Memari Municipality

Data source: Primary household survey of 2013, Memari municipality.

Zone-1: Industrial Area with Less Residential Building

This zone is smaller in radius, but fast growing. This zone consists of

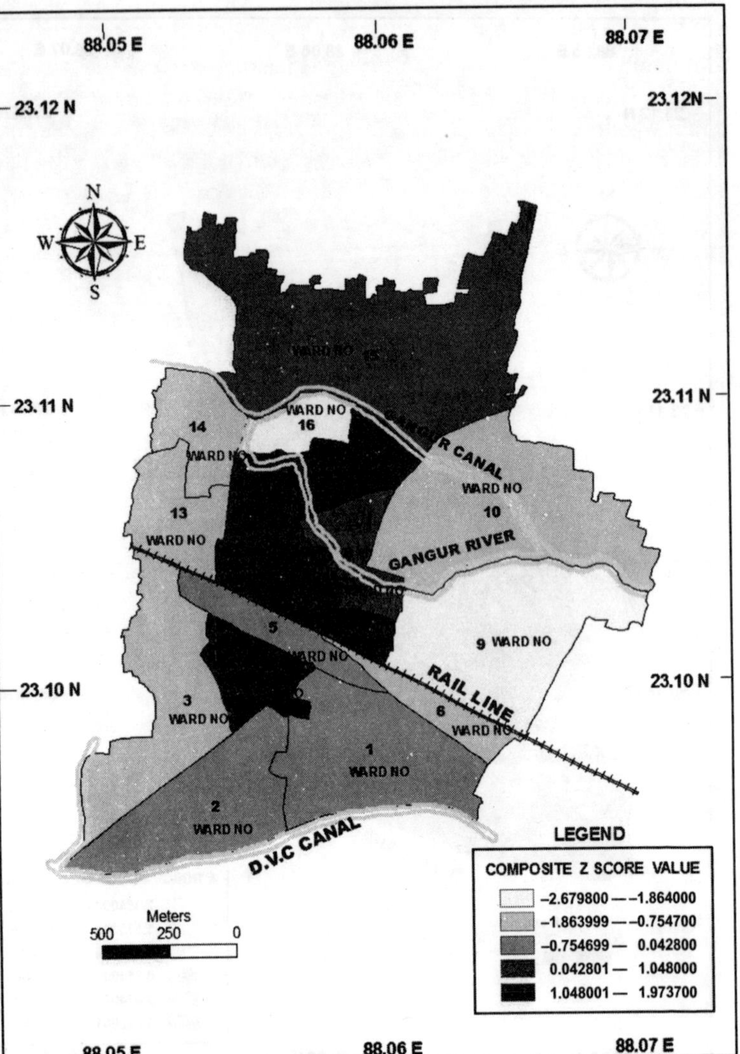

Fig. 12.5: Co-relation between Socio-Economic, Family and Ethnic Status by Composite 2 Score

Data source: Primary household survey of 2013, Memari municipality.

different factories and electronics goods making shops. In this area we found as many as 36 cold storage, serve as a reservoir of different food grain which is produced in surrounding rural area. Electric transformer factory and its associated office located in ward no. 9, rice mill, saw mill, factory for making electronic tools, different electronic parts, motor garage showroom of different two wheeler company like Bajaj, Honda, phonic and also some car showroom, small steel plant electronic parts making, small scale manufacturing products are produced here. The harmful gases from the mills and factory's chimneys created problem to the local residents and unhealthy living condition.

Zone-2: Residential zone with Better Municipal Facilities

This zone consists of mainly residential area out of industrial belt, density of population is much higher and big and beautiful complexes are there, mainly middle class residential population live in well decorated and big houses, houses are mainly 3 sorties or more than that. Municipal authority provide all the civic amenities like-safe drinking water, proper drainage system, street light, metal road etc. **Memari college**—is the centre of higher education, **Memari** hospital is major Centre for medical treatment situated here, Shops like glossary, carpentry, meat shop, fast food Centre is in this zone. A Muslim educational institution named Almodina madrasah is major centres of ARBI language study.

Zone-3: Mixed Rural-Urban Landuse Zone

This zone is also residential zone, but characteristics is different from previous residential area because rural type of housing and municipal facilities are not as good as in previous zone, municipal tube-well not well planned, water facilities does not reach every house, lack of metal road, lack of street lighting, drainage system is poor, the housing type is like rural household (storage of crops, domestic animal-cow), the occupation structure is totally changed people mainly engaged in primary activity like fishing, potter, agriculture labour or farmer, idol making etc. Some agricultural land also visible. Slum and squatter people, few tribal people live in this zone, depend mainly on agriculture. Other land-uses like B.D.O. office, Gramin Bank indicating that this zone is under Memari municipality, but their characteristic is rurban in nature.

Zone-4: Agricultural Landuse Zone

This zone mainly comprises of agricultural land with some tribal patches who live there because they are agricultural labour. Municipal dumping ground—where all municipal solid waste dumped there. Burial ground-side of D.V.C. canal. A proposed rural vegetable mark *et al.* most completed which serve as a market to the farmer of this area and also surrounding villages. Petrol Pump, Smog Examination Centre, Mother Teresa Seba Niketan these are the major land-use of that zone. Population density is low and characteristics is totally rural in nature.

Main Findings of the Study

After study the urban ecology of Memari town with the help of social area analysis techniques, we can conclude it with certain characteristics of social areas of Memari town:

1. Naturally grown this type of new cities have one C.B.D. Area or growth centre and in their initial phase all economic activities are concentrated in this area.
2. The radius of different zones of the city are different because it is dynamic in nature and always changing in shape with time.
3. C.B.D. Area always play a good major role for city's development, but it is depends on accessibility and connectivity with surrounding areas.
4. As the city originated from rural area we found some agricultural area inside city, but it is visible that in future this zone will be encroached by residential and other establishments.
5. This model of social area should be identical to study urban-ecology of small and new town.

Acknowledgements

I deem it to be my proud privilege to express my deep sense of gratitude and heartiest thanks to Ina Dhar Roy (Assistant Professor), Department of Geography, Chandannagore Government College for her valuable suggestion, her highly perceptive guidance and supervision enabled me to achieve my research objective till completion of my research work.

APPENDICES

Table 12.2: Socio-economic Status—Memari Municipality

Ward No.	*Single Earning Family*	*Income> 10,000 Per household*	*Female Population Engaged in Higher Education*	*Percentage of Women in Work Force*	*Population Engaged in non-Agricultural Activity*	*Percentage of B.P.L. Card Holder*
1.	68	27	13	2.24	29	35.61
2.	78	22	17	7.72	20	34.09
3.	65	18	1	1.20	37	31.38
4.	61	33	16	5.32	78	13.28
5.	69	17	12	1.30	80	34.91
6.	71	36	5	3.79	65	34.16
7.	63	38	16	1.71	63	15.29
8.	72	20	26	3.26	59	11.68
9.	61	21	24	7.20	40	35.21
10.	63	41	22	9.80	55	25.30
11.	76	33	12	4.68	75	26.88
12.	71	34	24	5.65	91	11.52
13.	67	14	8	3.68	66	20.93
14.	73	24	17	3.94	80	27.71
15.	60	12	5	8.44	24	67.90
16.	74	27	3	3.50	45	10.36

Source: Primary Survey by the Author, 2013.

Table 12.3: Correlation Matrix

	V1	*V2*	*V3*	*V4*	*V5*	*V6*
V1	1.000	0.042	–0.006	–0.183	0.130	–0.273
V2	0.042	1.000	0.286	0.126	0.376	–0.470
V3	–0.006	0.286	1.000	0.353	0.269	–0.347
V4	–0.183	0.126	0.353	1.000	–0.261	0.314
V5	0.130	0.376	0.269	–0.261	1.000	–0.546
V6	–0.273	–0.470	–0.347	0.314	–0.546	1.000

Source: Calculated by the Author.

Table 12.4: Table for Principal Component Analysis

	V1	V2	V3	V4	V5	V6	Sji
(1)	(2)	(3)	(4)	(5)	(6)	(7)	(8)
V1	1.00	0.42	0.006	0.183	0.130	0.273	2.012
V2	0.42	1.00	0.286	0.126	0.376	0.470	2.678
V3	0.006	0.286	1.00	.353	.269	.347	2.261
V4	0.183	0.126	0.353	1.00	.261	.314	2.237
V5	0.130	0.376	.269	.261	1.00	.546	2.582
V6	0.273	0.470	0.347	.314	.546	1.00	2.950

Source: Calculated by the Author.

Table 12.4 (*Contd.*)

	£ji	Sji'	£ji'	(£ji')2	PC1	(PC1)2
(1)	(9)	(10)	(11)	(12)	(13)	(14)
V1	0.682	1.59	0.613	0.375	0.554	0.3069
V2	0.908	2.30	0.888	0.788	0.7376	0.5440
V3	0.766	1.88	0.72	0.518	0.6223	0.3872
V4	0.758	1.81	0.700	0.490	0.6158	0.3792
V5	0.875	2.25	0.868	0.753	0.7108	0.5052
V6	1.000	**2.59**	1.000	1.000	0.8124	0.6600
				Σ = 3.924		Σ = 2.7825

Sji = Row-wise summation
£ji = value of sji ÷ Maximum value of sji
sji' = Row wise transformation
£ji' = Value of sji'÷ maximum value of sji'

Principal index for ward no. 1: $\frac{68\times 0.55427}{2.7825}+\frac{0.7376}{2.7825}+\frac{13\times 0.6263}{2.7825}+$

$$\frac{2.24\times 0.6158}{2.7825}+\frac{29\times 0.7108}{2.7825}+$$

$$\frac{35.61\times 0.8124}{2.7825}=41.8974$$

Table 12.5: Table for P.C. A Mapping

Ward No.	*Principal Index*	*Z- score*
1.	41.8974	–0.8213
2.	41.9283	–0.7331
3.	36.8102	–1.6522
4.	49.4426	0.9882
5.	51.8360	1.0598
6.	45.2326	–0.1398
7.	44.6482	–0.248
8.	43.1036	–0.529
9.	43.9636	–0.3726
10.	52.1483	1.1666
11.	52.3467	1.1166
12.	56.6069	1.9279
13.	42.6187	–0.6173
14.	51.6879	1.0328
15.	44.0613	0.0097
16.	37.8508	–1.1209

Mean = 46.0114 S.D. = 5.4958

Source: Calculated by the Author.

Table 12.6: Family Status

Ward No.	Female Sex-Ratio	Male Population (18-65)	Female Population (18-65)	No of Persons Per Household
1.	940	67	65	4.39
2.	934	62	60	4.48
3.	992	54	56	4.10
4.	995	52	58	4.33
5.	912	59	60	4.38
6.	932	67	61	5.02
7.	1002	69	62	4.25
8.	984	66	63	4.03
9.	977	58	56	4.28
10.	939	59	53	4.09
11.	967	68	63	4.55
12.	966	71	67	4.05
13.	922	58	55	4.37
14.	948	56	60	3.40
15.	991	59	53	6.32
16.	991	53	55	2.30

Source: Primary Survey by the Author, 2013.

Table 12.7: Correlation Matrix

	V1	*V2*	*V3*	*V4*
V1	1.000	–0.126	–0.098	–0.085
V2	–0.126	1.000	0.773	0.275
V3	–0.098	0.773	1.000	–0.065
V4	–0.085	0.275	–0.065	1.000

Source: Calculated by the Author.

Table 12.8: Principal Component Analysis

	V1	V2	V3	V4	Sji	£ji
(1)	(2)	(3)	(4)	(5)	(6)	(7)
V1	1.000	0.126	0.098	0.085	1.309	0.602
V2	0 126	1.000	0.773	0.275	2.174	1.000
V3	0.098	0.773	1.000	0.065	1.936	0.890
V4	0.085	0.275	0.065	1.000	1.425	0.655

Table 12.8 (*Contd.*)

(1)	(8)	(9)	(10)	(11)	(12)
	Sji'	£ji'	(£ji)2	PC1	(PCA)2
V1	0.870	0.447	0.200	0.410	0.1681
V2	1.943	1.000	1.000	0.9173	0.8414
V3	1.764	0.9078	0.824	0.8327	0.6934
V4	1.039	0.534	0.285	0.4898	0.2399
			Σ = 2.309		**Σ = 1.9428**

Source: Calculated by the Author.

Table 12.9: Table for P.C.A. Mapping

Ward No.	Principal Index	Z-Score
1.	258.936	+0.093
2.	253.189	–0.7315
3.	259.84	+0.2235
4.	260.444	+0.3103
5.	247.106	–1.605
6.	255.692	–0.3721
7.	271.641	+1.918
8.	266.800	+1.223
9.	258.609	0.0468
10.	249.729	–1.228
11.	264.288	0.8537
12.	267.082	1.2636
13.	246.598	–1.6781
14.	253.038	–0.7532
15.	261.263	0.4279
16.	258.275	–0.0011

Mean: 258.2831 S.D.: 6.9631

Source: Calculated by the Author.

Table 12.10: Ethnic Status of Memari Municipality

Ward No.	Percentage of Hindu Religion	Percentage of Muslim Religion	Percentage of Bengali as mother tongue	Percentage of Urdu as a mother tongue	Concentration of S.T Population in percentage	Concentration of S. C Population in percentage
1.	85	8	67	7	3.27	26.25
2.	65	31	61	26	0.28	22.34
3.	71	23	63	19	0.20	18.58
4.	69	27	59	25	0.47	16.82
5.	78	17	64	14	0.21	18.65
6.	36	51	41	34	1.42	14.61
7.	82	12	70	11	1.02	11.63
8.	81	9	72	8	0.42	12.42
9.	32	38	40	12	11.59	13.65
10.	39	43	38	23	4.69	11.38
11.	45	47	72	5	5.00	13.04
12.	84	10	74	10	2.91	7.32
13.	72	23	71	12	0.44	17.01
14.	63	5	61	3	10.19	13.59
15.	52	38	52	24	3.10	17.87
16.	36	50	36	38	5.37	8.09

Source: Primary Survey by the Author, 2013.

Table 12.11: Correlation Matrix

	V1	V2	V3	V4	V5	V6
V1	1.000	–0.891	0.842	–0.513	–0.546	0.309
V2	–0. 891	1.000	–0.716	0.687	0.156	–0.197
V3	0. 842	–0.716	1.000	–0.708	–0.428	0.198
V4	–0.513	0.687	–0.708	1.000	–0.235	–0.067
V5	–0.546	0.156	–0.428	–0.235	1.000	–0.308
V6	0.309	–0.197	0.198	–0.067	–0.308	1.000

Source: Calculated by the Author.

Table 12.12: Table for Principal Component Analysis

	V1	*V2*	*V3*	*V4*	*V5*	*V6*	*Sji*
(1)	(2)	(3)	(4)	(5)	(6)	(7)	(8)
V1	1.000	0.891	0.842	0.513	0.546	0.309	4.101
V2	0.891	1.000	0.716	0.687	0.156	0.197	3.647
V3	0.842	0.716	1.000	0.708	0.428	0.198	3.892
V4	0.513	0.687	0.708	1.000	0.235	0.067	3.21
V5	0.546	0.156	0.428	0.235	1.000	0.308	2.673
V6	0.309	0.197	0.198	0.067	0.308	1.000	2.079

Table 12.12 (*Contd.*)

	£ji	*Sji '*	*£ ji'*	*(£ ji')2*	*PC1*	*PC1)2*
(1)	(9)	(10)	(11)	(12)	(13)	(14)
V1	1.000	**3.504**	1.000	1.000	0.953	0.9087
V2	0.889	3.197	0.912	0.828	0.867	0.7524
V3	0.949	3.359	0.955	0.912	0.905	0.8200
V4	0.7827	2.764	0.7889	0.608	0.743	0.5527
V5	0.651	2.083	0.594	0.348	0.562	0.3162
V6	0.506	1.432	0.400	0.160	0.381	0.1453
				Σ = 3.856		**Σ =3.4953**

Source: Calculated by the Author.

Table 12.13: Table for P.C. A. mapping

Ward No.	*Principal Index*	*Z-Score*
1.	47.3755	+0.654
2.	49.2049	+1.078
3.	47.4641	+0.674
4.	48.0019	+0.800
5.	47.0899	+0.588
6.	42.1221	–0.564
7.	47.2212	+0.618
8.	46.0812	+0.354
9.	34.4035	–2.354
10.	38.0152	–1.516
11.	45.8511	+0.300
12.	47.9275	+0.7822
13.	48.1878	+0.842
14.	37.9630	–1.529
15.	44.608	+0.012
16.	41.3537	–0.742

Mean = 44.5544 S.D. = 4.3119

Source: Calculated by the Author.

Table 12.14: Co-relation Between Socio economic Family Ethnic statuses by Composite 'Z' Score

Ward No.	*Socio-Economic Status*	*Family Status*	*Ethnic Status*	*Composite Z Score*
1.	−0.8213	0.093	0.654	−0.0743
2.	−0.733	−0.7315	1.078	−0.3865
3.	−1.6522	0.2235	0.674	−0.7547
4.	0.9882	0.3103	0.8	2.0985
5.	1.0598	−1.605	0.588	0.0428
6.	−0.1398	−0.3721	−0.564	−1.0759
7.	−0.248	1.918	0.618	2.288
8.	−0.529	1.223	0.354	1.048
9.	−0.3726	0.0468	−2.354	−2.6798
10.	1.1666	−1.228	−1.516	−1.5774
11.	1.1166	0.8537	0.3	2.2703
12.	1.9279	1.2636	0.7822	3.9737
13.	−0.6173	−1.6781	0.842	−1.4534
14.	1.0328	−0.7532	−1.529	−1.2494
15.	0.0097	0.4279	0.012	0.4496
16.	−1.1209	−0.0011	−0.742	−1.864

Source: Calculated by the Author.

References

Ahmad, E. (1979) Social Area Analysis of Metropolitan Hyderabad, *Technical Bulletin No. 3*, Hyderabad: Osmania University.

Burgess, E.W. (1925) "The Growth of City" in R.E. Park, E.W. Burgess and R. Mekenzie (eds.) *The City*, Chicago: University of Chicago Press, pp. 46-47.

Bell, W. (1955) "Economics, Family and Ethnic Status: An Empirical Test", *American Sociological Review*, 20, pp. 45-52.

D'Souza, V.S. (1968) *Social Structure of a Planned City Chandigarh*, New Delhi: Orient Longman Limited.

Gopi, K.N. (1976) Socio-Economic Structure of a Metropolitan Fringe and its Patterns of Interaction with the Central City; in Alam, S.M. and V.V. Pokshishvsky (eds.) *Urbanisation in Developing Countries*, Hyderabad: Osmania University, pp. 134-143.

Harris, C.D. and E.L. Ullman (1945) "The Nature of Cities", *Annals of the American Academy of Political and Social Sciences*, 242, pp. 7-17.

Hoyt, H. (1939) *The Structure and Growth of Residential Neighbourhoods in American Cities*, Washington D.C. Printing Press.

Johnson, J.H. (1974) "Geographical Processes at the Edge of the City", in J.H. Johnson (ed.) *Suburban Growth. Geographical Processes at the Edge of the Western City*, New York: John Wiley & Sons, pp. 1-16.

Karan, P.P. (1957). The Pattern of Indian Towns: A Study in Urban Morphology. *Journal of American Institute of Planners*, Vol. 23, 70-75.

Knox, P. (1987) *Urban Social Geography: An Introduction*, Second Edition, New York: John Wiley & Sons Inc.

Murdie, R.A. (1969) *Factorial Ecology of Metropolitan Toronto: 1951-61*, Research Publication 116, Department of Geography, and University of Chicago.

Nangia, S. (1976) *Delhi Metropolitan Region: A Study in Settlement Geography*, New Delhi: K.B. Publications.

Rees, P. (1970) Concept of Social Space, in Berry, B. and Harton, F.E. (eds.), *Geographic Perspective on Urban Systems*, Prentice Hall, Englewood Cliffs, New Jersey.

Ramachandran, R., 1989, *Urbanization and Urban Systems in India*. Delhi: Oxford University Press.

Shevky, E. and Williams, M., 1949, *The Social Areas of Los Angeles*. Los Angeles: University of California Press.

Shevky, E. and W. Bell (1955) *Social Area Analysis: Theory Illustrative Application and Computational Procedure*, Stanford California: Stanford University Press.

Yadav, C.S. (ed.) (1987) *Contemporary City Ecology, Perspectives in Urban Geography*, Vol. 6, *Concept's International Series in Geography* No. 3, New Delhi: Concept Publishing Company.

13

Regional Pattern of Urbanisation in Bankura District, West Bengal, India

Madhumoy Pal and *Susmita Das*

1. Introduction

The term '*Urban*' refers to a spatial or areal unit having certain marked secondary and tertiary functions along with a municipality, corporation or cantonment or notified area committee etc. It concerns with the geography of towns, their situation, pattern layout, housing and hierarchical organization of population concentration and service centre. Besides, '*Urbanisation*' refers to increasing of urban population in an area which leads to physical growth of urban areas, be it horizontal or vertical. In other words, "the shift of population from village to city or town and the process of transformation of village into city or town are called urbanisation" (G. Trewartha). By definition the Census of India, 2011 treats those areas as urban which are either statutory town, i.e. all places with a municipality, corporation, cantonment board or notified town area committee etc. or census town which satisfies the following criteria—(a) A minimum population of 5000; (b) At least 75 per cent of the male main working population engaged in non-agricultural pursuits; and (c) A density of population of at least 400 per sq.km.

According to Census 2011, the state of West Bengal is one of highly urbanised states of India with 31.89 per cent of the total population residing in various urban areas. Besides, the district of Bankura is a less urbanised district of West Bengal, where the process of urbanisation begins in 19th century, but untill now, the district has not been able to achieve higher rate of urbanisation due to lack of industrialization and higher dependence on agriculture. According to 2011 Census, the district has only 8.3 per cent urban population and ranked last in the state. However, the two prominent features of urbanisation pattern in Bankura are: (1) The low level of urbanisation; and (2) The excessive concentration of the urban population in municipal areas. The present study has been made to analyse the regional pattern of urbanisation in Bankura district.

1.1 Objectives

Major objectives of this study are as under—

1. To identify the urban population of different towns.
2. To identify the share of urban population to the total population.
3. To analyse the class-wise and functional classification of different towns.
4. To identify the density of urban population.
5. To find out the overall pattern of urbanisation of the district.
6. To examine the urban structure of the present municipalities and census towns as well as their potentialities to growth.
7. To suggest some future direction on urban growth and development.

2. Database and Methodology

The present study is based upon Secondary data sources, which is collected from the following demographic data sources—1. Census of India (1951-2011), 2. Town Directory of West Bengal, 3. *District Census Handbooks* (DCH).

For the purpose of the study following methodology has been executed:

(i) Level of urbanisation, it expresses the percentage of urban population with respect to the total population for a particular time. Thus,

Level of Urbanisation =

$$(\text{Urban Population} \div \text{Total Population}) \times 100$$

(ii) Decadal growth of urban population, which indicates the degree of urbanisation with respect to time. Thus, for example,

Decadal growth of urban population (2001-2011) =

$$[\text{Urban Population (2011)} - \text{Urban Population (2001)}] \div \text{Urban Population (2001)} \times 100$$

(iii) Rate of Urbanisation, It indicates decadal change in percentage of urban population. Thus, Rate of Urbanisation (2001-2011) = (Per cent of Urban Population in 2011— Per cent of Urban Population in 2001) ÷ Per cent of Urban Population in 2001 × 100

(iv) Contribution of growth in urban population to total growth of population is an important measure for analyzing process of urbanisation also. Thus, contribution of Growth in Urban Population to total growth (2001-2011) = (Urban Population in 2011–Urban Population in 2001) ÷ (Total Population in 2011 – Total Population in 2001) × 100.

(v) Pattern of urbanisation to find the pattern of urbanisation composite score is used and for this the values of the indicators have been calculated for each town. The values of the towns have been given Weightage on the basis of the following formula:

$$Wji = \frac{VJi}{Vai}$$

Where Wji = Weightage on 'i'th indicator in the 'jth' own;
Vji = value of 'i'th indicator in 'jth' town; and
Vai = value of 'i' indicator in study area.

By summing the Weightage of all the indicators in a town composite score has derived to express the overall pattern of urbanisation of Bankura district.

3. The Study Area

Bankura district is one of the seven districts of Burdwan Division of West Bengal. The district may be described as the "connecting link between the plains of Bengal on the east and Chota Nagpur plateau on the west" (Census of India, 2011). The district of Bankura is also the important part of '*Junglemahal*' of West Bengal and included in the centre of area known as '*Rarh*' in Bengal. The district lies between 22°8′ N–23°38′ N latitudes and 86°36' E–87°46' E longitudes with the total area of 6882 sq.km. The Damodar River flows along the northern boundary of the district. Bankura is bounded by Burdwan district in the north, Purulia district in the west and Medinipur district in the south. The Survey of India (SoI) topsheets of 1:2,50,000 covering the district are 73I, 73J, 73M and 73N. Urbanisation in Bankura district has not been rapid. The district experienced a slower rate of urbanisation compared to all the other districts of West Bengal in the post-independence decades. The total urban population of Bankura district in 2011 was 2,99,773 which are distributed unevenly in different towns. The percentage of urban population to the total population has shown slow increasing trend from 7.17 per cent in 1951 to 8.36 per cent in 2011 at an average decadal rate of 27.43 per cent.

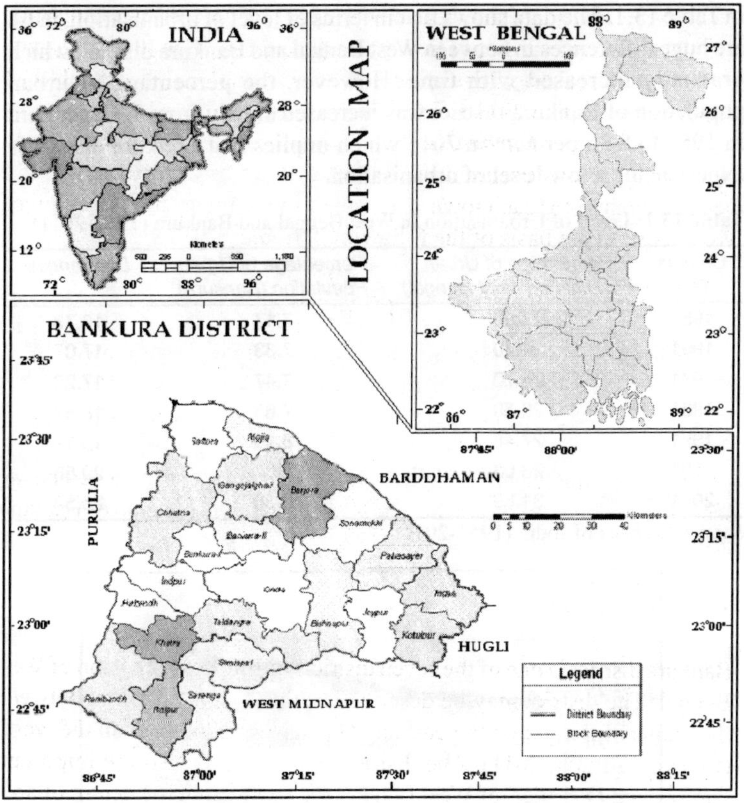

Fig. 13.1: Map of Bankura District

4. Results and Discussion

4.1 Level of Urbanisation (1951-2011)

Urbanisation in Bankura district has not been rapid. According to Census 2011, the district has an area of 6882 sq.km in which rural areas occupy largely 6791.53 sq.km and urban areas are only 90.47 sq.km. Besides, in Bankura district only 8.36 per cent of total population lives in urban area and share only 3.94 per cent of population in state's total population which is not at all encouraging. The level of urbanisation in Bankura district is very low, comprising 7.37 per cent in 2001 and 8.36 per cent in 2011 when the state level averages are 28.03 per cent in 2001 and 31.89 per cent in 2011 respectively. The comparative trends in Level of Urbanisation between West Bengal and Bankura district have been shown in Table 13.1. The data shows that in terms of level of urbanisation, there are huge differences in between West Bengal and Bankura district, which gradually increased with time. However, the percentage of urban population of Bankura district was increased slowly from 7.17 per cent in 1951 to 8.36 per cent in 2011 which implies that Bankura district is experiencing a low level of urbanisation.

Table 13.1: Level of Urbanisation in West Bengal and Bankura (1951-2011)

Census Year	*Percentage of Urban Population (West Bengal)*	*Percentage of Urban Population (Bankura)*	*Differences*
1951	23.90	7.17	16.73
1961	24.40	7.33	17.07
1971	24.70	7.47	17.23
1981	26.50	7.63	18.87
1991	27.48	8.29	19.19
2001	28.03	7.37	20.66
2011	31.89	8.36	23.53

Source: Census of India (1951-2011).

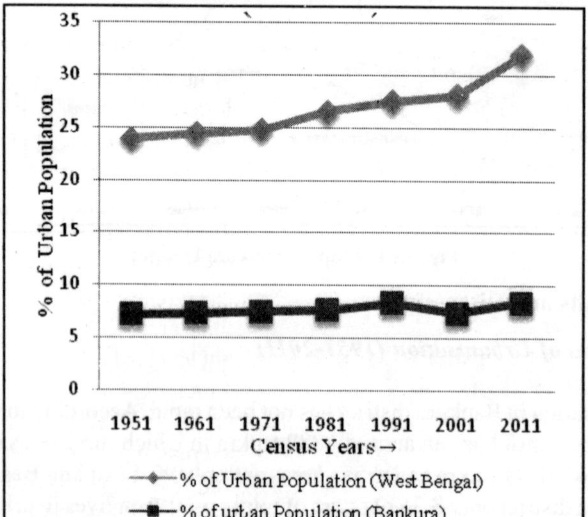

Fig. 13.2: Level of Urbanisation in West Bengal and Bankura (1951-2011)
Source: Census of India.

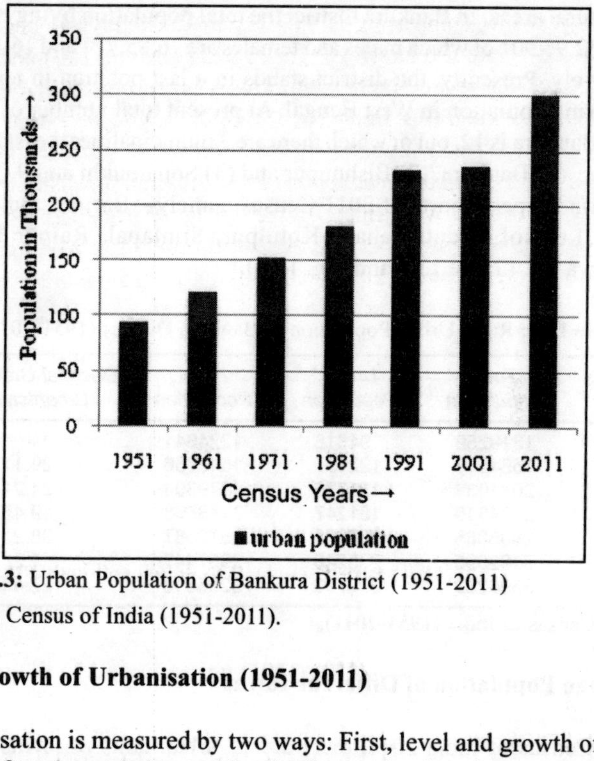

Fig. 13.3: Urban Population of Bankura District (1951-2011)
Source: Census of India (1951-2011).

4.2 Growth of Urbanisation (1951-2011)

Urbanisation is measured by two ways: First, level and growth of urban share of total population and its distribution by size classes of cities and towns. This is called demographic approach. Second, changes in number and growth of urban centres and an expansion of geographical boundaries of existing urban areas. This is called geographical approach. Growth of urbanisation depends on different social, economic, historical and political factors in different regions. So, the rate of urbanisation differs from region to region. This is universal. It has been already noted that Bankura district displays one of the lowest urbanisation rates compared to other districts in West Bengal. But, there are certain urban areas like Bankura and Bishnupur Municipality that record significant levels of urbanisation. The proportion of urban population to the total increased slowly from 7.17 per cent in 1951 to 8.36 per ce nt in 2011. In 1951 census, the total population of the district was 13,19,259 whereas the urban population was only 94,618 persons (7.17%). It is found that, there is a very slow positive increase in urban population of the district from 1951-2011. In 2011, the total urban population entered nearly to 3 lakh (2,99,773) persons. As per 2011 census, 91.64 per cent population of Bankura district lives in rural areas. In Bankura district the total population living in rural areas is 32,96,901 of which males and females are 16,85,777 and 16,11,124 respectively. Presently, the district stands in a last position in terms of total urban population in West Bengal. At present total number of urban units in Bankura is 12, out of which there are 3 municipalities, i.e. statutory towns *viz.* (1) Bankura, (2) Bishnupur and (3) Sonamukhi and 9 Census Towns *viz.* as per reports of 2011 Census namely—Barjora, Beliatore, Khatra, Ledisol, Jhanti Pahari, Kotulpur, Simlapal, Raipur Bazar, Ghutgarya etc. (Table 13.2 and Fig. 13.4).

Table 13.2: Rural Urban Population of Bankura District (1951-2011)

Census Year	Total Population	Urban Population	Rural Population	Decadal Growth of Urbanisation
1951	1319259	94618	1224641	–
1961	1664513	122157	1542356	29.11
1971	2031039	151735	1879304	24.21
1981	2374815	181247	2193568	19.45
1991	2805065	232478	2572587	28.27
2001	3192695	235248	2957447	1.2
2011	3596292	299773	3295613	27.43

Source: Census of India (1951-2011).

4.3 Urban Population of Different Towns

As per Census of India 2011, there are 12 urban units or towns in the district. Table 13.3 shows the town-wise trends of urbanisation in Bankura district from 1951-2011 and Figure 13.5 illustrates the present sharing condition of urban population among the different towns of Bankura district. The data reveals that the urbanisation processes are isolated throughout the district and spread in different municipality areas only. In fact, among the three municipalities, only Bankura municipality was able to achieve outstanding urban growth since the independence which is also the nodal town of Bankura district. Besides, it is also necessary to point out that there is a trend of continuous decrease in urban population growth of all the three municipalities. That means urban population slowly spreads into the newly build-up census towns of the district. This is the indication of spread of urbanisation.

According to Census of India 2011, there are only twelve urban units or towns in the district among which nine are census towns. Census towns are playing important role in Urbanisation of Bankura district. They are accounting 20 per cent of total urban population of the district. However,

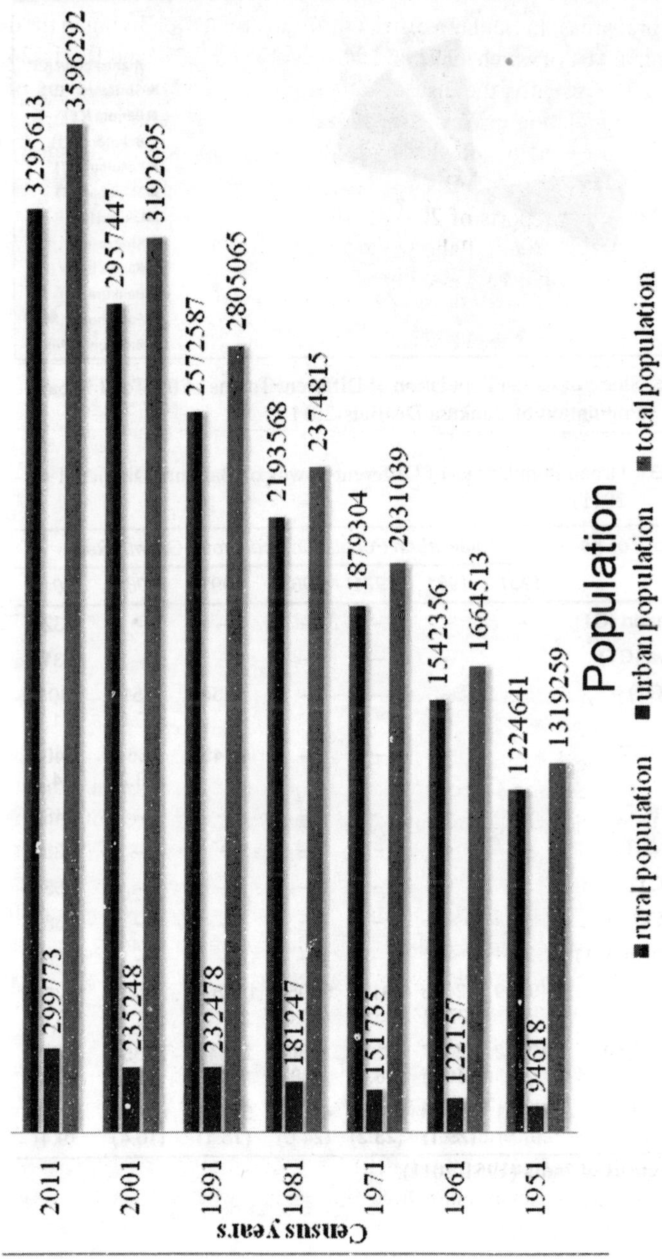

Fig. 13.4: Rural Urban Population of Bankura District (1951-2011)

Source: Census of India (1951-2011).

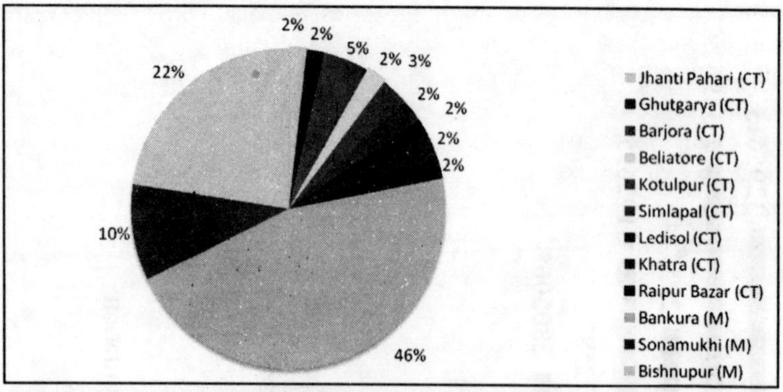

Fig. 13.5: Share of Urban Population of Different Towns of the Total Urban Population of Bankura Districts-2011

Table 13.3: Urban Populations of Different Towns of Bankura District (1951-2011)

Name of Towns	*Total Urban Population and Urban Growth Rate*						
	1951	*1961*	*1971*	*1981*	*1991*	*2001*	*2011*
Jhanti Pahari (CT)	–	–	–	–	–	–	5326
Ghutgarya (CT)	–	–	–	–	–	–	5311
Barjora (CT)	–	–	–	–	9554	11512 (20.5)	14012 (21.7)
Beliatore (CT)	–	–	–	–	4745	5654 (19.2)	6463 (14.3)
Kotulpur (CT)	–	–	–	–	–	–	8483
Simlapal (CT)	–	–	–	–	–	–	7206
Ledisol (CT)	–	–	–	–	–	–	5056
Khatra (CT)	–	–	–	–	–	–	7382
Raipur Bazar (CT)	–	–	–	–	–	–	6280
Bankura (M)	49369	62833 (27.3)	79129 (25.9)	94954 (20.0)	114876 (21.0)	128781 (12.1)	137386 (6.7)
Sonamukhi (M)	12352	15027 (21.7)	18974 (26.3)	19890 (4.8)	24640 (23.9)	27354 (11.0)	29085 (6.3)
Bishnupur (M)	23981	30958 (29.1)	38135 (23.2)	47529 (24.6)	56128 (18.1)	61947 (10.4)	67783 (9.4)

Source: Census of India (1951-2011).

according to Census of India 2011, the highest number of urban population is to be found in Bankura municipality comprising 1,37,386 persons followed by Bishnupur and Sonamukhi accounting 67,783 and 29,085 persons respectively. These three municipalities covering almost 80 per cent of district total urban population. Remaining 20 per cent urban population of the district are found in nine census towns. Among the census towns, highest number of urban population is found in Barjora, accounting 14,012 persons and the lowest number of urban population is found in Ledisol census town accounting only 5,056 persons.

4.4 Class-wise Classification of Towns

For the analysis of class-wise classification of towns, Census of India identified six categories of towns on the basis of population size. Table 13.4 provides the distribution of all the urban centre of the district among the six classes and Table 13.5 providing the number of urban centre of such classes on time scale. By applying this classification it is found that in 1951, there were only two (Bankura and Bishnupur municipality) Class III level towns and only one (Sonamukhi) was ranked class IV level town. After that, in 3 successive censuses of 1961, 1971, and 1981, the number of urban units in Bankura district remains unchanged. In 1991 census, two census towns, namely Barjora and Beliatore were identified as census towns which fell into Class-IV and Class-V level town. After that in 2011 Census, seven additional census towns are added in urban profile of the district and they all fall into Class-V level town. Tables 13.4 and 13.5 shows the entire picture of class-wise classification of towns of Bankura district from 1951 to 2011. Table 13.6 shows the numbers of towns and percentage of urban population in different size categories from 1951 to 2011.

In 1951, there were only three urban centres in the district of Bankura and this figure was unchanged up to 1981. It is also noted that in this time period only one town *viz.* Bankura municipality was able to change its position from Class-III to Class-II. After that, in 1991 it entered into Class-I. At present Bishnupur municipality belongs to Class-II and Sonamukhi municipality belongs to Class-III respectively.

4.5 Density of Urban Population

One of the most important indices of population concentration is the density of population. It is defined as the number of persons per sq.km.

Table 13.4: Class-wise Classification of towns, Bankura District, 2011

Class	*Size of Population*	*Number of Urban Centre (2011)*	*Urban Population (Thousand)*	*% of Total Urban Population*	*Name of the urban Centre/town*
I	>1,00,000	1	137.39	45.83	Bankura municipality
II	50,000-99,999	1	67.78	22.61	Bishnupur municipality
III	20,000-49,999	1	29.08	09.70	Sonamukhi municipality
IV	10,000-19,999	1	14.01	04.67	Barjora (CT)
V	5,000-9,999	8	51.51	17.18	Beliatore (CT), Jhantipahari (CT), Ghutgarya (CT), Kotulpur (CT), Simlapal (CT), Ledisol (CT), Khatra (CT), Raipur Bazar (CT)
VI	<5,000	Nil	Nil	Nil	Nil

Source: Census of India, 2011.

Table 13.5: Class-wise change in positions of towns from 1951-2011

Sl. No.	*Name of the Town*	*Census Years*						
		1951	*1961*	*1971*	*1981*	*1991*	*2001*	*2011*
1.	Bankura Municipality	III	II	II	II	I	I	I
2.	Bishnupur Municipality	IV	IV	IV	IV	III	III	II
3.	Sonamukhi Municipality	III	III	III	III	II	II	II
4.	Barjora (CT)	–	–	–	–	–	–	V
5.	Beliatore (CT)	–	–	–	–	–	–	V
6.	Jhantipahari (CT)	–	–	–	–	V	IV	IV
7.	Ghutgarya (CT)	–	–	–	–	VI	V	V
8.	Kotulpur (CT)	–	–	–	–	–	–	V
9.	Simlapal (CT)	–	–	–	–	–	–	V
10.	Ledisol (CT)	–	–	–	–	–	–	V
11.	Khatra (CT)	–	–	–	–	–	–	V
12.	Raipur Bazar (CT)	–	–	–	–	–	–	V

Source: Compiled by the authors.

Table 13.6: Number of Towns and Percentage of Urban Population in Different Size Categories

Census Year	Number of Towns						Percentage of Urban Population					
	Class I	*Class II*	*Class III*	*Class IV*	*Class V*	*Class VI*	*Class I*	*Class II*	*Class III*	*Class IV*	*Class V*	*Class VI*
1951	–	–	2	1	–	–	–	–	85.59	14.41	–	–
1961	–	1	1	1	–	–	–	57.74	28.72	13.81	–	–
1971	–	1	1	1	–	–	–	58.08	28.00	13.92	–	–
1981	–	1	1	1	–	–	–	58.48	29.27	12.25	–	–
1991	1	1	1	–	1	1	54.72	26.73	11.74	–	5.48	2.68
2001	1	1	1	1	1	–	54.74	26.33	11.63	4.89	2.40	–
2011	1	1	1	1	8	–	45.83	22.61	9.70	4.67	17.19	–

Source: Calculated by the Authors.

of area. It is expressed as the number of population divided by the total area. The average density of urban population in Bankura district is increasing since 1951. In 1951, the average density was 1539 persons/ sq.km. and it was more than double to 3826 persons/sq.km. Table 13.7 and Fig. 13.6 shows the population density of different towns of Bankura district (2011). Except Bankura municipality all other towns have medium to low urban density. Bankura municipality has high density because it is the district headquarters and various financial, political, other economic activities are still centralized in the town. Besides in the census towns of this district, moderate and low densities are to be found.

Table 13.7: Population Densities of Different Towns in Bankura District, 2011

Category	*Persons/ sq.km*	*Name of the town*	*Population Density (Persons/sq.km)*
Very high	Above 7000	Bankura (M)	7208
High	5001-7000	—	—
Medium	3001-5000	Ledisol (CT)	3599
		Khatra (CT)	4568
		Beliatore (CT)	4252
		Bishnupur (M)	3078
Low	Below 3000	Kotulpur (CT)	1503
		Simlapal (CT)	1799
		Raipur Bazar (CT)	2591
		Barjora (CT)	1933
		Jhanti Pahari (CT)	1370
		Ghutgarya (CT)	1458
		Sonamukhi (M)	1616
Bankura District			**3826**

Source: Census of India, 2011 (Calculated by the Authors).

4.6 Regional Pattern of Urbanisation

An important feature of urbanisation in Bankura district is dualism—the low level of urbanisation and the excessive concentration of the urban population in municipal areas. An analysis of the distribution of urban population across size categories (Table 13.8) reveals that the process of urbanisation in Bankura District has found to be Municipalities oriented. This is manifested in a high percentage of urban population being concentrated in class I, which has gone up systematically over the decades

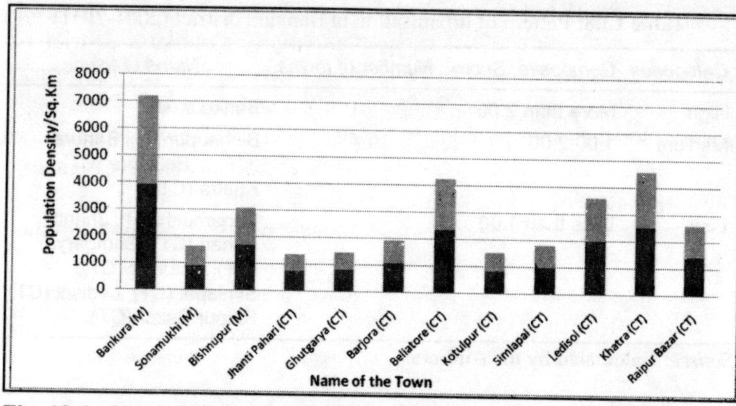

Fig. 13.6: Population Density of Different Towns in Bankura District, 2011

in the last century. A closer look on percentage of urban population by size class would show that the percentage share of urban population in Class-I continued to dominate the scene. In 2011, the share of urban population in Class-I cities is very high (45.83%) whereas the percentage share of urban population in Classes-II, III, IV, V cities are in decreasing trend except Class-VI towns. However, by summing the weightage of all the indicators in a town composite score has derived to express the overall picture of urbanisation. The variables used to construct the index of urbanisation are the level (% Urban), the degree of urbanisation (% share in country's urban population), decadal growth rate of urban population, density of urban population etc. The towns have been grouped into three categories on the basis of the composite score (Table 13.9) as following:

4.6.1 Areas having High Degree of Urbanisation

There is only one town namely, Bankura municipality fall in this category. It comprises 46 per cent of urban population of total urban population of the district. It has also a high density among all the towns within the district. The Bankura Municipality (District Headquarters) is most urbanised area of the district which is situated in the central part of the study area. All the major activities, such as economical, political, educational etc. are concentrated in this area. Besides, the town also well connected by rail and road network.

4.6.2 Areas having Moderate Degree of Urbanisation

There are four patches of moderate urbanisation which comprise 30 per

Table 13.8: Pattern of urbanisation in Bankura district (2001-2011)

Categories	*Composite Score*	*Number of towns*	*Name of towns*
High	More than 2.00	1	Bankura (M)
Medium	1.00-2.00	4	Bishnupur (M), Barjora (CT), Beliatore (CT), Khatra (CT).
Low	Less than 1.00	7	Sonamukhi (M), Jhanti Pahari (CT), Ghutgarya (CT), Kotulpur (CT), Simlapal (CT), Ledisol (CT), Raipur Bazar (CT).

Source: Calculated by the Authors.

Table 13.9: Composite Index of Weightage Indicators (2001)

Sl. No.	*Name of the Town*	*A*	*B*	*C*	*D*	*TOTAL*
1.	Bankura (M)	0.46	0.46	0.24	1.88	3.04
2.	Sonamukhi (M)	0.09	0.09	0.23	0.42	0.83
3.	Bishnupur (M)	0.23	0.23	0.34	0.80	1.60
4.	Jhanti Pahari (CT)	0.02	0.02	–	0.36	0.40
5.	Ghutgarya (CT)	0.02	0.02	–	0.38	0.42
6.	Barjora (CT)	0.05	0.05	0.79	0.50	1.39
7.	Beliatore (CT)	0.02	0.02	0.52	1.11	1.67
8.	Kotulpur (CT)	0.03	0.03	–	0.39	0.45
9.	Simlapal (CT)	0.02	0.02	–	0.47	0.51
10.	Ledisol (CT)	0.02	0.02	–	0.94	0.98
11.	Khatra (CT)	0.02	0.02	–	1.19	1.23
12.	Raipur Bazar (CT)	0.02	0.02	–	0.64	0.68

Note: A = Urban Population (in thousands), B = Percentage of urban population, C= Decadal urban growth, D= Density of urban population.

Source: Calculated by the Authors.

cent of urban population of the district. The first patch comprising the Bishnupur municipality situated in the north-east part of the study area. It consist 22 per cent of total urban population of the district. The second patch consisting Barjora census town, which is situated in northern part of the study area. It consisting 4.67 per cent of urban population of the district. The third one is Khatra Census town which is situated in south of the study area and consists 2.46 per cent of urban population. The last one is Beliatore which is situated nearby to Barjora CT and comprising 2.15 per cent of urban population of the district.

4.6.3 Areas having Low Degree of Urbanisation

There are 25 per cent of towns which fall into this category. Seven newly formed Census towns in 2011 census fall mainly into this category. These towns are—Jhanti Pahari (CT), Ghutgarya (CT), Kotulpur (CT), Simlapal (CT), Ledisol (CT), and Raipur Bazar (CT). Besides, Sonamukhi Municipality also falls into this category.

5. Conclusion

Bankura District experienced a slower rate of urbanisation compared to all other districts in West Bengal in the post-independence decades. The gap between urbanisation level of Bankura and West Bengal increased sharply from 16.73 percentages in 1951 to 23.53 percentages in 2011. The district of Bankura has a low level of urbanisation due to mainly agriculture based economy. The study shows that the areas with a high level of urbanisation have relatively high level of socio-economic development, nearness to the major transportation routes, rapid industrial development and in-migration of workers from the surrounding areas and recorded a high growth in their urban population. Contrary to this, the areas with a low level degree of urbanisation have low level of socio-economic development, peripheral location, low level of industrial development, and experiencing continuous outmigration recorded a slow growth in their urban population. In fact, the areas of moderate growth in urban population can be identified as areas of transition from low to high level of urbanisation and played an important role in diffusion of ideas and cultural values from urban to rural areas and *vice versa*. However, these urban areas or towns of the district are the important centre of education, administration, trade and commerce as well as the service centre and market of their hinterland. All these towns are unplanned and suffering for haphazard growth where primary activities are still dominating. Migration of rural people to these areas triggering them to migrate these areas for better employment, educational opportunities, communication and infrastructure leads to create several urban problems like—housing problems, sanitation problems, traffics jam due to overcrowding, waste and sewage disposal, lack of drinking water supply, narrowness of road due to hookers' problems etc. Besides, these towns have the potentialities to grow and serve as cultural town, tourist town, market town, industrial town in near future.

Acknowledgement

The Authors expresses special thanks to Dr. Subrata Pan, Assistant Professor and Head, Department of Geography, Bankura Christian College for supporting help and providing guidelines during writing this paper.

References

Bikramjit Saha (2012), Regional Pattern of Urbanisation in Koochbehar District, West Bengal. *International Journal of Social Science Tomorrow*. Vol. I, No. 3. May, 2012.

Census of India, (1951-2011), Relevant Issues.

Md. Anisujjaman, (2015), Urbanisation and Human Development: A Study of West Bengal. *International Journal of Humanities and Social Science Invention*. Volume 4. Issue 7. July 2015, pp. 01-08.

Nasim Aktar and Chand Sultana, (2014) Trends and Pattern of Urbanisation in West Bengal. Pratidhwani the Echo. *A Peer-Reviewed Indexed International Journal of Humanities and Social Science*. Volume III, Issue II. October, 2014.

R.B. Bhagat, (2011), Emerging Pattern of Urbanisation in India. *Economic & Political Weekly*. Vol. XIVI. No. 34. August 20, 2011.

R.B. Mondal, (2000), *Urban Geography: A Textbook*. Concept Publishing Company, New Delhi, 2000.

Ramachandran, R. (2007), Urbanisation and Urban System in India, Oxford University Press, New Delhi.

Saurav Chakraborty, Soumendu Chatterjee, Kakoli Das, Utpal Roy, (2015), Changing Pattern of Urbanisation in West Bengal: An Analysis of 2011 Census of India Data. *Asian Journal of Research in Social Sciences and Humanities*, Vol. 5, No. 5, May 2015, pp. 169-181.

Siddhartha, K. and Mukherjee, S. (2009), *Cities Urbanisation and Urban Systems*. Kisalaya Publications Pvt. Limited, N. Delhi.

14

The Impact of Industrial Growth on Environment Quality of Haldia, West Bengal

Mahua Chatterjee

Introduction

Haldia, an important industrial town of West Bengal is the "Gateway of South-east Asia". Prior to the industrialization, the area was called *Dordubnan*, merely a village inhabited by fishermen and salt producers. With the commencement of Haldia port, the landscape of Haldia began to a rapid change. Between 1981 and 2001, Haldia radically transformed from an agricultural village to an industrial town. The newly developed port, oil refinery, petro-chemical and other industries attracted more and more people in Haldia in search of job in different industries and factories which opened a new vista in the field of employment. The number of employees had increased more than four times in a decade (1971-1981). Petrochemical and downstream industries employed nearly 70 per cent of working population and who helped to usher a boom in industrialization. But the rapid industrialization in its earlier phase did not take much care of the environment and thus invited a rapid rise in pollution which ultimately compelled the Government and industrialists to take actions for maintaining environment quality and also to customize and regulate the rate of pollution. Initially, policies focusing on the regulatory measures which basically aimed at reducing the emission came into effect. Industries preferably big industries have already introduced new technology and industrial processes to reduce pollution and other adverse environmental impacts. But in Haldia, there are so many small factories, the owners of which still have not installed pollution control measures due to the constraint of capital. Environmental Impact Assessment (EIA) survey had been carried out by the Pollution Control Board at regular intervals to protect, conserve and manage the environment in a sustainable manner. This study puts focus on some measures to protect the environment from increasing air and water pollution caused by burgeoning industrial development in Haldia.

Objectives

Considering the environmental condition, there are many aspects seem to include but this study is limited to focus on two factors—air and water for discussion. Therefore, the chapter has the following four objectives:

1. To show the industrial growth in Haldia during last three decades.
2. To identify the causes of industrial pollution in the town.
3. To study the impact of industrialization on air and water quality of the area.
4. To state some measures in order to minimize the pollution effect of industries.

Data Base and Methodology

The present study is based on secondary data. The data are mainly taken from Central and State Government documents, such as the type and number of industries from Annual Report of Haldia Development Authority and from the Department of Commerce and Industries, Government of West Bengal. The information regarding the pollution used here is collected from the reports of Central Pollution Control Board. The nature of data in most cases annual time series for all the key factors of analysis. The study combines both descriptive and empirical method.

Study Area

Haldia (22°03″-43°93′N, 88°07′-53°15′E) is situated at the confluence of Hooghly and Haldi rivers near the Bay of Bengal, about 56 nautical miles downstream of Calcutta in the *Purba* (East) Midnapur (Medinipur) district of West Bengal. It has access to railways, roadways (NH-41, SH-6) and even waterways that lead across the country. Haldia Municipality is divided into 26 wards with a population of 2,00,762 persons and area of about 109.6 sq. km. as per 2011 Census. The industrial growth in Haldia is very much dependent on port. Presently, there are about 388 industrial units with an estimated investment of about Rs. 108 billion where 45,000 people are directly employed and nearly double are indirectly employed (*see* Fig. 14.1).

Industrial Growth in Haldia

Haldia port acts as the triggering factor for setting-up of industries at Haldia. Central Government took initiative to open an oil refinery near the port. This is the eleventh refinery of India and fourth for Indian Oil Corporation (IOC). The production was started commercially from 1975. Crude Oil from Iraq is received at the port and then transmitted through pipeline to the refinery storage tank from where it is refined. IOC manufactured some of the bi-products of petroleum such as Liquefied Petroleum Gas (LPG), Motor gasoline, Naptha, High Speed Diesel (HSD), Aviation Turbine Fuel (ATF), Jute Batching Oil (JBO), Kerosene, Bitumen etc. at their different plants in Haldia which were developed from 1982 onwards. Refinery supplies the raw-materials for other plants too. Swal Corporation is one of such factory which came up in 1979. Tata Chemicals Ltd. set-up their plant in 1979 and started the production within two years. They produce Industrial phosphate and Acids which again used as raw-materials for other industries. During the period from January 1998 to December 2001, a total 492 number of Petrochemicals Downstream Industries have been set-up in Haldia. Plastic and Polymer has observed an attractive rate of growth among downstream industries and State Government provides constant support. Industrialization in Haldia gets speeded up during the decades of 1990s and 2000. On one side several new projects came into being and on the other side the industries which are already been existed made expansion of the units. Indian Oil Corporation Ltd. (IOC), IOC Petronas Ltd., Manaksia Ltd., South Asian Petrochemicals Ltd. expanded their units, while Marcus Oils Chemicals Private Ltd., Sanjana Cryogenic Storages Ltd., RDB Rasayans, Adani Wilmar Ltd., Reliance Industries Ltd., Hindustan Unilever Ltd. opened-up new plants in Haldia. As one of the Mega projects, Haldia Petrochemicals Ltd. has started commercial production in 2000. The Project involved Rs. 5175 crore. Japanese Multinational Company, Mitsubishi Chemicals opened Purified Terephthalic Acid Plant (PTA) at the cost of Rs. 1600 crore in Haldia almost at the same year. These all are the assets of any industrial town (*see* Fig. 14.2).

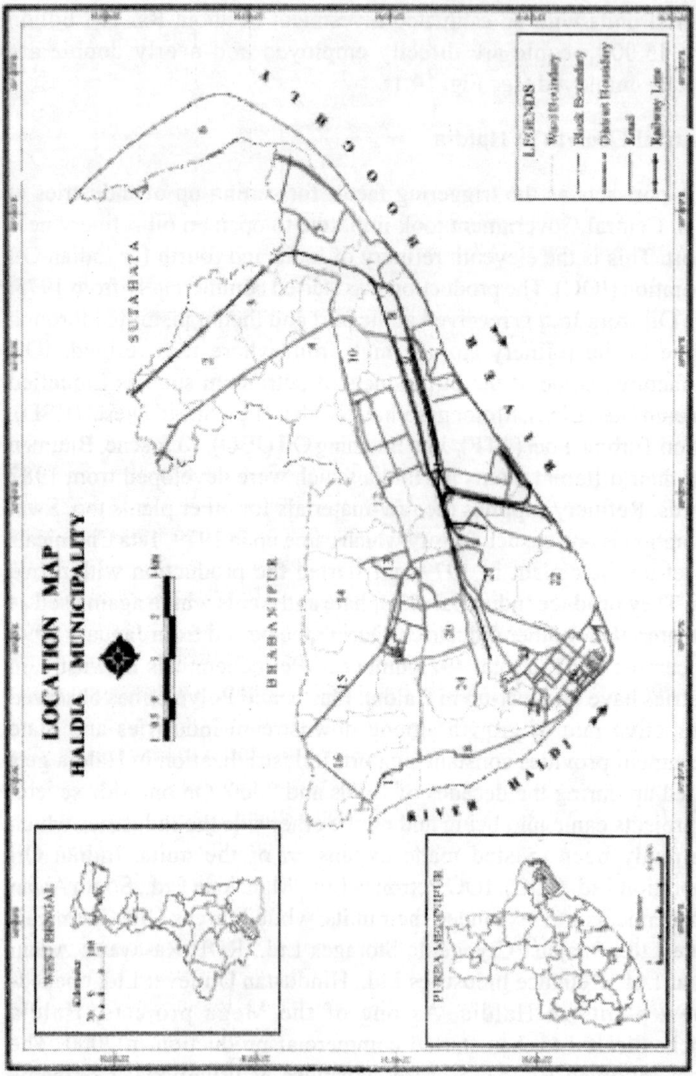

Fig. 14.1: Location Map of Haldia Municipality

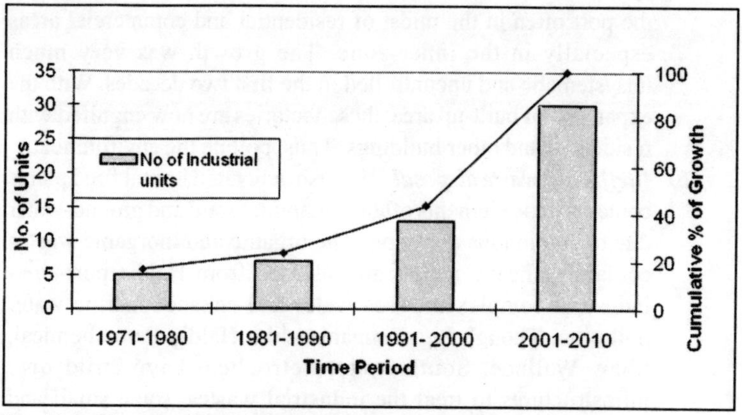

Fig. 14.2: Growth of Industries in Haldia Municipality, 1971-2010

Source: Haldia Municipality.

Industrial Pollution in Haldia

Industrial development is considered as an indicator measuring economic progress of an area by providing opportunities of employment and better quality of living. Such economic success is however not free from environmental consequences in terms of pollution and degradation. The establishment of industries in Haldia has no doubt brought about material wealth, but the industrialization of predominantly rural areas has led to degradation of environment due to industrial pollution. Atmospheric emissions have increased rapidly. Petrochemical smog, carbon mono-oxide, nitrous oxide, sulphur, lead etc. are some of the unwelcome by-products of rapid industrialization. At Haldia, effluents from the companies like Indian Oil, Haldia Petrochemical, Eureka Chemicals, Hindustan Fertilizers and smoke from marine vessels pollute the atmosphere.

In earlier periods of industrialization, since the number of factories was limited, the levels of pollution did not grow significantly. But when these factories increased both numerically and spatially, the issue of pollution started to gain importance. The Indian scientists have drawn-up an Index of Atmospheric Purity (IAP) using lichens growing on tree trunks and rocks to classify levels of pollution in various places of Haldia. They found that the lichens are disappearing within the core zone of highly industrialized Haldia Township due to increasing air pollution. The causes as identified responsible for environmental pollution in Haldia are listed as follows:

- *(a)* ***Unplanned industrial growth***—Haldia's industrial development is absolutely port centred. All the factories had been located near the port often in the midst of residential and commercial areas especially in the inner zone. The growth was very much unsystematic and uncontrolled in the first two decades. With the expansion of built-up area, these factories are now engulfed with residential and other buildings. Thus, pollute the environment.

(b) ***Inefficient waste disposal***—Fly ash generated in coal fired plants contains toxic elements often contaminate soil and ground-water due to continuous dumping. The organic and inorganic wastes containing heavy metals are released from Haldia port-*cum*-industrial complex into sea water and enhance marine water pollution. Though big companies like Haldia Petrochemical, Shaw Wallace, South Asian Petrochem have build own infrastructures to treat the industrial wastes, some small and medium scale industries still do not possess such system.

(c) ***Lack of monitoring to control pollution***—Poor enforcement drive allowed many industries to bypass laws made by Pollution Control Board which resulted large scale pollution. The Comprehensive Environmental Pollution Index (CEPI) score used by Central Pollution Control Board (2009) is a measure of pollution of industrial areas after taking into account the source, magnitude and scale of pollution; the number of people affected and pollution control measures in place. A high score indicated high levels of pollution and environmental degradation. Of the three sites in Bengal, Haldia was found to be the most polluting with a CEPI score of 75.43. Howrah came next (74.84), followed by Asansol (70.20).

Impact of Industrialization on Air Quality

Air quality in the natural environment is manifested in terms of identified parameters such as sulphur di-oxide (SO_2), Nitrogen di-oxide (NO_2), carbon mono-oxide (CO), lead, heavy metals, respiratory particulate matter (RPM) etc. Any change of these parameters over the time is the effect of air pollution. The main sources of air pollution in Haldia industrial region are—(a) stationary sources (mainly industries), (b) mobile sources (transport such as motor vehicles and marine vessels), and (c) area sources (e.g. waste burning and dust). Air Pollution is noticeably common in areas where industries are located within or adjacent to the settlement. Table 14.2 shows the ambient air quality of Haldia municipality area for 2001-2008. It is monitored through two manual stations at WBIIDC building and Durgachak Super Market (*see* Figs. 14.3 and 14.4).

Table 14.2: Ambient Air Quality of Haldia Industrial Region

Sl. No.	Location	SPM/ SO_2	2001	2002	2003	2004	2005	2006	2007	2008
1	WBIIDC Building	SPM	97	135	101	135	202	222	128	127
		SO_2	13	7	5	7	8	10	10	9
2	Durgachak Super Market	SPM	154	118	139	155	190	198	121	122
		SO_2	18	9	7	7	7	8	9	9

Source: West Bengal Pollution Control Board, 2009.

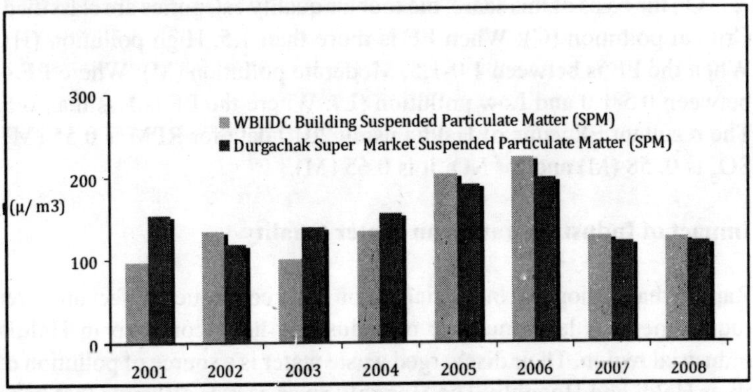

Fig. 14.3: Trend of SPM Concentration in Haldia Industrial Region
Source: West Bengal Pollution Control Board, 2009.

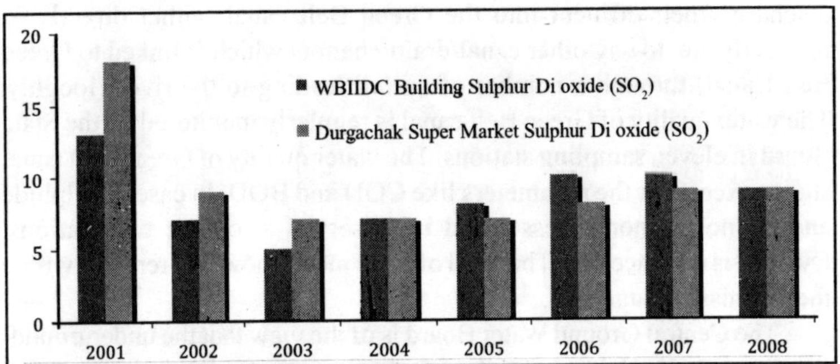

Fig. 14.4: Trend of Sulphur di-Oxide Concentration in Haldia Industrial Region
Source: West Bengal Pollution Control Board, 2009.

With a view to ascertain the ambient air quality at various locations of Haldia, a monitoring network has been established. The air pollutants SO_2, NO_2 and RPM are regularly monitored through four manual stations using Respirable Dust Samplers at Durgachak Supermarket, WBIIDC Building,

Bhabanipur and Bhunia Raichak. The monitoring results indicate that levels of sulphur di-oxide and nitrogen di-oxide are within the stipulated standards, whereas the level of RPM occasionally exceed, especially in winter months.

An Exceedence Factor (EF) can be calculated by the following ratio—

EF = (Observed Mean Annual Concentration of a Pollutant/Its Standard Annual Value)

On the basis of this score, the four air quality categories are classified. Critical pollution (C): When EF is more than 1.5, High pollution (H): When the EF is between 1.0-1.5, Moderate pollution (M): Where EF is between 0.5-1.0 and Low pollution (L): Where the EF is less than 0.5. The resultant EF value of Haldia using 2010 data for RPM is 0.55 (M), SO_2 is 0. 58 (M) and for NO_2 it is 0.65 (M).

Impact of Industrialization on Water Quality

Rapid urbanisation and industrialization has a consequent effect on water requirement. A large number of industries have come up in Haldia industrial region. Their discharged waste water is a source of pollution of river Haldi and Hooghly. The Hooghly river carries effluents that have contaminated fish and shell fish with heavy metals such as Nickel (Ni), Copper (Cu), Cadmium (Cd) and Zinc (Zn). All the industrial units discharge their effluent into the Green Belt canal (either directly or indirectly, i.e. to any other canal/drain/channel which is linked to Green Belt Canal) through a number of outfall leading to the river Hooghly. The water quality of Green Belt canal is regularly monitored by the State Board in eleven sampling stations. The water quality of Green Belt canal shows excess for the parameters like COD and BOD. In case of sulphide and phenol, minor excess could be observed at one or two stations. Cyanide is not traceable. The level of toxic metals however remains within the permissible standard.

The Central Ground Water Board is of the view that the underground-water situation in Haldia is fragile and advices against indiscriminate sinking of tube-wells for fresh water. The quality of ground-water utilized for drinking purpose and irrigation nearby is deteriorating in some wards. Salinity and iron make the taste of water and vegetable cooked in it unappealing and long term usage of this water with fluoride can lead several health hazards.

Some Measures to Minimize the Pollution Effect

Union Ministry of Environment and Forest in September, 2011 imposed a moratorium on development of new industries and extension of existing units in Haldia based on Comprehensive Environmental Pollution Index calculated by Central Pollution Control Board. However, considering the potential growth in Haldia region, the West Bengal Pollution Control Board has already taken necessary steps for appropriate environment management in that region. Some of the major initiatives of the State Board are listed below:

1. Operating an ambient air quality monitoring network of five (5) stations (including one continuous automatic ambient air monitoring station) within Haldia region.
2. Monitoring of surface water quality of Green Belt Canal, which receives major industrial discharges.
3. Monitoring of ground-water quality at three (3) locations.
4. Abstraction of ground-water has been restricted by the Central Ground Water Board through a notification in 2002, as sufficient water will be made available through Geonkhali project not only for the presently operating units, but also for the projected industrial development in the area.
5. Prepared an Area-wide Environmental Quality Management Plan for Haldia with the help of The Energy and Resources Institute (TERI), New Delhi in 2005.
6. Setting-up a Common Treatment, Storage and Disposal Facility for industrial hazardous wastes.
7. Encouraging the industries for setting-up of automatic ambient air quality monitoring stations.

Enterprises in Haldia were becoming increasingly active in dealing with pollution issues in collaboration with the related government departments, the state pollution control board, local authorities and industry bodies. The Central Government has lifted the moratorium two years later as the report submitted by state government shows marginal improvement.

Conclusion

It can be said without any doubt that under the existing industrial set-up and operating systems, a cent per cent pollution-free environment is almost a utopian dream. Acknowledging this fact, it is absolutely necessary to ensure that each of the industrial unit in Haldia does cause the least possible pollution. Industrial productions in Haldia are gradually moving into capital intensive designs with increasing adaptation of new processes and technologies. The large industries in Haldia took adequate steps to reduce waste disposal, small and medium industries (SMI), yet to take such measures towards the reduction of pollution at source. Mere Government legislation on the pollution control would not serve the purpose as all these anti-pollution laws and measures, become ineffective if proper monitoring system would not be developed. So, all-round initiatives and measures are solicited for eco-friendly industrialization in Haldia and ensuring the local people a better quality of environment.

References

Basu, J. (ed.) (1997): *The Industrial Scenario in West Bengal: Significant Progress*, but miles to go National Book Agency, Kolkata, pp. 160-217.

Bose, D.K. (1971): Planning for Development of Haldia, *Indian Journal of Regional Science*, 3(2), pp. 59-68.

Brahmachari, B. (1986): *Haldia r Itikatha*, Vols. 1 and 2.

Chakraborty, S. (2012): Bengal Government wants industry ban to be lifted from Haldia and Asansol, *Times of India*, November 18, 2012.

Chaudhury, M.R. (1971): *The Industrial Landscape of West Bengal*, Oxford and IBH Pub. Co., Calcutta.

Estall, R.C. and R.O. Buchanan (1973) *Industrial Activity and Economic Geography,* London, pp. 15-131.

Haldia Development Authority: *Annual Reports*, 2005, 2006, 2007, 2008, 2009, 2010.

Indian Institute of Port Management, Kolkata (2006): *Rapid EIA of Multipurpose Riverine Jetties at Haldia Dock Complex* published in August, pp. 206-209.

Kiely, R. (1998) *Industrialisation and Development: A Comparative Analysis*, UCL Press, London.

Mishra, A. (2007): *Silpayane Haldia, Apanjan Patrika*, Haldia, 21st July, 2007.

Sau, S. (2007): Development of Haldia Industrial Urban Complex, *Occasional Paper No.* VU/ECO/01/2007, pp. 3-21, Department of Economics and Rural Development, Vidyasagar University, Midnapore, West Bengal.

West Bengal Pollution Control Board (2011): *Comprehensive Environmental Pollution, Abatement Action Plans for the Industrial Clusters in West Bengal,* 2009, pp. 1-34.

Agriculture, Industry and Environment

15

Use of Chemical Equipments in Agriculture and Its Impacts on Environment

A Study of Bankura District, West Bengal, India

Sanjib Chakraborty

Introduction

In modern agriculture system chemical equipments play a major role in increasing the agricultural productivity and changing of agricultural land-use pattern. This chemical equipment includes chemical fertilizers, insecticides, herbicides, pesticides etc. Use of these chemical equipments started in India since 1960 and at present it becomes a essential factor of agricultural development.

The fertility status is very low in this district which resulted a huge amount use of chemical fertilizers for more crop production.

No doubt that chemical fertilizer boosted the crop production more than our imagination. Insecticides and pesticides decrease the rate of damaging crops due to the insects and pests, but at the same time these chemicals play a major role in vast changes of our environment. These chemicals are absorbed not only by the crops, but also mixed with the soil and percolating in the underground water. Through, the process of bio-accumulation these chemicals stored in each and every tropic level and through the process of bio-magnification, the stored chemicals are transforming from one tropic level to another.

In various parts of this district there was found fluoride in groundwater which is the result of overusing of phosphate. Beneficial micro-organisms are badly affected by these chemicals. Plants can not gain the micro-nutrients from chemical fertilizers; they take it from the soil in huge amount. Thus, it has created a deficiency of the micro-nutrients in the soils. Already there have a deficiency of zinc and boron in this district. By following organic farming we can use bio-fertilizers which could reduce the bad impacts of the chemical fertilizers by reducing the usage amount.

Objectives of the Study

The main objectives of the present study are enunciated hereunder:

1. To identify the causes responsible for overusing of chemical equipments in agricultural land.
2. To know the spatio-temporal pattern of the uses of chemical equipments in this study area.
3. To identify the changes of agricultural productivity due to the use of chemical equipments.
4. To examine the impacts of use of chemical equipments on agricultural production.
5. To examine the environmental changes due to the use of chemical equipments in agriculture.

Study Area

Bankura district is situated in eastern part of India. Its latitudinal extent is from 22° 38′N to 23° 38′N and longitudinal extent from 86° 36′E to 87° 46′E. This district holds a great strategic significance from socio-cultural aspect. It comprises 6,882 sq. km. area. On the north and north-east the district is bounded by Barddhaman district, from which it is separated by the Damodar river. On the south-east, it is bounded by Hooghly district, south by Paschim Medinipur district and on the west by Purulia district. Administratively the district is divided into three sub-divisions and twenty two blocks. The district is the homeland of 35,96,292 persons, out of which urban and rural population comprises 8.36 per cent and 91.64 per cent respectively. According to 2011 census population density of this district is 523 persons per sq. km.

The major part of this district is characterized by undulating topography. The average slope of land varies from 0.4 per cent to 10 per cent. The soil is mostly lateritic, light in texture and acidic in nature. The fertility status is also very low. The sol is light and porous in nature with low organic matter and low water holding capacity. However, eastern and southern part of this district is more productive than western part (*see* Fig. 15.1).

Methodology and Sources of Data

The present study is empirical in nature. It is based on both long time primary observation and on secondary data. District has been taken as unit of study. Office of the Deputy Director of Agriculture (Administration), Bankura, Department of Agricultural Chemist, Soil Testing Laboratory, Bankura, State Water Investigation Department, Bankura, West Bengal has provided the necessary data.

Simple statistical techniques are used for deriving the results and cartographic method are applied for mapping the derived results.

Factors Influencing the Use of Chemical Equipments in Bankura

Factors influencing the increasing rate of the use of chemical equipments in agricultural land are discussed with the following points:

Temporal Changes in the Land-Use Pattern of Bankura during 2010-2014

A vast change has been occurred between 2010 to 2014 about land-use pattern in Bankura. Culturable wasteland decreases totally 91.74 per cent and included under productive cultivated land. Gross cropped area increases to 84.12 per cent and all of the above tends to more use of chemical fertilizers to increase the fertility rate of the soil. The changes in the land-use pattern are shown in Table 15.1.

Low Availability of Nitrogen, Phosphorus and Potassium in Soil

Availability of nitrogen is low (<280 kg ha^{-1}) in 27.0 per cent area. Phosphorus for plant growth is low (<45kg ha^{-1}) in 74.4 per cent area while availability of potassium for plant growth was found to be low (below 200 kg ha^{-1}) in 61.2 per cent area of the district (Tables 15.2, 15.3 and 15.4).

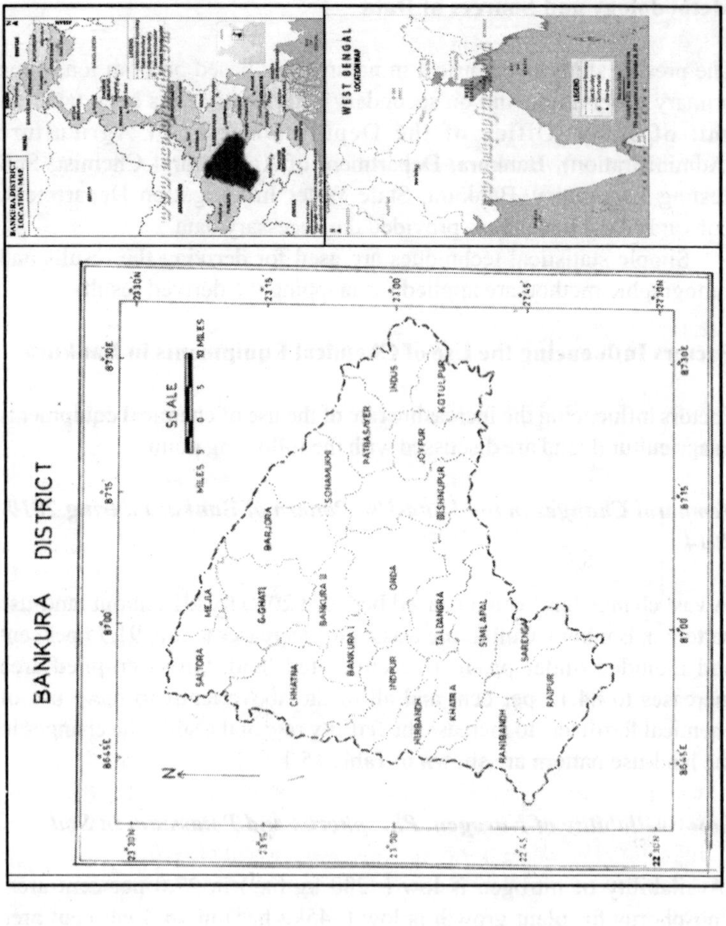

Fig. 15.1: Location Map of Bankura District

Table 15.1: Changes of Land-use Pattern in Bankura District (Area in hectare) during 2010-2014

Land-Use Pattern	*2010-2011*	*2013-2014*	*Volume of Changes (%)*
Geographical Area	688100	688100	—
Forest	148350	148350	—
Area under Non-Agricultural use	109621	109621	—
Barren and Un-culturable Land	3302	3302	—
Permanent Pasture	633	633	—
Area under Fruit Crops, Misc. Tree crops and others	284.49	5523.54	Nearly 20 times
Culturable Waste Land	2337	2337	—
Fallow other than Current Fallow	1386	1386	—
Culturable Waste Land	255679.40	21106.46	–91.74%
Net Area Cultivated	161507.11	396841.00	2.45 times
Area Cultivated More than Once	149985.00	177684.50	18.47%
Gross Cropped Area	**311492.11**	**573525.50**	**84.12%**

Source: Office of the Deputy Director of Agriculture (Administration), Bankura, West Bengal.

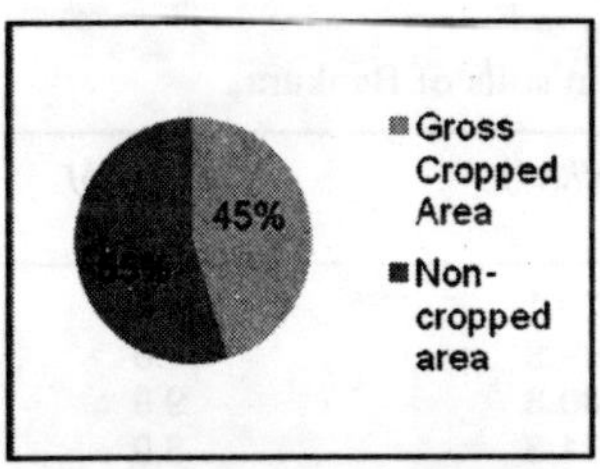

Fig. 15.2: Land-Use Pattern in Bankura District (Area in hectare) in 2010.

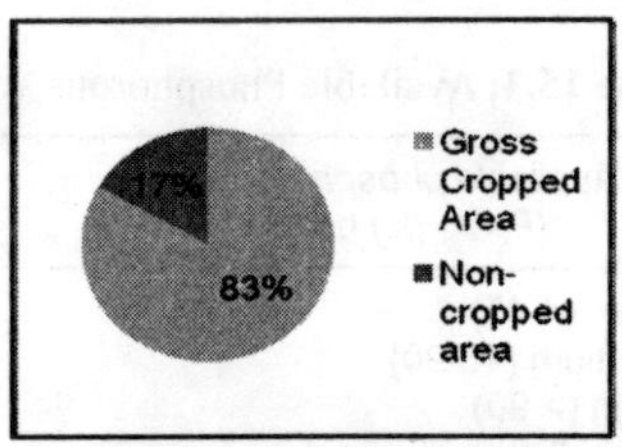

Fig. 15.3: Land-Use Pattern in Bankura District (Area in hectare) in 2014.

This deficiency also becomes a fact behind the increasing amount of using of chemical fertilizers by the farmers and day-by-day overusing of fertilizers become a common practice by the farmers of both low and high nitrogen, phosphorus and potassium available areas.

As a result of which overusing of nitrogen in the nitrogen sufficient areas causes the accumulation of nitrate in groundwater while overusing of super phosphate in the phosphorus sufficient areas causes the contamination of fluoride, cadmium in ground-water. Overusing of Muriates of potash in the potassium sufficient areas causes the contamination of chlorine in groundwater.

Table 15.2: Available Nitrogen status in soils of Bankura

Available Nitrogen(kg ha^{-1})	*Area (km^2)*	*Area (%)*
Low (< 280)	1673.4	24.3
Medium (280-450)	3082.1	44.8
High (> 450)	1855.2	27.0
Miscellaneous	271.3	3.9
Total	**6882.0**	**100.0**

Source: Department of Agricultural Chemist, Soil Testing Laboratory, Bankura, West Bengal.

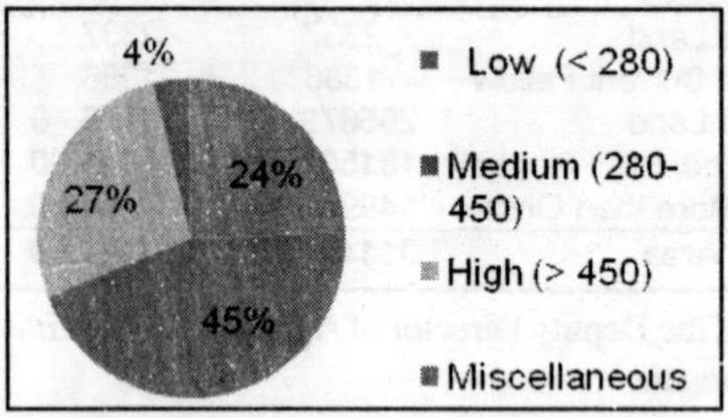

Fig. 15.4: Available Nitrogen (kg ha^{-1}) Status in Soils of Bankura (Area in %)

Table 15.3: Available Phosphorous status in soils of Bankura

Available phosphorous (P_2O_5) (kg ha^{-1})	*Area(km^2)*	*Area (%)*
Low (< 45)	5120.1	74.4
Medium (45-90)	809.8	11.8
High (> 90)	680.8	9.9
Miscellaneous	271.3	3.9
Total	**6882.0**	**100.0**

Source: Department of Agricultural Chemist, Soil Testing Laboratory, Bankura, West Bengal.

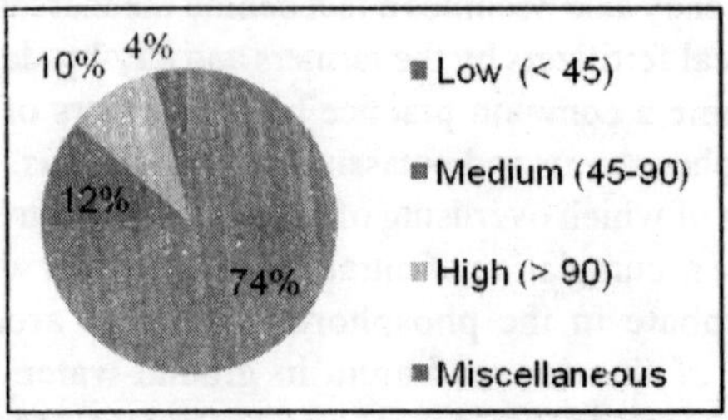

Fig. 15.5: Available Phosphorous (kg ha^{-1}) Status in Soils of Bankura (Area in %)

Table 15.4: Available Potassium status in soils of Bankura

Available potassium (K_2O)(kg ha^{-1})	*Area (km^2)*	*Area (%)*
Low (< 200)	4209.8	61.2
Medium (200-350)	1758.5	25.6
High (> 350)	642.4	9.3
Miscellaneous	271.3	3.9
Total	**6882.0**	**100.0**

Source: Department of Agricultural Chemist, Soil Testing Laboratory, Bankura, West Bengal.

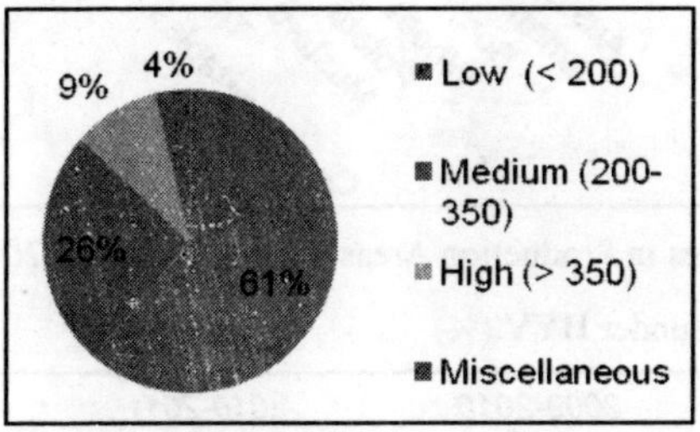

Fig. 15.6: Available Potassium (kg ha^{-1}) Status in Soils of Bankura (Area in %)

Temporal Changes of Production Areas

Area under production increases overall 87.30 per cent. Aman rice production area increases 182.59 per cent. Production area increases more than 40 per cent for Aus, boro, *Til* etc. crops (Table 15.5). As HYV seeds are used nearly in 100 per cent production area, it creates a greater demands of chemical equipments (Table 15.6). This makes a greater change in using of more chemical equipments (Table 15.5).

Table 15.5: Area under production (Hectares)

Crops	*2010-2011*	*2013-2014*	*Volume of Changes (%)*
Aus	20358.00	31252.00	53.51
Aman	123563.00	349184.00	182.59
Boro	30856.00	47624.00	54.34
Wheat	7830.00	3157.00	-59.68
Potato	47142.00	52924.00	12.26
Mustard	18380.00	17475.00	-4.92
Til	21706.00	30867.00	42.20
Vegetables	30128.00	29351.00	2.57
Total	**299963.00**	**561834.00**	**87.30**

Source: Office of the Deputy Director of Agriculture (Administration), Bankura, West Bengal.

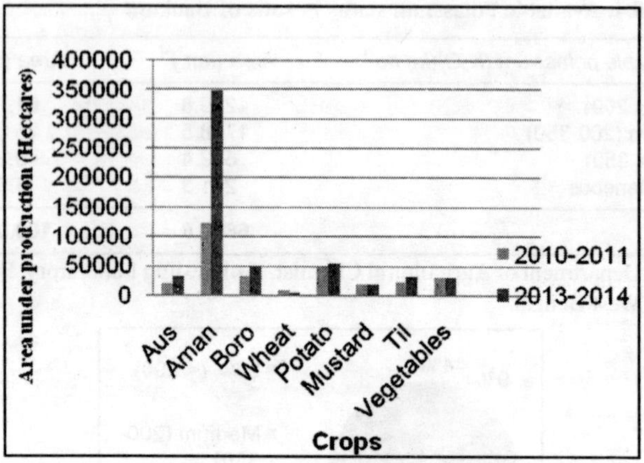

Fig. 15.7: Changes in Production Areas (Hectares) during 2010-14 in Bankura

Table 15.6: Area under HYV (%)

Crops	*2009-2010*	*2010-2011*	*2013-2014*
Aus	99.95	100	100
Aman	98.20	96.55	96.59
Boro	100	100	100

Source: Office of the Deputy Director of Agriculture (Administration), Bankura, West Bengal.

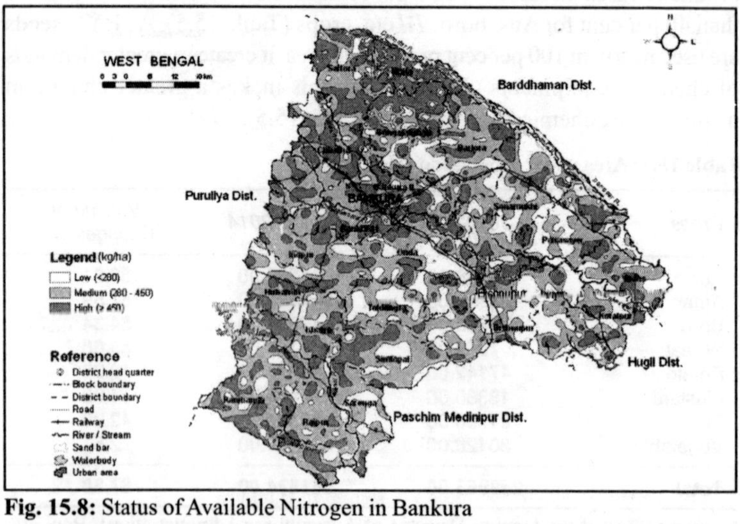

Fig. 15.8: Status of Available Nitrogen in Bankura

Source: Department of Agricultural Chemist, Soil Testing Laboratory, Bankura, West Bengal.

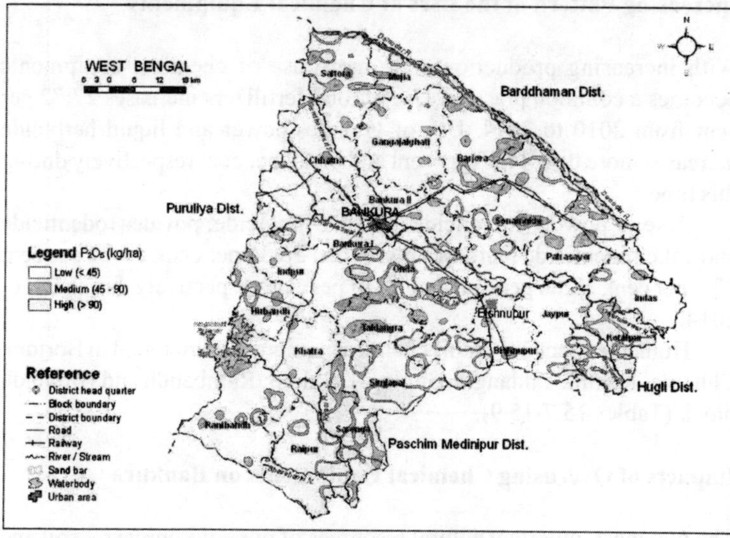

Fig. 15.9: Status of Available Phosphorous in Bankura

Source: Department of Agricultural Chemist, Soil Testing Laboratory, Bankura, West Bengal.

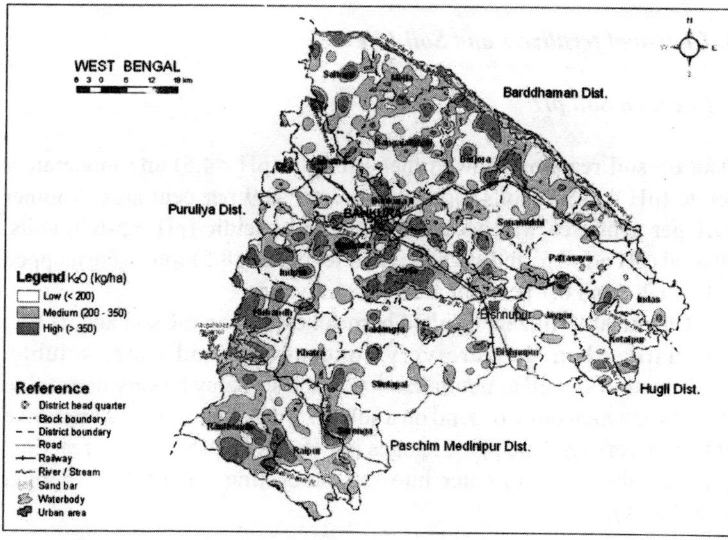

Fig. 15.10: Status of Available Potassium in Bankura

Source: Department of Agricultural Chemist, Soil Testing Laboratory, Bankura, West Bengal.

Increasing Pattern of the Uses of Chemical Equipments

With increasing production area, more use of chemical equipments becomes a common practice. Use of total fertilizers increases 27.72 per cent from 2010 to 2014. Use of granules/power and liquid herbicide increases more than 44.30 per cent and 85.22 per cent respectively during this time.

Use of powder insecticide, powder fungicide, powder rodenticide and cake rodenticide increases more than 56.34 per cent, 24.74 per cent 37.7 per cent, 12.06 per cent and 19.19 per cent respectively during 2010-2014.

Higher amount use of this chemical equipments are found in Borjora, Chhatna, Khatra, Taldangra, Simlapal, Raipur, Ranibandh and Hirbandh block (Tables 15.7-15.9).

Impacts of Overusing Chemical Equipments on Bankura

The two most important natural resources of our environment—soil and groundwater of Bankura are badly affected by overusing of these chemical equipments which are discussed below.

A. Chemical fertilizers and Soil Life

1. Effect on Soil pH

Data on soil reaction showed that strongly (pH <4.5) and moderately acidic (pH 4.5-5.5) soils together covered 73.9 per cent area. Another 19.1 per cent area was occupied by slightly acidic (pH 5.5-6.5) soils. Neutral (pH 6.5-7.5) and slightly alkaline (pH 7.5-8.5) soils were mapped only on 2.4 and 0.7 per cent area, respectively.

Chemical fertilizers resulted harmful effects on the soil and its life, especially when they are very concentrated and water soluble. Acidification as well as neutralization of the soil may be very harmful to microbes, which often depend on a sole enzyme. And enzymes are active only in a very specific pH. Changes in pH slow down enzyme reaction, and microbes have to enter into rest, encysting, or die from hunger (Fig. 15.14).

Table 15.7: Increasing Pattern in the Use of Chemical Fertilizers (in MT) and Herbicides in Different Blocks of Bankura District during 2010-2014

Sl. No.	Name of the Block	Chemical Fertilizers						Herbicides			
		Nitrogen (N)		Phosphorous (P)		Potash (K)		Granules/Powder (Kg.)		Liquid (Lit.)	
		2010-2011	2013-2014	2010-2011	2013-2014	2010-2011	2013-2014	2010-2011	2013-2014	2010-2011	2013-2014
1.	Bankura I	125.00	705.00	85.00	412.00	58.00	308.00	20	110	22	60
2.	Bankura II	240.00	856.00	150.00	466.00	98.00	395.00	85	180	42	80
3.	Chhatna	230.00	1152.00	155.00	718.00	138.00	612.00	52	160	30	90
4.	Saltora	168.00	896.00	95.00	505.00	83.00	426.00	30	120	18	65
5.	Mejhia	146.00	695.00	62.00	356.00	58.00	305.00	25	115	12	55
6.	Gangajal Ghati	285.00	1247.00	182.00	784.00	145.00	616.00	80	240	22	60
7.	Barjora	3124.50	2108.00	1120.30	1235.00	956.00	1057.00	510	1080	85	280
8.	Onda	1550.00	2804.00	820.00	1702.00	590.00	1328.00	700	1190	100	298
9.	Indpur	810	865.00	390	445.00	510	520.00	50	170	25	90
10.	Khatra	820	895.00	440	450.00	510	520.00	210	465	70	160
11.	Hirbandh	790	850.00	465	460.00	470	475.00	70	230	21	105
12.	Ranibandh	825	890.00	405	425.00	410	435.00	55	170	18	78
13.	Taldangra	1600	1675.00	725	780.00	735	760.00	430	860	290	755
14.	Simlapal	1625	1685.00	710	755.00	715	745.00	440	875	280	760
15.	Raipur	1410	1535.00	660	665.00	675	760.00	300	735	260	620
16.	Sarenga	1300	1430.00	610	690.00	615	705.00	280	750	210	630
17.	Bishnupur	2077.80	2577.55	1170.60	1469.60	1171.80	1469.76	3800	4690	900	1510
18.	Sonamukhi	2987.40	4437.88	1696.00	2464.09	1700.40	2457.51	6200	7280	1100	1615
19.	Patrasayer	2806.40	3880.97	1608.00	2150.21	1609.80	2145.95	2860	4580	880	1490
20.	Indus	2742.90	2207.18	1523.40	1256.55	1526.10	1255.31	3800	5175	930	1495
21.	Joypur	3347.40	3896.45	2009.00	2381.64	2009.30	2380.28	2000	3080	1020	1675
22.	Kotulpur	5728.70	6283.06	3581.20	3925.94	3587.30	3927.00	5200	6990	1100	1800
	Total	**34739.10**	**43571.09**	**18662.50**	**24496.03**	**18370.70**	**23602.81**	**27197**	**39245**	**7435**	**13771**

Source: Office of the Deputy Director of Agriculture (Administration), Bankura, West Bengal.

Table 15.8: Increasing pattern in the use of chemical fertilizers (in MT) in Bankura District during 2010-2014

Fertilizers	*2010-2011*	*2011-2012*	*2012-2013*	*2013-2014*
Nitrogen (N)	34739.10	43615.75	42531.91	43571.09
Phosphorous (P)	18662.50	24027.01	23707.17	24496.03
Potash (K)	18370.70	23493.25	22834.98	23602.81
Grand Total	**71772.30**	**91136.01**	**89074.06**	**911669.93**

Source: Office of the Deputy Director of Agriculture (Administration), Bankura, West Bengal.

Table 15.9: Increasing pattern in the use of Granular/Powder and Liquid Herbicides in Bankura District during 2010-2014

Herbicides	*2010-2011*	*2011-2012*	*2012-2013*	*2013-2014*
Granular/ Powder (in Kg.)	27197	31750	38177	39245
Liquid (in Lit)	7435	9404	12886	13771

Source: Office of the Deputy Director of Agriculture (Administration), Bankura, West Bengal.

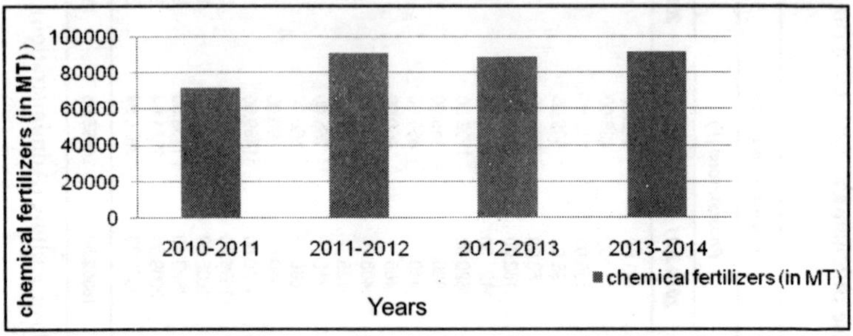

Fig. 15.11: Changes in the Use of Chemical Fertilizers (in MT) during 2010-2014 in Bankura

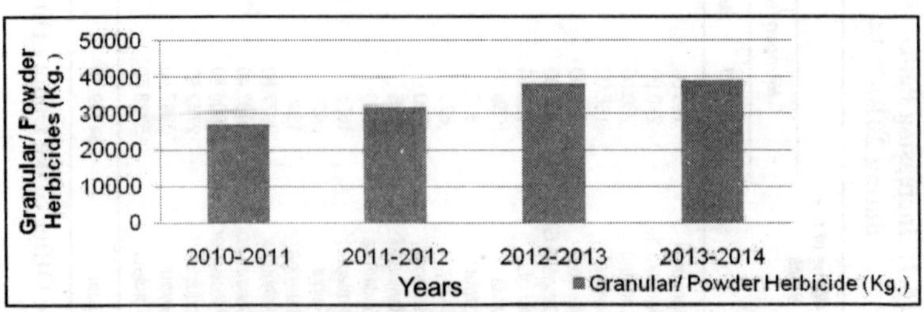

Fig. 15.12: Changes in the Use of Granular/Powder Herbicides (in Kg.) during 2010-2014 in Bankura

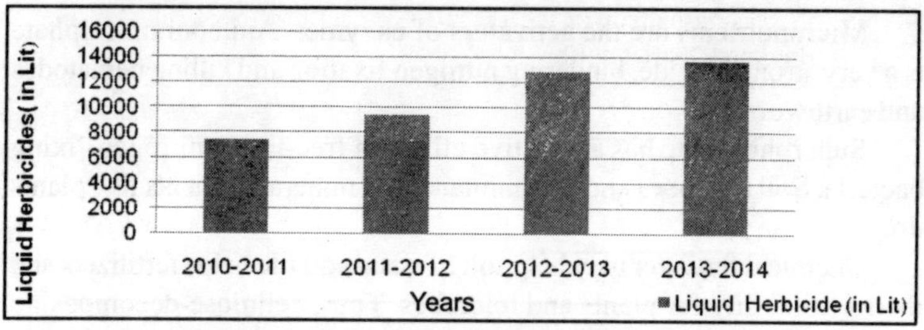

Fig. 15.13: Changes in the Use of Liquid Herbicides (in Lit.) during 2010-2014 in Bankura

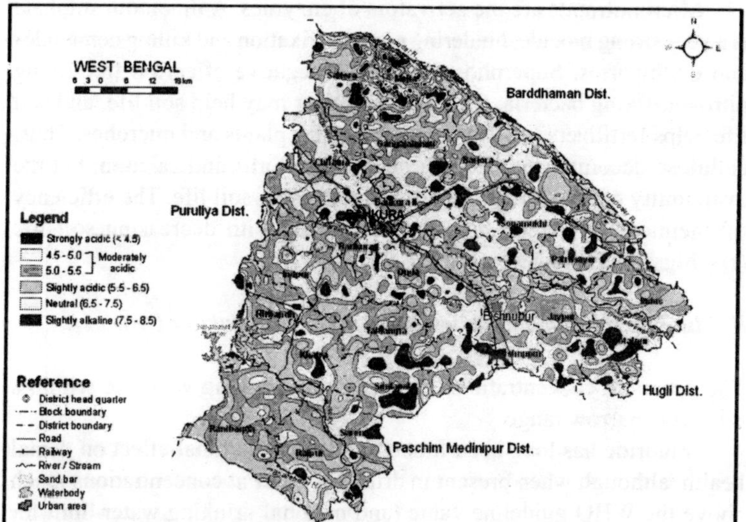

Fig. 15.14: Soil pH Status in Bankura

Source: Department of Agricultural Chemist, Soil Testing Laboratory, Bankura, West Bengal.

2. Effect on Soil Micronutrients

Results highlighted that soils of 31.0 per cent area of the district is with low (<0.50%) organic carbon, Results on the status of micro-nutrients signalled that deficiency of zinc occurred in 3.9 pe. cent area. Deficiency of boron (<0.36 mg kg^{-1}) was observed in 86.7 per cent area of the district, 2.8 per cent area in the district is found deficient (<0.05 mg kg^{-1}) in molybdenum nutrition content.

Micronutrients are the activators of enzymes. Ammonium sulphate is a very strong biocide, hindering nitrogen fixation and killing nematodes and earthworms.

Superphosphate has a negative effect on free-living nitrogen-fixing bacteria. Soil microbes and soil animals need mineral nutrients like plants do.

Chemical fertilizer may help soil life, and soil life helps fertilizers and their availability for plants and microbes. Thus, cellulose-decomposing bacteria need phosphorus and calcium, but the availability of zinc and phosphorus depends on soil life. The efficiency of chemical fertilizers, however, decreases with decreasing soil life.

Micronutrients are the activators of enzymes. Ammonium sulphate is a very strong biocide, hindering nitrogen fixation and killing nematodes and earthworms. Superphosphate has a negative effect on free-living nitrogen-fixing bacteria. Chemical fertilizer may help soil life, and soil life helps fertilizers and their availability for plants and microbes. Thus, cellulose-decomposing bacteria need phosphorus and calcium, but the availability of zinc and phosphorus depends on soil life. The efficiency of chemical fertilizers, however, decreases with decreasing soil life (*see* Figs. 15.15-15.19).

B. Fluoride Contamination in Groundwater in Bankura District

The optimum concentrations of fluoride in drinking water lie within a relatively narrow range.

Fluoride has long been found to have a beneficial effect on dental health, although when present in drinking water at concentrations much above the WHO guideline value (and national drinking water limit for most countries) of 1.5 mg/L, long term use can result in development of dental fluorosis or at its worst, crippling skeletal fluorosis.

High value of fluoride (>1.5 mg/L) found in various places of Borjora, Gangajalghati blocks where value between 1-1.5 mg/L found mainly in Saltora, Simlapal block and less than 1mg/L floride is observed in various places of Bankura I, Bankura II, Gangajalghati, Chatna, Taldangra, Simlapal, Indpur Block (*see* Tables 15.10 and 15.11).

Conclusion and Suggestions

The present study confirms that the application of chemical fertilizer has greater influence on soil and groundwater quality of this district.

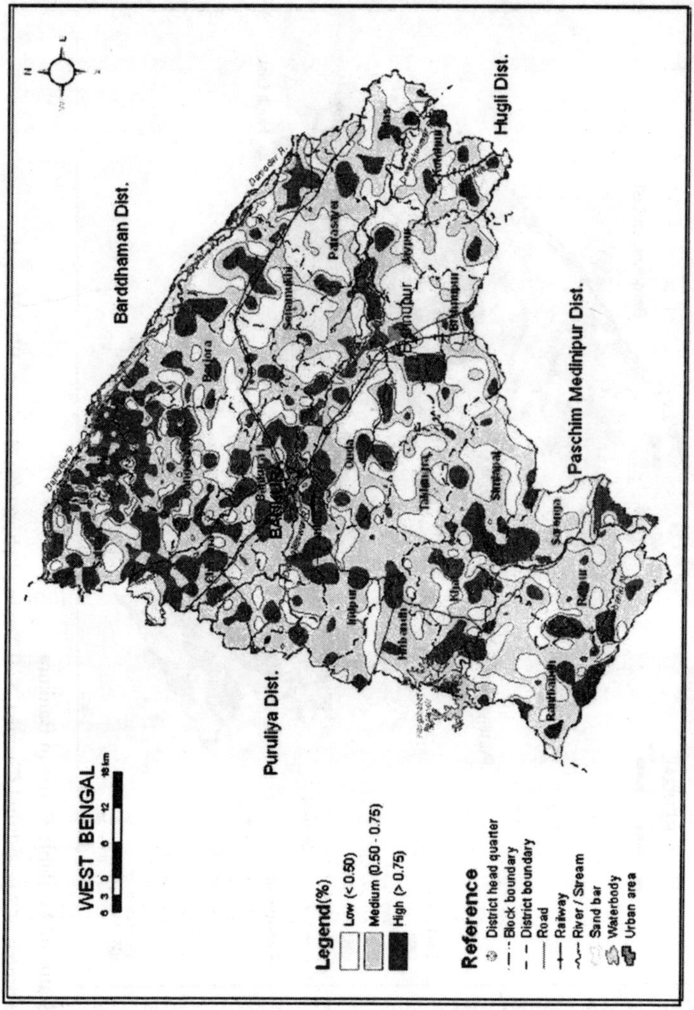

Fig. 15.15: Status of Available Organic Carbon in Bankura

Source: Department of Agricultural Chemist, Soil Testing Laboratory, Bankura, West Bengal.

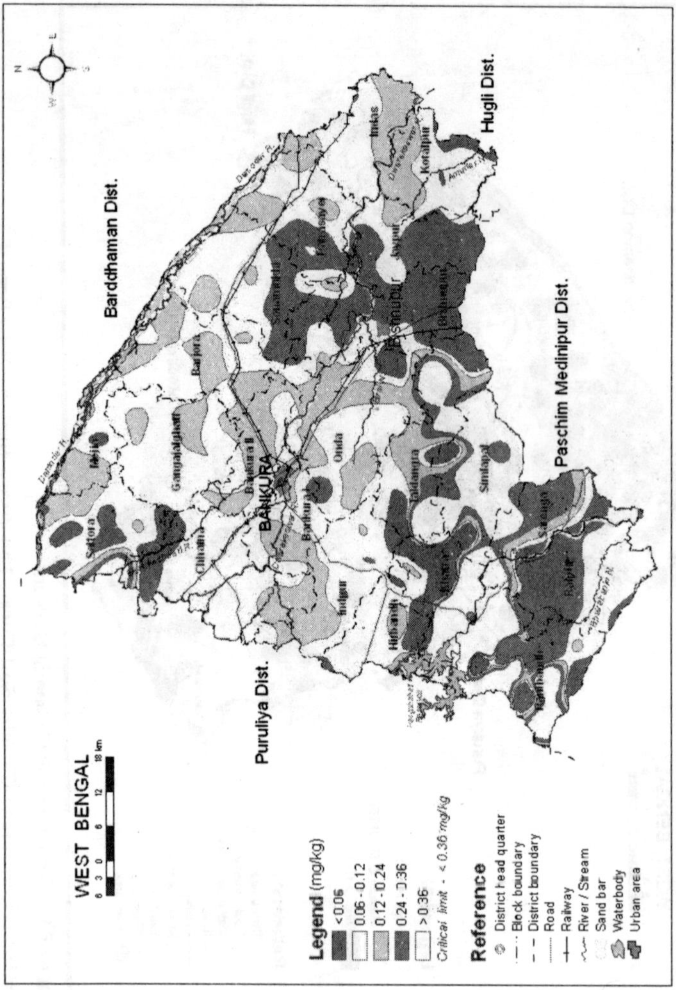

Fig. 15.16: Status of Available Boron in Bankura

Source: Department of Agricultural Chemist, Soil Testing Laboratory, Bankura, West Bengal.

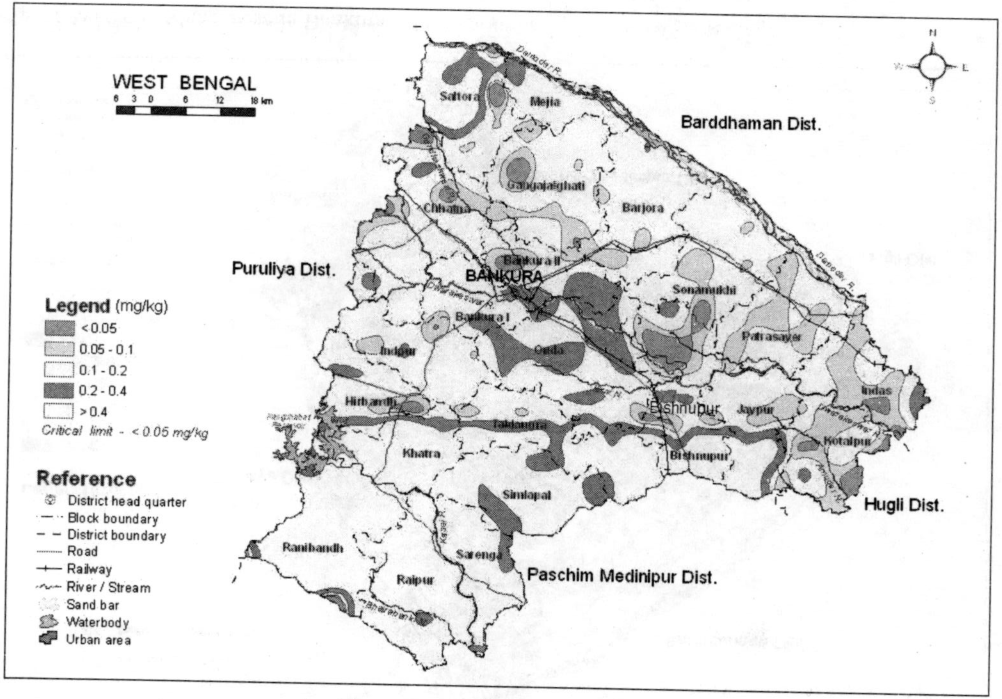

Fig. 15.17: Status of Available Molybdenum in Bankura

Source: Department of Agricultural Chemist, Soil Testing Laboratory, Bankura, West Bengal.

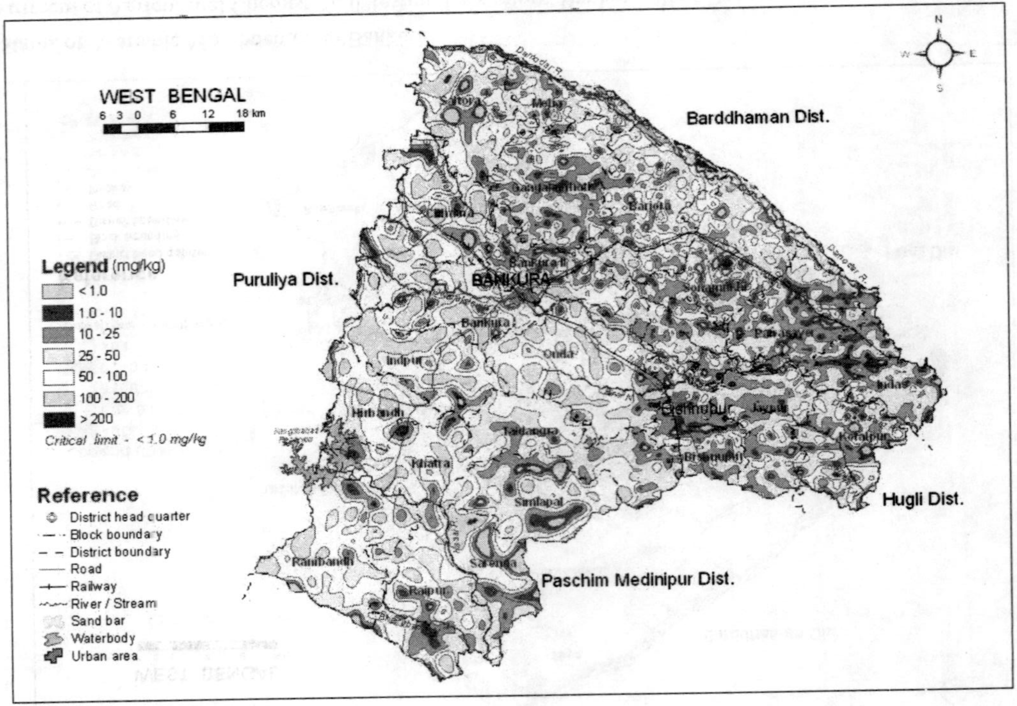

Fig. 15.18: Status of Available Manganese in Bankura

Source: Department of Agricultural Chemist, Soil Testing Laboratory, Bankura, West Bengal.

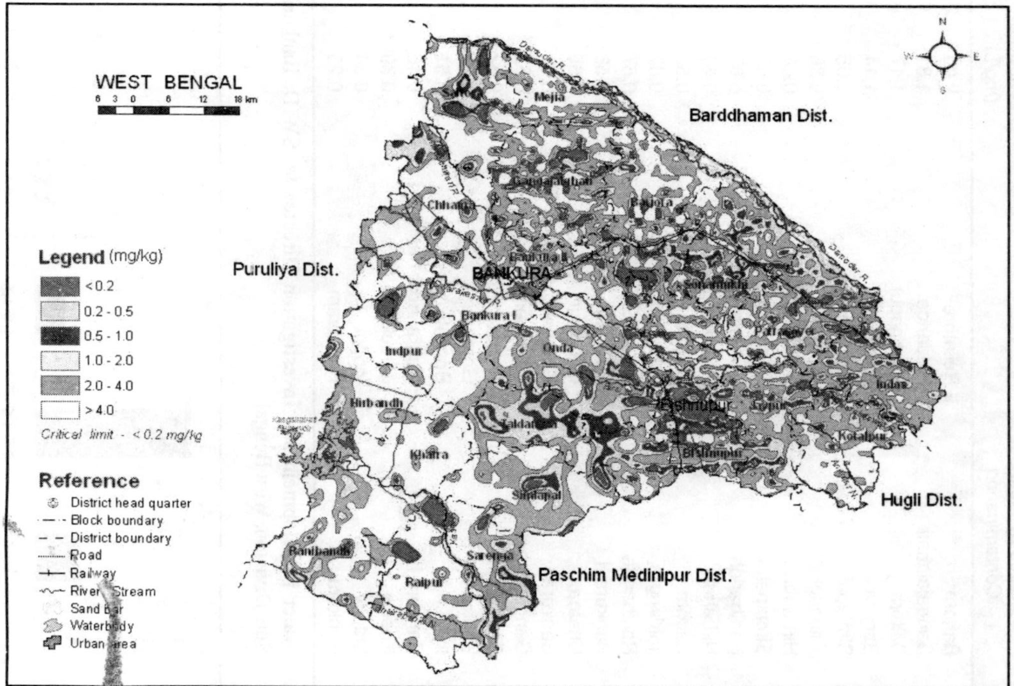

Fig. 15.19: Status of Available Copper in Bankura

Source: Department of Agricultural Chemist, Soil Testing Laboratory, Bankura, West Bengal.

Table 15.10: Pattern Distribution of Flouride in Groundwater in studied blocks of Bankura District

Sl. No.	*Name of the Blocks Affected by Flouride Contamination*	*Location*	*Flouride (F) in Groundwater (mg/L)*
1.	Barjora	Beliatore	2.00
2.	Gangajalghati	Beldanga	1.81
3.	Saltora	Krishnapur	1.17
4.	Barjora	Dhabani	1.14
5.	Simlapal	Ruabagan	1.05
6.	Taldangra	Dulangoa	0.86
7.	Hirbandh	Brahmandanga	0.68
8.	Simlapal	Sunukpahari	0.67
9.	Ranibandh	Gurpara	0.67
10.	Hirbandh	Jamdahara	0.65
11.	Saltora	Saltora	0.65
12.	Taldangra	Taldangra	0.62
13.	Ranibandh	Jhilimili	0.57
14.	Bankura II	Bankathi	0.56
15.	Chatna	Gopalpur	0.55
16.	Bankura I	Gorabari	0.54
17.	Gangajalghati	Bamagari	0.52
18.	Chatna	Hatyar	0.52
19.	Khatra	Gorabari	0.51
20.	Indpur	Bonkata	0.51
21.	Bankura II	Magra, near harimandir	0.46
22.	Khatra	Jentulchita	0.39
23.	Indpur	Indpur	0.34
24.	Bankura I	Royagram	0.23

Source: Water Development and Investigation Directorate, SWID, Bankura Sub-Division, West Bengal.

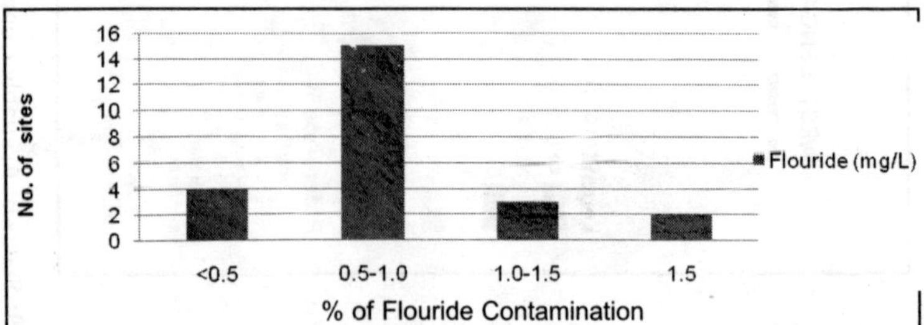

Fig. 15.20: No. of Flouride Contamination Sites Found in Bankura District

Table 15.11: Average Fluoride Concentration in groundwater in studied blocks of Bankura District

Sl. No.	*Name of the Blocks Affected by Average Fluoride Contamination*	*Average Fluoride Concentration (F) in Groundwater(mg/L)*
1.	Barjora	1.57
2.	Taldangra	1.26
3.	Gangajalghati	1.17
4.	Saltora	0.91
5.	Simlapal	0.86
6.	Hirbandh	0.67
7.	Ranibandh	0.62
8.	Chhatna	0.54
9.	Bankura II	0.51
10.	Khaira	0.49
11.	Indpur	0.43
12.	Bankura I	0.39

Source: Water Development and Investigation Directorate, SWID, Bankura Sub-Division, West Bengal.

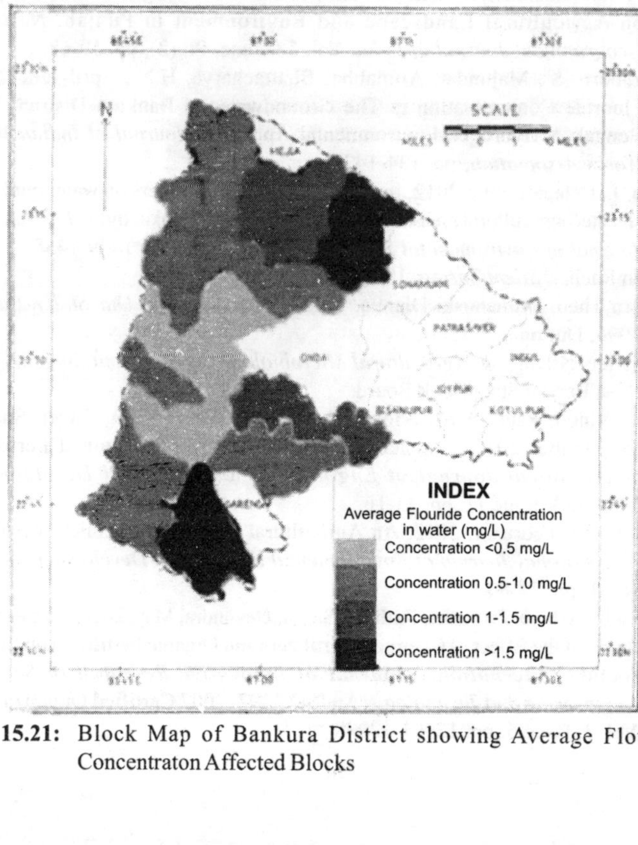

Fig. 15.21: Block Map of Bankura District showing Average Flouride Concentraton Affected Blocks

If we do not want to disturb the soil health and groundwater quality, we have to emphasize more on organic farming. We have to emphasis more on using of bio-fertilizers and biological pest control method instead of chemical equipments. Instead of overusing of chemical fertilizers we have to think and follow more about Integrated Nutrient management. So, we have to think and follow about Integrated Pest Management to control the pests. Already various N.G.Os have started to help the farmers by their Micro-Enterprise Development Programme.

Organic farming in one way which can reduce the uses of chemical equipments and in another way it can make the agricultural system more eco-friendly.

References

Mandal Kumar Aananda, Organic Farming.2012, Anima Prakashani.

Rana, Pooja and Sohal, K.S., 2012, Changes in Extent if Irrigation and its Impacts on Agricultural Landscape and Environment in Punjab, *National Geographical Journal of India*, Vol. 58, June, Pt. (2), pp. 59-68.

Chakraborti, S., Majundar, Arunabha; Bhattacharya, H.N., April-June 2012, Fluoride Contamination in The Groundwater of Bankura District, West Bengal: A Hydrogeo-Environmental Appraisal, *Journal of Indian Water Works Association*, pp. 134-142.

Divya, J., Belagali, S.L., 2012, Impact of chemical fertilizers on water quality in selected agricultural areas of Mysore District, Karnataka, India, *International Journal of Environmental Sciences*, Vol. 2, No. 3, pp. 1449-1458.

Carson Rachel, *Silent Spring*, 1962, Mariner Books.

Colborn Theo, Dumanoski Dianne, Myers Peterson John, *Our Stolen Future*, 1996, Dutton.

Mukherjee, Nilangshu, *Agricultural Microbiology (Krisi Jibanu Biggan)*, 1982 West Bengal State Book Board.

Dubey, Vinod; Patel, A.K.; Shukla, Archna: Shukla, Sonam, Singh, Shalini, (September 2012), Impact of Continuous use of Chemical Fertilizer, *International Journal of Engineering Research and Development*, Volume 3, Issue 11, pp. 13-16.

Savci Serpil, February, 2012, An Agricultural Pollutant: Chemical Fertilizer, *International Journal of Environmental Science and Development*, Vol. 3, No. 1, pp. 77-80.

Rai, Nidhi; Ashiya, Priyanka; Rathore, Singh, Devendra, May, 2014, Comparative Study of the Effect of Chemical Fertilizers and Organic Fertilizers on Eisenia foetida, *International Journal of Innovative Research in Science, Engineering and Technology* (An ISO 3297: 2007 Certified Organization), Vol. 3, Issue 5, pp. 12991-12998.

16

Agricultural Regionalisation

A Study of Purba Medinipur District

Jayanta Kumar Maity

Introduction

> "Agriculture is the most constituent of man's primary occupations and form of first vital link of human interaction with his environment."
> —*Mishra,* 1992

Agriculture is a primary activity in Purba Medinipur district where about 80 per cent to total population is engaged in agricultural activities. Agriculture plays an important role in rural economic development. This is because most of the rural people are poor and their basic needs of food, water and shelter are mostly met by agricultural production. There are different types of cereals (grain food such as paddy, wheat), vegetables (potato, onion, ginger, tomato, garlic, pumpkin, sponge gourd, beet, cauliflower, lady's finger, bitter gourd, arum, celery, spinach, beans, brinjal, snake gourd, squash, peas, cabbage, gourd, betel, basil etc.). Oil seeds (mustard, *til*, sunflower, ground nut etc.) fruits, fibres (jute, hemp, silk etc. produced in the field. Lifestyle, standard of living, food habit, housing condition, health condition, sanitation facility of the villagers depends on the economic status of the villagers which in turn depends on agriculture. Agricultural diversification is very high in the district but the standard of living is not as good as required. Thus, the nutritional level is very poor of the villagers.

Floriculture is increasingly regarded as a viable diversification from the traditional field crops because of higher returns per unit area. Floriculture is a discipline of horticulture concerned with the cultivation of flowering and ornamental plants for gardens and for floristry, comprising the floral industry. Floriculture is reliable economic option of Purba Medinipur district. Large amount of money come from floricultural activities of the villagers. Major type of flowers produced in this district are: Rose, Gladious, Balsam, Marigold, Chrysanthemum, Aster, Tuberose, Jarbera, Jasmine, Lotus, Karan, Murgai, Baby, Jipsi, China rose, Foal-fool, Clitoris, Dalia, Gulbahar, bel etc.

Location and Selection of the Study Area

The study area includes all the block of Purba Medinipur districts. Purba Medinipur district is the southernmost district of Burdwan division of West Bengal. The study area is bounded by 22° 57′ 10″ N to 22° 36′ 35″ N latitude and 88° 12′ 40″ E to 86° 33′ 50″ E longitude. It covers an area of 4736 sq.km. (1829 sq. mile). The headquarters is located at Tamluk. It was formed on January 1, 2002 after the partition of Medinipur into Purba Medinipur and Paschim Medinipur which lies at the northern and western border of it. The Odisha is at the south-west border whereas the Bay of Bengal lies in the south; the Hooghly River and South 24 Parganas district to the east and Howrah district to the north-east.

Purba Medinipur is formed of the sub-division of Tamluk, Contai, and Haldia of erstwhile Medinipur district. Another sub-division, Egra has been created out of the erstwhile Contai sub-division during the partition of Medinipur. There are 25 blocks and 5 municipals in the district. In 2011, the State Government has proposed to rename the district as Tamralipta district after the ancient port city of Tamralipta which used to lie near the modern district headquarters (Fig. 16.1).

Methodology

Investigator has followed well defined methodology. Among the all districts of West Bengal, Purba Medinipur district is the most agriculturally diversified district. Investigator used the secondary data collecting from the Office of the Deputy Director of Agriculture, Purba Medinipur District. Investigator also used the formula of cropping intensity, Weaver's method of crop combination, Bhatia's method of agriculture efficiency.

Objectives of the Study

The present work will emphasize the following objectives of Purba Medinipur district, West Bengal:

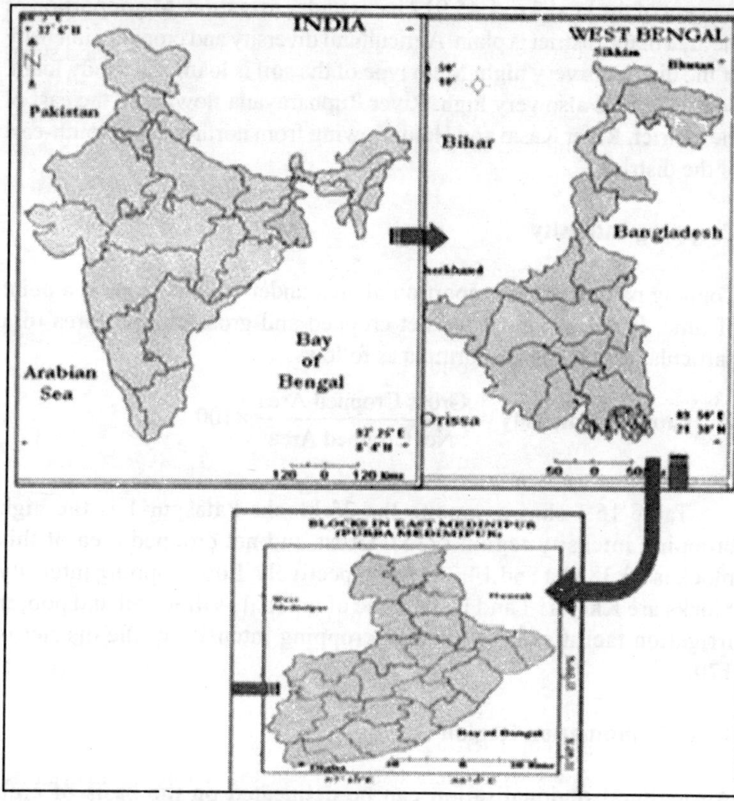

Fig. 16.1: Location Map of Study Area

- To analyse the agricultural land-use and crop production in the different parts of the district.
- To analyse the cropping intensity of the different blocks of the district.
- To find out the crop productivity.
- To find out the crop combination region of different blocks.
- To analyse the agricultural efficiency.

Discussion and Result

Agriculture is the main economic activity of Purba Medinipur district. This district has a land area of 4,30,140 ha. The net cultivated area of the district, i.e. 3,04,800 ha. and gross cropped area is 5,18,076, having 48 per cent of the land, i.e. 1,45,917 ha. is under irrigation. Major portion of the area of the district is plain. Agricultural diversity and cropping intensity of the district is very high. Main type of the soil is loam and sandy loam. Soil fertility is also very high. River Rupnarayana flowing to the east of the district. River Kasai and Haldi flowing from north-west to south-east of the district.

Cropping Intensity

Copping pattern is the proportion of area under various crops at a point of time. It is considered the net cropped and gross cropped area of a particular area using the formula as follows:

$$\text{Cropping intensity} = \frac{\text{Gross Cropped Area}}{\text{Net Cropped Area}} \times 100$$

Table 16.1 shows, among the 25 blocks Pataspur-1 is the high cropping intensity region (235). Gross and net cropped area of this block is 33,388 ha and 14,200 ha respectively. Low cropping intensity blocks are Khejuri-I and II, because of unfertile saline soil and poorer irrigation facilities. The average cropping intensity of the district is 170.

Crop Combination Region

Agricultural regionalisation can be delineated on the basis of crop combination region. It is also an important aspect of Agriculture geography. Crop combination is the dynamic concept. Crops are generally grown in combination in the study area at a season or time. In Purba Medinipur district, Paddy is the main crop. Other important crops are vegetables, pulses, oil seeds, potato etc.

There are various statistical methods to calculate the crop combination region; of these Weaver's method of crop combination is more acceptable. Weaver computed the percentage of total harvested cropland occupied by each crop that held as much as 1 per cent of cultivated land. Weaver calculated deviation of the real percentage of crops against a theoretical standard. The theoretical curve for the standard measurement was employed as shown in Table 16.2.

Table 16.1: Cropping Intensityof Purba Medinipur District (Area in ha)

	Name of The Block	Geographical Area	Net Cropped Area	Gross Cropped Area	Cropping Intensity
1.	Tamluk	13182	9500	17140	180
2.	Sahid Matangini	11158	6400	18850	185
3.	Panskura-I	24556	18600	39420	212
4.	Kolaghat	15514	11150	20700	185
5.	Nandakumar	17740	12100	21195	175
6.	Nandigram-III	16464	12800	18885	147
7.	Moyna	14840	10900	22334	205
8.	Mahisadal	14610	10700	18692	175
9.	Sutahata	17600	8600	14280	166
10.	Haldia	15370	7850	12485	159
11.	Nandigram-I	20523	14100	18760	133
12.	Nandigram-II	12483	8400	13360	159
13.	Kanthi-I	17064	13100	17347	132
14.	Kanthi-II	18032	13500	17475	129
15.	Kanthi-III	15694	13300	24375	183
16.	Ramnagar-I	13323	9800	14215	145
17.	Ramnagar-II	16957	12350	19255	156
18.	Bhagwanpur-II	17896	12900	23625	183
19.	Khejuri-I	13052	10920	13510	124
20.	Khejurl-II	29628	11480	14250	124
21.	Bhagwanpur-I	18364	14600	25275	173
22.	Egra-I	20479	16150	27956	173
23.	Egra-II	19821	16200	26151	161
24.	Pataspur-I	17169	14200	33388	235
25.	Pataspur-II	18621	15200	32153	211
Total		**430140**	**304800**	**518076**	**170**

Source: District Statistical Handbook, Purba Medinipur, 2011.

Table 16.2: Theoritical Curve for the Standard Measurement

Monoculture	100% of the total harvested crop land in one crop.
2-crop combination	50% in each crop of two crops.
3-crop combination	33.3% in each of three crops.
4-crop combination	25% in each of three crops.
5-crop combination	20% in each of three crops.

Source: www.shodganga.inflibnet.ae.in

For the determination of the minimum deviation the standard deviation method was

$$SD = \sqrt{d2}/n$$

Where, d = difference between the actual crop percentage in a given region and Theoretical percentage

n = no. of crop in a given combination.

Table 16.3: Crop Combination Region of Purba Medinipur District—2012-13

Sl. No.	Name of The Block	Paddy	Paddy-vegetable	Pad-Veg-pul	Pad-Veg-pul-Oil	Pad-Veg-pul-oil-potato	Crop-combination Region
1.	Tamluk	676.8458	1045.892	957.1446	830.0011	747.819	Paddy
2.	Sahid Matangini	620.4694	1197.262	1016.691	872.0177	778.4283	Paddy
3.	Panskura-I	1940.926	838.8282	663.4351	419.1603	405.2158	Pad-Veg-Pul-Oil-Potato
4.	Kolaghat	954.5132	925.0515	835.626	691.6888	630.6341	Pad-Veg-Pul-Oil-Potato
5.	Nandakumar	550.1692	1308.597	1006.703	924.188	823.7308	Paddy
6.	Nandigram-III	1003.633	1045.732	766.8502	666.8336	604.8891	Pad-Veg-Pul-Oil-Potato
7.	Moyna	313.0812	1549.462	1327.493	1140.569	995.6273	Paddy
8.	Mahisadal	605.5448	1266.079	965.4876	879.1247	788.0072	Paddy
9.	Sutahata	1315.599	999.1669	555.0621	592.4829	558.1506	Pad-Veg-Pul
10.	Haldia	1663.494	907.9896	446.3049	491.9237	474.3177	Pad-Veg-Pul
11.	Nandigram-I	998.2235	1114.635	720.9964	697.2208	628.9892	Pad-Veg-Pul-Oil-Potato
12.	Nandigram-II	1274.971	964.9495	578.5762	586.6777	545.0693	Pad-Veg-Pul-Oil-Potato
13.	Kanthi-I	486.0706	1309.143	1142.062	993.391	864.7242	Paddy
14.	Kanthi-II	509.8855	1239.663	1091.639	969.859	846.6472	Paddy
15.	Kanthi-III	503.3845	1248.117	1103.966	970.7393	847.1291	Paddy
16.	Ramnagar-I	1794.34	820.9231	574.4106	399.7078	386.264	Pad-Veg-Pul-Oil-Potato
17.	Ramnagar-II	1141.221	965.7884	774.5112	604.455	557.4659	Pad-Veg-Pul-Oil-Potato
18.	Bhagwanpur-II	369.257	1453.47	1248.085	1081.276	934.9738	Paddy
19.	Khejuri-I	604.9657	1270.407	1032.291	898.7948	781.8298	Paddy
20.	Khejuri-II	635.6895	1246.196	1007.1	878.0318	764.4413	Paddy
21.	Bhagwanpur-I	223.2661	1647.076	1435.442	1233.636	1069.295	Paddy
22.	Egra-I	309.5864	1522.106	1357.139	1123.343	984.1789	Paddy
23.	Egra-II	226.2635	1625.868	1435.79	1232.723	1068.212	Paddy
24.	Pataspur-I	227.7077	1667.383	1454.832	1225.507	1065.172	Paddy
25.	Pataspur-II	254.9611	1622.845	1418.809	1192.92	1037.875	Paddy

Source: Calculated by the Author.

Table 16.4: Purba Medinipur district: weaver's method—crop combination

No. of Crops	*No. of Blocks*	*Name of Districts*
Monoculture	16	Tamluk, Sahidmatangini Nandakumar, Moyna, Mahisadal, Kathi I, II & III, Khejuri I & II, Bhagawanpur I & II, Egra I & II, Pataspur I &II.
2 crop combination	0	–
3 crop combination	2	Sutahata, Haldia.
4 crop combination	0	–
5 crop combination	7	Panskura I, Kolaghat, Nandigram I, II & III, Ramnagar I & II.

Source: Calculated by the Author.

After the calculation of Weaver's method of crop combination, Table 16.3 and 16.4 show that there are 16 monoculture blocks among the 25 blocks. Paddy is the dominant crop in this area because of low plain area and also developed the boro cultivation due to irrigation facilities. Three crop combination regions are Sutahata and Haldia blocks. Five crop combination regions are Panskura I, Kolaghat, Nandigram I, II and III, Ramnagar I and II because of better irrigation facilities and loamy fertile soil.

Crop Diversification

Crop diversification and crop specialisation is important criteria to delineate an agricultural region. Bhatia (1965) developed a formula based on gross cropped area. This formula is as follows:

$$\text{Index of crop diversification} = \frac{\text{Percentage of sown area under x crop}}{\text{Number of x crop}}$$

Where, x crop are those crop that individually occupy 10 per cent or more of the gross cropped area in the area under study.

Tables 16.5 and 16.6 shows that high degree of crop diversification blocks are Panskura-I, Kolaghat, Nandigram-III, Ramnagar-I and II. Medium degree of crop diversification blocks are Tamluk, Nandakumar, Mahisadal, Sutahata, Haldia, Nandigram-I and II. And low degree of diversification blocks are Sahidmatangini, Moyna, Kathi-I, II and III, Bhagawanpur-I and II, Khejuri-I and II, Egra-I and II, Pataspur-I and II.

Table 16.5: Crop Diversification of Purba Medinipur District

Sl.No.	*Name of the Block*	*Crop Diverslfication*
1.	Tamluk	42.5
2.	Sahid Matangini	75
3.	Panskura-I	30.3
4.	Kolahat	40
5.	Nandkumar	44.5
6.	Nandigram-III	40
7.	Moyna	82
8.	Mahisada	44
9.	Sutahata	43.5
10.	Haldia	42.5
11.	Nandigram-I	43
12	Nandigram-II	41
13.	Kanthi-I	78
14.	Kanthi-II	77
15.	Kanthi-III	78
16.	Ramnagar-I	37
17.	Ramnagar-II	39
18.	Bhgwanpur-II	80
19.	Khejuri-I	75
20.	Khejuri-II	75
21.	Bhgwanpur-I	85
22.	Egra-I	82
23.	Egra-II	85
24.	Pataspur-I	85
25.	Pataspur-II	84

Source: Calculated by the Author.

Table 16.6: Crop Diversification

Crop Diversification	*Value*	*Blocks*
High	<40	Panskura-I, Kolaghat, Nandigram-II, Ramnagar-I & II
Middle	41–70	Tamluk, Nandakumar, Mahisadal, Sutahata, Haldia, Nandigram-I & and II
Low	>70	Sahidmatangini, Moyna, Kathi-I, II & III, Bhagawanpur-I & II, Khejuri-I & II, Egra-I & II, Pataspur-I & II

Source: Calculated by the Author.

Agriculture Productivity and Agricultural Efficiency

According to Majid Husain, "the measurement of production and inputs required for the production of that output is known as agricultural productivity." Agricultural productivity depends on physical, socio-economic, political, institutional and organizational factors. There are various sophisticated tools and techniques to determine the agriculture productivity. S.S. Bhatia has been considered suitable to measure the agricultural efficiency. The method is based on the weightage of acre yield in respect to the total crop acreage of any areal unit. It is as follows:

$$\text{Agricultural Efficiency} = \frac{\sum_{j}^{p} = Eij.Cij}{\sum_{j}^{p} = 1Cij}$$

$$Eij = \frac{Yij}{yij} \times 100$$

Where, Yij = Yield per acre of jth crop in ith district

yij = Yield per acre of jth crop in the region

Cij = Proportionate share of land under jth crop in the total cropped area of the ith district.

Table 16.7 and 16.8 shows that Panskura is the high agricultural efficiency block because of soil fertility, irrigation facilities both sallow tube well and water tank, marketing facilities etc. Middle agricultural efficiency blocks are Tamluk, Sahid Matangini, Kolaghat, Nandakumar, Mahisadal, Sutahata, Nandigram-I, Ramnagar-I, Bhagwanpur-I, Bhagwanpur-II, Egra-I, Pataspur-I, Pataspur-II. Low agricultural efficiency blocks are Nandigram-III, Moyna, Haldia, Nandigram-II, Kanthi-I, Kanthi-II, Kanthi-III, Ramnagar-II, Khejuri-I, Khejuri-II, Egra-II because of lower plain land, coastal saline soil, poorer drainage system and agriculture land converted into fishing land.

Table 16.7: Agricultural Efficiency-2012-13

Sl. No.	*Name of the Block*	*Agricultural Efficiency*
1.	Tamluk	101
2.	Sahid Matangini	105
3.	Panskura-I	114
4.	Kolaghat	103
5.	Nandakumar	104
6.	Nandigram-III	100
7.	Moyna	103
8.	Mahisadal	156
9.	Sutahata	95
10.	Haldia	101
11.	Nandigram-I	92
12.	Nandigram-II	93
13.	Kanthi-I	92
14.	Kanthi-II	92
15.	Kanthi-III	103
16.	Ramnagar-I	98
17.	Ramnagar-II	101
18.	Bhagwanpur-II	94
19.	Khejuri-I	93
20.	Khejuri-II	93
21.	Bhagwanpur-1	101
22.	Egra-I	103
23.	Egra-II	99
24.	Pataspur-I	106
25.	Pataspur-II	106

Source: Calculated by the Author.

Table 16.8: Agricultural Efficiency Region-2012-13

Agricultural Efficiency	*Range*	*No. of Districts*	*Districts*
High	>110	1	Panskura
Medium	101-110	13	Tamluk, Sahid Matangini, Kolaghat, Nandakumar, Mahisadal, Sutahata, Nandigram-I, Ramnagar-I, Bhagwanpur-I, Bhagwanpur-II, Egra-I, Pataspur-I, Pataspur-II
Low	<100	11	Nandigram-III, Moyna, Haldia, Nandigram-II, Kanthi-I, Kanthi-II, Kanthi-III, Ramnagar-II, Khejuri-I, Khejuri-II, Egra-I!

Source: Calculated by the Author.

References

Husain, Majid, 1996, *Systematic Agricultural Geography*, New Delhi: Rawat Publication.

Singh, Jasbir, 1976. *Agriculture Atlas of India: A Geography Analysis*, Haryana: Visal Publication.

Bhatia, S.S., 1965, "Pattern of crop concentration and diversification in India", *Economic Geography*, Vol. 11, p. 56.

Draft Annual Plan on Agriculture—2012-2013, Office of the Deputy Director of Agriculture, Purba Medinipur, Tamluk.

Census of India, Government of India, 1991, 2011.

Appendix

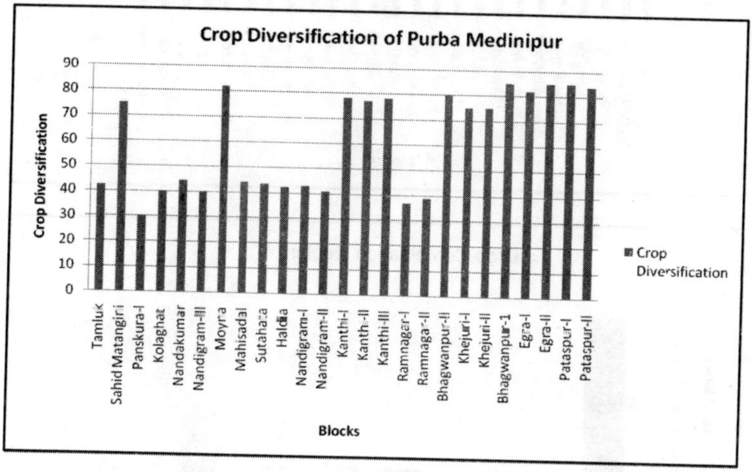

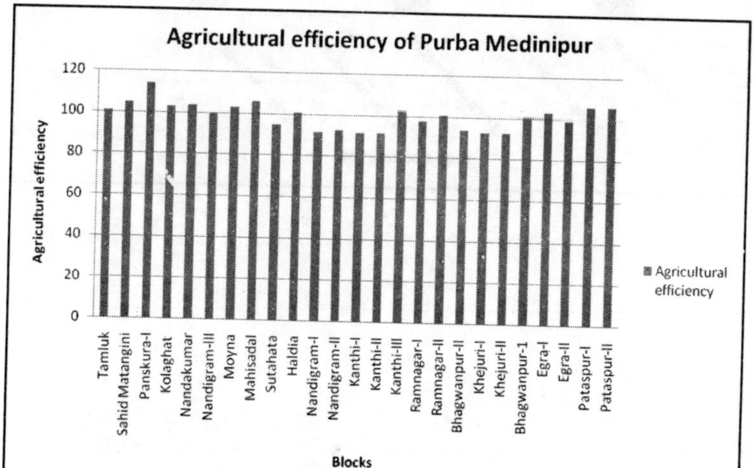

Source: Based on Author's Calculation.

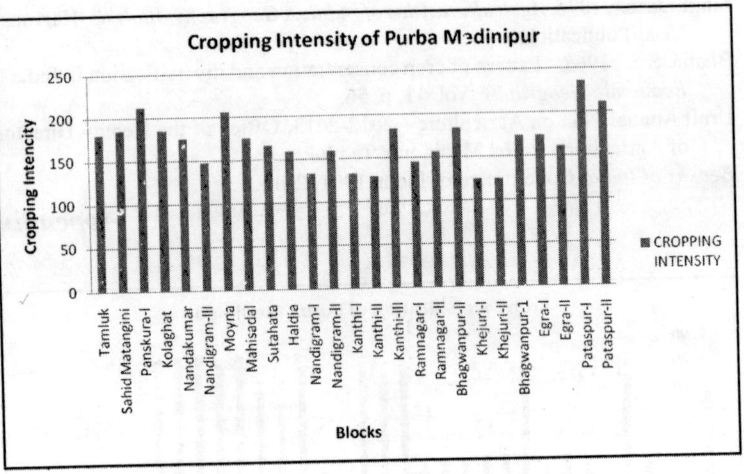

Cropping Intensity of Purba Medinipur
Cropping Intencity
250
200
150
100
50
0
Tamluk
Sahid Matangini
Panskura-I
Kolaghat
Nandakumar
Nandigram-III
Moyna
Mahisadal
Sutahata
Haldia
Nandigram-I
Nandigram-II
Kanthi-I
Kanthi-II
Kanthi-III
Ramnagar-I
Ramnagar-II
Bhagwanpur-II
Khejuri-I
Khejuri-II
Bhagwanpur-1
Egra-I
Egra-II
Pataspur-I
Pataspur-II
Blocks
CROPPING INTENSITY

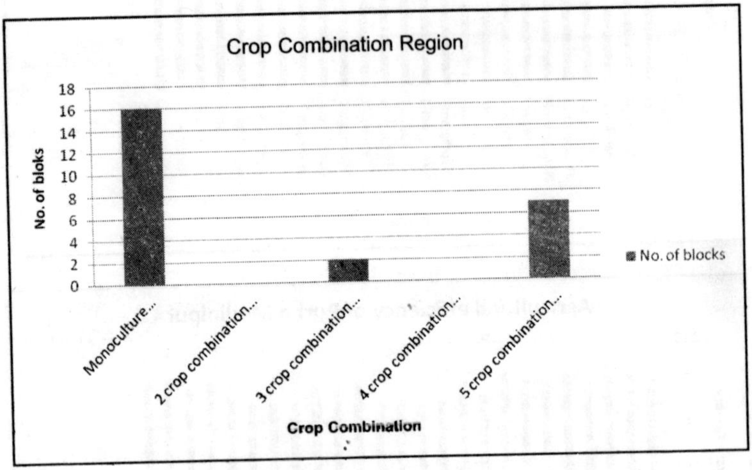

Crop Combination Region
No. of bloks
18
16
14
12
10
8
6
4
2
0
Monoculture...
2 crop combination...
3 crop combination...
4 crop combination...
5 crop combination...
Crop Combination
No. of blocks

17

Unscientific Agricultural Practices and Its Impact on Rural Livelihood in Burdwan-I C.D. Block, Barddhaman, West Bengal

Kshudiram Chakraborty and *Biswaranjan Mistri*

1.0. Introduction

Agriculture is the main stay of livelihood of 60 per cent Indians (Paul, 2015). A farmer cultivates his land on the basis of his experience and most of them are untrained about modern agriculture. In India, new agricultural technologies like HYV technology, together with use of fertilizer, irrigation and improved machinery have been adopted to increase crop yields while ignoring the subsequent ecological and sociological consequences (Chattopadhyay, 1984; Brown, 1982). After green revolution, mono-crop cultivation has rampantly been proliferated and resulting into the destruction of crop sequence, traditional crop calendar and crop rotation (Thapar, 1973). "Millions of people have enjoyed no benefit" from the new technology (Tangley, 1987) and the fruit of green revolution are pocketed mainly by rich and prosperous farmers (Bhattacharya and Majid, 1976). Disparity between big and small farmers has been increased because the productivity of large farms has been increased more with new technology than small farm (Oommen, 1971; Dhanagare, 1987). "The green revolution has not only made agriculture economically unviable but also destroyed the environmentally rich biodiversity" (Nellithanam, 1997), with inflation of rural displacement, increasing poverty and loosing biodiversity (Brown, 1982). In reality, food grain production has been increased less than 2.5 per cent during 1965-70 (Paddock, 1970), but the area under pulse has been declined by 49.7 per cent during 1965-71 (Thapar, 1973). Ultimately, the revolution was green as it was seen through green coloured glasses where "nothing is sacred but everything has a price" (Paddock, 1970; Shiva, 1991).

Presently, with the decline of the productivity of crop and ever increasing cost of agricultural inputs, return from agriculture has been declined considerably and agriculture has become a low profitable sector which cannot provide basic livelihood of farmers in rural areas in Burdwan-I C.D. Block, Barddhaman.

2.0. Study Area

The area of the block is 250.54 km^2 of which 206.95 km^2 (82.4%) is used for agriculture. Population density is 718 person/km^2. *Aman* and *boro* paddy are cultivated in 87 per cent land. Single cropping, double cropping and triple cropping lands are 3.36 per cent, 83.65 per cent and 12.98 per cent of the agricultural land respectively. Cropping intensity of the block is 205. Agricultural density is 59 cultivator/km^2 whereas physiological density is 1067 person/km^2 (Population Census, 2011). The latitudinal and longitudinal extension of the block are from 23°12′ 4″ N to 23° 22′ 48″ N and from 87°47′ 8″ E to 88°4′ 24″ E respectively.

3.0. Objectives

The objectives of the research study are as follows:

(i) To measure nutrient indices of the block.
(ii) To compare between amount of applied nutrients and recommended amount of nutrients.
(iii) To estimate cost-benefit for *aman*, *boro*, potato and *khas* cultivation.
(iv) To find out the pattern of earning and expenditure of the farmer.
(v) To calculate deficit or surplus income of the farmer; and
(vi) To know alternative earnings of the farmer's family to sustain livelihood.

4.0. Materials and Methods

4.1 Soils

The study has been done on the basis of primary data. For collecting of soil samples, the block has been divided into grids of one sq. km. On the basis of grid, 208 soil samples have been collected from arable land of the block in June, 2014 and detailed interview has been done with the concerned cultivators about their techniques of cultivation, production of crops, problems and management practices of agriculture.

4.2 Soil Testing

The collected soil samples have been dried in air and total nitrogen (N), has been measured after the method of Subbiah and Asija, (1956). Phosphate (P) and potassium (K) have been tested through soil kit method. Nutrient indices have been calculated with this formula, NI= (L×1+M×2+H×3)/T. Here, L, M and H are number of samples falling in low, medium and high categories of nutrient status respectively and T is total number of soil samples (Motsara *et al.*, 1982). ... (i)

4.3 Statistical Analysis

To analyse the data, linear regression, curvilinear regression and multiple regression have been computed in MS Excel, 2007 and Statistical 10.0. Principal component has been analysed and histograms have been prepared using Past 3.0. The equations of regression analysis are:

$$Yc = a + bx \quad \text{... (ii)}$$

$$Yc = a + bx_1 + cx_1^2 \quad \text{... (iii)}$$

$$Yc = a + bx_1 + cx_2 + dx_3 \quad \text{... (iv)}$$

Earning of farmer's family has been calculated by the equation as E = Σ (profit in *aman* × area of cultivation + profit in *boro* × area of cultivation + profit in potato × area of cultivation) ... (v)

5.0. Results and Discussion

Nutrient Indices have been calculated using equation no. (i). Nutrient Indices of the block are as follows:

Nutrient Index for Nitrogen = $(1\times62+2\times107+3\times39)/208 = 1.88$
Nutrient Index for Phosphate = $(1\times105+2\times73+3\times30)/208 = 1.49$
Nutrient Index for Potassium = $(1\times68+2\times117+3\times23)/208 = 1.78$

From the above calculated value, the nitrogen, phosphate and potassium status are found as medium, low and medium respectively. These values can be treated as medium, low and medium fertility of nutrients of the soil.

5.1. Fertilizer Recommendation

The main objective of test of the soil is to find out the soil fertility to recommend suitable crop and fertility application rate. "Soil Test based Fertilizer Recommendations for Principal Crops and Cropping Sequences in West Bengal" edited and complied by Dr. B.K. Bhattacharyya has mentioned recommendation of fertilizer rate to be applied in crops in West Bengal.

Table 17.1: Fertilizer Recommendation for Paddy and potato Cultivation.

Crops	*Fertility Class*	*Quantity of NPK Nutrients required in kg/ha*			*Time of Application*
		N	*P_2O_5*	*K_2O*	
Rice, *Kharif*, Medium duration (125-135 days) HYV, *Jaya*, *Ajaya*, IR-20, *Kunti*	High Medium Low	50 **60** 80	25 30 **40**	25 **30** 40	Basal- ¼ N, full P and K Topdressing of N ½ at 15 DAT ¼ at 40-45 DAT
Rice Boro, HYV, IR-64, iR-36, *Shasyasree*	High Medium Low	80 **100** 120	40 50 **60**	40 **50** 60	Basal- ¼ N, full P & K Topdressing of N, ½ at tillering, ¼ at P.I.
Potato K. *Jyoti*, K. *Chandramukhi*, K *Badsha*	High Medium Low	150 **200** 250	100 125 **150**	100 **125** 150	Basal-3/4 N, full Pand K. Topdressing of N ¼ at 1st earthing up

Source: Bhattacharyya, 2000.

From Table 17.1, it has found out that fertilizer requirement varies with crop varieties along with fertility class of the soil. The three soil nutrients (NPK) are supplied by chemical fertilizer in different proportion. But chemical fertilizer does not supply any micronutrient.

In *kharif* paddy cultivation, 80 kg ha^{-1} N is required for medium duration (125-135 days) crop production of HYV seeds of Jaya, IR-20 in low fertile soil and 50 kg ha^{-1} N is required to cultivate in high fertile soil. 40 kg ha^{-1} phosphate is required to cultivate HYV seeds while 25 kg ha^{-1} is required to cultivate in high fertile soil. In the block, 60 kg ha^{-1} N, 40 kg ha^{-1} P and 30 kg ha^{-1} K is recommended in *kharif* cultivation. In the *boro* paddy cultivation, fertilizer requirement is greater than *kharif* paddy cultivation as it is a production in short time period with HYV seeds (IR-36, IR-64). 100 kg ha^{-1} N, 60 kg ha^{-1} P and 50 kg ha^{-1} K are required to cultivate in medium fertile and low fertile soil in the block. In potato cultivation, K. *Jyoti*, K. *Chandramukhi,* 200 kg ha^{-1} N, 150 kg ha^{-1} P and 125 kg ha^{-1} K is recommended for cultivation in the block.

Chemical fertilizer is inorganic substance which contains mainly one or two nutrients. Urea is the main supplier of nitrogen. It contains 46 per cent of nitrogen. Di-ammonium Phosphate [DAP $(NH_4)_2HPO_4$] is the main supplier of phosphate as it serves 46 per cent of phosphate. DAP also contains 18 per cent of nitrogen. Urea $CO(NH_2)_2$ is the supplier of nitrogen, 46 per cent of its weight. Muriate of potash, MoP (KCl) is one of the potassium supplier, 60 per cent of its weight. To provide 60 kg N, 40 kg P and 30 kg K per hectare, DAP, urea and MoP requirement are 86.95 kg, 96.39 kg and 50 kg respectively in *kharif* cultivation. In *boro* paddy cultivation, to provide 100 kg N, 60 kg P and 50 kg K per hectare, DAP, urea and MoP requirement are 130.43 kg, 166.34 kg, and 83.333 kg respectively. In potato cultivation, to provide 200 kg N, 150 kg P and 125 kg K per hectare, NPK (10:26:26), DAP and urea requirement are 480.769 kg, 54.34 kg and 309 kg respectively.

5.2. Application of Nutrients in Kharif Season

In *kharif* season, recommended amount of nitrogen is 60 kg ha^{-1} whereas 40-50 kg ha^{-1} N is applied by 4.8 per cent farmers. 5.28 per cent farmers apply 50-60kg N ha^{-1}. 60-70 kg and 70-80 kg N per ha are applied by 7.21 and 28.36 per cent farmer respectively. So, 12.49 per cent farmers apply standard amount of nitrogen. 21.15 per cent and 12.5 per cent farmer apply 80-90 and 100-110 kg ha^{-1} which is twice of standard amount. 140-150 kg and 150-160 kg ha^{-1} N is applied by 1.44 and 0.96 per cent farmers (Fig. 17.1).

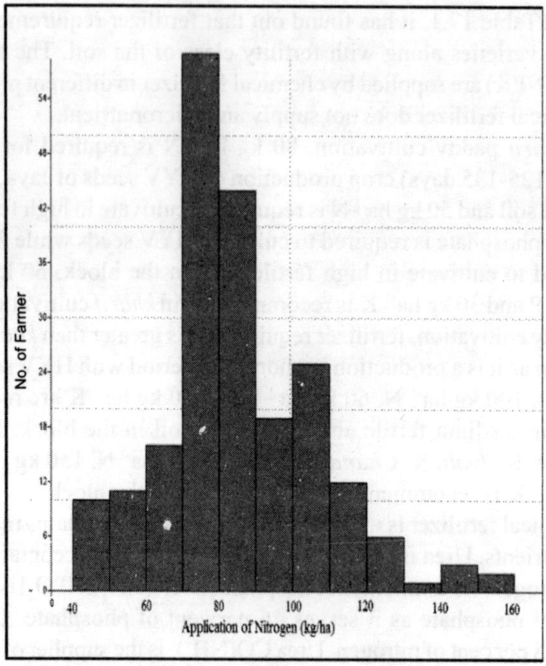

Fig. 17.1: Application of Nitrogen in *Kharif*, Burdwan-I C.D. Block, 2014
Source: Field Survey by the Authors.

Amount of recommended phosphate fertilizer is 40 kg ha^{-1} for low fertile land. In the block, 25-45 kg ha^{-1} is applied by 11.05 per cent farmer. This may consider as standard in *kharif*. 45-65 per cent and 65-85 kg ha^{-1} are applied by 22.59 per cent and 34.61 per cent of farmer. 85-105 kg ha^{-1} and 105-125 kg ha^{-1} P, triple than recommended amount, are applied by 19.23 and 10.96 per cent farmer. 10.44 and 0.48 per cent farmer apply 125-145 and 145-165 kg ha^{-1} P, five times than recommended amount (Fig. 17.2).

In *kharif*, recommended amount of potassium is 30 kg ha^{-1} as nutrient index of potassium is medium. In the block, 20-40 kg ha^{-1} is applied by 13.46 per cent farmer. This amount may judge as standard in *kharif*. 40-60 kg ha^{-1} and 60-80 kg ha^{-1}, more than double of recommended amount, are applied by 59.61 per cent and 21.15 per cent farmers respectively. 3.36 per cent and 1.44 per cent farmer apply 80-100 kg ha^{-1} and 140-160 kg ha^{-1} K which are four to five times more than recommended amount (Fig. 17.3).

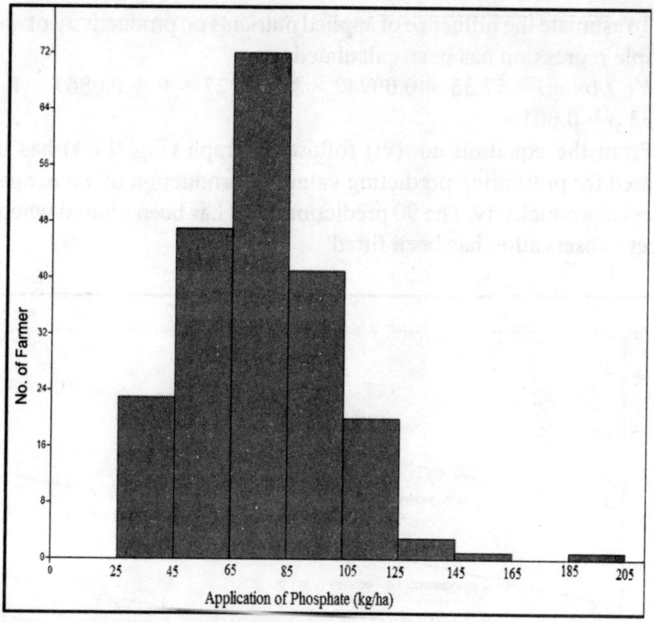

Fig. 17.2: Application of Phosphate in *Kharif*, Burdwan-I, 2014
Source: Field Survey by the Authors.

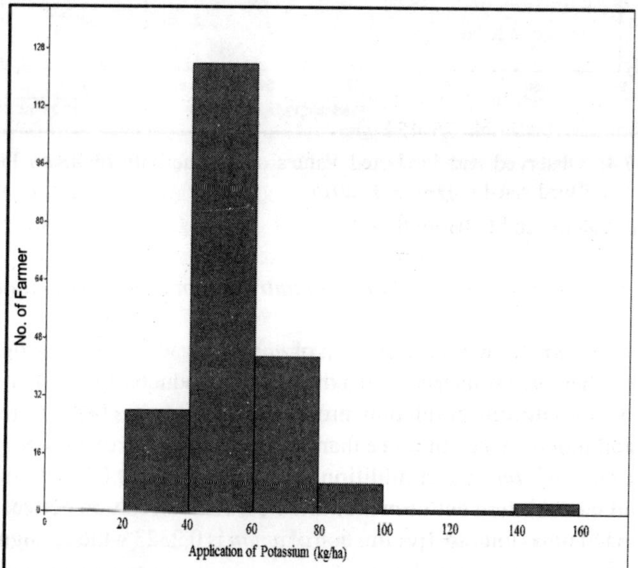

Fig. 17.3: Application of Potassium in *Kharif*, Burdwan-I, 2014
Source: Field Survey by the Authors.

To estimate the influence of applied nutrients on productivity of *aman,* multiple regression has been calculated.

Yc *(Aman)* = 57.35 + 0.00942 × N-0.0227 × P + 0.0867 × K r = 0.2433 p=<0.001 ...(vi)

From the equation no. (vi) following graph (Fig. 17.4) has been prepared for presenting predicting values of production of *aman* against observed productivity. The 90 prediction level has been plotted where 95 per cent observation has been fitted.

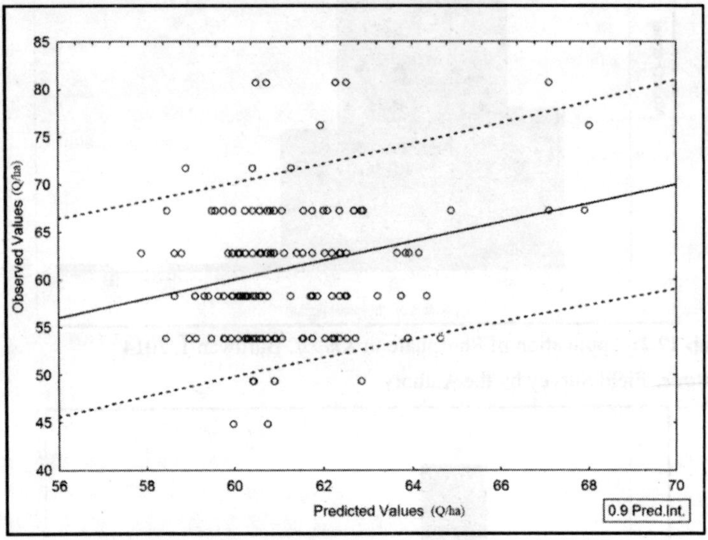

Fig. 17.4: Observed and Predicted Values of Productivity of *Aman* Paddy, Burdwan-I C.D. Block, 2014

Source: Calculated by the Authors.

5.2.1. Correlation among addition of nutrients and Aman production

The correlation between production of *aman* and addition of nitrogen is 0.1095 where 93 kg/ha has shown the highest productivity as about 63.2 Q/ha. In this curvilinear relation, production of *aman* has been decreased with addition of nitrogen more than 93 kg/ha. The correlation between production of *aman* and addition of phosphate is 0.0342 which is insignificant relation between the variables. The correlation between the addition of potassium and production of *aman* is 0.2323 which is signified at 95 per cent confidence level.

$$Yc\ (aman) = -0.000 \times N^2 + 0.161 \times N + 53.10 \quad r = 0.1095\ \ldots\ (vii)$$
$$= -1.05471E\text{-}06 \times P^2 + 0.009166211 \times P + 60.35706768 \quad r = 0.0342\ \ldots (viii)$$
$$= 0.079 \times K + 56.90 \quad r = 0.2323\ \ldots\ (ix)$$

5.3. Application of Nutrients in Boro Season

In *boro* season, recommended amount of nitrogen is 100 kg ha^{-1}. In the block, 4.80 per cent and 8.65 per cent farmer apply 60-80 kg and 80-100 kg N per ha respectively. 24.03 per cent and 20.67 per cent farmer apply 110-120 kg ha^{-1} and 120-140 kg ha^{-1} respectively. So, 32.69 per cent farmer apply standard amount of N in *boro*. 140-160 kg ha^{-1} is applied by 18.755 farmer. This amount is 1.5 times of recommended amount. 4.80 per cent and 1.44 per cent of farmer apply 160-180 kg and 180-200 kg ha^{-1}, double of recommended level (Fig. 17.5).

In *boro*, recommended amount of P is 60 kg ha^{-1}. In the block, 40.55 kg and 55.70 kg N per ha are applied by 2.88 per cent and 11.53 per cent farmer. 23.55 per cent and 24.51 per cent farmer apply 70-85 kg P and 100-115 kg P ha^{-1}. 115-130 kg ha^{-1} and 130-145 kg ha^{-1} are applied by 10.09 per cent and 4.32 per cent farmer. This amount is more than double of recommended amount. Three times of P, 175-190 kg ha^{-1} is applied by 1.44 per cent farmer (Fig. 17.6).

In *boro*, recommended amount of potassium is 50 kg ha^{-1}. In the block, 24.51 per cent and 5.28 per cent farmer apply 40-50 kg and 50-60 kg ha^{-1} K. So, these 29.79 per cent farmer applies standard amount of K. The 29.80 per cent of farmer applies 60-70 kg ha^{-1} N. Nearly double amount than recommedation, i.e. 90-100 kg ha^{-1} is applied by 14.90 per cent farmer. Triple amount than recommendation, i.e. 140-150 kg ha^{-1} is applied by 0.961 per cent farmer (Fig. 17.7).

To estimate the influence of applied nutrients on productivity of *boro,* multiple regression has been calculated.

$$Yc\ (Boro) = 62.863 - 0.013 \times N + 0.299 \times P + 0.081 \times K$$
$$r = 0.2704\ p = <0.001\ \ldots\ (x)$$

From the equation no. (x), a graph has been prepared for presenting prediction values of production of *boro* against observed productivity (Fig. 17.8). The 90 prediction level has been plotted where more than 95 per cent observation has been fitted.

The correlation between N-addition and *boro* production is 0.1048 where 126 kg/ha N-addition has shown the highest productivity of 71.712

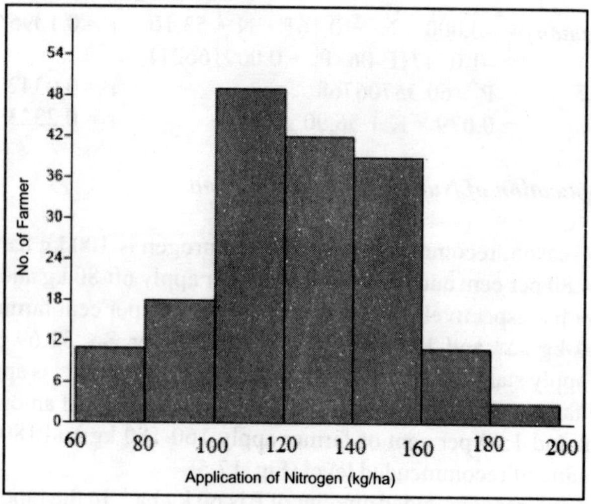

Fig. 17.5: Application of Nitrogen in *Boro*, Burdwan-I C.D. Block, 2014
Source: Field Survey by the Authros.

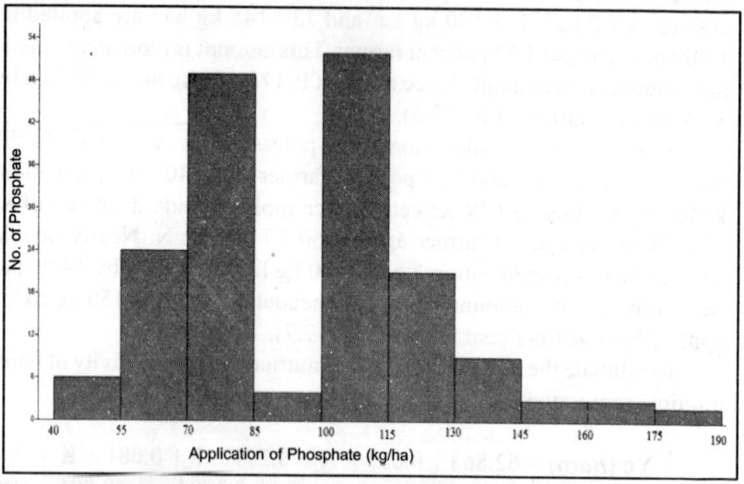

Fig. 17.6: Application of Phosphate in *Boro*, Burdwan-I, 2014
Source: Field Survey by the Authros.

kg/ha. With the addition of more than 126 kg/ha N, *boro* productivity is declined. The correlation between addition of phosphate and production of *boro* is 0.2408. This relation is significant at 98 per cent level. The correlation between addition of K and production of *boro* is 0.054 which is not satisfactorily significant.

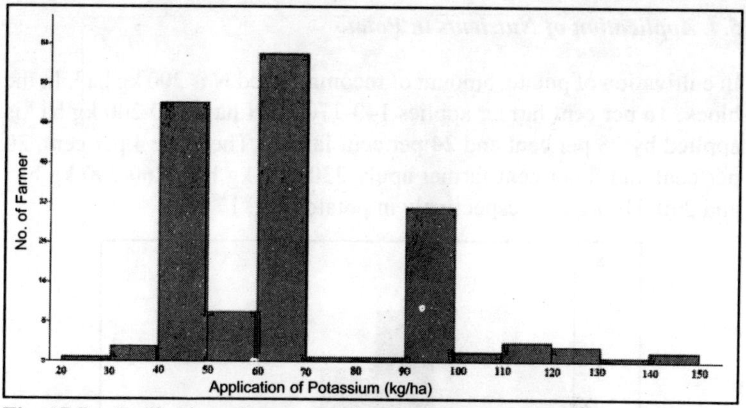

Fig. 17.7: Application of Potassium in *Boro*, Burdwan-I, 2014

Source: Field Survey by the Authros.

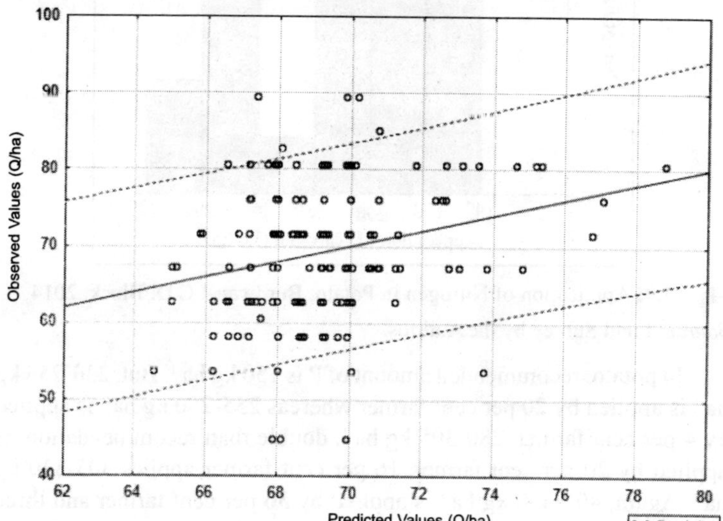

Fig. 17.8: Observed and Predicted Values of Productivity of *Boro* Paddy, Burdwan-I C.D. Block, 2014

Source: Field Survey by the Authros

$$\text{Yc } (Boro) = -0.001 \times N^2 + 0.253 \times N + 53.47 \quad r = 0.1048 \quad \ldots \text{(xi)}$$

$$= 0.076 \times P + 61.52 \quad r = 0.2408 \quad \ldots \text{(xii)}$$

$$= -0.000 \times K^2 + 0.104 \times K + 65.56 \quad r = 0.0547 \ldots \text{(xiii)}$$

5.4. Application of Nutrients in Potato

In cultivation of potato, amount of recommended N is 200 kg ha^{-1}. In the block, 16 per cent farmer applies 140-170 kg N ha^{-1}. 170-200 kg ha^{-1} is applied by 28 per cent and 24 per cent farmer. There are 4 per cent, 20 per cent and 8 per cent farmer apply 230-260 kg ha^{-1}, 260-290 kg ha^{-1} and 290-310 kg ha^{-1} respectively in potato (Fig. 17.9).

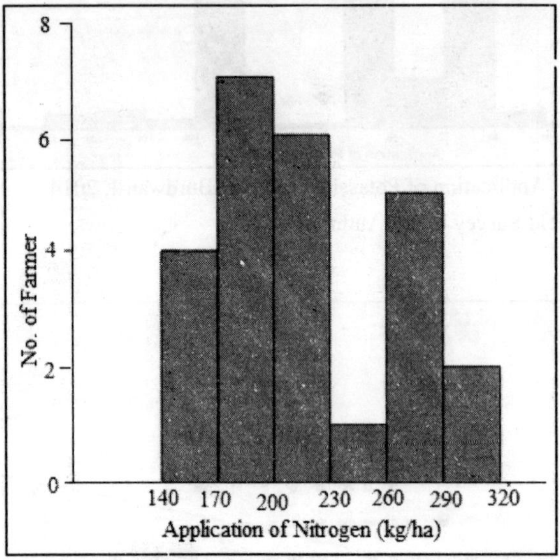

Fig. 17.9: Application of Nitrogen in Potato, Burdwan-I C.D. Block, 2014
Source: Field Survey by the Authros.

In potato, recommended amount of P is 150 kg ha^{-1}. But, 230-255 kg ha^{-1} is applied by 20 per cent farmer whereas 255-280 kg ha^{-1} is applied by 4 per cent farmer. 280-305 kg ha^{-1}, double than recommendation, is applied by 20 per cent farmer. 16 per cent farmer applies 305-330 kg ha^{-1}. Again, 405-430 kg ha^{-1} is applied by 36 per cent farmer and three times of recommended P, 430-450 kg ha^{-1} is applied by 4 per cent farmer (Fig. 17.10).

In cultivation of potato, 125 kg ha^{-1} is recommended for medium index of K in the block. But, in the block, 225-250 kg ha^{-1}, twice than recommendation, is applied by 20 per cent farmer. 275-300 kg ha^{-1} is applied by 20 per cent farmer double than recommendation. 300-325 kg and 375-400 kg ha^{-1} are applied by 16 per cent and 24 per cent farmer. Three times of recommended amount of K, 425-450 kg ha^{-1} is applied by 16 per cent farmer (Fig. 17.11).

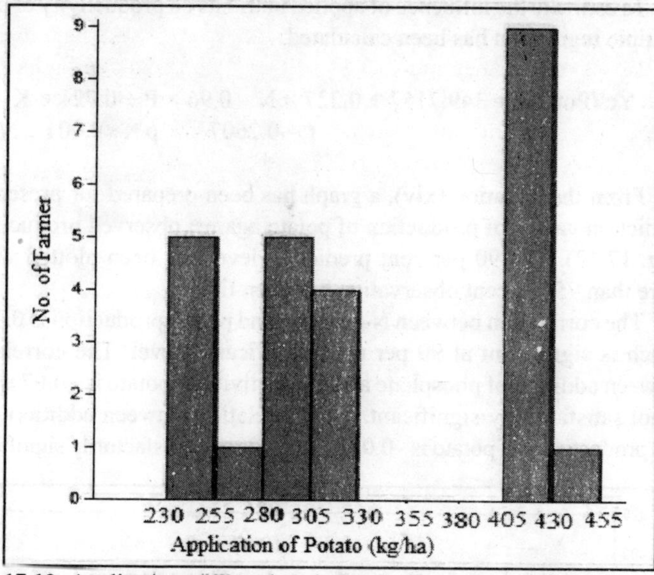

Fig. 17.10: Application of Phosphate in Potato, Burdwan-I, 2014

Source: Field Survey by the Authros.

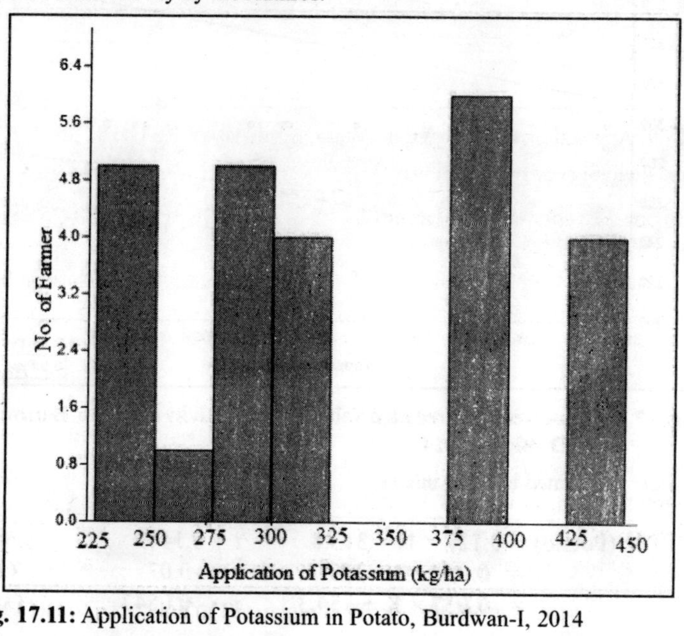

Fig. 17.11: Application of Potassium in Potato, Burdwan-I, 2014

Source: Field Survey by the Authros.

To estimate the influence of applied nutrients on productivity of *boro,* multiple regression has been calculated.

$$Yc\ (Potato) = 349.7157 + 0.227 \times N - 0.96 \times P + 0.721 \times K$$
$$r = 0.2607 \qquad p = <0.001 \quad \ldots \text{(xiv)}$$

From the equation (xiv), a graph has been prepared for presenting prediction values of production of potato against observed productivity (Fig. 17.12). The 90 per cent prediction level has been plotted where more than 95 per cent observation has been fitted.

The correlation between N-addition and potato production is 0.1449 which is significant at 90 per cent significance level. The correlation between addition of phosphate and productivity of potato is –0.07 which is not satisfactorily significant. The correlation between addition of K and productivity of potato is –0.0547 which is not satisfactorily significant.

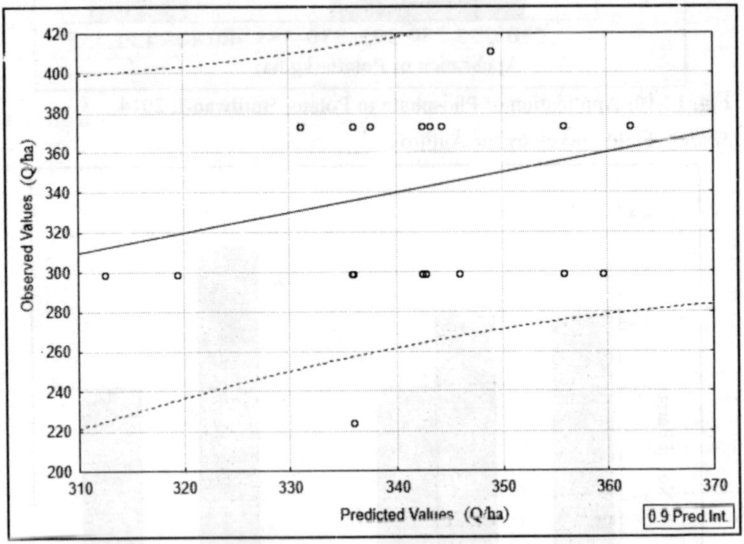

Fig. 17.12: Observed and Predicted Values of Productivity of Potato, Burdwan-I C.D. Block, 2014

Source: Calculated by the Authors.

$$Yc\ (Potato) = 0.127 \times N + 313.8 \qquad r = 0.1449 \qquad \ldots \text{(xv)}$$
$$= -0.054 \times P + 359.7 \qquad r = -0.07 \qquad \ldots \text{(xvi)}$$
$$= -0.037 \times K + 354.3 \qquad r = -0.0547 \qquad \ldots \text{(xvii)}$$

5.5. Cost-Benefit Analysis of Different Crops

In this study, calculation of cost of production and return from cultivation of *aman*, *boro*, potato and *khas* have been measured from detailled interview with the cultivator and market survey, June, 2014. *Khas* (*Gobindobhog*) is actually a type of *aman* paddy, cultivated with traditional organic based techniques.

Table 17.2: Cost-Benefit Analysis of Different Crops, Burdwan-I C.D. Block, 2014

Inputs/Production		*Seasons of Crops and Values are in*			
		Modern Chemical Based Agriculture			*Traditional Cultivation (Aman Season)*
	Fertilizer Name	*Aman*	*Boro*	*Potato*	*Khas (Gobindabhog)*
Seed		2241	2141	22410	224
Tillage		7470	7470	7470	7470
Fertilizer	DAP	3585	5019		1792
	Urea	1030	1411	1703	373
	MoP	1210	1561		1494
	NPK			28684	
	Organic manure (oil cake)				1120
Labour		33615	33615	37350	33615
Pesticide		5229	5976	7470	3735
Submersible		0	8964	7470	0
Total		54381	66258	112557	49824
Productivity		60.95	69.47	336.15	30
Saling price (Q)		1200	1200	560	3300
Total Return		73146	83365	188244	99000
Profit		18765	17107	75687	49176

Source: Calculated by the Authors.

5.6. Yearly Expenditure of the Farmer's Family

Monthly or yearly expenditure of a farmer's family is dependent on number of family members of the family; larger the family members, higher the expenditure of the family in rural areas. In this study, 13.94 per cent family expenses ₹ 36,000-63,000 yearly where 2-3 members are in the family. ₹ 63,000-90,000 is the expenditure of 18.27 per cent family with 4-5 members. 37.5 per cent family spends ₹ 90,000-1,17,000 yearly with 6 members in the family. 9.13 per cent, 10.57 per cent and 10.57 per cent family's expanses are ₹ 1.17-1.44 lakh, ₹ 1.44-1.71 lakh and ₹ 1.71-1.98 lakh yr^{-1} where family members are 7, 8-9 and 10 respectively. ₹ 3.06-3.33 lakh yr^{-1} and ₹ 3.33-3.60 lakh yr^{-1} are the expanditure of one each family where 17 and 20 family members are in joint family (Fig. 17.13).

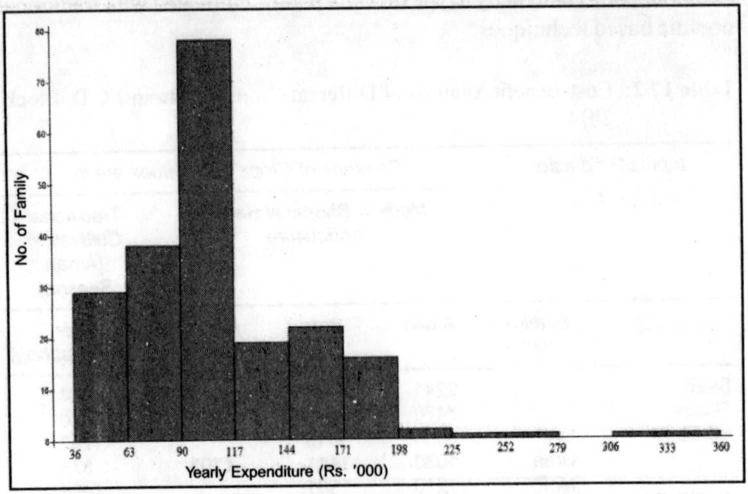

Fig. 17.13: Yearly Expenditure of the farmer's Family, Burdwan-I, C.D. Block, 2014

Source: Field Survey by the Authros

5.7. Landholding of Farmer's Family in the Block

Present landholdings is a function of societal evolution and influence. Within the surveyed farmers, 11.53 per cent farmer has less than 0.5 ha land where 16.34 per cent has 0.5-1.0 ha agricultural land. 25.48 per cent farmer has 1-1.5 ha land. So, 27 per cent farmer has less than one ha land. 1.5-2 ha land is owned by 10.57 per cent farmer. So, more than 50 per cent farmers have marginal landholdings in the block. 6-6.5 ha is controlled by 1.44 per cent farmer. 14-14.5 ha land is held by one farmer. In this study, 93.75 per cent farmer are small farmer who has less than four ha agricultural land (Fig. 17.14).

5.8. Yearly Earning of the Farmer's Family

The earning of the farmer's family has been calculated by equation (v). In the study area, 21.15 per cent farmer has yearly earning of less than

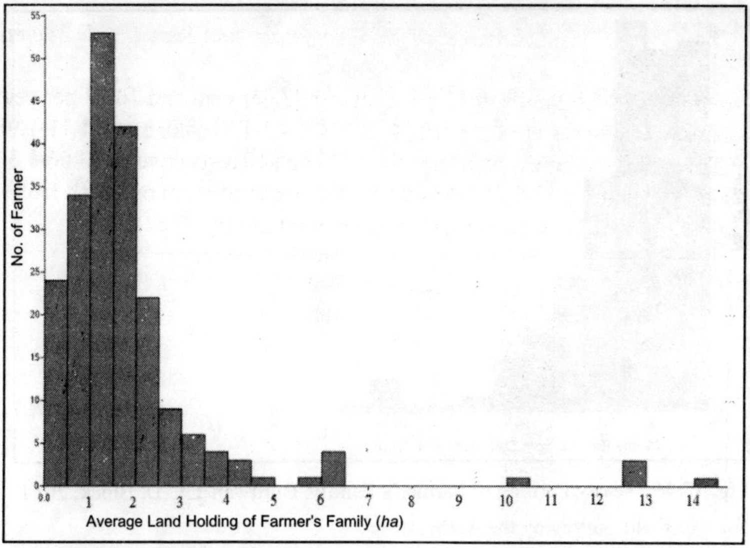

Fig. 17.14: Landholding of Farmer's Family, 2014

Source: Field Survey by the Authros.

₹ 21,000, those who have landholding of <0.6 ha. 20.67 per cent and 21.59 per cent farmer have yearly earnings of ₹ 21-42 thousand and ₹ 42-63 thousand due to landholding of 0.6-1.33 ha and 1.33-1.8 ha respectively. Yearly ₹ 63-84 thousand and ₹ 84-105 thousand are the earning of 13.46 per cent and 7.69 per cent family for landholding of 1.8-2.5 ha and 2.5-3 ha respectively. ₹ 1.05-1.26 lakh and ₹ 1.26-1.47 lakh are the earning of 4.08 per cent and 3.84 per cent respectively. Highest earnings (₹ 4.41-4.62 lakh) have been found in 0.89 per cent farmer's family where landholding is >15 ha (Fig. 17.15). In this context, profit from agriculture has been considered as the earning of agriculture and as a mode of the rural livelihood.

5.9. Deficit or Surplus Budget of the Farmer's Family

In the study area, 82 per cent family have deficit budget in their family earnings from agriculture. 21.15 per cent farmer's family has deficit of ₹ <24000 whereas 16.82 per cent and 19.23 per cent family have faced deficit of ₹ 24-48 thousand and 48-72 thousand because of low landholding (<2 ha) with 5-6 family members. 11.06 per cent and 5.28 per cent farmer's family has deficit budget of ₹ 72-96 thousand and ₹ 96-120 thousand due to landholding of 2 ha and family member of 6-7.

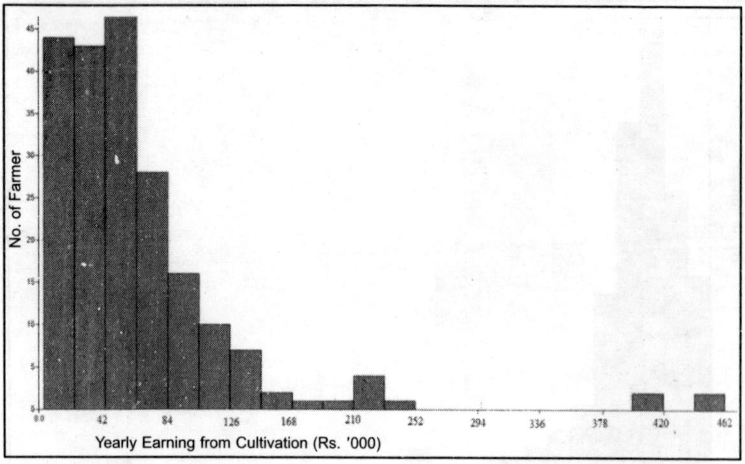

Fig. 17.15: Yearly Earning of Farmer's Family, Burdwan-I, C.D. Block, 2014
Source: Field Survey by the Authros.

There are ₹ 1.68-1.92 lakh deficit has been found in 3 farmer's family who have <1 ha land with 8-9 members in the family. Inversely, 8.17 per cent farmers have surplus of income (₹ 0-24 thousand) from agriculture due to landholding of >3 ha with 3-4 family member. 3.36 per cent and 3.84 per cent farmers have surplus budget of ₹ 24-48 thousand and ₹ 72-96 thousand respectively due to average landholding of 4-5 ha and 3-5 members in the family. Highest surplus income has been found in one family due to landholding of 13 ha with 5 members in family (Fig. 17.16). Grossly, a family with three members cannot survive only on agriculture with less than one ha land.

5.10. Engagement in Alternative Earning Opportunities of Farmer's Family

In the study area, farmers are also engaged in alternative source of income other than agriculture. There is 7 per cent farmer, holding more than 4 ha of land, do not have deficit budget as they are big farmer. But, 21 per cent farmer are engaged in different types of services of governmental or private service sector. Agricultural labour is the occupation of 14 per cent farmer. Different types of business like grocery, agricultural shop, cloths are the occupation of 24 per cent farmer. 3 per cent farmer is the owner of warehouse. 2 per cent farmer is engaged in miscellaneous activity like poultry farming and horticulture. But, 2 per cent farmer tries to sell their

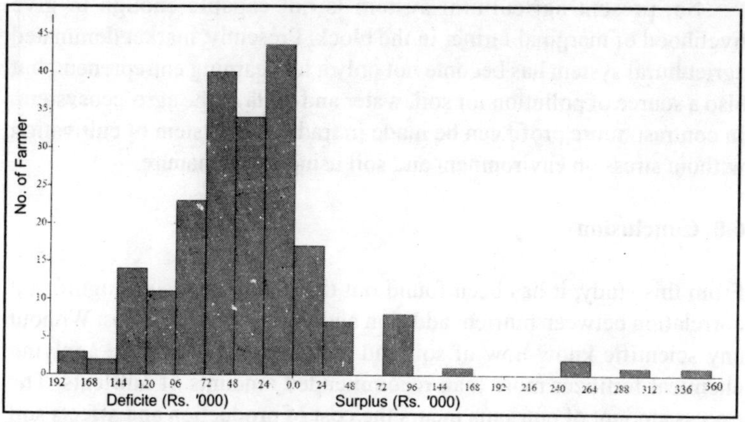

Fig. 17.16: Deficit or Surplus Budget of Farmer's Family, Burdwan-I, C.D. Block, 2014

Source: Field Survey by the Authros.

land for reluctant of agriculture. Lastly, 29 per cent farmer has no alternative opportunity of employment and they face vicious cycle of poverty. Few big farmers have installed submersible to withdraw excessive groundwater to sale as water for irrigation in other's agricultural land in commercial motives (*see* Fig. 17.17).

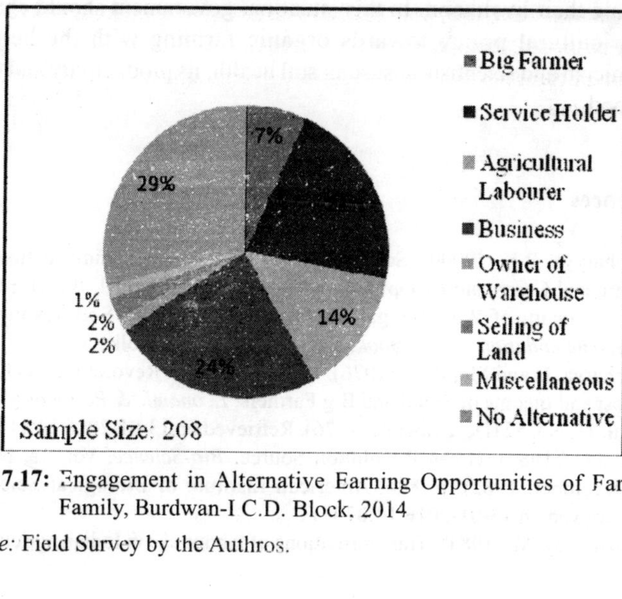

Fig. 17.17: Engagement in Alternative Earning Opportunities of Farmer's Family, Burdwan-I C.D. Block, 2014

Source: Field Survey by the Authros.

So, present agricultural system is not capable enough to give livelihood of marginal farmer in the block. Presently, market dominated agricultural system has become not only a low earning entrepreneur, but also a source of pollution for soil, water and biota of the agro-ecosystem. In contrast, more profit can be made in traditional system of cultivation without stress on environment and soil using green manure.

6.0. Conclusion

From this study, it has been found out that there is no such significant correlation between nutrient addition and productivity of crops. Without any scientific know-how of soil and agriculture, farmers are applying chemical fertilizer more than recommended amounts of nutrients. The excess amount of nutrients incurs the cost of production and affects soil health. Again, though the profit is higher in *khas* cultivation than *aman* or *boro*, farmers cultivate market based HYV seeds like I.R.-36, *Lalswarna* which has higher cost of production and low market price. In spite of higher profit in potato, 27 per cent farmer cultivates *boro* in coarse textured soil with the use of submersible irrigation instead of potato due to vague ideology on chemical farming. In present system of cultivation, 82 per cent family cannot survive with the earnings from agriculture and 71 per cent farmer seeks alternative earning opportunities to sustain their livelihood. In this situation, government should change the agricultural policy towards organic farming with the help of academician and scientists to sustain soil health, its productivity and rural livelihood.

References

Bhattacharyya, B.K., (2000), Soil Test-Based Fertilizer Recommendations for Principal Crops and Cropping Sequences in West Bengal, Bulletin No. 2 Government of West Bengal in Basak, R.K. (2000), Soil Testing and *Recommendation: A Text Book*, Kalyani Publishers, Kolkata.

Bhattacharya, P. and Majid, A. (1976). Impact of Green Revolution on Output, Cost and Income of Small and Big Farmers, *Economic & Political Weekly*, Vol. 11, No. 52 (December 25, 1976), Retrieved on 13-01-2016 14:11 UTC.

Brown, J.C. (1982). Green Revolution Source, *Bio-Science*, Vol. 32, No. 11 (December, 1982), p. 836, American Institute of Biological Sciences, Retrieved on 13-01-2016 14:07 UTC.

Chattopadhyay, M. (1984). Transformations of labour use in Indian agriculture,

Cambridge Journal of Economics, Vol. 8, No. 3 (September 1984), pp. 289-296, Retrieved on 13-01-2016 13:56 UTC.

Dhanagare, D.N. (1987). Green Revolution and Social Inequalities in Rural India, *Economic & Political Weekly*, Vol. 22, No. 19/21, Retrieved on 13-01-2016 14:06 UTC.

Motsara, M.R., Singh, J. and Verma, K.P.S. (1982) *Fertilizer News* 27 (9) *in* Basak, R.K. (2000), *Soil Testing and Recommendation: A Text Book*, Kalyani Publishers, Kolkata.

Nellithanam, J. (1997). Green Revolution and Subsistence Agriculture: You Reap as You Sow, *Economic & Political Weekly*, Vol. 32, No. 18, pp. 930-932, Retrieved on 13-01-2016 14:08 UTC.

Oommen, T.K. (1971). Green Revolution and Agrarian Conflict, *Economic & Political Weekly*, Vol. 6, No. 26, Retrieved on 13-01-2016 14:07 UTC.

Paddock, W.C. (1970). How Green Is the Green Revolution? *Bio-Science*, Vol. 20, No. 16 (August 15, 1970), pp. 897-902, American Institute of Biological Sciences, Retrieved on 13-01-2016 14:07 UTC.

Paul, A. (2015). *Banglar Krishi O Krishak Samasya O Sombhabana*, Naya Udyog Publication, Kolkata.

Shiva, V. (1991). The Violence of the Green Revolution: Third World Agriculture, Ecology and Politics *in* Smith, R. (2007). Review, on behalf of Taylor and Francis, Ltd., *Agenda Feminist Media*, Volume 1, No. 1 (2007), pp. 141-145, Retrieved on 13-01-2016 14:09 UTC.

Tangley, L. (1987). Beyond the Green Revolution, *Bio Science*, Vol. 37, No. 3, Whence Seeds for the Future? *Biologists Address Global Agricultural Issues*, pp. 176-180, Oxford University Press, Retrieved on 13-01-2016 14:09 UTC.

Thapar, R. (1973). Backwash of Green Revolution, *Economic & Political Weekly*, Vol. 8, No. 34 (August 25, 1973), p. 1547, Retrieved on 13-01-2016 14:10 UTC.

18

Land Suitability Analysis for Coconut through Geoinformatics for Sustainable Agriculture in Koraiyar Watershed, Coimbatore District, Tamil Nadu

P. Masilamani, S. Abdul Rahaman and *S. Aruchamy*

Land evaluation is formally defined as "the assessment of land performance when used for a specified purpose, involving the execution and interpretation of surveys and studies of land forms, soils, vegetation, climate and other aspects of land in order to identify and make a comparison of promising kinds of land-use in terms applicable to the objectives of the evaluation" (FAO, 1976).

The Aims of Land Evaluation

Land evaluation may be concerned with present land performance. Frequently however, it involves change and its effects: with change in the use of land and in some cases change in the land itself.

Evaluation takes into consideration the economics of the proposed enterprises, the social consequences for the people of the area and the country concerned, and the consequences, beneficial or adverse, for the environment. Thus land evaluation should answer the following questions:

- How is the land currently managed, and what will happen if present practices remain unchanged?

- What improvements in management practices, within the present use, are possible?
- What other uses of land are physically possible and economically and socially relevant?
- Which of these uses offer possibilities of sustained production or other benefits?
- What adverse effects, physical, economic or social, are associated with each use?
- What recurrent inputs are necessary to bring about the desired production and minimize the adverse effects? What are the benefits of each form of use?

If the introduction of a new use involves significant change in the land itself, as for example in irrigation schemes, then the following additional questions should be answered:

- What changes in the condition of the land are feasible and necessary, and how can they be brought about?
- What non-recurrent inputs are necessary to implement these changes?
- The evaluation process does not in itself determine the land-use changes that are to be carried out, but provides data on the basis of which such decisions can be taken.

Principles of the FAO Revised Framework for Land Evaluation

(i) Land suitability should be assessed and classified with respect to specified kinds of land-use and services;

(ii) Land evaluation requires a comparison of benefits obtained and the inputs needed on different types of land to assess the productive potential, environmental services and sustainable livelihood;

(iii) Land evaluation requires a multidisciplinary and cross-sectoral approach;

(iv) Land evaluation should take into account the biophysical, economic, social and political context as well as the environmental concerns;

(v) Suitability refers to use or services on a sustained basis; sustainability should incorporate productivity, social equity and environmental concerns;

(vi) Land evaluation involves a comparison of more than one kind of use or service;

(vii) Land evaluation needs to consider all stakeholders; and

(viii) The scale and the level of decision-making should be clearly defined prior to the land evaluation process.

Land Evaluation for Land Use Planning

Land evaluation, in general refers to matching land qualities with requirements of a particular landuse system. Remote sensing derived soil and terrain information are prerequisite for optimal landuse planning. The most widely used indices and approaches for land evaluation are land capability, land productivity and FAO Framework of land evaluation based soil and land suitability analysis. Remote sensing and GIS technique based integrated techniques were used for assessing land capability, land productively and soil suitability for various Land Utilization Types (LUTs) which are vital components for suggesting suitable cropping and farming system for sustainable agriculture development (Martin and Saha, 1999).

Land Suitability

Land suitability is the fitness of a given type of land for a defined use. The land may be considered in its present condition or after improvements. The process of land suitability classification is the appraisal and grouping of specific areas of land in terms of their suitability for defined uses.

Land Suitability Classes

Land suitability classes reflect degrees of suitability. The classes are numbered consecutively, by arabic numbers, in sequence of decreasing degrees of suitability within the Order. Within the Order Suitable the number of classes is not specified. There might, for example, be only two, S1 and S2. The number of classes recognized should be kept to the minimum necessary to meet interpretative aims; five should probably be the most ever used.

If three classes are recognized within the Order Suitable, as can often be recommended, the following names and definitions may be appropriate in a qualitative classification:

Class S1 Highly Suitable:	Land having no significant limitations to sustained application of a given use, or only minor limitations that will not significantly reduce productivity or benefits and will not raise inputs above an acceptable level.
Class S2 Moderately Suitable:	Land having limitations which in aggregate are moderately severe for sustained application of a given use; the limitations will reduce productivity or benefits and increase required inputs to the extent that the overall advantage to be gained from the use, although still attractive, will be appreciably inferior to that expected on Class S1 land.
Class S3 Marginally Suitable:	Land having limitations which in aggregate are severe for sustained application of a given use and will so reduce productivity or benefits, or increase required inputs, that this expenditure will be only marginally justified.

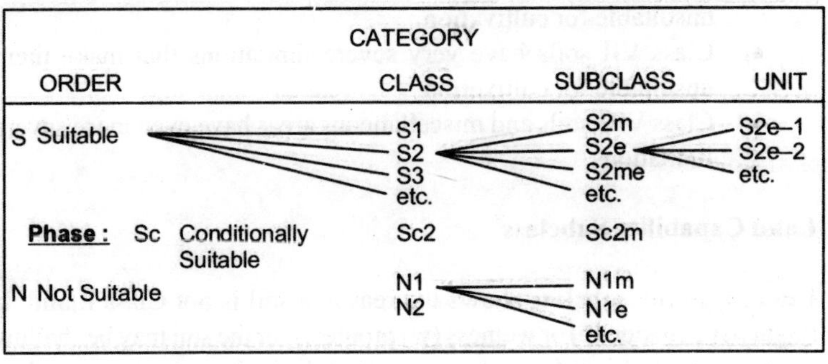

Land Capability Classification

Land capability classification involves an evaluation of the degree of limitation posed by permanent or semi-permanent attributes of land to one or more landuse. It is essentially a negative approach whereby the degree of constraint increases, the capability of land decreases. The land capability scheme was developed during the 1930s in USA, but the widespread adaptation of this scheme only began after 1960. The technique was evolved by the soil conservation service of the US

Department of agriculture and is referred to as the USDA system of land capability classification.

Land capability classification shows, in a general way, the suitability of soils for most kinds of field crops. In the capability classification system, soils are grouped at two levels: capability class and capability subclass.

Capability classes, the broadest groups, are designated by Roman numerals I through VIII. The numerals indicate progressively greater limitations and narrower choices for practical use. The classes are defined as follows:

- Class I soils have few limitations that restrict their use.
- Class II soils have moderate limitations that reduce the choice of plants or that require moderate conservation practices.
- Class III soils have severe limitations that reduce the choice of plants and/or that require special conservation practices.
- Class IV soils have very severe limitations that reduce the choice of plants and/or that require very careful management.
- Class V soils are not likely to erode, but have other limitations such as frequent flooding that limit their use.
- Class VI soils have severe limitations that make them generally unsuitable for cultivation.
- Class VII soils have very severe limitations that make them unsuitable for cultivation.
- Class VIII soils and miscellaneous areas have even more severe limitations.

Land Capability Subclass

Land capability subclass shows the reason a soil is not Class I land. It might have erosion (e) or wetness (w) problems, or the soil may be shallow or droughty (s). Class I soils have no capability subclasses because they have no severe limitations for crop production.

The letter "e" shows that the main limitation is risk of erosion unless close-growing plant cover or heavy plant residue cover is maintained.

The letter "w" shows that water in or on the soil interfere with plant growth or cultivation. In many soils, the wetness can be partly corrected by artificial drainage.

The letter "s" shows that the soil is limited mainly because it is shallow, droughty, or stony. For soil evaluation, Class II through VIII soils have one or more subclasses.

Land Irrigability

Land irrigability classification is an interpretative grouping of soils based on physical and socio-economic factors in addition to the soil irrigability and is primarily concerned with predicting the behaviour of soils when they are brought under irrigation (IARI, 1971).

Land suitable for irrigation are grouped under classes 1 to 4 according to their limitations. Lands not suited for irrigation are grouped under classes 5 and 6.

Land Irrigability Classes and their Definition

Class	*Definition*
1	Land that have few limitations of soils, topography or drainage for sustained use under irrigation.
2	Lands that have moderate limitations of soil and drainage for sustained use under irrigation.
3	Lands that have severe limitations of soil, drainage and slope for sustained use under irrigation.
4	Lands that have very severe limitations of topography and soil for sustained use under irrigation.
5	Land that are temporarily classed as not suitable for sustained use under irrigation.
6	Lands not suitable for irrigation due to topographic, soil and rock exposure limitations.
Miscellaneous	Water bodies, urban area.

References

FAO, 1976. A framework for land evaluation. *FAO Soils Bulletin* No. 32. Rome.

FAO. 1983. Guidelines: Land evaluation for rainfed agriculture. *FAO Soils Bulletin* No. 52. Rome.

Martin, D. and Saha, S.K. (1999). Land evaluation by integrated use of Remote Sensing and GIS for cropping pattern analysis. *Pro. Trends in Geoinformatics Technology and Applications, IIRS*, Dehradun, pp. 134-142.

Water and Environment

19

Fluoride Contamination in Drinking-Water and Related Health Hazards

In Some Parts of Lakshmisagar G.P., Simlapal Block of Bankura Dist., West Bengal: A Study in Medical Geography

Shrabani Dutta Sinha and *Ramamrita Singha Mahapatra*

Introduction

Medical-Geography is a recent sprout of health research that primarily deals on the co-relation between health-condition and its effective elements on Geo-spatial grounds and it also studies the natural and social factors that condition the varied frequency of certain diseases among population in different localities.

For maintenance of good health, safe and pure drinking water is very essential. For existence of all living elements in the universe, pure water is very significant. But sometimes it is contaminated with different elements like fluoride etc. Fluoride is a compound form of fluorine and other minerals like fluorspar, apatite, cryolite, fluorapatite etc. and this element exists in ground-water (Agarwal *et al.*, 1997).

The effect of fluoride on human health is now a crucial problem causing fluorosis. It threatens the health of millions of human beings in India. Therefore, extensive studies have been done on this national health problem (Johnson *et al.*, 2008, UNICEF, 2008). Fluoride in drinking water has both positive and negative impacts on human physical health. Both lower and higher concentration of fluoride is harmful to human body (Hussain *et al.*, 2004). So, the permissible limit of fluoride is 0.5-1.0 mg/ltr which is good for bones and teeth. But the excessive fluoride concentration causes dental and skeletal fluorosis and other disturbances on human body.

According to the report of BIS (Bureau of Indian Standards, 1991) and ICMR (Indian Council of Medical Research), the highest desirable limit of fluoride is specified as 1.0 mg/ltr and maximum permissible limit is 1.5 mg/ltr. According to the report by WHO, 20 states in India are affected by fluoride contamination, among which 09 states are much affected including West Bengal. In the map (Fig. 19.1) of West Bengal, 07 districts including Bankura have been highlighted as fluoride affected districts and through an intensive field-survey few parts of Lakshmisagar G.P. under Simlapal block have been noticed as fluoride affected zone. It is a natural hazard and also a public-health problem. In fine, the paper prescribes certain relevant measures to combat with the problem.

Objectives

The specific objectives of this study are as follows:

1. To present a snapshot for the causes of fluoride-contamination in drinking water.
2. To identify the nature and extent of disease through the drinking of fluoride-contaminated water.
3. To co-relate the relationship of fluoride-contamination of ground-water with geo-spatial context.
4. To find out some remedies to alleviate the problem in study area.
5. Finally, to request the elite group of researchers working on fluorosis to take-up well designed studies to answer some of the puzzles of interaction of fluoride.

Study Area

Geographically, the study area comes under Lakshmisagar gram panchyet which is under Simlapal community development block of Bankura district. The latitudinal and longitudinal coordinates of the area is 22°30' north and 87°38' east respectively. Total area of Lakshmisagar is 330.14 hec. The villages—Jamda, Tilabani and Maidhara are surrounded by river Shilabati and are located in west part of Simlapal block.

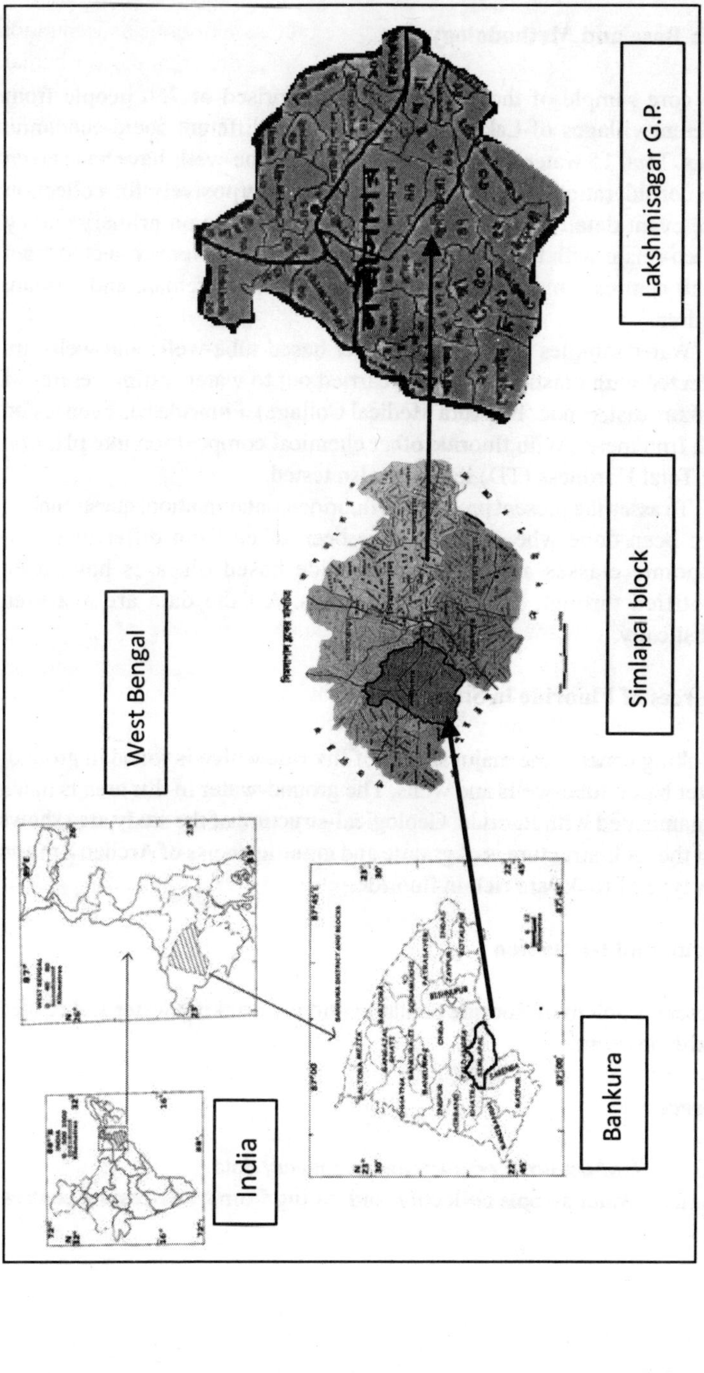

Fig. 19.1: Location of Study Area

Data Base and Methodology

The core sample of the present study comprised of 750 people from different villages of Lakshmisagar G.P. with different socio-economic status. Total 15 water samples from wells and tube-wells have been taken into consideration. The sample was selected purposively for collection of relevant data. This research work has been done on primary survey and co-relate with the results some secondary data were collected from health centres. Out of 750, 350 are male, 256 are female and 144 are children.

Water samples from ground-water based tube-wells and wells are collected with plastic bottles and carried out to water testing centres of Bankura dist. (under Bankura Medical Collage). Fluoride has been tested with Iron meter. With fluoride other chemical composition like pH, iron and Total Hardness (TD) level are also tested.

To asses the present problem of fluoride-contamination, questionnaire have been done where people have been taken from different socio-economic classes and different fluoride based diseases have been identified through signs and symptoms. All the data are analysed statistically.

Sources of Fluoride in Study Area

Drinking water is the major source of fluoride which is found in ground-water based tube-wells and wells. The ground-water in this area is much contaminated with fluoride. Geological-structure of the study area shows that the rock-structure is of granite and granitic gneiss of Archen Era and this type of rocks are rich in fluoride.

Result and Discussion

Present problem of fluoride contamination in drinking water and related health problem.

Source

1. Collection of primary and secondary data.
2. Water sample collection and testing from water-testing centres.

Methods

1. Door to door survey from Jamda, Maidhara and Tilabani villages.
2. Primary Health Centres (PHCs) from above villages.

Table 19.1: Population of the Villages

	Person	*Male*	*Female*	*Children*
Total sample population	750	350	256	144
Non-scheduled categories	650 (87%)	300	250	100
Scheduled categories	100 (13%)	50	06	44

Table 19.2: Percentage of the Population Pattern of the Villages

	Person	*Male*	*Female*	*Children*
Total sample population	750	350	256	144
Non-scheduled categories	87%	86%	97%	70%
Scheduled categories	13%	14%	0.3%	30%
Total (%)	**100%**	**100%**	**100%**	**100%**

Source: Field Survey by the Authors.

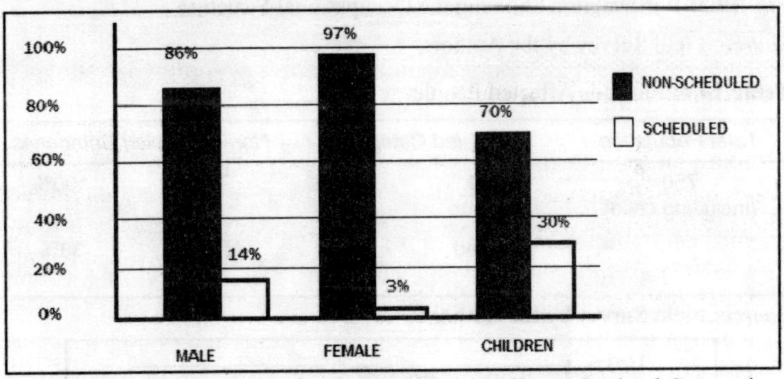

Fig. 19.2: Bar-Diagram Showing Population of Different Societal Categories

Source: Field Survey by the Authors.

Socio-Economical Status of the Study Area

One of the most important factors that affect the human health is socio economic condition of the people. Moreover, recurrence of disease due to poor environmental condition especially in rural area affects the various indicators of growth and development of health.

Our study area is not exception of that above statements. Among 750 people, 350 are male, 256 are female and 144 are children. Among

Table 19.3: Occupational Structure of the People

Total Population	*Service Holder*	*Agricultural Labour*	*Other Workers*	*Non-workers*
606 (Excluding Child)	40	200	200	166
100%	7%	33%	33%	27%

Source: Field Survey by the Authors.

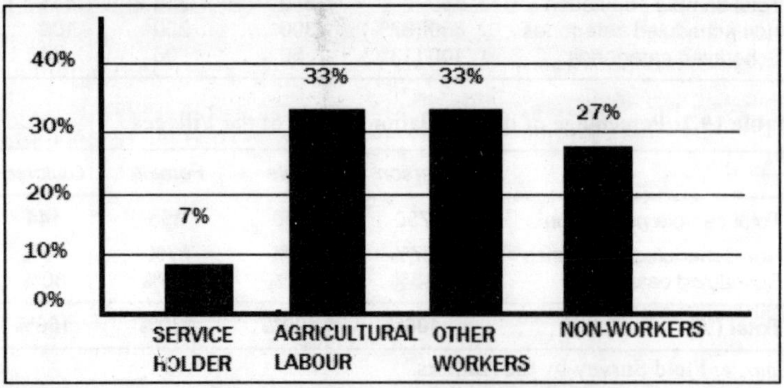

Fig. 19.3: Bar-Diagram Showing the Occupational Structure

Source: Field Survey by the Authors.

Table 19.4: Fluoride Affected People

Total Population	*Scheduled Categories*		*Non-scheduled Categories*	
750 (including child)	Total 100	100%	Total 650	100%
	Affected 80	80%	Affected 250	38%

Source: Field Survey by the Authors.

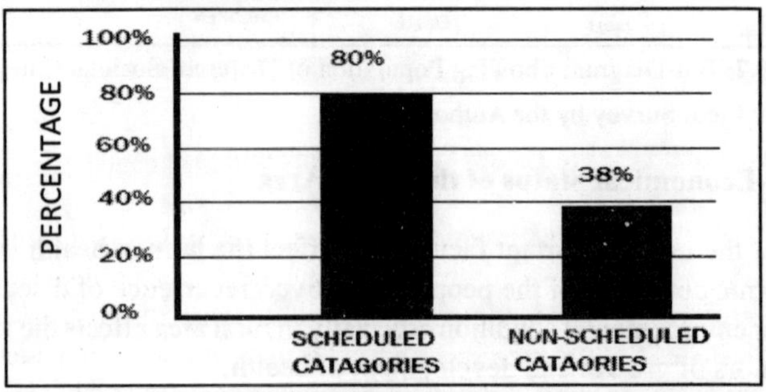

the adult age groups, only 7 per cent are service holder, 33 per cent are agricultural labour, other 33 per cent are engaged in other economic activities with few amount of wages or having small shops, but 27 per cent are totally non-workers.

Among the total sample-people, 87 per cent are non-scheduled categories and 13 per cent are of scheduled categories. From survey, it is clear the fluoride affected people are of poor-financial-conditions and they mainly belong to tribal category and few of them are of non-scheduled caste. Due to poor financial condition, they cannot afford nutritious foods, calcium rich foods etc. Moreover lack of proper education, they are also indifferent about their disease. It is painful truth, the minor symptoms (dental-fluorosis) are found in about 80 per cent of total sample-population.

Fluoride Level of Ground-Water

In our study area, out of total 15 samples highest fluoride level of 8.5mg/ltr has been found in a tube-well from Jamda-gram. It was first observed at the time of water testing of "SAJAL DHARA PRAKALPA"(two years ago). Tube-wells and wells were seized from then and now water supply has been started from "Shilabati river". According to the viewpoint of local people, fluoride is present in soil also. The water having fluoride level below 1 mg/ltr. is good for teeth and bones, but when it exceeds, becomes curse (*see* Table 19.5 and Fig. 19.5).

Table 19.5: Fluoride Level of Ground-Water of Study-Area

No. of Samples	*0.5-1 mg/Ltr*	*1-1.5 mg/ltr*	*1.5-2 mg/ltr*	*2-2.5 mg/ltr.*	*2.5-3 mg/lt*	*>3mg/ltr.*
15 100%	2 13%	5 34%	3 20%	2 13%	2 13%	1 7%

Source: Field Survey by the Authors.

Nature of Fluoride Based Diseases in Study-Area

Any kind of disease entirely depends on climate, socio-economic condition, food habits, living-styles and type of drinking water also. varying conditions of these, diseases also vary from place to place. Medical geography mainly studies the natural and social factors that condition the varied frequency of certain disease among populations in different localities.

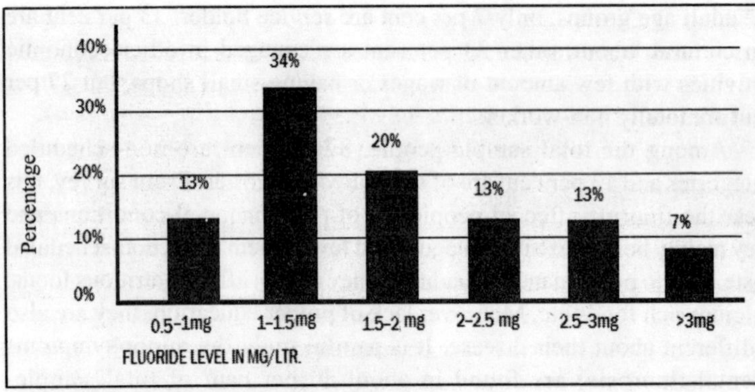

Fig. 19.5: Fluoride-Level of Water-Samples

Source: Field Survey by the Authors.

We all listen the slogan "drink pure water", "drink clean water, save life" etc. but inspite of all these, fluoride contamination in drinking water is a public health problem in many areas of the globe. Few areas in West Bengal have been declared as fluoride-affected-zone. Our study area of Bankura dist. has been suffering from such curse.

In major part of Jamda, Tilabani and Maidhara (western part) are affected by fluoride. Out of total 15 samples, more than 50 per cent tube-wells and wells (number of tube-wells and wells is 08), fluoride levels are more than 1.5 mg/ltr. A tube-well has been found where fluoride level is more than 8.5 mg/ltr. As a result more than 70 per cent people are fluoride affected and suffered by different diseases caused by drinking the contaminated water. Female and children are more affected than male. Tables 19.6 and 19.7 showing % of Fluoride Affected People.

Tables 19.6: Percentage of Fluoride Affected People (Population)

Total Population	*Fluoride Affected*
750 100%	533 71%

Source: Field Survey by the Authors.

Table 19.7: Percentage of Fluoride Affected People

Fluoride Affected	*Male*	*Female*	*Children*
533 100%	160 30%	171 32%	202 38%

Source: Field Survey by the Authors.

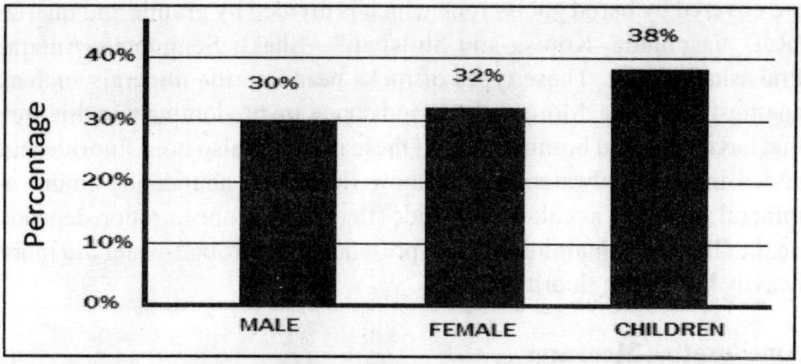

Fig. 19.6: Bar-Diagram Showing Percentage of Fluoride Affected People
Source: Field Survey by the Authors.

Different types of fluoride based diseases are found in my study area. Mainly dental fluorosis (pitted enamel and discolouration of teeth), skeletal fluorosis (pain and stiffness of joints, chronic joint pain, arthritis and calcification of ligaments), fluoride-toxicity (nausea, vomiting, diarrhea, abdominal pain, numbness, tingling extremities etc.) are very common. Children are mainly affected by dental-fluorosis. In spite of these, gastro-intestinal problem, neurological problem, problem on forward flexion of spine are also seen. Thyroid malfunctioning are also noticed among the female and it is assumed that it is due to fluorosis because fluorosis negetively affects thyroid function. Different types of fluoride based diseases and percentage of affected people are shown in the Table 19.8.

Table 19.8: Diff. Types of Fluoride Based Diseases and % of Affected People

Name of the Diseases	*Percentage of the People Suffered*
Dental Fluorosis	35%
Skeletal Fluorosis	25%
Fluoride Toxicity	15%
Gastrointestinal Problem	15
Neurological Problem	5%
Thyroid Mal-functioning	5%

Source: Field Survey by the Authors.

Relation Between Geological Structure and Fluoride

Geological structure of underground-water of Bankura dist. is much prone to fluoride contamination. The area is underlain by pre-Cambrian igneous (granite) and metamorphic (gneiss) rock. Both sides of river Shilabati are covered by bared gneiss rock which is divided by granite and quartz. (Ref. "Damunda, Kopisa and Shilabati"—Shakti Sengupta—Antaral Prakashan, 2002). These types of rocks bear fluoride minerals such as apatite-fluorite etc. More ancient sandstones are predominant in this area that have mica and hornblende and these minerals also hold fluoride and added into groundwater. We all know fluoride is abundantly found in mineral salts such as calcium fluoride (fluorspar). Concentration depends on the fluorine containing mineral present. Underground-water are more heavily laden with fluorine.

Ameliorative Measures

From the above discussion the fact is that, in our study area a major number of villagers are suffering from different types of fluorosis. The problem is highly alarming to the society.

Most of sufferers are economically poor and ill-educated also. They do not know the acute and proper way to solve the problem. They do not have proper medical treatment.

Now, Government supply different types of calcium tablets to the fluorosis patients through health-centres. But is it the only solution? So, we draw attention to the government planners, policy-makers, other societies and also to the villagers to solve the curse.

1. Calcium in diet, reduces the absorption of fluoride. So, government should take care of economically poor people and also affected people to enhance their financial condition so that they can purchase food because medicine is not the only solution of such problem.
2. Hard water rich in calcium reduces the fluoride toxicity. In some patients with calcium deficiency OSTEOMALACIA (found in our study area) type changes are seen. Constriction of vertebral canal and intervertebral foramen may ultimately cause paralysis. So, trace elements like molybdenum enhances the effect of fluoride.
3. Since the major source of fluoride is drinking water, de-fluoridation is the best preventive measure which can be carried out at domestic as well as community-level.
4. Vitamin C, D, fresh fruits, calcium rich foods also reduce fluorosis. These may be arranged from health department for poor people.

5. All the tube-wells are not fluoride-affected. So, people can use the tube-wells which are fluoride free.
6. Medical team can be formed for the treatment of fluorosis affected villagers and for counselling about fluorosis.
7. Resin and other filter beds are also available filtering through which reduces the amount of fluoride.
8. Changing of living style is urgent. Wine, excess tea, *gutkha* etc. should be checked.
9. Pipe water supply from river Shilabati is needed. Although, it has been started, yet it has not reached to the every villager.
10. Awareness programme must be taken from school-level and it must be carried on at a certain span of time to all the villagers.
11. Alum is used at domestic level for removal of fluoride. In India, a scientific method "NALGONDA TECHNIQUE" in which based on the amount of fluoride in drinking water and alkalinity of the water (expressed as $MgCaCO_2$), amount of alum to be mixed with water is calculated.

Conclusion

The source of fluoride in drinking water is natural but fluorosis disease is a social problem. We all try to lead a disease free life. So, we can conclude with this hope that if all the above measures can be taken in proper way, although the affected people will not be cured properly but the problem can be reduced in number. Moreover, other villagers will have to lead a fluorosis-free-healthy life. We all come forward unitedly to establish "Jamda, Tilabani, Maidhara"—a complete fluorosis-free area.

Acknowledements

The authors are thankful to the villagers, teachers and school-staffs, staffs of B.D.O. Office, P.H.C. of Lakshmisagar, B.P.H.C. of Simlapal block and Lakshmisagar G.P. for their generous help to collect the relevant informations and datas.

References

Agarwal, V., Vaish, A.K., Vaish, P. (1997). Groundwater Quality: Focus on Fluoride and Fluorosis in Rajasthan, *Current Science*, 73(9), pp. 743-746.

WHO—Monograph of fluoride and human health, WHO Geneva, 1970.

Susheela, A.K., 2001. *A Treatise on Fluorosis;* Fluorosis Research and Rural Development Foundation, New Delhi.

Shiv Chandra, *et al.*, 1980. *Determination of Optimal Fluoride intake, Community Dental and Oral Epidemiol*, 8:35-40.

Handa, B.K., 1975. *Geochemistry and Genesis of Fluoride Containing Groundwaters in India.*

Gupta S.K. and R.D. Deshpande, 1998. Depleting groundwater levels and increasing fluoride concentration in villages of Mehsana dist., Gujarat, India: Cost to economy and health, report sponsored by Habitat International Coalition.

20

Impact of Fluoride on Human Life

A Case Study on a Tribal Village of Purulia District

Somnath Rudra

Introduction

Groundwater is the major source of drinking water for many of the Indian population. More than 90 per cent of the rural population use groundwater for domestic purposes. But, this water becomes contaminated with various elements and by using this contaminated water, considerable damages occur on human health. Fluoride is one of the elements which contaminate water and human health hazards occur.

Fluoride is the compound form of fluorine. Fluoride is a common element and exists in a number of minerals, like fluorspar, cryolite, apatite, mica and fluorapatite (Agarwal *et al.*, 1997). Fluoride ions from these minerals leach into the groundwater and contribute to high fluoride concentrations. Therefore, handpumps, dug and borewells have been very much contaminated with fluoride. Though fluoride enters the body through food, water, industrial exposure, drugs, cosmetics, etc., drinking water is the major contributor (75-90% of daily intake) (Sarala and Rao, 1993). Fluoride is important for tooth and bone formation. Deficit of fluoride in human body causes dental caries. But, if the concentration of fluoride in water exceeds the limit then many problems are created in our health.

According to BIS (Bureau of Indian Standards, 1991) and ICMR (Indian Council of Medical Research, 1975), the highest desirable limit of fluoride is specified at 1.0 mg/litre and the maximum permissible limit is 1.5 mg/litre. According to WHO (1997), the permissible limit for fluoride is 1.5 mg/litre.

Contamination of drinking water with fluoride is a public health problem in many parts of the world as well as in India. Endemic fluorosis occurring due to consumption of groundwater contaminated with fluoride is threatening the health of millions of people in India and therefore is a challenging and extensively studied national health problem (Fawell, *et al.*, 2006). High fluoride concentrations and fluorosis in the country are commonly associated with rural areas, arid and semi-arid climate, granites and gneisses, and advanced stage of groundwater development (Handa, 1988; Subba Rao, 2008). The community living in rural or semi-urban areas are most severely affected as they are dependent on groundwater drawn by handpumps, tube-wells, open well water for consumption. Water quality is seldom tested in rural areas because of the strong conviction that water drawn from the deepest crust of the earth has to be safe or pure.

At present, fluorosis is endemic in at least 20 states in India, affecting more than 65 million people, including 6 million children (Gupta *et al.*, 2006). In West Bengal, fluoride was first detected at Bhubanandapur in Nalhati-I Block in Birbhum District in 1996. In 2005, 729 sources were found to be contaminated with fluoride above 1.5 ppm in 43 blocks of seven districts *viz*. Purulia, Birbhum, Bankura, Malda, South Dinajpur, North Dinajpur and South 24-Parganas.

Juludi village of Babugram Gram Panchayat of Raghunathpur-I CD Block is highly affected by fluoride contamination in drinking water. So, large numbers of people are affected by dental, skeletal and different non-skeletal fluorosis diseases.

Objective

The study has been done to achieve the following objectives:

(1) To identify the natural, socio-economic and habitual causes of fluoride contamination in drinking water and onset of fluorosis in the village.
(2) To analyse the relation between fluorosis patients and other socio-economic factors.
(3) To measure the nature and extent of fluorosis diseases suffered by the people through the drinking of fluoride contaminated water.

(4) To find out some remedial measures suitable for this area to alleviate the problem.

Study Area

Juludi village is located at Babugram gram panchayat of Raghunathpur-I CD block of Purulia district. Total area of the village is 94.7 hectare. Total number of households in the village is 96. According to 2011 census, total population of the village is 478, out of which male and female populations are 264 and 214 respectively. As far as the caste composition of the village is concerned the village is fully settled by tribal community mainly *Santal.*

Highest level of fluoride concentration in the tube-wells is 4.08 mg/litre. As the people are mostly from tribal community, who are poor and their education level is very low, more than 70 per cent people are still illitreate. That is why, people are very much suffering from the problems of fluorosis disease. No human intervention has been taken so far to tackle the problem. So, the people are suffering acutely from this disease (*see* Fig. 20.1).

Methodology

The present study has been made by both primary and secondary data. For secondary data, information regarding fluoride contamination has been collected from different books, journals, websites, census report etc. The drinking water from different tube-wells have been taken for testing at an interval of two years. These samples are tested at the fluoride testing labs located at Purulia. Household survey has been conducted with well defined schedules and questionnaires. The questionnaire has two sets of questions. The first set of questionnaire includes the questions on the socio-economic conditions of the affected families of the villagers. The second set includes the questions on the different fluorosis diseases suffered by the people. These collected data are then tabulated and statistically analysed by choosing different variables and the relationships between different variables are found out.

Causes of Fluoride Contamination

Fluoride contamination in drinking water and thereby onset of fluorosis diseases have several natural as well as socio-economic causes. In Purulia

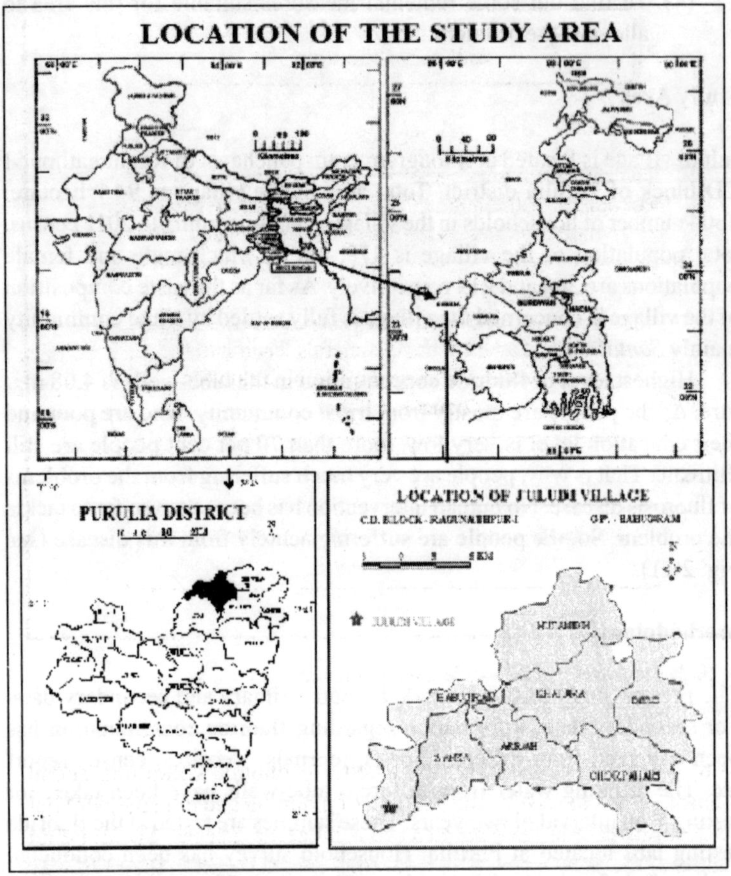

Fig. 20.1: Location Map of the Study Area

district, minerals like fluorite, topaz, apatite, rock phosphate, phosphatic nodules and phosphorites are widespread and contain high percentage of fluorides. Abnormal level of fluoride in water is common in fractured hard rock zone with pegmatite veins. Fluoride ions from these minerals leach into the groundwater and contribute to high fluoride concentrations. Thus, the drinking water of the handpumps, dug and bore-wells are contaminated with fluoride (Fig. 20.2).

Social factors like caste status, belief, tradition etc. play important role to the onset of fluorosis. People from high caste social group are

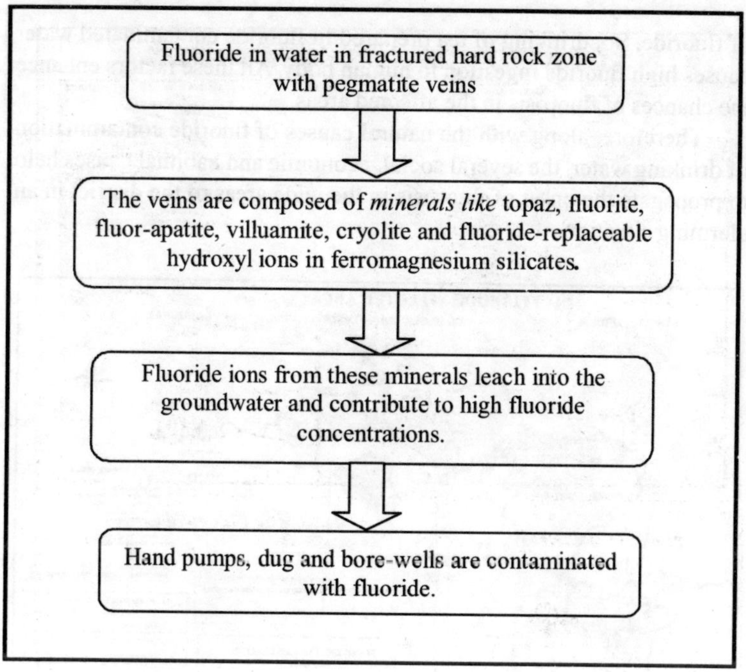

Fig. 20.2: Mechanism of Fluoride Contamination

Source: Rudra, S., 2014.

able to combat fluorosis with their better economic condition, social influence, power to receive the benefits of planning and management but poor destitute people have no mean to combat the disease. Social belief or habits of the people also play important role to retain in their old way of life and take the contaminated water long time. In this way fluorosis disease persists long time in the village. On the other hand, people have erroneous concept that contaminated water is safe for cooking, as boiling of this water may reduce the level of contamination. But, it is not true and fluoride contaminated water is not safe for both drinking and cooking purposes because cooking or boiling of it increases the concentration level.

Several bad habits of the people of the fluoride endemic areas may accelerate fluorosis more intensively. People of the affected villages of the study area have habit of chewing *supari*, *gutkha*, *pan masala*, tobaco etc. which have high amount of fluoride content. Tea contains high amount of fluoride. So, drinking of tea prepared in fluoride contaminated water causes high fluoride ingestion to human body. All these factors enhance the chances of fluorosis in the affected areas.

Therefore, along with the natural causes of fluoride contamination of drinking water, the several social, economic and habitual causes help to propagate the onset of fluorosis in the wide areas of the district in an alarming situation.

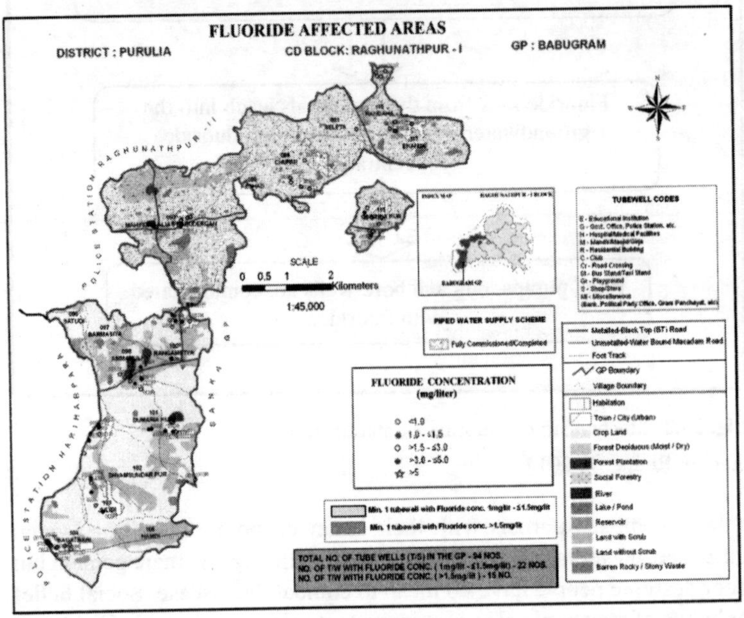

Fig. 20.3: Fluoride Affected Villages of Babugram G.P.

Source: WBPHED.

In Babugram GP of Raghunathpur-I CD block, out of total 10 villages, fluoride contamination in tube-wells are recorded in 6 villages. In Rangametya and Juludi villages, above 4 mg/litre fluoride in tube-wells are recorded (Table 20.1).

In Juludi village the main source of drinking water is from ten tube-wells. Out of these ten tube-wells 40 per cent tube-wells are fluoride contaminated above the level of 1.5 mg/litre. One interesting feature is that in all the tube-wells fluoride level has been increased in two years interval. This is shown in Table 20.2.

Table 20.1: Fluoride levels in Different Villages of Babugram G.P.

Village	*Maximum Level of Fluoride (mg/litre)*
Rangametya	4.41
Juludi	4.08
Gobinapur	2.77
Shyamsundarpur	1.82
Churmi	1.70
Dumariakuri	1.54
Ekanja	1.48
Manihara	1.01
Nandaha	0.64
Bagatbari	0.54

Source: WBPHED.

Table 20.2: Fluoride Level of the Tube-Wells

Sl. No.	*Ground water based Tube-wells*	*Changes in the Fluoride level (mg/litre)of tube-wells*	
	Location	*26.10.10*	*29.08.12*
1.	Near the House of Somnath Besra	1.15	1.46
2.	Near the House of Sunil Majhi	1.12	1.33
3.	Near the House of Mantulal Majhi	1.09	1.31
4.	Near Transformer	**3.66**	**4.08**
5.	Near the House of Nambar Majhi	**3.34**	**3.57**
6.	Inside of Primary School	**3.15**	**3.89**
7.	Beside of Junior High School	**3.91**	**3.42**
8.	Namo Para; Near Tetul Tree	1.22	1.24
9.	Namo Para; Near the House of Dasharath Majhi	0.85	0.89
10.	Namo Para; Near the House of Banku Majhi	1.32	1.43

Source: Compiled by Author from Field Survey.

Socio-economic Status of the Villagers

Socio-economic status like occupation, income, level of education, caste, family size, house type, assets and amenities etc. play important role on any kind of health problems. Proportion of fluorosis patients of the family is also determined by these factors.

Occupation is an important factor of the socio-economic status of the family because it determines the income level, purchasing capacity, education, dietary status, capacity to treat the patients etc. All these factors may also influence to protect fluorosis disease to human being. In this village, the tribal people are engaged in main occupations like cultivation and agriculture labourer and household industries. 82 per cent families are dependent on cultivation of their small proportion of land, 16 per cent are dependent of daily labour on the others agriculture works and only 2 per cent families depend on household industries like *sal* leaves plate making and *beedi* making. Other subsidiary occupations are animal rearing, rickshaw puller etc. As for example, agricultural labourers are the poor sections of the society who suffer from undernutrition, malnutrition and less immunity power. Most of the agricultural labourers are illitreate and not aware of the problems of fluorosis. That is why, they can not confront with the attack of fluorosis. On the other hand, the cultivator class of people cultivates their own chunk of land and they have substantial access to monetary capital. With this economic advantage, they can protect and prevent themselves from the attack of fluorosis.

In this village, all the patients belong to Scheduled Tribe communities where poverty, malnutrition, undernutrition, less immunity power and dirty physical environment invite fluorosis.

Education status of the villagers is very poor. Only 43 per cent male population is literate. Female literacy is very poor, 71 per cent females are illiterate. Only 1.42 per cent male gets their higher education but no female person of the village still has crossed the level of higher secondary education. Due to becoming illiterate, they are not aware of any kind of fluorosis diseases. They cannot be mobilized and inspired against the protection and prevention of fluorosis.

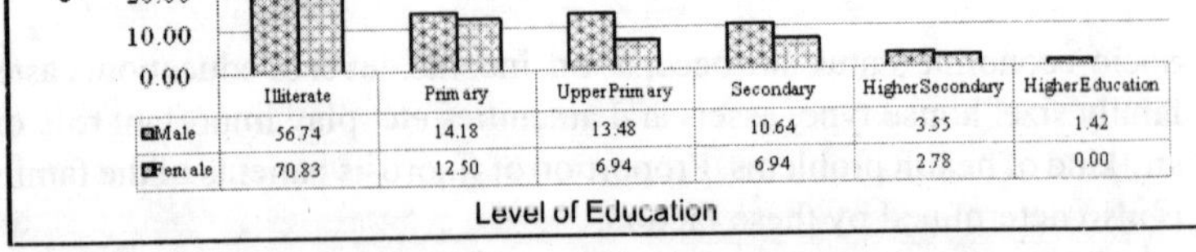

Fig. 20.4: Level of Education of Juludi Village

House type may indicate the numerical strength of fluorosis patients in an indirect manner. As for example, rich literate people may reside in large number in brick built houses whereas the poor illiterate sections of the community have no other alternatives but to stay at their mud built huts. Therefore, the brick built house dwellers have better access to the infrastructure facilities and amenities to resist, prevent and protect from fluorosis diseases. Likewise, the concrete roofed house dwellers can resist fluorosis to a larger extent than the asbestos, tile and thatched roofed dwellers.

Availability of infrastructure, facilities and amenities indicates the comfort of the people. If the people have well access to the services from various infrastructure, facilities and amenities, then they can maintain their daily life more easily and comfortably. Under such a situation, an effort can be made to resist fluorosis. Generally, the socio-economically well to do families have well access to the services from infrastructure, facilities and amenities, so that, they can protect themselves from fluorosis. The situation of the poor people is just the reverse as they have inadequate access to infrastructure, facilities and amenities. That is why, poor people are very much susceptible to fluorosis.

Impact of Fluoride Contamination on Human Health

The impact of fluoride contamination on human health is related not only to deficiency of fluoride in human health but also to their excessive intake. Fluoride in drinking water has both beneficial and detrimental effects on human health. Thus, the fluoride concentration in drinking water is like a two-edged knife, both its higher and lower concentration is not safe (Hussain *et al.,* 2004a). Impact of fluoride on human health depends on the level of concentration of fluoride in drinking water. The intake of fluoride in permissible limits of 0.5-1.0 mg/litre is known to be beneficial for human health in production and maintenance of healthy teeth and bones (Wood, 1974). Excess fluoride intake causes diseases of dental fluorosis, skeletal fluorosis and other non-skeletal fluorosis like muscular problem, gastro-intestinal, neurological problem, painful skin rashes and allergy, abnormal thyroid function and other hormonal disturbances.

A detailed account regarding different fluorosis diseases on various limbs of human being are studied here which is shown in Table 20.3. Here, 30.18 per cent people are affected by different types of fluorosis diseases. The present study indicates that proportion of different fluorosis diseases vary considerably. In this village, dental and skeletal fluorosis are the most important diseases among all types of fluorosis diseases.

Dental fluorosis is the major disease followed by skeletal fluorosis. Here, 51 per cent fluorosis patients are from dental fluorosis out of which proportion of male is more than female. Male dental fluorosis patients are 54.55 per cent while female are 47.62 per cent. This form of fluorosis affects the teeth and mainly occurs in children. Children under nine years of age exposed to levels of fluoride greater than 1.5 mg/liter may develop a condition known as *dental fluorosis.* First, the enamel of the teeth is eroded and the teeth become chalky white in appearance. Then, yellowish and white spots develop which then, transform into dark brown mottling or spotting of the permanent teeth. With due time, the spots become blank and cavities are formed which leads to breaking of teeth.

Skeletal fluorosis affects the bones or skeleton of the body. It can affect both young and old people. One can have aches and pain in the joints. The joints which are normally affected by skeletal fluorosis are neck, hip, shoulder and knee that makes it difficult to walk and movements, and painful rigidity or stiffness of joints also sets in. A patient with fluorosis in the terminal stages may be crippled and paralysed. Here, out of total fluorosis patients, 34.88 per cent patients are affected by skeletal fluorosis where male proportion is 38.10 per cent and female proportion is 31.82 per cent.

Other important non-skeletal fluorosis patients are below 10 per cent in the village. This can be observed from Table 20.3.

Table 20.3: Comparison between Proportions of Different Fluorosis Diseases

Sl. No.	*Patients*	*Total*	*Male*	*Female*
1.	% of fluorosis patient to population	30.18	31.21	29.17
2.	% of Dental fluorosis to total fluorosis patient	51.16	54.55	47.62
3.	% of Skeletal Adult fluorosis patient to total patient	34.88	38.10	31.82
4.	% of fluorosis patient with muscular problem to total patient	3.49	4.55	2.38
5.	% of patient with neurological problem to total patient	3.49	2.27	4.76
6.	% of patient with gastrointestinal problem to total patient	6.98	6.82	7.14
7.	% of patient with polyurea & polydipsia problem to total patient	3.49	2.27	4.76
8.	% of patient with allergy problem to total patient	5.81	4.55	7.14

Source: Compiled by the Author from Field Survey.

Other Socio-economic Problems Due to Fluorosis

Large number of peoples have now become the fluorosis patients in the village. This disease causes not only the health problems but also causes several socio-economic problems to the society as well as in the families. These are:

- Large numbers of children in between 6-18 year have dental fluorosis with whitish and brown pitted teeth. Children having dental fluorosis suffer from dental pain.

- Young people at the age of 20-40 years have been affected by skeletal fluorosis with heel pain and swollen hill, pain in back, neck, stiffness in spine and bent frontward. They cannot sit properly without any high base support. They cannot sit in cross leg situation and sometimes fall backward suddenly.
- Some people cannot stand erect and even walk properly without any support of log of sticks. They cannot bent forward quickly during their walking.
- Fluorosis makes the people physically weak and adversely affects the economy of the family. The earning members of the family remain unemployed as nobody is willing to hire the physically weak fluorosis patients as labourer.
- Poor people do not have sufficient money to treat the disease at proper place. In this way the family earning stops, as the main earning member is in bedridden and on the other hand, they sell off their last assets also to treat the patients. So, they go to the local doctor and most of the time they spent money but without any result.
- The young boys and girls having dental fluorosis face many problems at their school. Their friends do not allow them to sit beside them and talk to them, as they consider this disease as communicable disease. They laugh at them due to having brown teeth.
- Head of the fluorosis affected households faces the problem of marrying off their young girls because the fluorosis affected girls are refused in many cases to get married as the brown strain or pitting teeth lose their facial beauty and the grooms do not select a girl of that area for marry.
- The relatives of the villagers do not want to visit and stay at their home. If they come they do not want to take water of their home as they consider it as poisonous water.
- The affected people feel fear to take part in any social gatherings because they become the matter of jokes and laugh with bending body.

Recommendation

The Juludi village is fully tribal village. Here, education level is very low and the people are drinking the fluoride contaminated water throughout the long time. That is why, the people are suffering from fluorosis diseases very much. There is no human intervention taken in the village from any sector of the Governmental or non-Governmental organization. The following programme can be taken:

1. The fluoride contaminated tube-wells should be identified and marked by red label and people should be prevented to use that water for drinking purpose.
2. Fluoride free water from other sources should be supplied. If it is not possible immediately, then Domestic fluoride filter may be supplied to the affected families.
3. Fluoride filter should be made up by local sanitary marts and should be distributed to the affected households.
4. Proper training should be given to the people to use and maintenance of the filters.
5. Rain water harvesting plant should be installed at the school building of the village to provide fluoride free water for cooking and drinking purpose.
6. The community defluoridation unit has been installed by UNICEF but, functioning of the project is not started yet. It should be started very soon to provide fluoride free water.
7. Food habit should be changed. Food should be enriched with vitamin C, D, protein and calcium as these food protect health from fluorosis.
8. Dental screening and health survey at regular interval should be performed to monitor the fluorosis patients.
9. A medical team should be formed to regular check up the patients and supply proper medicine and regular monitoring the progress of health status.
10. Emphasis should be given to the people having low income and low education level.
11. Awareness programme should be performed to aware the people about the source of their problems, personal remedial measures, changing of bad habits and food habits.

Conclusion

So, it can be concluded that source of fluoride in drinking water is natural but its impact on human health depends on its level of concentration in water, socio-economic factors and food habits etc. Due to low availability of fresh drinking water, the contamination of it with fluoride is very dangerous. People have no other option, but to take such contaminated water for drinking purpose. Fluorosis disease not only affects badly the health of the people, but also it adversely affects the economy of the family and society. Economically, the affected people are most backward. Access of modern facilities and social amenities to them are not sufficient. All these factors make the problem more acute. But, if the recommended measures are implied holistically, then the problems can be reduced remarkably.

References

Agarwal, V., Vaish, A.K., Vaish, P. (1997), Groundwater quality: focus on fluoride and fluorosis in Rajasthan, *Current Science*, 73(9), pp. 743-746.

BIS (1991), Bureau of Indian Standards, Drinking Water Specification (First Revision) IS 10500.

Census of India, 2011.

Fawell, J., Bailey, K., Chilton, J., Dahi, E., Fewtrell, L. and Magara, Y. (2006). *Fluoride in Drinking Water*, World Health Organisation, IWA Publishing, Alliance House, 12 Caxton Street, London SW1H 0QS, UK.

Gupta, S., Banerjee, S., Saha, R., Datta, J.K., Mondal, N. (2006). Fluoride geochemistry of groundwater in Nalhati-1 block of the Birbhum district, West Bengal, India. *Fluoride*, 39 (4): 318-320.

Handa, B.K. (1988). Fluoride occurrences in natural water in India and its significance. *BHU-Jal News*, 3, 21-24.

Hussain, J., Sharma, K.C., and Hussain, I. (2004a). Fluoride in drinking water and its ill effect on Human Health: A review. *Journal of Tissue Research,* 4(2), 263-273.

ICMR (1975). Indian Council of Medical Research, Manual of standards of quality for drinking water supplies, Special Report Series No. 44.

Rudra, S. (2014). Problems of Fluoride Contamination in Drinking Water: A Case Study in Patamputra Village of Purulia District. *J. Practising Geographer,* 18(2): pp. 71-81.

Sarala, K., P.R. Rao (1993), Endemic fluorosis in the village Ralla, Anantapuram in Andhra Pradesh an Epidemiological study, *Fluoride*, 26, pp. 177-180.

Short, H.E., G.R., McRobert, T.W., Bernard and Mannadinayar, A.S. (1937). "Endemic Fluorosis in the Madras Presidency". *Indian Journal of Medical Research*, 25, 553-561.

Subba Rao, N. (2008). Fluoride in Groundwater, Varaha River Basin, Visakhapatnam District, Andhra Pradesh, India. *Environmental Monitoring and Assessment, 152*, 47-60.

UNICEF (1999): States of the Art Report on the Extent of Fluoride in Drinking

Water and the Resulting Endemicity. In India, Report by Fluorosis and Rural Development, Foundation for UNICEF, New Delhi.

WHO (1971): *International Water Standards*, Geneva.

Wood, J.M. (1974). Biological cycles for toxic elements in the environment. *Science*, 183, 1049-1052.

World Health Organization (1997): *Guideline for Drinking Water Quality Health Criteria and Other Supporting Information*, Vol. 2, 2nd Ed., World Health Organization, Geneva.

21
Health Risk Associated with Fluoride Contaminated Groundwater
Some Facts on Health

Prithviraj Karak

1. Introduction

Being the most electronegative of all chemical elements, fluorine is highly reactive chemically, it is rarely available in nature as elemental fluorine. Fluoride is an ion of the chemical element fluorine (F), which belongs to the halogen family. Fluoride ion is an ionic form of the element fluorine, which is found in abundance in nature, primarily in water and soil. It is found only in the form of compounds known as fluorides. All living organisms are exposed to inorganic fluorides mainly through food and water. The most relevant inorganic fluorides are hydrogen fluoride (HF), calcium fluoride (CaF_2), sodium fluoride (NaF), sulphur hexafluoride (SF_6) and silicofluorides which are present naturally in the environment. They are mainly the focus of this digest. There are many natural products such as tea and fish contain significant quantities of fluorides.[1]

1.1. Sources of Fluoride

Natural

Fluoride as an element is found in the environment and it constitutes 0.06-0.09 per cent of the total earth's crust. Most of the fluoride found in groundwater is naturally occurring from the breakdown of rocks and soils or weathering and deposition of atmospheric volcanic particles and gases emitted from earth's crust.

Human Activities

Fluorides released into the environment are mainly the mining and processing of phosphate rock. It also uses as agricultural fertilizer, as well as the manufacture of aluminium. The other sources include the combustion of coal and other manufacturing processes such as steel, copper, nickel, glass, brick, ceramic, glues and adhesives. In addition, small amount comes from the use of fluoride-containing pesticides in agriculture.

1.2. Fluoride Content in Groundwater

Eight five per cent of rural population of our country uses ground-water for drinking and domestic purposes. According to World Health Organization (WHO), the guideline value and the permissible limit of fluoride as per guidelines of Bureau of Indian Standard (BIS) is 1.5 mg/l. It becomes toxic when the drinking water beyond the maximum permissible limit of 1.5 mg/l.[2] Chronic exposure to fluoridated ground-water in drinking creates a health problem in human beings[3, 4] as well as diverse species of domestic animals[5, 6] in the form of osteo-dental fluorosis.

1.3. Fluoride Affected Areas

In India 62 million of people, including 6 million of children are affected with fluoride related health disorders. The problem of high groundwater fluoride concentration resources has become one of the most important toxicological and geo-environmental issues in India. In India, about 20 states out of the 35 States and Union Territories of the Indian Republic are highly affected with high groundwater fluoride (Fig. 21.1). 40-70 per cent districts are affected in Bihar, National Capital Territory of Delhi, Haryana, Jharkhand, Karnataka, Maharashtra, Madhya Pradesh, Odisha, Tamil Nadu and Uttar Pradesh. In India 10-40 per cent affected districts are Assam, Jammu & Kashmir, Kerala, Chhattisgarh and West Bengal. While the endemicity for the remaining states are not known.

In West Bengal, fluoride contamination of groundwater was first detected during 1997 at Nasipur area of Nalhati-I Block in the district of

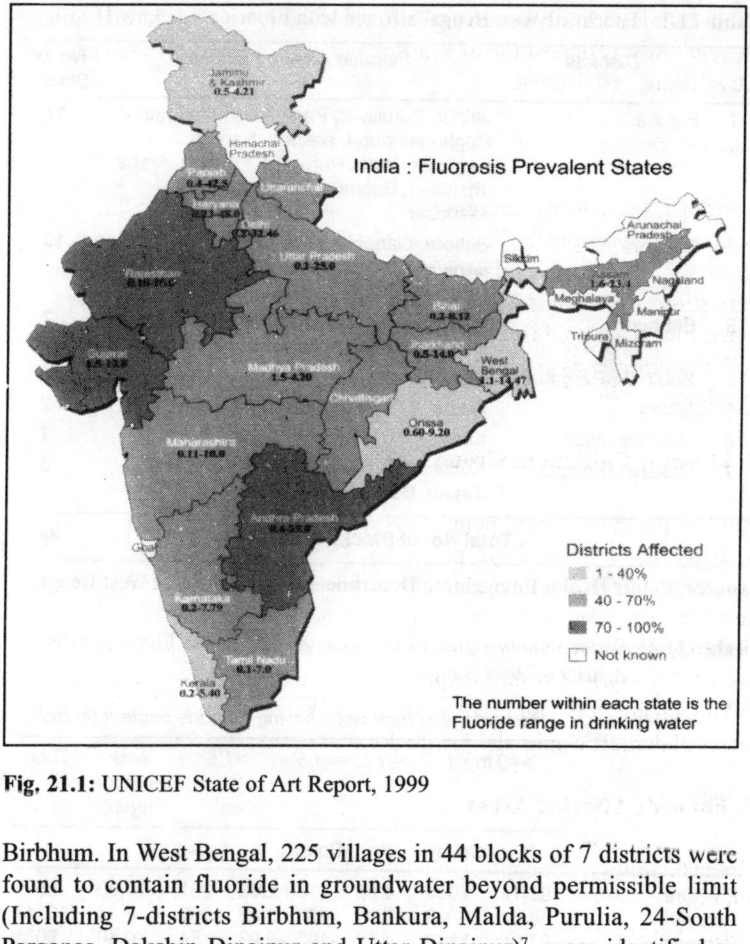

Fig. 21.1: UNICEF State of Art Report, 1999

Birbhum. In West Bengal, 225 villages in 44 blocks of 7 districts were found to contain fluoride in groundwater beyond permissible limit (Including 7-districts Birbhum, Bankura, Malda, Purulia, 24-South Parganas, Dakshin Dinajpur and Uttar Dinajpur)[7], were identified as endemic for fluorosis and people in these regions are at risk of fluoride contamination (Tables 21.1, 21.2 and 21.3). It was also observed that in West Bengal at South 24-Pargana, Baruipur is a place where both arsenic and fluoride has found in groundwater.[8]

It is observed that the sub-surface environment of Bankura is appreciably contaminated with the deadly poison of fluoride. Out of the 8521 tube-wells surveyed in 10 affected blocks, 667 sources are detected with fluoride above the desirable limit of 1 mg/l (Table 21.3).

Table 21.1: Blocks of West Bengal affected with Fluoride > 1.5 mg/l

Sl. No.	Districts	Fluoride Affected Blocks	No. of Blocks
1.	Purulia	Jaipur, Purulia–II, Para, Raghunathpur–II, Raghunathpur–I, Neturia, Santuri, Kashipur, Hura, Purulia–I, Puncha, Arsha, Jhalda– I, Bagmundi, Balarampur, Arabazar	17
2.	Bankura	Saltora, Gangajalghati, Chhatna, Indpur, Bankura–II, Barjora, Taldangra, Simlapal, Hirbandh, Raipur,	10
3.	Birbhum	Nalhati–I, Rampurhat–I, Mayureswar–I, Rajnagar, Suri– II, Sainthia, Khoyrasol,	7
4.	South 24-Parganas	Baruipur	1
5.	Malda	Ratua–II, Bamangola	2
6.	Uttar Dinajpur	Itahar	1
7.	Dakshin Dinajpur	Kushmundi, Gangarampur, Kumarganj, Tapan, Bansihari	5
		Total No. of Blocks	**44**

Source: Public Health Engineering Department, Government of West Bengal.

Table 21.2: Water quality status of the spot sources in the Fluoride affected district of West Bengal

Districts	Percentage of tube-wells having Fluoride content (in mg/l)							
	>=0 to <1		>=1 to <=1.5		>1.5		Max Fluoride (ppm)	Total
	%	Count	%	Count	%	Count		
Bankura	92.17	7854	4.88	416	2.95	251	10.80	8521
Purulia	88.88	9525	7.71	826	3.42	366	8.28	10717
Birbhum	97.91	8842	1.16	105	0.93	84	20.40	9031
South 24 Parganas	98.85	1120	0.79	9	0.35	4	1.81	1133
Uttar Dinajpur	97.33	3897	2.27	91	0.40	16	1.87	4004
Dakshin Dinajpur	77.34	11254	15.54	2261	7.13	1037	7.58	14552
Maldah	96.05	2333	2.18	53	1.77	43	4.53	2429

Source: Public Health Engineering Department, Government of West Bengal.

2. Environmental Levels and Human Exposure of Fluoride

Fluoride is widely distributed in the lithosphere mainly in the form of fluorspar, fluorapatite and cryolite, and is also recognised as the thirteenth most common element in the earth's crust. The principal

Table 21.3: Water quality status of the spot sources in the Fluoride affected different blocks of Bankura district, West Bengal

Bankura	*Percentage of tube-wells having Fluoride content (in mg/l)*							
	>=0 to <1		*>=1 to <=1.5*		*>1.5*		*Max Fluoride (ppm)*	*Total*
	%	*Count*	*%*	*Count*	*%*	*Count*		
Saltora	96.32	497	2.33	12	1.36	7	3.41	516
Gangajalghati	86.12	732	11.53	98	2.35	20	2.32	850
Chhatna	96.07	1,419	2.91	43	1.02	15	4.25	1,477
Indpur	94.20	779	5.44	45	0.36	3	1.63	827
Bankura-II	93.41	893	4.71	45	1.88	18	5.10	956
Barjora	93.59	788	5.23	44	1.19	10	2.51	842
Taldangra	95.52	939	2.85	28	1.63	16	3.65	983
Simlapal	79.23	698	3.52	31	17.25	152	2.00	881
Simlapal	79.23	525	8.70	51	1.71	10	10.80	586
Raipur	96.85	584	3.15	19	0.00	0	1.50	603
Total	**92.17**	**7,854**	**4.88**	**416**	**2.95**	**251**		**8,521**

Source: Public Health Engineering Department, Government of West Bengal.

sources of entry of fluoride to the physiology of human are: (a) water, (b) air (dust), (c) some species of vegetations, (d) certain edible marine animals, and (e) certain industrial processes. It is also found in seawater at a concentration of around 1.2-1.4 mg/litre, in groundwaters at concentrations up to 67 mg/litre, and in most surface waters at concentrations less than 0.1 mg/litre.[9] Fluoride is also found in foods particularly fish and tea.

While almost all foodstuffs contain traces quantity of fluoride. Water and non-dairy beverages are the main sources of ingested fluoride, accounting for 66 to 80 per cent of fluoride intake in US adults according to the concentration of fluoride in the public drinking water. Other significant sources of ingested fluoride are toothpaste in very young children (who tend to swallow most of their toothpaste), tea in tea-drinking communities, and inhaled fluoride in some communities in China where coal containing very high levels fluoride is burned indoors. Absorption of ingested fluoride is via the stomach and small intestine.[10]

3. Absorption of Fluoride on Human Body

Fluoride absorption in human body mainly occurs due to chronic exposure.

The absorption mainly occurs in mucosal and enteral, inhalational and dermal part of the body.

3.1 Mucosal and Enteral Absorption

The currently accepted theory on fluoride absorption is that inorganic fluoride in the form of the undissociated molecule, Hydrofluoric acid (HF), is absorbed by rapid passive diffusion along the entire gastrointestinal tract (stomach and intestine), without any apparent active transport mechanisms being involved.[11, 12, 13] Since soluble ionic fluorides dissociate to release free F^- in solution and protonate to form HF in the acid milieu of the gastrointestinal tract. In this form readily absorbed in the stomach.

3.2 Absorption through Inhalation

When fluorides in gaseous or particulate form are breathed in the respiratory tract, they are partially or completely absorbed depending on how soluble they are or on how big the fluoride-containing particles are.

3.3. Dermal Absorption

Different group of researcher shows only hydrofluoric acid is absorbed through the dermis. Liquid hydrofluoric acid is either a strong or weak acid, depending on its aqueous concentration.[14, 15] Dermal exposure to concentration of hydrofluoric acid solutions can result in severe chemical burns.[16, 17]

4. Distribution of Fluoride on Human Body

Once fluoride is absorbed, either by ingestion, inhalation, or dermal absorption, it passes into the blood for distribution throughout the body and for partial excretion. In plasma, fluoride exists in two distinct forms: a non-ionic form covalently bonded to carbon-containing, lipid-soluble molecules and in an unbound ionic form.[18] Fluoride is then rapidly distributed in tissues. From plasma, fluoride complexes with calcified tissues and is distributed to either the extracellular or intracellular spaces of the soft tissues or is excreted. Most of the ionic fluoride retained in the body enters into the calcified tissues (bone and dentition), either by substituting for the hydroxyl ion (OH^-) or bicarbonate ion (HCO_3^-) in hydroxyapatite in bone or enamel to form fluoroapatite, or as an ionic exchange within the hydration shell of the crystalline surface.[19, 20] In humans fluorides mostly build-up in bones and teeth, which retain about 99 per cent of the total fluoride body burden. It is eliminated from the body primarily through the urine. Infants retain 80 to 90 per cent of fluoride ingested, while adults retain approximately 60 per cent.

5. Excretion of Fluoride on Human Body

Renal excretion is the predominant route for removal of inorganic fluoride from the body. Approximately 50 per cent of the daily intake of fluoride is cleared by the kidneys.[21] Renal excretion and deposition in calcified tissues account for almost 100 per cent of the clearance of inorganic fluoride from plasma.[22] As fluoride deposition in bone decreases with age, fluoride levels in plasma increase.[23]

However, the balance of fluoride in the body (i.e. the difference between the amount of fluoride ingested and the amount excreted) can be positive or negative. This physiological balance is determined by earlier fluoride exposure, the degree of accumulation in bone, the rate at which it is released from bone and the efficiency of the kidneys in excreting fluoride. When fluoride intakes are low excretion through urine can exceed intake. Fluoride can be transferred from mother to foetus through the placenta.

6. Effect of Groundwater Fluoride on Human Health

India is among 23 Nations where health problems occur due to consumption of fluoride contaminated water. Fluorine has been found to be an essential element for animal species. A number of organizations around the world have examined the effects of fluoride on human health. It has both beneficial and detrimental effects on human health. In terms of dental health, the prevalence of dental caries is inversely related to the concentration of fluoride in drinking water. While there is a dose-response relationship between the concentration of fluoride in drinking water and the prevalence of dental fluorosis.[24]

6.1 Beneficial Effects of Fluoride on Human Health

Fluoride is not considered to be essential for human growth and development but it is considered to be beneficial micronutrient for the proper development of teeth and bones. It has beneficial effects on teeth at low concentrations of 1 mg/l by preventing and reducing the dental caries (tooth decay).

Dental caries occurs when sugar-containing foods are metabolised by oral bacteria in the mouth, resulting in acid production on the tooth surface. It causes the removal of minerals from the tooth enamel and ultimately produces dental caries. As a local effect, fluoride in saliva interacts with the minerals on the tooth surface and replaces all the lost enamel and so prevents dental caries. Fluoride at an optimal level (as per WHO permissible range) in the water supply provides the ideal, constant "repair kit" for teeth.

Since the early 20th century in several parts of the world as a public health protective measure against tooth decay, intentionally fluoridation of drinking water (it is the adjustment of the natural concentration of fluoride in drinking water to the optimal recommended level for the prevention of dental caries) and the development of fluoride containing oral care products (toothpastes and mouth rinses), foods (fluoridated salts) and supplements (fluoride tablets) have been employed. Additional amount of exposure to fluoride comes from naturally occurring water (tap and mineral), beverages, food, and to a lesser extent, from other environmental sources.

6.2. Adverse Health Effects of Fluoride

Depending on the level of exposure of fluoride, it has two effects. The effects are acute effects (i.e., short term effects) and chronic effects (i.e., long term effects) on human body.

6.2.1 Short-Term (Acute) Effects

Acute toxicity of fluoride is quite rare and occurrs principally as a result of exposure to excess fluoride in accidental poisonings. The symptoms of acute toxicity include severe nausea, vomiting, excess saliva production, abdominal pain, and diarrhoea. Severe cases of exposure can result in convulsions, irregular heartbeat, and coma. Young children are potentially at risk for acute effects because of the often attractive taste of fluoridated toothpaste. They should always be supervised when brushing and, as is appropriate for their age, made aware of the danger in swallowing excessive amounts.

6.2.2 Long-Term (Chronic) Effects

The major manifestation resulting from chronic ingestion of excessive amounts of fluoride. Chronic exposure of fluoride causes dental fluorosis and systemic effects such as reproductive or developmental health effects, cardiovascular system, skeletal system (i.e., structure and function of skeletal muscle)[25-27], brain[28] and spinal cord. Recent studies also shows the accumulation of fluoride in the hippocampus of the brain[29] causes degeneration of neurons and decreased aerobic metabolism[30] and altered free-radical metabolism in the liver, kidney, and heart.[31-34]

Dental Fluorosis

Excessive, chronic ingestion of the fluoride ion can cause a condition known as enamel fluorosis. Depending on the amount of fluoride exposure (the dose) and the period of tooth formation at which the exposure occurs. This causes enamel fluorosis which can range from mild discolouration of the tooth surface to severe staining, enamel loss, and pitting. Fluoride-related fluorosis usually starts appearing in children between birth and age of 3 years, most significantly on the permanent central incisors[35], which are the most important teeth from an esthetic standpoint. This condition is permanent after it develops in children during tooth formation (from birth until about the age of 8).

Depending on the amount of fluoride exposure it may by very mild, mild or moderate form, is not considered to be a toxic effect. According to WHO Oral Health Surveys Manual Scores Table 21.4 shows that mild or very mild fluororis is often unnoticeable to the normal (untrained) eye, but moderate fluorosis, caused by the ingestion of large quantities of fluoride during tooth formation and affect tooth appearance. If large quantities of fluoride are ingested during tooth formation it can lead to severe fluorosis and enamel erosion, making teeth more vulnerable to decay. This undesirable effect is generally associated with water fluoride concentrations in excess of 4 mg/l (*see* Fig. 21.2)[36].

Skeletal Fluorosis

In chronic exposure of fluoride also causes it readily incorporated into the crystalline structure of bone, and accumulates during the course of time. Fluoride ions are readily incorporated into bone by substituting hydroxyl groups in the carbonate-apatite structure to produce

Table 21.3: Levels of dental fluorosis (Sources from WHO Oral Health Surveys Manual Scores)[37]

Level of Exposure	*Dental effects*
0 = Normal	Enamel surface is smooth, glossy and usually a pale creamy-white colour.
1 = Questionable	The enamel shows slight aberrations in the translucent normal enamel and which may range from a few white flecks to occasional spots.
2 = Very mild	Small opaque, paper-white areas scattered irregularly over the tooth but involving less than 25% of the labial tooth surface.
3 = Mild	White opacities of the enamel involving more than 25%, but less than 50% of the tooth surface.
4 = Moderate	The enamel surfaces show marked wear, and brown staining.
5 = Severe	The enamel surfaces are severely affected and the hypoplasia is so marked that the general form of the tooth may be affected. There are pitted or worn areas and brown stains are widespread; the teeth often have a corroded appearance.

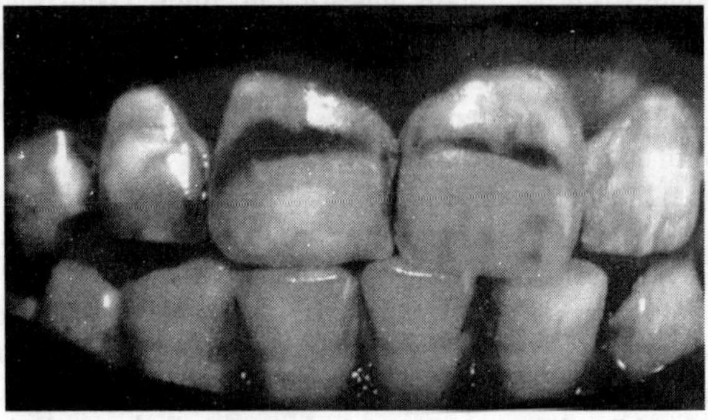

Fig. 21.2: Dental Fluorosis

Sources: Subrata Ghosh (2010): *et al.*, *Journal of Environmental Protection Science*, Vol. 4, pp. 13-21.

fluorohydroxyapatite. Therefore, it alters the mineral structure of the bone. As the bone strength is thought to derive mainly from the interface between the collagen and the mineral[38], alteration in mineralization affects bone strength. Such condition is called skeletal fluorosis. It is extremely rare, and this condition is characterized by increased bone brittleness and a greater risk of fractures. Usually occurs when exposure to fluoride in drinking water exceeds 4 mg/l over a lifetime.[39]

Skeletal fluorosis is categorized into a preclinical stage and stages I, II, and III and the last of which is referred to as the "crippling" stage because mobility is affected. At stage II, mobility is not significantly affected, but it is characterized by sporadic pain, stiffness of joints, and osteosclerosis (bone thickening) of the pelvis and spine.

Osteosarcoma

Researchers have found that there is a potential link between fluoride and cancer-osteosarcoma. Since fluoride is deposited in the bones during bone formation, some researchers hypothesized that this phenomenon may induce osteosarcoma in growing children.[40] But this hypothesis is still on debate, whether fluoride might be associated with bone cancer or not. Some researcher, on animal studies has suggested the possibility of increased risk of osteosarcoma (a bone cancer) in male rats, but no new animal bioassays have been performed to evaluate this further. Overall, the results obtained were mixed, as some studies reporting a positive association and others no association. The National Toxicology Programme concluded that the evidence to date is tentative and mixed as to whether fluoride has the potential to initiate or promote cancers, particularly of the bone.

Developmental and Reproductive Toxicity

Few research on human studies have reported that fluoride might be associated with alterations in reproductive hormones and fertility, but limitations in the study design make them of limited value for risk evaluation. Many researchers worked on animal studies and observed no reproductive toxicity. Effects of fluoride on the morphology of reproductive organs and reproductive function have been reported in male and female rabbits and mice, where given doses of greater than 4.5 mg kg^{-1} body weight per day for varying periods, either orally or by injection. However, in recent studies on laboratory animals, no effects have been observed on reproduction, reproductive organs or the development of the foetus.[41]

Fluoride and Intelligence

Different group of researchers from China and other areas where fluoride levels in groundwater are naturally very high (fluorosis endemic regions) claiming that an association between high water fluoride levels and slightly reduced intelligence (measured as IQ) in four to seven year-old children.[42] Afterwards, reviewed and meta-analysed by Choi *et al.*,[43] who concluded that the results supported a possibility of adverse neuro-developmental effects of high fluoride intake.

Endocrine Effects

Fluoride has suppressive effect on the thyroid function, and is more severe when iodine is deficient. Mostly fluoride is associated with lower levels of iodine. Different studies on animals with iodine deficiency showed effects on thyroid function at fluoride doses of 3-6 mg/kg/day, and in one study, at doses in the range of 0.4-0.6 mg/kg/day.[44-46] The levels of thyroid hormones T_3, T_4, and TSH are altered in response to excess fluoride in rodents.[47]

Thyroid effects in humans were observed when fluoride levels 0.05-0.13 mg/kg/day when iodine intake was adequate and also 0.01-0.03 mg/kg/day when iodine intake was inadequate. The mechanisms and effects of fluoride on the endocrine system are still remaining unclear.

Effect on Phagocytosis

Fluoride also plays an important role in the breakdown of phagocytosis process. It depletes the energy reserves and the ability of white blood cells to properly destroy foreign agents by the process of phagocytosis. It was observed that as little as 0.2 ppm fluorides stimulate free radical production (super oxide) in resting white blood cells, virtually abolishing phagocytosis. Even micro-molar amounts of fluoride, <1 ppm, may seriously depress the ability of white blood cells to destroy pathogenic agents.

Effect on Cardiovascular System

Fluoride has also found to accumulate the cardiovascular system. This causes in increased blood pressure (i.e., hypertension)[48], arterial calcifications[49], arteriosclerosis[50, 51], and myocardial damage.[52, 53] Electrocardiogram abnormalities observed on chronic exposure of fluoride on both human and animals.[54, 55] Recent research shows that patients with cardiac failure have significantly elevated levels of fluoride in their blood, even more than patients with kidney disease.

Effect on other Organ System

Different scientific organization also considered the effects of fluorinated groundwater on human body such as the gastrointestinal system, kidneys, liver, and immune system. Still now there were no research findings which shows that the effect of fluoride at 4 mg/l on human studies on drinking water containing fluoride at 4 mg/l in which gastrointestinal, renal, hepatic, or immune system. Different case reports and *in vitro* and animal studies indicated that exposure to fluoride at concentrations greater than 4 mg/l can be irritating to the gastrointestinal system, affect renal tissues and function, and alter hepatic and immunologic parameters. Such effects are unlikely to be a risk for the average individual exposed to fluoride at 4 mg/l in drinking water.

Conclusion

Preventive and curative measures against pollution and contamination of groundwater may continue to receive low priority for many years. The major reasons which contribute to elevated concentration of fluoride in groundwater are weathering of rocks and leaching of fluoride bearing minerals. Different researchers have observed different concentrations of fluoride for the different diseases. This study confirms the dreaded impact of fluoride toxicity, in particular, on human health.

Fluorosis is dreaded disease caused by consumption of excess amount of fluoride. This is mainly due to the consumption of water which having excess fluoride content. As per WHO standards prescribe 1.5 ppm as maximum level of fluoride in drinking water. However, deep bore-wells do carry excess fluoride causing various bone and physical deformities. There is no new clear evidence found from human studies indicating that fluoride in drinking water influences male and female reproductive capacity. Few research work on human studies have suggested that fluoride might be associated with alterations in reproductive hormonal functions and fertility control.

Particularly, this problem is severe in India and need immediate attention of Government, donors and philanthropists to save our people. Suitable measures such as defluorinating the groundwater before use and recharging the groundwater by rainwater harvesting need to be practiced to improve the quality of groundwater. Groundwater of a particular area should be thoroughly analysed before its use for domestic purposes and accordingly a suitable method can be chosen for its treatment.

Notes

1. *Environmental Health Criteria,* 227. Fluorides. International Programme on Chemical Safety. World Health Organization, Geneva 2002, Available at: http://www.inchem.org/documents/ehc/ehc/ehc227.htm
2. World Health Organization. *Guidelines for Drinking Water Quality*, Geneva: World Health Organisation, 1984.
3. Choubisa, S.L., 2001, Endemic fluorosis in southern Rajasthan, India. *Fluoride*, 34(1):61-70.
4. Choubisa, S.L., (2012), Fluoride in drinking water and its toxicosis in tribals, Rajasthan, India. *Proc. Natl. Acad. Sci. India Sect. B. Biol. Sci.*, 82(2):325-30. doi: 10.1007/s 40011-012-0047-8.
5. Choubisa, S.L. (1999), Some observations on endemic fluorosis in domestic animals of Southern Rajasthan (India). *Vet. Res. Commu.*, 23(7):457-65.
6. Choubisa, S.L. (2017), Fluoridated groundwater and its toxic effects on domesticated animals residing in rural tribal areas of Rajasthan, India. *Int. J. Environ. Stud.,* 64(2):151-59.
7. Gupta, S., Banerjee, S., Saha, R., Datta, J.K., Mondal, N., (2006), Fluoride geochemistry of groundwater in Nalhati-1 block of the Birbhum district, West Bengal, India. *Fluoride*, 39:318-20.
8. Central Ground Water Board, Ministry of Water Resources, Government of India, "Bhu-Jal News", *Quarterly Journal*, Volume No. 24, Number 1, Jan-March 2009.
9. Smith, F.A., Ekstrand, J. (1996), The occurrence and the chemistry of fluoride. *In:* Fejerskov, O., Ekstrand, J., Burt, B.A., (eds.) *Fluoride in Dentistry,* 2nd ed. Copenhagen: Munksgaard, 20-21.
10. IPCS. *Environmental Health Criteria 227 Fluorides*. Geneva: World Health Organisation, 2002.
11. Singer, L., and Ophaug, R., (1982), "Ionic and Non-ionic Fluoride In Plasma (or Serum)". *Crc. Crit. Rev. Clin. Lab. Sci.*, 8(2): 111-40.
12. Barbakow, F., (1983), "Intake, Absorption, and Excretion of Dietary Fluoride". *Int. J. Vitam, Nutr., Res. Suppl.*, 25:83-94.
13. Whitford, G.M., and Pashley, D.H., (1984), "Fluoride Absorption: The Influence of Gastric Acidity", *Calcif. Tissue Int.*, 36(3):302-7.
14. Leech, H.E., (1956), "The Physical and Chemical Properties of Fluorine and the Physical and Chemical Properties and Uses of Hydrogen Fluoride". *Mellor's Comprehensive Treatise on Inorganic and Theoretical Chemistry,* London: Longmans, *Green*, (Suppl. II); 1:46-146.
15. Rudge, A.J., (1982). "*The Manufacture of Fluorine and Its Compounds,*" Oxford University Press, London.
16. Dale, R.H., (1951), "Treatment of Hydrofluoric Acid Burns". *Br. Med. J.*, 1:728-32.
17. Greco R.J., Hartford C.E., *et al.*, (1988), "Hydrofluoric Acid-Induced Hypocalcemia". *J. Trauma.*, 28(11):1593-99.

18. Guy, W.S., "Inorganic and Organic Fluorine in Human Blood", in *Continuing Evaluation of the Use of Fluorides, AAS Selected Symposium*, 11, 1979, Johansen, E., Taves, D.R., and Olsen, T.O., Eds., Boulder, C.O.; Westview Press, 124-47.
19. McCann, H.G., and Bullock, F.A., (1957), "The Effects of Fluoride Ingestion on the Composition and Solubility of Mineralized Tissues of the Rat". *J. Dental Res.*, 36:391-8.
20. Neuman, W.F., and Neuman, M.W., (1958), *"The Chemical Dynamics of Bone Mineral"*. University of Chicago Press, Chicago, 75-100.
21. Whitford, G.M., (1990), "The Physiological and Toxicological Characteristics of Fluoride". *J. Dent, Res.*, 69:539-57.
22. Jamberg, P.O., Ekstrand, J., *et al.*, (1983), "Renal Excretion of Fluoride During Water Diuresis and Induced Urinary pH-Changes in Man". *Toxicol, Lett.*; 18(1-2):141-6.
23. Parkins, F.M., Tinanoff, N., *et al.*, (1974), "Relationship of Human Plasma Fluoride and Bone Fluoride to Age". *Calcif. Tissue Res.*, 16(4):335-8.
24. McDonagh, M., Whiting, P., Bradley, M., Cooper J., Sutton A., Chestnut I., Misso K., Wilson P., Treasure E., Kleijnen J. *A systematic review of public water fluoridation*. York: The University of York NHS Centre for Reviews and Dissemination; 2000.
25. Jolly, S.S., Prasad, S., Sharma, R., (1970), Review of 25 years research on fluoride. *Journal Association of Physicians of India*, 18:459-71.
26. Kaul, R.D., Susheela, A.K. (1974), Evidence of muscle fibre degeneration in rabbits treated with sodium fluoride. *Fluoride*, 7(4):177-81.
27. Shashi, A., Singh, J.P., Thapar, S.P. (1992), Protein degradation in skeletal muscle of rabbit during experimental fluorosis. *Fluoride*, 25(3):155-8.
28. Shashi, A., Singh, J.P., Thapar, S.P. (1994), Effect of long-term administration of fluoride on levels of protein, free aminoacids and RNA in rabbit brain. *Fluoride*, 27(3):155-9.
29. Mullenix, P.J., Denbesten, P.K., Schunior, A., Kernan, W.J. (1995), Neurotoxicity of Sodium fluoride in rats. *Neurotoxicology and Teratology*, 17(3):169-77.
30. Spittle, B. (1998), Comments on the finding of toxin-induced blood vessel inclusions and alterations in neuronal and cerebrovascular integrity following the chronic administration of aluminium fluoride and sodium fluoride. *Fluoride*, 31(2):89-90.
31. Sharma, A., Chinoy, N.J., (1998), Role of free radicals in fluoride-induced toxicity in liver and kidney of mice and its reversal. *Fluoride*, 31(3): S26.
32. Patel. D., Chinoy, N.J. (1998), Influence of fluoride on biological free radical reactions in ovary of mice and its reversal. *Fluoride*, 31(3): S27.
33. Chinoy, N.J., Patel, D. (1998), Influence of fluoride on biological free radicals in ovary of mice and its reversal. *Environmental Sciences*, 6(3):171-84.
34. Sun, G., Qiu, L., Ding, G., Qian, C., Zheng Q. (1998), Effects of â-carotene and SOD on lipid peroxidation induced by fluoride: An experimental study. *Fluoride*, 31(3): S29.

35. Hong, L., Levy, S.M., Broffitt, B., *et al.*, (2006), Timing of fluoride intake in relation to development of fluorosis on maxillary central incisors. *Community Dent Oral Epidemiol.*, August, 34(4): 299-309.
36. Fluoride in Drinking Water: A Scientific Review of EPA's standards: National Research Council of the National Academies. The National Academy Press. Washington, DC. March 2006.
37. World Health Organization, *Oral Health Surveys: Basic Methods*. Fifth ed. 2013, Geneva: World Health Organization.
38. Catanese, J., Keavney, T.M. (1996), Role of collagen and hydroxyapatite in the mechanical behaviour of bone tissue. *J. Bone Miner Res.*, 11: S295.
39. Fluoride in Drinking Water: A Scientific Review of EPA's standards: National Research Council of the National Academies. The National Academy Press. Washington, DC. March 2006.
40. Morry, D.W. and C. Steinmaus, (2011), Evidence on the carcinogenicity of fluoride and its salts, Office of Environmental Health Hazard Assessment's Reproductive and Cancer Hazard Assessment Branch, California Environmental Protection Agency.
41. IPCS. Fluorides—Environmetal Health Criteria 227. International Programme on Chemical Safety. Geneva, Switzerland: World Health Organization, 2002.
42. Guojian Wang, Delong Yang, Fengge Jia, Huiqin Wanga Shehezi, Xinjiang. (2008), A study of the IQ levels of four-to seven-year-old children in high fluoride areas. *Fluoride*, 41(4): 340-343.
43. Choi, A.L., *et al.*, (2012), Developmental fluoride neurotoxicity: a systematic review and meta-analysis. *Environ Health Perspect*, 120(10): 1362-68.
44. Bobek, S., S. Kahl, and Z. Ewy, (1976), Effect of long-term fluoride administration on thyroid hormones level blood in rats. *Endocrinol Exp.*; 10(4): 289-95.
45. Guan, Z.Z., *et al.*, (1998), Synergistic action of iodine-deficiency and fluorine-intoxication on rat thyroid. *Chin. Med. J. (Engl);* 101(9): 679-84.
46. Zhao, W., *et al.*, (1998), Long-term Effects of Various Iodine and Fluorine Doses on the Thyroid and Fluorosis in Mice. *Endocr. Regul.*, 32(2): 63-70.
47. International Programme on Chemical Safety. World Health Organization, Fluorides. *Environmental Health Criteria*, 227, 2002, World Health Organization, Geneva.
48. Amini, H., *et al.*, (2011), Drinking water fluoride and blood pressure: an environmental study. *Biol. Trace. Elem. Res.*, 144:157-63.
49. Tuncel, E., The incidence of Moenckeberg calcifications in patients with endemic fluorosis. *Fluoride*, 17(1):4-8.
50. Varol, E., *et al.*, (2010), Impact of chronic fluorosis on left ventricular diastolic and global functions. *Sci. Tot. Environ.*, 408:2295-98.
51. Song, A.H., *et al.*, Observations on fluorotic aortosclerosis by two-dimensional echocardiography. *Endemic Diseases Bulletin*, 5(1): 91-94.

52. Basha, M.P., Sujitha, N.S. (2011), Chronic fluoride toxicity and myocardial damage: antioxidant offered protection in second generation rats. *Toxicol. Int.*, 18(2):99-104.
53. Cicek, E., *et al.*, (2005), Effects of chronic ingestion of sodium fluoride on myocardium in a second generation of rats. *Human Exper. Toxicol.*, 24:79-87.
54. Ji F., *et al.*, (2004), Study on the cardiovascular damage of skeletal fluorosis patients. *Chin. J. Ctrl. Endem. Dis.*, 19(6):321-23 (Abstract).
55. Xu, R.Y., Xu, R.Q. (1997), Electrocardiogram analysis of patients with skeletal fluorosis. *Fluoride*, 30(1):16-8.

Society, Culture, Tourism and Environment

22

Dynamics of GRT Concerning Culture, Society and Environment

Premangshu Chakrabarty and *Krishna Biswas*

Introduction

Women workforce is a tremendous resource which no society can undervalue. Involving women at all levels of development will make a world of difference but it is only possible by dismantling of century-old structures of thought and practice (Young, 1997). Gender Responsible Tourism (GRT) is a concept of the new millennium arising out of it. Advancing women's best interest in the tourism sector is the declared aim of GRT (http://www.g-r-t.org/index.php/en/about-grt/the-six-pillars) in terms of:

(i) quality and quantity of women engagement;
(ii) equal access to opportunities;
(iii) fair and equitable sharing of benefits;
(iv) upholding the rights;
(v) minimize the gender based exploitation; and
(vi) raising voices and leadership.

The most promising industry of the 21st century is tourism with huge job opportunities absorbing skilled, unskilled, semi-skilled, formal and informal labour force. The benefits of tourism include foreign exchange influx, infrastructural development, regional development and upgradation in standard of living in the host societies. Apart from these advantages, it rejuvenates the lost traditions and preserves the heritages. International tourist movement have increased from 25 million globally in 1950 to 1133 million in 2014. Tourism is reported to contribute 9 per cent of the world's GDP and one in every eleven jobs worldwide (UNWTO, 2015). In tourism sector, the job provided to women can be divided into three broad categories (Pureell, 2005):

- Family tourism business, running accommodation unit/ farmhouse.
- Contingently gendered jobs, happen to be mainly done by women especially in restaurant, cafe etc.
- Sex related usually subjected to ethical concern of the host society; employing women as sex workers has been approved by some of the governments (Amsterdam is well known for Sex Tourism).

Women participation in this industry manifesting the level of gender empowerment in the respective host society is increasingly conceived as an indicator of its status worldwide.

Theoretical Considerations on Global Scenario

Worldwide investigation shows an increasing trend of women participation in tourism sector. However in most of the countries, their involvement is found mainly on part-time basis and also seasonal. "The Global Report on Women in Tourism 2010", published by United Nations World Tourism Organisation (UNWTO, 2011) incorporates the following observations on women participation in this industry:

- One in five tourism ministers worldwide are women.
- Women are largely absorbed in customer service and clerical level jobs but poorly represented at managerial levels.
- Women in tourism are on average earning 10 per cent to 15 per cent less than their male counterparts.
- A large amount of unpaid work is being carried out by women in family tourism businesses e.g. in home stays.

Highest absorption of women labour force is found in accommodation and catering sector of tourism worldwide. An UK based study of United Nations Environment and Development (UNED) in the year 2002 claimed that on an average 46 per cent of the tourism workforce are women absorbed in HCT (hotels, catering and tourism) sector (UNED, 2002). Women participation rate is remarkably high in the HCT sector in countries like Lithuania, Latvia, Russia, Peru, Switzerland, Norway etc. The participation rate is found quite well in New Zealand, Japan, Australia, Spain, United States, United Kingdom, Italy, France, Greece, Israel etc. (Baum, 2013). It is noteworthy that most of the above mentioned countries are considered as 'Core Countries' of the world according to Wallerstein's World System Theory of the "Core-Periphery concept" introduced in the early 1980s in order to explain the dependency relationship between core and periphery countries. As the core countries control the global market, the periphery and semi-periphery countries have to depend upon them. Ranking of these core countries in Gender Development Index (GDI) are high enough while the situation is just the reverse in case of the peripheral and semi-peripheral countries as represented in Table 22.1.

It is noteworthy to mention that the as higher is the GDI value, there is more opportunity of women participation in HCT. Further, if the opportunity of women participation increases in a country with the development of newer types of tourism, it will ultimately contribute positively in changing GDI and thereby the problem of gender disparity in these countries can be addressed.

The status of women participation in tourism industry is already satisfactory in core countries. Now-a-days, with introduction of different kind of tourism activities like community based tourism, eco-tourism, homestay, agro-tourism/rural tourism etc. participation status of women in tourism industry is steadily increasing particularly in the peripheral and semi-peripheral countries. A team of researchers from Wageningen University of Netherlands, under the supervision of Dr. I. Ateljevic, in their project publication entitled "Women Empowerment Through Tourism" (2008) pointed out that women involvement in tourism in Third World countries brings many positive impacts in terms of promoting development especially in economically marginalised regions, encouraging sustainable use of natural resources and enhancing the control of local people over development. In African countries, under different ecotourism projects, women are maintaining the establishments like a library of nature, a shop of community manufactured items etc. Southern Asia and South-east Asian sub-regions appear to be outstanding where women are found empowered intensively with the progress of tourism industry. For example in Nepal under the project called EWN (Empowering Women in Nepal), the women are provided with training for the specialized jobs like trekking guide to serve the changing demand

Table 22.1: Women Participation in HCT and GDI

Core Countries with High Women Participation in HCT		Countries in Periphery with Less Women Participation in HCT	
Name of the Country	*GDI Rank (2013)*	*Name of the Country*	*GDI Rank (2013)*
Norway (66.2%)	5	Indonesia	98
Sweden (56.1%)	6	Madagascar	99
United States (53.1%)	7	Tanzania	100
Finland (74.2%)	8	Nepal	102
United Kingdom (53.6%)	13	Cambodia	105
France (47.5%)	17	Zimbabwe	105
Canada (59.7%)	24	Bangladesh	107
Spain (55.9%)	25	Kenya	107
Israel (42.1%)	29	Saudi Arabia (1.5%)	112
Australia (55.9%)	40	Turkey (14.8%)	118
New Zealand (60.1%)	47	Egypt (2.4%)	125
Singapore (55.3%)	52	Iran (8.1%)	128
Germany (57.8%)	61	Jordan	130
Italy (50.3%)	61	India	132
Russia (79.1%)	61	Iraq (3.6%)	137

Source: Compiled from ILO, UNDP and UNWTO websites.

of the market. In the Middle East and Latin American countries, different NGOs are found working for placement of the trained female folk in different spheres of tourism industry.

In spite of socio-economic differences among Core and Peripheral countries, tourism has opened the door of income and employment for women coming from different background. Even in peripheral regions where a number of socio-cultural and political factors restrict womens' free movement, tourism industry becomes useful to empower women by encouraging pursuit like crafts making, running small catering business etc. According to Wallerstein's World System view regarding the Core and Periphery Model, position of any country is interchangeable with time either because of the introduction of new resources or scarcity of available resources. By the sustainable optimum use of tourism resources and involving women into this activity, a peripheral country may move forward to achieve the status of a core country.

In patriarchal societies men occupies the central place and women are dependent on them. Women empowerment through tourism can at least bring positive change in the status of women in society. Tourism is increasingly being considered as one of the most promising avenues in order to empower women irrespective age, skill, background, educational qualification etc. In Japan, it has been observed that holidays based around weaving activities helped the women to gain increased control over their lives (Creighton, 1995). It is noteworthy to mention that although considered unethical in the most parts of the globe, sex tourism in many countries of the world are increasingly becoming so popular and significant that it has attracted the attention of developers and a number of governments have consequently accepted it as one of the informal sectors of female absorption.

Women's work is found largely concentrated in the retailing, hotel and catering sector throughout the world and tends to be seasonal, part time and low-paid. Work participation of women in the UK tourism industry demonstrates considerable flexibility (Bagguley, 1990). In Eastern Europe, a policy has been undertaken which says that at least 40 per cent of the employees should be female within a company (Ateljevic, 2008). In case of Greece, the introduction of agro-tourism alters the prevailing gender norms in its rural society and enables Greek women to gain increased income and power (Castelberg-Koulma, 1991). Spain in July, 2015 has been awarded with the first rank by the World Economic Forum for being the best tourist destination and most accessible country for tourist. A large number of women of the country are found successfully working in almost all kinds of tourism related works. Actually in Spain, catering tourists who stay in farms is conceived as an extension of women's domestic job (García-Ramón *et al.*, 1995). It is another manifestation of informal sector of employment but ethical in all sense. Many women in West Java are engaged in managing small-scale accommodation establishments and simultaneously cater the visitors with local food items and fruits. Income from such ventures improves the standard of living in the host society (Sinclair, 2005). In case of the Caribbean Islands, women participation is largely appreciated in the accommodation sector (Momsen, 1994). From the world trend of women participation in tourism, the following have been derived—

1. More is the GDI (Gender Development Index) value of regional unit concerned, the better is the situation of women participation in tourism industry.
2. More is the Star value of the hotel, better is the scenario of absorption of women as employees in accommodation sector.
3. There is wide scope of female employment in souvenir industry associated with tourism.
4. Policy orientation is vital to ensure female participation in tourism sector as well as for promoting GRT (Gender Responsible Tourism).

Discussion on Indian Scenario

The objectives of the present study in Indian context are to—

1. Highlight the level of women participation in tourism industry with special reference to accommodation sector.
2. Relate between gender development and women participation in tourism of different states in India.
3. Explore the role of souvenir industry in providing employment and income to female folk.
4. Evaluate the tourism policy from the standpoint of promoting GRT.

According to the World Tourism Organization, India will be the leader in the tourism industry in South Asia with 8.9 million arrivals by 2020. India is gradually emerged as the second most rapidly increasing (8.8 %) tourism economy in the world during the time period of 2005-14

(Deshwal, 2015). Position of India in global tourism scenario is reflected in the Travel and Tourism Competitiveness Index-2015 designated India as 52nd among 141 countries. About 5 per cent of India's employment already comes from this sector and its future employment potentiality is bright as revealed from the statistical reports.

The report entitled "Report of the Committee for Evolving a Composite Development Index of States", submitted by the Raghuram Rajan Committee in the year 2013 identified Arunachal Pradesh, Assam, Bihar, Chhattisgarh, Jharkhand, Madhya Pradesh, Meghalaya, Odisha, Rajasthan and Uttar Pradesh as the 'least developed' states. On the other hand, Goa, Kerala and Tamil Nadu are among the better developed states (Rajan Committee Report, 2013). These aforementioned developed states have high GDI values and characteristically providing better scope of employment to women in tourism sector than other states in India.

A survey was conducted by the authors involving the government tourism officials of different states of India during Travel and Tourism Fair (TTF), 2015 at Kolkata. The followings are the outcomes in the context:

- Goa has achieved maximum success among Indian States in the field of women participation in travel and tourism business. It is noteworthy that Goa ranks 2nd in Gender Development among the states of the country. Goa has already introduced lady tourist police for providing better security perception among its female travellers. Female guides and cab drivers are also available on demand in popular tourist destinations in Goa.
- Kerala (ranked 3rd in Gender Development Index among Indian States) absorbs a large number of women in its health tourism sector, especially in its Ayurvedic Treatment Centres. Ayurveda is traditionally being practiced in Kerala from ancient time. This state has earned international reputation for its Ayurvedic clinics. According to a CII (Confederation of Indian Industries) estimate, medical tourism will make a business of worth US$ 4 billion by 2017. Kerala is forerunner in this field due to its unique combination of ancient Indian health care structure with the modern system of surgery and medicine. For its advancement, CII celebrated 2006-07 as medical tourism year in Kerala. In rural Kerala, SHGs (Self-Help Groups) of women folk are very much involved in tourism sector. Women participation scenario in hotel industry of urban areas is good enough in Kerala which

however varies from district to district. As for example, women participation in hotel industry is better in Thiruvananthapuram, the capital city than Kochi where more star category hotels are situated.

- Regarding medical tourism, the other southern states of India like Maharashtra, Tamil Nadu, Karnataka, Andhra Pradesh (ranked 10th, 15th, 23rd, and 25th in Gender Development Index respectively) experience the presence of a large number of women employees to serve the medical tourists coming from different parts of the world. Some renowned hospitals such as Hiranandani Hospital, Asian Heart Institute at Maharashtra, MIOT International, Christian Medical Collage at Tamil Nadu, Columbia Asia Referral Hospital, B.G.S. Global Hospital at Karnataka, Sri Sathya Sai Institute of Higher Medical Science, Apollo at Andhra Pradesh etc. offer employment to women especially for serving medical tourists because of their gender attributed inherent caring nature and compassion towards patients which are among the fundamental demands of medical tourists coming from foreign countries as well as other states of India.
- In Himachal Pradesh (ranked 12th in Gender Development Index), women participation in conventional HCT sector among popular destinations is remarkably low but in unorganized sectors (like craft industry and homestays) women participation rate is found high. According to "Indian Hotel Industry Survey 2013-2014" in Shimla, called the "Queen of all Hill Stations", women participation in hotels is basically restricted in non-managerial posts and overall participation rate is comparatively poor enough.
- Punjab (ranked 13th in Gender Development Index) is noted for the entrepreneurial skill of women serving the tourism industry. Women are found as owner of many travel agencies in the region. Apart from craft and hotel industry, women are serving visitors by getting absorbed even in fuel stations.
- Women participation rate in tourism sector of Gujarat (ranked 21st in Gender Development Index) is recently increasing with the effort of Gujarat Government. Cities like Ahmedabad, Vadodara etc. are noteworthy for providing women employment in star category hotels.
- States more backward in Gender Development like Rajasthan (29th), Odisha (30th) or Madhya Pradesh (31st) shows the

increasing trend of women absorption in travel and tourism industry which in turn generate positive feedbacks to their backward economies as well as gender inequalities. Highest level of female absorption is recorded in cultural performance followed by engagement in craft making for souvenir industry. Different cultural festivals like Mewar Festival, Gangaur Festival, Mount Abu Festival of Rajasthan, Ekamra Utsav, Kalinga Mahotsav, Rajarani Music Festival of Odisha, Lokrang Festival, Khajuraho Festival of Madhya Pradesh etc. are drawing the large number of female artists in the arena of tourism every year.

- Many states including West Bengal (ranked 22nd in Gender Development Index), Assam (ranked 24th in Gender Development Index), Jammu & Kashmir (ranked 26th in Gender Development Index) etc. have adopted the policy to train village women to enable them in making their attractive traditional handcrafts in such a way that these can be marketed on the eve of international and national tourist festivals. These indigenous products have great appeal to tourists particularly from overseas as souvenirs. Tourists are also found interested in visiting the craft villages to experience the process of the respective craft making where women folk are directly involved.

As the tourism industry in India is flourishing rapidly, the rate of women participation in its different spheres has increased day-by-day. The hotel industry is identified as the largest job provider in this field as evident from Fig. 22.1 and Fig. 22.2 while Fig. 22.3 represents the status of the job provided to women in the four Metro-Cities of the country.

Tourism sector mainly provide part-time, casual as well as seasonal basis job opportunities. It is very much welcomed especially by those women who are interested to be self-dependent economically but cannot materialize their desire in time due to family responsibilities like bearing and rearing children, caring for the elderly, or/and doing household work. On the other hand students as well as retired women also capitalize the scope of additional income and employment opportunities arising from this industry. Uneducated, unskilled rural women on the other hand may also avail various economic and social opportunities with the growth of village tourism.

The unique craft making of folk attracts the attention of both domestic and international tourists. Linkage between craft industry and tourism is

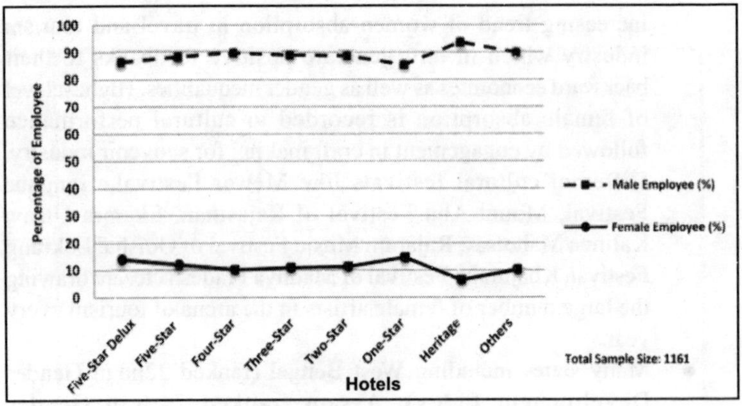

Fig. 22.1: Percentage of Male and Female Employees in Star Category Hotels in India

Source: Prepared by the authors after *Indian Hotel Industry Survey Report* (2014-2015) by FHRAI.

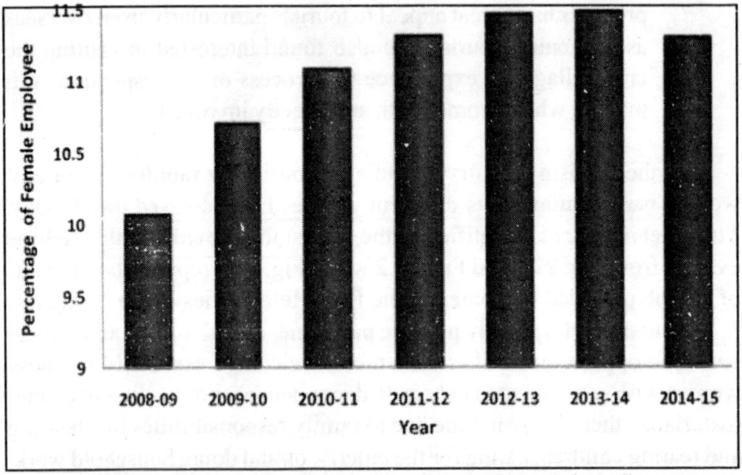

Fig. 22.2: Female Participation Rate in Star Category Hotels in India

Source: Prepared by the authors after FHRAI reports on *Indian Hotel Industry Survey.*

vital in respect of women empowerment arising from their inherent ability and skills. Most of the souvenir industries are characteristically village oriented and suitable for female artisans. Another reason for women

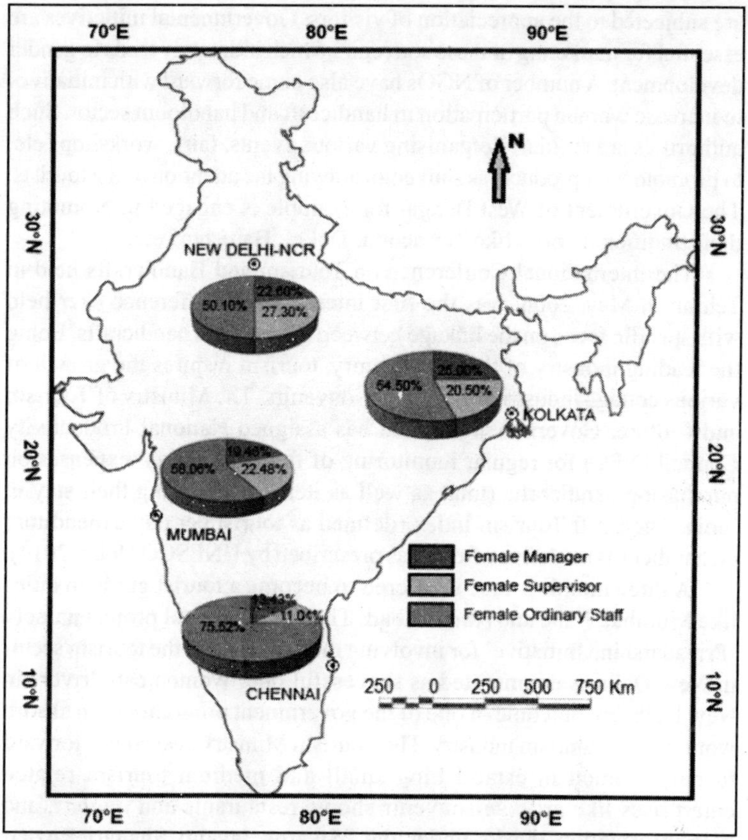

Fig. 22.3: Status of Female Staff Absorbed in Star Category Hotels in Four Metro Cities of India (2014-2015)

Source: Prepared by the authors after FHRAI report on *Indian Hotel Industry Survey 2014-2015*.

dominance in craft industry is nothing, but the availing of opportunity of making additional income for the family while the male members are engaged in traditional pursuits but not able in earning enough for running respectable livelihood. Even the rural women of Jammu & Kashmir despite of prolonged insurgency are found participating in activities like food processing or making, handicrafts and handlooms which are closely associated with tourism industry (Suri, 2013). For religious and social restrictions imposed upon them, they are not usually allowed to make contact directly with the outsiders. But products manufactured by them are subjected to the appreciation of visitors. Governmental initiatives are essential for marketing of these souvenirs which ultimately leads to gender development. A number of NGOs have also come forward with initiatives to increase women participation in handicraft and handloom sector. Such authorities are regularly organising various events, fairs, workshops etc. to promote their products as souvenirs drawing the attention of the tourists. The Government of West Bengal for example is engaged in promoting their traditional crafts like Terracotta, Dokra, Baluchuri etc.

The International Conference on Tourism and Handicrafts held in Tehran in May, 2006, was the first international conference ever held with specific focus on the linkage between tourism and handicrafts. Being the leading industry of the 21st century, tourism inspires the growth of various cottage industries producing souvenirs. The Ministry of Tourism and Culture, Government of India has assigned National Productivity Council (NPC) for regular monitoring of foreign tourists' expenses on purchasing handicrafts (total as well as item-wise) during their stay in India. The Craft/Tourism Index (defined as tourist per day expenditure on handicrafts) is derived from it as prescribed by UNESCO (John, 2014).

A three month course is offered to become a tourist guide in cities like Mumbai, Pune and Ahmedabad. The governmental project namely 'Priyadarshine Initiative' for involving more women in the tourism sector in New Delhi is enumerated as successful one. Women cab drivers in New Delhi are outcome of one of the government programmes to absorb women in the tourism industry. The Tourism Ministry also comes forward to help women in establishing small and medium tourism related enterprises like art-*cum*-souvenir shops, restaurants and *dhabas*, and help/information kiosks under the "Swarna Jayanti Shahari Rozgar Yojana" (SJSRY) of the Urban Development Ministry (Rani, 2013). The Women Self-Help Group (SHG) of different states like Goa, Odisha etc. are also very much active in this context. Even in the Tourism Development Plan of remotest north-eastern state like Arunachal Pradesh, female leadership in tourism industry is advocated for representing the bright future.

In May, 2002, the Department of Tourism, Government of India introduced its National Tourism Policy identifying seven key areas namely *Swaagat* (welcome), *Soochana* (information), *Suvidha* (facilitation), *Suraksha* (safety), *Sahyoga* (cooperation), *Samrachana* (infrastructure) and *Safai* (cleanliness). The scope of women participation under this model is exclusive as outlined below:

- Women are considered better receptionists by nature to be engaged for *Swaagat* (welcome). In hotel industry maximum number of receptionist and call operator are found women.
- Appropriate and reliable information (*soochana*) is very important for safety and security of tourists. Tourists of today feel most comfortable if the on line service is available. Tourist Information Centres well equipped with all modern communication facilities (phone, fax, internet etc.) providing computerized services demand skilled labour and as the very nature of the work is more suitable for women, they are agreed in accepting lower wages than the males having same skills and abilities.
- The *Suvidha* (facilitation), *Suraksha* (safety), *Sahyoga* (cooperation) are among the priorities for tourist visiting alone or in group. By ensuring women participation in different services provided to them, gender tourism may advance. In rural tourism sector for example, particularly in homestays, women are found contributing a lot in the advancement of tourism economy.
- For protecting, maintaining and managing tourism resources (like heritage building, archaeological remains, ancient temples etc.), there is an urge for well trained employees. Presently women incorporation is emphasized for protection and maintenance of natural tourism resources which is originally derived from the concept of eco-feminism advocating women as better conservers. Coastal and Marine Biosphere project is an example where Tamil Nadu Government has indulged on empowering local women to manage the coastal ecosystem and wildlife resources (ICT, 2005).
- The *Safai* (cleanliness) is very much important for overall impression of a tourist destination. For making a Zero Waste Zone and clean tourist spot, Women's Self-Help Groups are given responsibilities in different states for obtaining better result.

The potentialities of the employment of female workers in different tourism sectors may be described on the basis of the concept of 5A's of tourism. For the first 'A', i.e. attraction, women may play the role of being a protector or conservator. The role of women in sustaining second 'A', i.e. accommodation has already been discussed in the context of hotel industry and homestays. It is noteworthy to mention that homestays may absorb the highest number of women workforce in tourism sector. The inherent quality of gender makes them a better service provider in such activities. Some famous examples of Indian homestays include Ladakh, Spiti of Jammu & Kashmir, Kullu, Shimla, Chamba, Solan in Himachal Pardesh, Nanda Devi Valley and Valley of Flower of Uttarakhand, various village of Sikkim and Assam in the North-East, Rajasthan, Madhya Pradesh and in southern states like Kerala, Karnataka and Tamil Nadu which are increasingly absorbing female workforce in tourism sector. Regarding third 'A', i.e. accessibility, the potentiality of women participation as tour operator is high prosperous. Amenities which have been considered as the fourth 'A' provide the scope of women involvement in many sectors such as souvenir industry, food services, recreational activities etc. The fifth 'A' is administration, the rate of women absorption in which is manifested through the number of lady tourist police employed in managing destinations.

Recommendations

The following are a few recommendations on improving gender participation scenario in tourism industry:

1. In the gender sensitive societies, culturally acceptable uniform may be introduced following the model of Jordon which stands very successful.
2. Vocational Training centres with well trained female instructors who are successfully working in tourism sector are very much required for future human resource development, specially for accommodation sector.
3. More handicraft training centres for female folk are needed.
4. Appointments like guide, tourist police, cab driver etc. for women may encourage more female participation in tourism sector.
5. Strengthening laws of the land against physical and mental harassment of women in workplace may be helpful in drawing more female participation in tourism industry.

Conclusion

Gender And Development (GAD) has been emerged as a model in the 1980s adopting a holistic approach following Boserup's (1970) documentation of the regressive impact of development on womens' lives and livelihoods (Visvanathan,1997). Making a review on four decades of development policy, Moser (1993) found five distinct "Women In Development" (WID) approaches namely welfare, equity, anti-poverty, efficiency and empowerment. The Women And Development (WAD) model was previously emerged in the Marxist world with the belief that gender disparity was intensified with the spread of capitalism. Capital accumulation in tourism industry and the social relations of gender bound to spatial affinity make interplay between the perspectives of WAD, WID and GAD deriving the nature of women participation in tourism industry worldwide. WITEP (Women in Tourism Empowerment Programme) initiated by UNWTO is nothing but a step forward to address inequalities and gender related discrimination in tourism industry.

References

Ateljevic, I. (2008): "Women empowerment through tourism", accessed from http://dtxtq4w60xqpw.cloudfront.net/sites/all/files/pdf/reportwomen_empowerment_through_tourism_by_irena_ateljevic_2008.pdf on 31/08/2015 at 11.25 PM, pp. 7-98.

Bagguley, P. (1990): "Gender and labour flexibility in hotels and catering", *Service Industries Journal*, Vol. 10, No. 4, pp. 737-747.

Baum, T. (2013): "International Perspectives on Women and Work in Hotels, Catering and Tourism", *Bureau for Gender Equality and Sectoral Activities*, ILO, Geneva, pp. 19-58.

Castelberg-Koulma, M. (1991): "Greek women and tourism: women's cooperatives as an alternative form of organization", Redclift, N. and Sinclair, M.T. (eds.), Working Women: International Perspectives on Labour *and Gender Ideology*, Routledge Publications, London and New York.

Creighton, M.R. (1995): "Japanese craft tourism; liberating the crane wife", *Annals of Tourism Research*, Vol. 22, No. 2, pp. 463-478.

Deshwal, P. (2015): "Tourism Industry: An Instrument of Indian Economic Growth through FDI", *International Journal of Scientific Research and Management* (IJSRM), Vol. 3, No. 2, p. 2137.

García-Ramón, M.D., Canoves, G. and Valdovinos, N. (1995): "Farm tourism, gender and the environment in Spain", *Annals of Tourism Research*, Vol. 22, No. 2, pp. 267-282.

Indian Institute of Public Administration (IIPA) (2009): "Gendering Human Development Indices: Recasting the Gender Development Index and Gender Empowerment Measure for India", Ministry of Women and Child Development, Government of India, New Delhi, p. 12.

Intercontinental Consultants and Technocrats Pvt. Ltd. (ICT) (2005): "Documentation of Best Practices Adopted by the State Governments for the Development of Tourism", Ministry of Tourism (MR Division), Government of India, *Final Report*, Vol. 1, New Delhi.

John, S. (2014): "A Study on the role of tourism in promoting arts and crafts—A case study on Channapatna toys", Proceedings of the Second International Conference on Global Business, Economics, Finance and Social Sciences, Chennai, India, pp. 1-4.

Momsen, J.H. (1994): "Tourism, Gender and Development in the Caribbean", Kinnaird, V. and Hall, D. (eds.), *Tourism: A Gender Analysis*, Wiley, Chichester.

Moser, C.O.N. (1993): *Gender Planning and Development*, Routledge Publications, London.

Pureell, K. (2005): "Women Employment in UK Tourism: Gender Roles and Labour Markets" Sinclair, M.T. (ed.), *Gender, Work and Tourism*, Routledge Publications, London, p. 39.

Rajan, G.R. (2013): *Report of the Committee for Evolving a Composite Development Index of States*, Government of India, New Delhi, pp. 1-58.

Rani, G.S. (2013): "Recent Trend in Tourism Industry and Women", *Indian Journal of Applied Research*, Vol. 3, No.10, pp. 1-3.

Sinclair, M.T. (2005): "Issues and Theories of Gender and Working Tourism", Sinclair, M.T. (ed.) *Gender, Work and Tourism*, Routledge Publications, London, pp. 2-6.

Suri, K. (2013): "Rural Entrepreneurship Development and Women in Jammu & Kashmir", *International Journal of Scientific Research*, Vol. 2, No. 6, pp. 542-545.

UNED (2002): "Gender and tourism: Women's employment and participation in tourism—Summary of UNED-UK", UN, London.

United Nations Development Programme (UNDP) (2014): "*Human Development Report 2014—Sustaining Human Progress: Reducing Vulnerability and Building Resilience*", New York, pp. 176-179.

UNWTO (2011): *"Global Report on Women in Tourism 2010"*, Madrid.

UNWTO (2015): "Tourism Highlight 2015" accessed from http://www.e-unwto.org/doi/book/10.18111/9789284416899 on 30/08/2015 at 11:27:13 AM, pp. 2-3.

Visvanathan, N., *et al.* (1997): *The Women, Gender and Development Reader*, *Zubaan*, New Delhi, pp. 18-23.

World Economic Forum (2015): *The Travel and Tourism Competitiveness Report 2015*, *WEF*, Geneva, pp. 178-179.

Young, K. (1997): "Planning from a Gender Perspective: Making a World of Difference" in *ibid.*, p. 336.

www.gendrresponsibletourism.org accessed on 01/07/2015 at 12.14 AM.

www.g-r-t.org/index.php/ en/about-grt/the-six-pillars accessed on 04/08/2016 at 2.30 PM.

www.http://ethics.unwto.org accessed on 01/07/2015 at 11.34 PM.

www.ilo.org accessed on 5/07/2015 at 10.30 PM.

23

A Geographical Inquiry on Sustainability of the *Purulia Chhau* Dance

An Intangible Cultural Heritage, in West Bengal

Ayanika Sarkar and *Biswaranjan Mistri*

1. Introduction

The way of life is always reflected in various forms of socio-cultural traditions. Tribal people from all-over the world, depend upon nature, not only for deriving substantial livelihood needs but also for the development of invisible characters of their cultural milieu (Reck, 1972). When characteristics of tribal culture are sustained with the changing time and pass through the generations as a hereditary tradition, it gets the characteristics of a folk culture (Ghosh, 2011). If one investigates to the bottom of the belief system which exists in a tribal folk society, he or she may be able to dig into a whole range of benefits that the society is seeking. These include intangible ones, often impacting at spiritual or psychological levels and tangibles that sustain their livelihood needs or both together, contributing to the larger human well-being as well as developing the true nature-culture linkages and interactions (Ramakrishnan, 2008). Different tribal communities have made an influential role on framing a multifaceted web of the socio-cultural traits by developing some unique folk regions in different ecological set-up of West Bengal in general and Purulia District in particular (Baké,1949). In time gradient, these cultural expressions develop a unique cultural identity, which is sustained by the hereditary traditions (Satpathi, 1999). Folk dances are considered to be the most attractive form which represents the particular folk culture (Buckland, 1983). Most of these dances, have taken birth in the doctrine of natural environment (Ghosh, 2014). Purulia District holds its *Chhau* dance tradition throughout its geographical boundary (Acharya, 2013). *Purulia Chhau* is mainly performed by the Kurmis and Mahatos. In this district, *Chhau* dance troupes are seen in every Community Development Blocks (C.D. Blocks) (Satpathi, 1999). Masks and music are essential part of this dance form (Bhattacharyya, 1968 and Arden, 1971). Many people sustain their livelihoods through this folk culture (Ghosh, 2012). Due to the extension of the new economic policy (liberalisation, privatisation, and globalisation), the age old folk culture is sometimes threatened to extinction. *Purulia Chhau* dance has failed to keep itself away from this trickledown effect of the homogenisation process. The changes in accordance with the emergence of globalization, the key components of *Chhau* dance are seemed to be modified (Bandyopadhyay, 2009). It is continuously changing itself for keeping pace with the changing environmental circumstances (Mishra, 2012).

2. The Study Area

2.1 Location of the Study Area

Purulia District is situated within the extension from 22°42′ 35″ N to 23°42′ 00″ N latitude and 85°49′ 25″ E to 86°54′ 3″ E longitude (Map 23.1). The state of Jharkhand demarks the Northern boundary of the district, while Western, Southern and the Eastern boundaries are bounded by Barddhaman, Bankura and Medinipur districts of West Bengal respectively.

2.2 Ecological and Demographic Features of Purulia District

The district, physiographically, is situated in a transitional zone between the Damodar Plains of West Bengal and Chhotanagpur Plateau of South-eastern Bihar. The elevation of Purulia from Mean Sea Level (MSL) is 677 m. It belongs to a subtropical climatic zone with average temperature of 52 °C and 3.8 °C in summer and winter respectively. Average rainfall varies from 1050 mm. to 1420 mm. Rivers, mainly Kasai, Damodar, Darakeswar, Kumari and Subarnarekha form the drainage system of the district. Lateritic soils are found in the uplands and Clay-loam to Loam in the valley areas. The nature of forest (under 11.9955 per cent forested

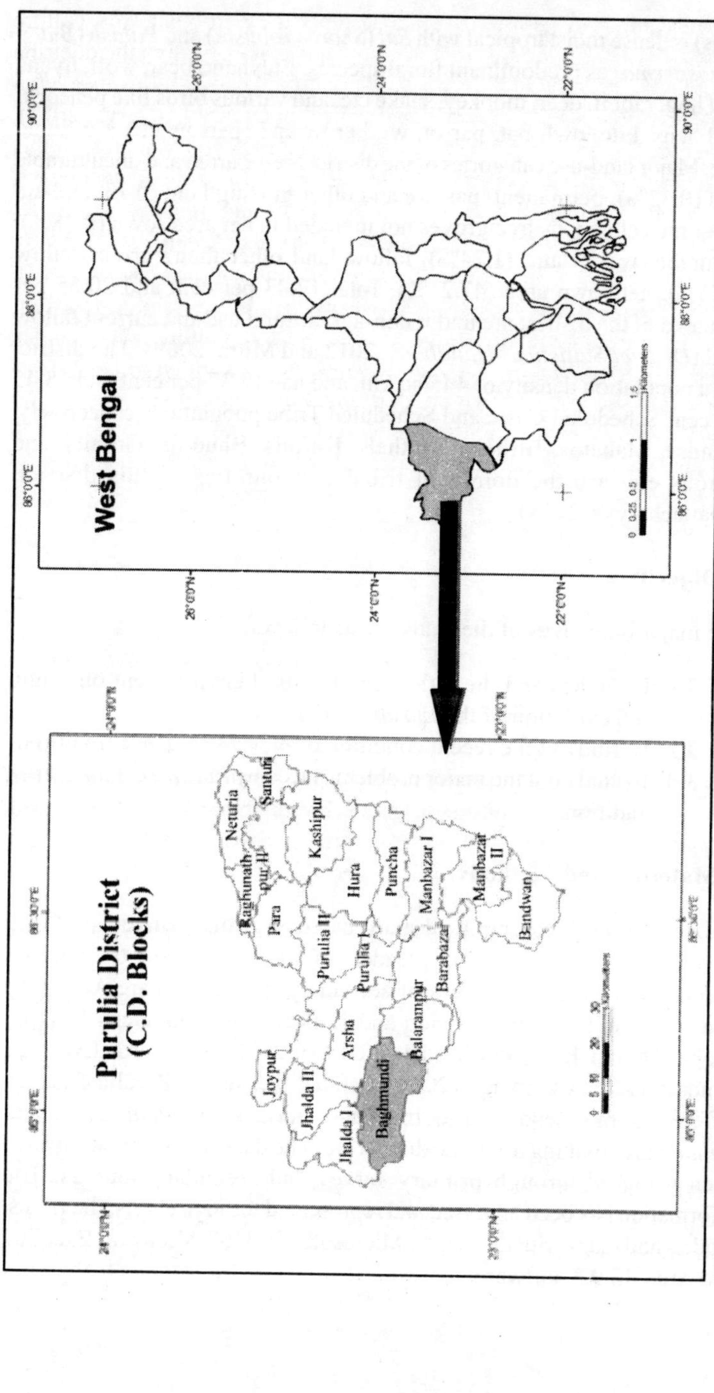

Map 23.1: Location Map.

areas) is dense moist tropical with *Sal* (*Shorea robusta*) and *Palash* (*Butea monosperma*) as predominant floral species. Elephant, bear, wolf, hyena wild hog, rabbit, deer, monkey, snake etc. and various birds like peacock, wild hens, kite, owl, bat, parrot, wild crow and sparrow etc. are found here. Major land-use categories of the district are—barren and unculturable land (0.32%), permanent, pasture and other grazing land (0.13%), land under miscellaneous tree groves not included in net area sown (0.38%), culturable waste land (1.24%), fallow land other than current fallow (0.75%), net sown area (47.21%). Total 17.43 per cent and 20.55 per cent area of the district are under non-agricultural use and current fallow land (*District Statistical Handbook*, 2012 and Mitra, 2009). The district has a population density of 445/sq.km. and has 19.37 per cent and 18.45 per cent Scheduled Caste and Scheduled Tribe population respectively. Mundas, Mahatos, Birhors, Santhals, Kurmis, Bhumijs, Goraits, and Oraons etc. are the dominant tribal communities of this district. (Bhattacharyya, 2014).

3. Objectives

The major objectives of the study are as follows:

3.1 To understand the influence of natural environment on origin and evolution of the *Purulia Chhau*.

3.2 To find out the recent condition of the *Chhau* dance tradition.

3.3 To chalk out the major problems faced by *Purulia Chhau* Dance tradition.

4. Materials and Methods

It is a grassroots level empirical study, based on primary survey involving selected *Chhau* dancers (233), leaders of 10 *Chhau* dance troupes and *Chhau* mask makers. Sources of secondary information are Advanced Space Borne Thermal Emission and Reflection Radiometer (ASTER) Global Digital Elevation Model (GDEM), 2011 from Earth Explorer, Landsat TM SFCC Image (2011), Official website of Purulia District, different books, reports, e-journals and journals on *Chhau* dance and *Chhau* mask making art of the district etc. The data and information have been gathered through primary survey and secondary sources. The information has been analysed and represented through charts, diagrams, models and maps with the help of Microsoft Word '07, Microsoft Excel'07 and Arc GIS 9.3 software.

5. Results and Discussions

5.1 Influence of Natural Environment on Purulia Chhau *Dance Tradition*

5.1.1. Origin of Purulia Chhau Dance in the Doctrine of Natural Environment

In earlier days, the tribal people residing in or around the Ajodhya hills of Purulia District, have been dependent upon forest based hunting and food gathering activities (Fig. 23.1). While going to the dense forested uplands for hunting, they have to face various wild animals. To rescue themselves from those animals they have started worshipping different natural phenomena like hills, trees, springs, rain as well as animals and birds. Being guided by the primitive animistic religion, the tribal people have started following different moods, attitudes and activities of the wild animals or birds for a safe and smooth life and livelihood. Finally, these nature based hunting activity has become a way to express worship to the tribal gods and goddess (e.g. Local Hill God) (Bhattacharyya, 1961). Still now, the nature dependent primitiveness is observed in the form of various *Chal*, and *Deg* (different kinds of steps used while dancing) which still represents the original tribal activities that were acquired at the time of their hunting activity in the olden days. Different *chal*s named *Sial chal, Bagh chal, Valuk chal, Sarpa chal, Bak chal, Mayur chal, Morog chal* etc. are examples of the mimicry of the animals like fox, tiger, bear, snake and birds like peacock, hen respectively. With the passage of time these dance form has become an integral part of the tribal culture of this district. Preliminary form of *Chhau* dance, i.e. *Kapjhanp* has originated in the Baghmundi area and then has diffused to Seraikella and Mayurbhanj Districts of Jharkhand and Odisha. It has reshaped as a hinduised war dance by getting support from the erstwhile royal nobility of Baghmundi area (Mahato, 2002 and Santra, 2002).

5.1.2. Spatial Pattern of Nature-culture Linkage in the Form of Chhau Dance Tradition (*see* Map 23.2)

Variation in elevation from Mean Sea Level can be observed from the Eastern part (less than 300 m.) to the Western part (more than 600 m.) of the district. Forest cover (dense mixed deciduous forest) also decreases eastward with the lowering of relief. The forested upland of Ajodhya Hill

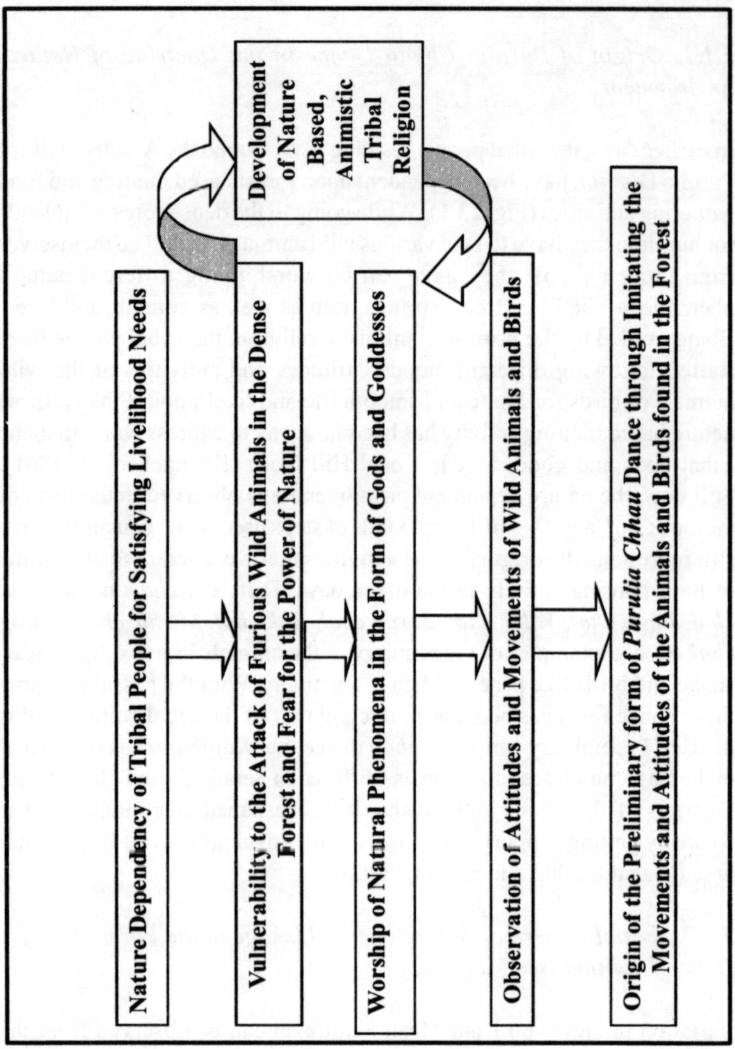

Fig. 23.1: Origin of *Purulia Chhau* Dance in the Doctrine of Natural Environment

Area, located at the extreme west of the district, is mainly comprised of the parts of Baghmundi, Jhalda-I, Jhalda-II, and Arsha Community Development Blocks (C.D. Blocks). Noticeable influence of geo-ecological set-up in general and relief as well as forest cover in particular on the spatial pattern of distribution of *Chhau* dance troupes can be understood by analysing Maps. 23.2, 23.3 and 23.4. Maximum number of *Chhau* dance troupes (25 to 30) can be observed in Baghmundi and Jhalda-I C.D. Blocks whereas in the eastward direction, where forest cover is lesser and relief is lower, concentration of *Chhau* dance troupes is found to be lesser. Baghmundi area is considered as the birthplace of the *Chhau* dance. The geo-ecological settings of this area have influenced the unique characteristics of the *Chhau* dance performance in this area. From the point of originality and dignity, *Chhau* dancers of Baghmundi have become successful to get much attention from local as well as national and international viewers. Many small *Chhau* dance troupes have been established in every C.D. Block of the district for some extra earning by utilising the flourishing popularity of *Chhau* dance even in the national and international level. But these newly developed troupes fail to maintain the originality and dignity of *Chhau* dance like the practitioners of Baghmundi and Jhalda. So, it can be said that micro-spatial differences in physiography and forest cover have major role to play upon the variation in the distribution of *Chhau* dance troupes throughout the district.

5.2 Condition of *Purulia Chhau* Dance Tradition

Performing *Chhau* dance is still not regarded as the primary source of income of the dancers. Main occupation of the dancers shows a range of variation. But still now, the largest proportion depends upon agricultural activities and most of them are agricultural labour (35.62%). After introduction of Mahatma Gandhi National Rural Employment Guarantee Scheme (MGNREGS, after passing NREGA Act in 2005) many dancers have involved themselves for earning money from the 100 days work programme. The second largest proportion (13.3%) of dancer belongs to the other categories which include fuelwood collection from the forests, *bidi* binding and household labour etc. Engagement in different Government (Government) and Non-government (Non-Government) services (2.15%) and business (0.85%) are very less (Fig. 23.2). *Chhau* dance troupes get most of the contracts from different places within Purulia District. Now-a-days, it has become a fashion to organize *Chhau* performance for enjoyment even in many small cultural programmes like—

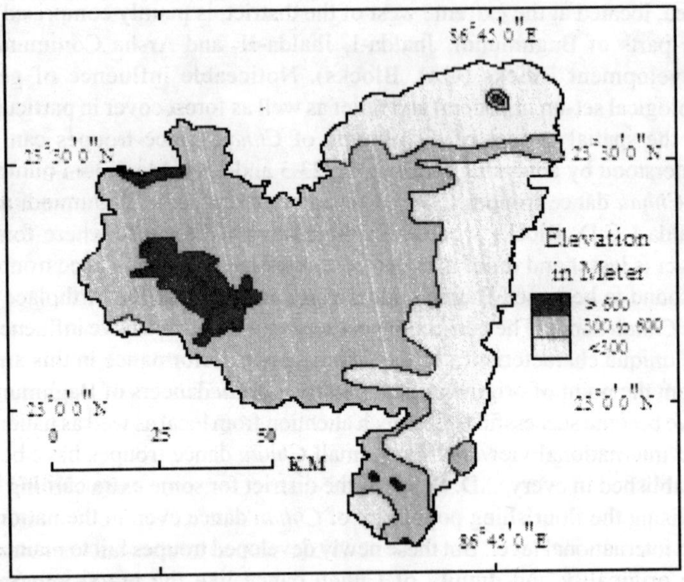

Map 23.2: Elevation Map of Purulia District, 2011.

Source: ASTER GDEM, Earth Explorer, 2011

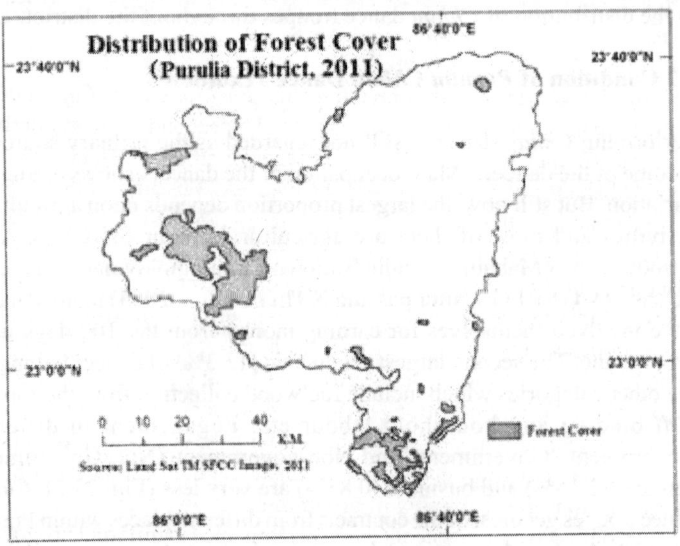

Map 23.3: Distribution of Forest Cover, Purulia District, 2011.

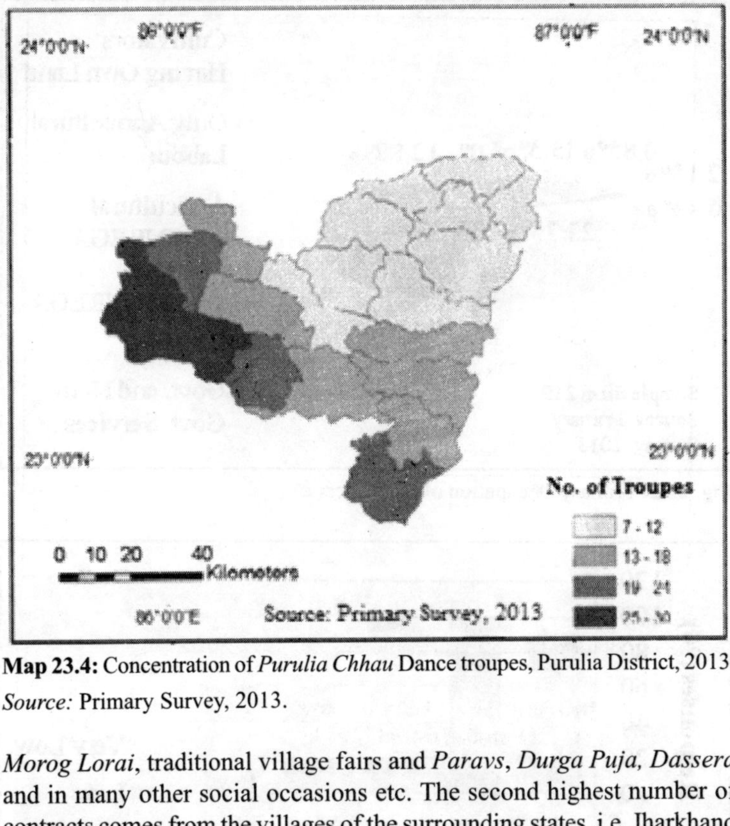

Map 23.4: Concentration of *Purulia Chhau* Dance troupes, Purulia District, 2013.
Source: Primary Survey, 2013.

Morog Lorai, traditional village fairs and *Paravs*, *Durga Puja, Dassera* and in many other social occasions etc. The second highest number of contracts comes from the villages of the surrounding states, i.e. Jharkhand and Odisha. Even another forms of *Chhau* exist in both of the states but still demand for the *Purulia Chhau* is very high in that regions. Though every troupe gets chance to perform *Chhau* in different districts of West Bengal, but it is not very high. In case of visiting different metro cities across India and foreign countries, maximum *Chhau* troupes get very less scope as most of the programmes in different metro cities of India and foreign countries are organized by different Governmental and Non-Governmental Organizations (Fig. 23.3). A very few number of dance troupes which are able to make contracts with the organizations and which are popular get the opportunity to make regular contacts with those organizations gets a number of programmes.

Month-wise variation of *Chhau* performance in different programmes shows that every troupe gets maximum number of contracts at the month of March and April (*Chaitra Parva* or *Gajan*) as this is the period when

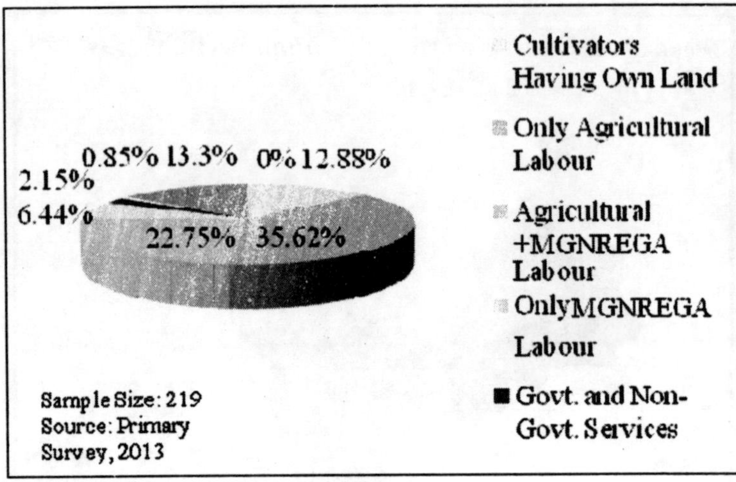

Fig. 23.2: Primary Occupation of the Dancers

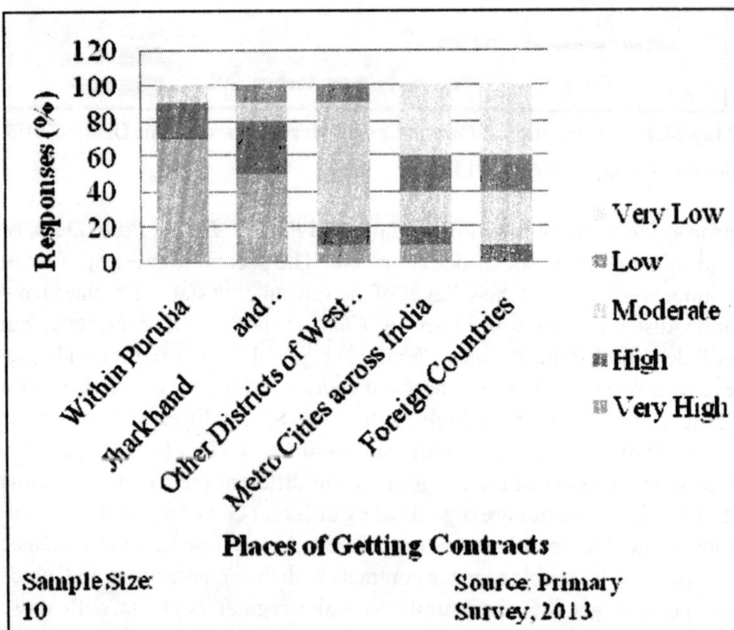

Fig. 23.3: Places of Getting Contracts for *Chhau* Performance

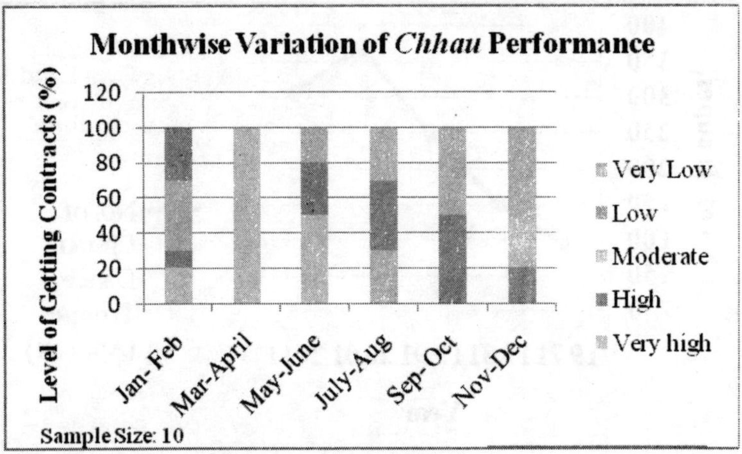

Fig. 23.4: Month-wise variation of *Chhau* Performance

Source: Primary Survey, 2013.

traditionally this dance form is performed. This craze continues up to the month of July. But after the arrival of Monsoonal rainfall, the number of programmes becomes low and even sometimes becomes very low in the month of July and August as the rural people including the large proportion of dancers who are depending upon agricultural activity become busy in cultivating crops (Fig. 23.4).

Though now-a-days, a fewer programmes are being held at the time of *Dassera* and *Durgapuja* but the number is very less. The number of programmes becomes lowest in the month of November and December though very few numbers of popular troupes get contracts in different Government and Non-Governmental programmes. In January and February, the number of programmes organised for *Chhau* dance is average (Fig. 5.4).

5.3 Problems of Sustaining *Chhau* Dance in Purulia

There is an increasing trend in number of troupes from the year 1971 to 2001. The highest increase in total number of *Chhau* dance troupes can be traced between the year 1991 and 2001, but it should be noticed that there is a sharp decline in the number of *Chhau* dance troupes from 370 to 306 between 2001 to 2011 and in 2013 the number have been reduced to 303 (Fig. 23.5).

There are various factors behind the situation. The main reasons have been identified on the basis of ranks as (major the problem represents

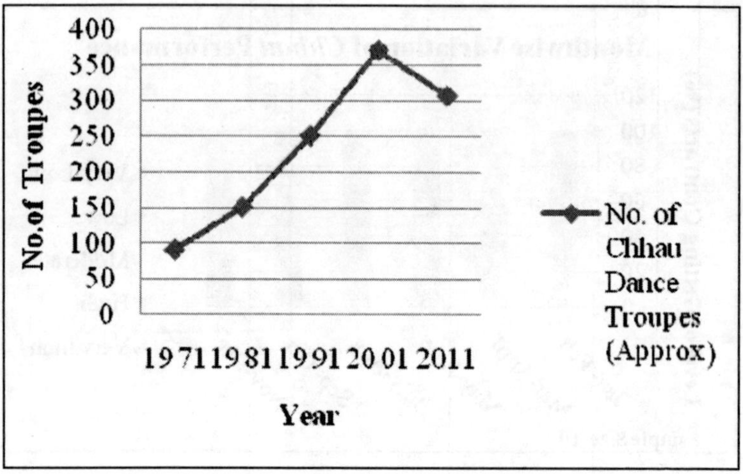

Fig. 23.5: Temporal Change in No. of *Chhau* Dance Troupes (Only in C.D. Blocks)

Source: Royal Chhou Academy, Balarampur, 2013.

lower the rank) given by the leaders of 10 dance troupes about the various problems of the *Chhau* dance perceived (Table 23.1).

5.3.1 Lack of Interest among the New Generation in Maintaining Hereditary Tradition

Lack of interest among the new generation in maintaining their hereditary tradition is the major problem (Fig. 23.6). The dancers below the age group of 20 years are taking this as only extra source of income. Moreover, a new problem has been raised in this respect that after performing a dance, a very little amount of money comes in the hands of the dancers. Sometimes engagement in different works as labour helps the young boys to earn more money than performance in *Chhau* dance (47.27%). Many of them (14.54%) will not continue *Chhau* dance in future as some of them migrate in other places either for job or for education (Fig. 23.7). Thus, there is loss of interest among the young boys in performing *Chhau* (Fig. 23.7). Most of the dancers from the age group of above 40 years take *Chhau* as profession as it is their age-old hereditary tradition and passion (42.06%) as they want *Chhau* to be developed and sustained. This trend is also noticed among the age group of 20 to 40 years but less among the performers of the age group of less than 20 years (Fig. 23. 7).

Table 23. 1: Major Problems Faced by *Purulia Chhau* Dance Troupes

Parameters	Major Problems Faced by Purulia Chhau Dance Troupes														
	Allotted Ranks by Troupe Leaders												Total No. of troupes Opined	Total Rank for Each Parameter	
	Rank	No. of Troupes	Rank	No. of Troupes	Rank	No. of Troupes	Rank	No. of Troupes	Rank	No. of Troupes	Rank	No. of Troupes		No.	%
A. Lack of Establishment Fund	1	4	2	1	3	4	4	1	5	0	6	0	10	22	10.47
B. Increase in Expenditure than Earning	1	0	2	1	3	0	4	7	5	2	6	0	10	40	19.05
C. Lack of Interest among New Generation	1	3	2	3	3	4	4	0	5	0	6	0	10	21	10
D. Lack of Govt. Initiatives	1	1	2	5	3	2	4	1	5	1	6	0	10	26	12
E. Lack of Interest among Rural Viewers	1	0	2	0	3	0	4	1	5	6	6	3	10	48	22.85
F. Miscellaneous	1	1	2	0	3	0	4	0	5	2	6	7	10	53	25.24
Total														**210**	**100**

Source: Primary Survey, 2013.

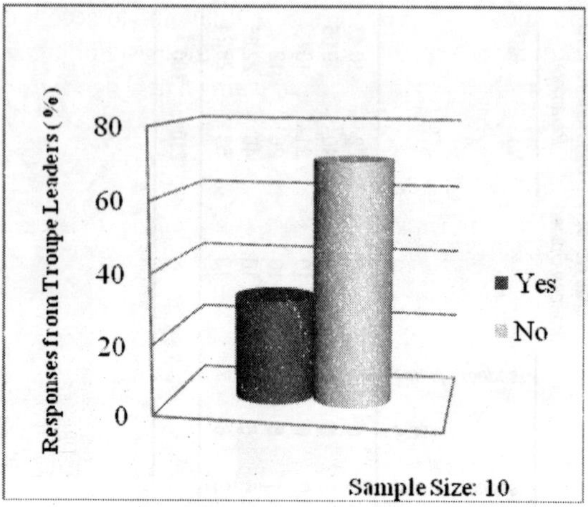

Fig. 23. 6: Willingness of New Generation to Join *Chhau* Troupes
Source: Primary Survey, 2013.

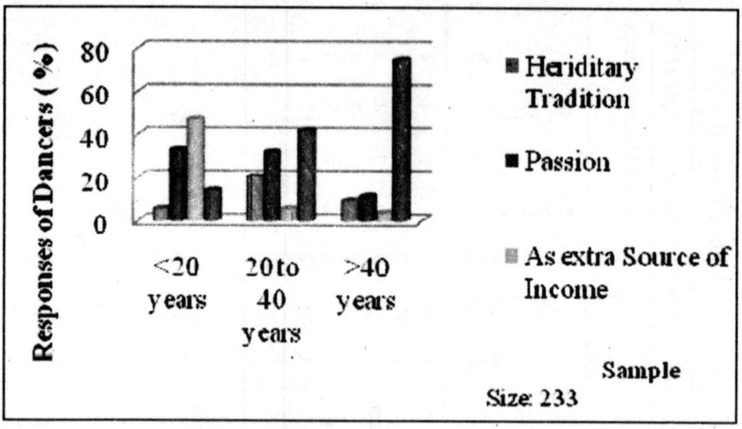

Fig. 23. 7: Reasons behind Taking *Chhau* as a Profession
Source: Primary Survey, 2013.

5.3.2 Lack of Fund for Establishing New Dance Troupe

Temporal change in the average establishment cost (from ₹ 35,000 to ₹ 1,50,000) for starting a new troupe has experienced a very sharp increase from 1970-80 to 2000-10 (Fig. 23.8). For initial organization, buying different musical instruments, communicating with the middlemen for getting contracts in the initial stages etc. a large amount of money is needed.

It is very difficult for the poor agricultural labours to accumulate such a huge amount of money for establishing new troupes. For this reasons, the people again lose their interest in establishing a new dance troupes.

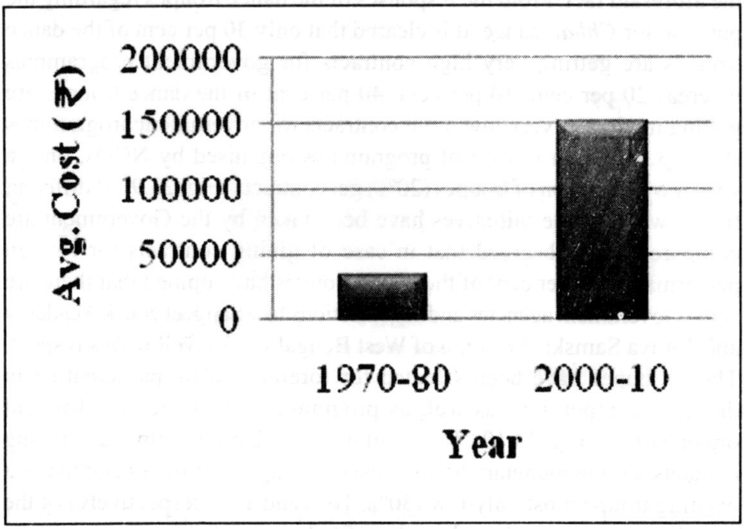

Fig. 23. 8: Temporal Change in Avg. Establishment Cost (₹)

Source: Primay Survey, 2013.

5.3.3 Lack of Government Initiatives

Though, there are many schemes and programmes both in international as well as national level for promoting or safeguarding the age old intangible cultural heritage. But the small and less popular dance troupes hardly get any facility. There are many eminent *Chhau* dancers like Guru Gambhir Singh Murha and Nepal Mahato who have been awarded many times for their contribution but in real scenario (according to their family members and dance troupe members) the awards have no gain in enhancing the economic condition of the poor dancers and their family. If any programme is organized by the Central or State Government the opportunity to show the skill of dancing is given to those popular troupes and the large number of troupes remains untouched from the scope. Some of the troupes (20%) have opined that it is better to perform in programmes organized by various NGOs as they pay more for a performance. Most of the dance troupes have opined that they get hardly any help from Government for any kind of improvement of the dance. Only the big and popular dance troupes are getting facilities of government initiatives. This

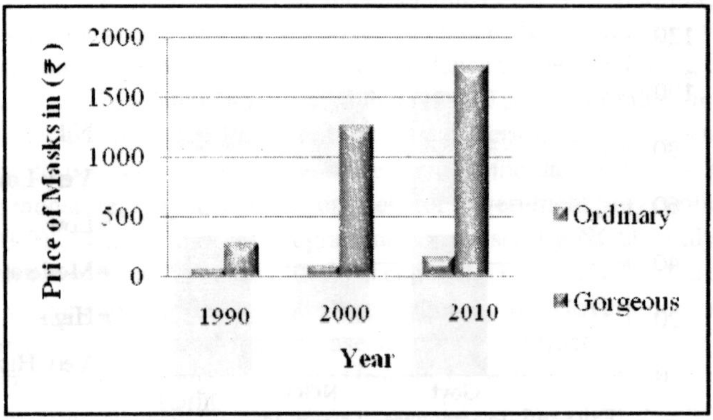

Fig. 23.11: Temporal Change in Avg. Price of Masks (₹)
Source: Primary Survey, 2013.

5.3.5 Lack of Interest among the Rural Viewers

Lack of interest among viewers is another problem faced by the traditional *Chhau* dance in the rural areas (Fig. 23.12). Rural people are now paying more interest in watching *Chhau* with glamorous outlook and filmy effects. According to the troupe leaders and managers of *Chhau* dance troupes, they have to modify their themes of performance according to the choice of viewers.

Most of the dancers (70.35%) have opined that the rural viewers of *Chhau* dance do not like traditional speechless and instrumental *Chhau* rather than prefer to *Pala*s of traditional mythological stories with some filmy effects. On the other hand, when the troupes perform in different urban areas or in foreign countries, they use to perform the traditional dance form. But it has been already discussed that there are very small number of troupes which get chance to perform in urban areas or in foreign countries. So, the small troupes are forced to inject modern filmy effects in the performance to attract rural viewers as the small troupes mainly gets contract for performing in different rural areas of Purulia as well as in surrounding districts of West Bengal, Jharkhand and Odisha. Consequently, the trend further leads to the destruction of traditional fervour of the *Purulia Chhau* dance (Fig. 23.12).

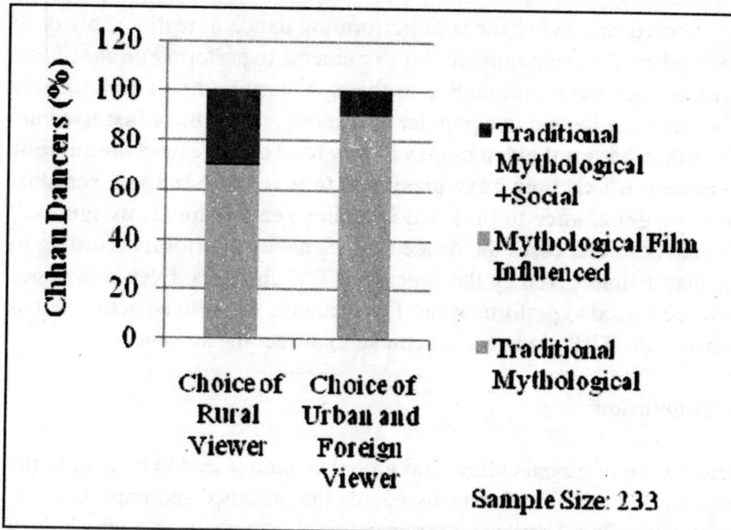

Fig. 23.12: Viewers' Choice on Theme of *Chhau* Performance

Source: Primary Survey, 2013.

5.3.6 Miscellaneous Problems

There are many other problems which create hindrances in the tradition of Purulia *Chhau* dance to be flourished:

(i) *Chhau* dance is mainly based on physical stunts and for this purpose a lot of energy is needed for a single performance. But *Chhau* dance are performed mainly on the rural areas of Purulia and surrounding districts. The poor rural people fail to pay a huge amount for a performance. Thus, performers fail to earn according to their labour and hard work.

(ii) *Chhau* dance needs regular practice. It is very difficult to make 25 to 35 people together at same time. Moreover, according to Anil Sutradhar, an elder *Chhau* dancer from Guru Gambhir Singh's dance troupe, there is lack of potentiality in the leaders to run the group in organized way and lead the other members of the troupes.

(iii) The artists do not even get extra insurance facilities in case of accidents or health problem etc.

(iv) Sometimes, *Chhau* Dancers are exploited by different mass-media agencies or dance choreographers.

Sometimes, the chances of performing dance in reality show or to teach others for entertainment show or cinema to perform *Purulia Chhau* have become very exploitative to them. According to a *Chhau* dancer who has been invited in a popular T.V. show, **"They have just used us. Even they have not given money to buy food or have paid the amount of money which they have promised to give us. For these reasons, even we get chance to perform in dance reality shows, we ignore."** Moreover in that cases the dance troupes have to perform according to the instructions given by the concerned T.V. channels. Even sometimes they are forced to perform as the T.V. channels wants to be performed to increase the TRP rating and of course to attract the audience.

6. Conclusion

Penetration of global culture and global economy lead to a threat to the regional variations and thus disregards the presence and importance of local level cultural heritage. Moreover this phenomenon, through a hidden path, is leading to discrimination and stratification among the dance troupes themselves. Already popular dance troupes are getting more and more scope to flourish and threatening the existence of the numerous small dance troupes. Change of a system is an indispensable factor, but the change should always accommodate the sustainability for the further betterment of the concerned community. For the purpose of protection, promotion and revitalization of *Purulia Chhau* some strategies can be taken. Some small scale strategies including community development through small scale organisations, fund allocation for conservation purpose and revitalization activity, skill upgradation and capacity building, encouraging economic enhancement through self-help groups, creation of bilateral agencies for programme contracts and monetary managements and broad scale strategies including using tools for spreading global culture as a tool of revitalizing folk culture, creation of tangible products for archival of intangible components, promotion of *Chhau* dance by encouraging education opportunities and research work, promotion of folk tourism as well as by galvanizing popular awareness can be fruitful for the betterment of this cultural heritage of Purulia District.

References

Acharya, I. (2013). Aesthetizing Without Agenda: A Counter-reading of the Western Approach to *Chhau* Dance. *Rupkatha: Journal on Interdisciplinary Studies in Humanities*, *5* (2), pp. 89-97.

Arden, J. (1971, Spring). The *Chhau* Dancers of Purulia. *The Drama Review, 15*, pp. 64-75.

Baké, A. (1949). Indian Folk Dances. *Journal of the International Folk Music Council*, 1, pp. 47-48.

Bhattacharyya, A. (1961). *Chhow* Dance of Purulia. In *District Census Handbook, Purulia.* Government of West Bengal. pp. 22-23.

Bhattacharyya, A. (1968, January to March). Mask Dances of Bengal. *Sangeet Natak, 7*, pp. 5-12.

Bhattacharyya, T. (2014). *Paschimbanga Darshan* (Vol. 3): *Purulia.* Firma KML Private Limited, Kolkata.

Bandyopadhyay, S. (2009). *Banglar Tin Rananritya Natua, Raibenshe O Paik.* Natnam, Kolkata.

Buckland, T. (1983). Definitions of Folk Dance: Some Explorations. *Folk Music Journal, 4*(4), pp. 315-332.

Government of India. (2011). *Census of India: West Bengal Series.* Kolkata.

Ghosh, C. (2011). *Bharatiya Shastriya Nritya Ebong Chhou O Banglar Loknritya.* Dey's Publishing, Kolkata.

Ghosh, B. (2014). *Paschimbanger Sanskriti.* Prakash Bhaban, Kolkata.

Government of West Bengal. (2012). *District Statistical Handbook, Purulia,* Bureau of Applied Economics and Statistics. Kolkata.

Mahato, P.P. (2002). The Anthropology of the Manbhum School of *Chho*: Its origin, development and creative excellence. In *Folk Culture of West Bengal,* Institute of Art and Handicraft, Kolkata. pp. 19-47.

Mishra, M. (2012). Globalisation and Folk Culture: A Qualitative Study on the Decaying Heritage of *Chhau* Dance of Purulia district in West Bengal, India. *Asian Journal of Research in Social Sciences and Humanities, 2* (3), pp. 151-159.

Mitra, S. (July, 2009). Jela Porichoy-Purulia Jela. *Yojona.* pp. 39-48.

Ramakrishnan, P.S. (2008). *The Cultural Cradle of Biodiversity.* National Book Trust, New Delhi.

Reck, D. (1972). The Music of Matha "Chhau". *Asian Music*, 3(2), pp. 8-14.

Santra, T. (2002). Paschimbanglar Gajon Nrityer Patabhumikay Anchalik Nritya Chhou. In B.D. Gupta (Ed.), *Folk Culture of West Bengal: Chhou.* Institute of Art and Handicraft, Kolkata. pp. 67-72.

Satpathi, I.D. (1999). *Chhou.* Loksamskriti O Adivashi Samskriti Kendra, Calcutta.

Satpathi, S.K. (2002). Purulia—The Home for *Chhou* Dance. In B.D. Gupta (Ed.), *Folk Culture of West Bengal: Chhou*. Institute of Art and Handicraft, Kolkata. pp. 13-18.

24
Tourism and Its Impact on Coastal Environment
A Case Study of Digha, (E) Midnapur, West Bengal

Biswajit Roy Chowdhury and *Bumba Khan*

Introduction

Human impact on the land surface can be seen in different forms. Tourism is one of them. It is now regarded as an industry that can generate a number of social and economic benefits. It also helps to promote employment opportunities and arguments foreign exchange earnings. Tourism is an integral part of socio-economic development of any city as any other relevant activities. Generally, people choose those places as a tourist spot where they can enjoy the scenic beauty of nature as well as can get all. kinds of facilities that can smoothen their leisure period. The law of tourism said that the activity of tourism should be in such a way that it should not hamper the existing environmental conditions of the concerned tourist area. This is termed as **Eco-tourism.** There have some basic rules and principles of eco-tourism and we should maintain them. But most of the people visit any place without getting any proper knowledge about eco-tourism. As a result of which the natural environment of the tourist spots are getting degraded day-by-day. Not only that to promote the tourism business most of the country in the world give some lucrative offers to the travellers in expense of their natural resources. This also helps to create another problem on both the natural and social environment of the tourist area.

Plate-I: Panoramic View of Digha Beach.

In respect of tourism, West Bengal is considered as a mini India. Almost all kinds of tourist spots (from Mountain to Sea) can be found in this state. As per Government tourism data in 2012, West Bengal stands fifth in terms of foreign tourist inflow and sixth in terms of domestic tourist inflow in the country. Digha, located in the southern coastal belt of West Bengal, is regarded as an important and attractive tourist place to both the domestic and international travellers. Every year almost 26,00,000 tourists come here to enjoy the scenic beauty of this sea city and the figure is still increasing day-by-day. This is mainly due to the improved transport and communication system and amusement facilities as well as the growing number of hotels and resorts on the coastal belt. But the fact is that this increasing pressure of population and the changing pattern of coastal landscape pose serious threat to the biodiversity and the coastal environment of that concerned region.

Objectives

The main objectives of the study are—

1. To study the existing tourism status and feasibility and effectiveness of environmental contingencies for sustainable development of tourism in the study area.
2. To study the community attitude towards tourism development and the impacts caused by the tourism in the above mentioned area.

3. To suggest the measures for the sustainable Tourism development in the region.

Data Base and Methodology

For conducting this research both the primary and secondary data have been collected through intensive field survey and from different Government and Non-Governmental organizations.

The data collected from various sources either by primary or secondary format has to be arranged and analysed properly in such a way that it can show the desired results of the concerned project. Thus to analyse the collected data we use relevant quantitative and cartographic techniques and concluding remarks have been drawn on the basis of such analysis.

Study Area at a Glance

Digha (previously known as '**Beerkul**'), a seaside resort city of West Bengal, lies between East Midnapore district and at the northern end of the Bay of Bengal and have sprung up on the East coast (Western sector) of Bengal. The geographical extension of this region (old and New Digha) ranges from 21°36'50" N latitude, 87°29' E longitude to 21°39' N latitude, 87°37' E longitude from the Odisha border to Jaldha mouja with an elevation of 7m from the mean sea level. It has a low gradient with a shallow sand beach with gentle waves extending up to 14 km in length. The climate of this region is not very harsh (annual average rainfall is 1750 mm, with annual mean temperature 27° C) rather more pleasant. Besides that the different types of aquatic life, flora-fauna, rolling seas, sand dunes, casuarinas forest, red crabs, eye catching beautiful scenario, have made this coastal town as an important tourist destination. During the last four decades road connections have improved and a fleet of transport operations with the incorporation of railway connectivity led to significant influx of tourists, which in turn necessitated development of hotels, holiday houses, private lodges etc. (Mandal, Dandapath and Shukla, 2013). As well as other basic infrastructures like—medical facilities, market, electricity, post office, library, health centre etc. also make this destination attractive for tourists as well as different interest groups (Fig. 24.1).

According to 2001 census, the total number of population in this region was 30,336 which become almost 46,532 according to the 2011 census. With the onset of such development the number of tourists (both domestic

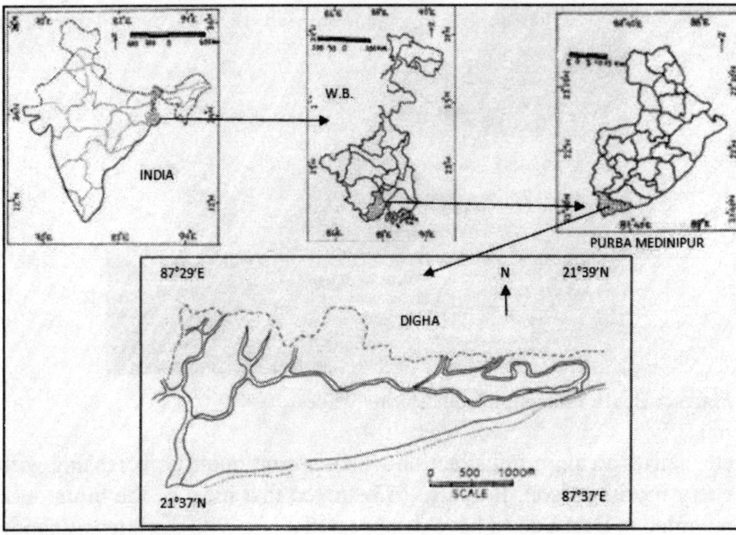

Fig. 24.1: Study Area.

and foreign) also increases day-by-day. According to the report of West Bengal Tourism Department (2011) approximately 25,47,017 tourists are coming in this region per year and the figure is still increasing day-by-day. This voluminous increase of tourist population has led to change the coastal environment of this geomorphologically dynamic, ecologically sensitive, biologically rich and economically profitable tourist spot.

Statement of the Problems

As I said earlier the natural environment of this region provide a unique combination of resources and contains of beaches, sand dunes, wetlands, Barrier Island, reefs etc. which may be considered to explore the opportunities for development of coastal tourism. But environmentally Digha is now remaining in a fragile condition. Coastal erosion is a major problem in this region. A report of GSI (Geological Survey of India) said that this erosion and accretion have been accelerated due to several anthropogenic activities near the coastline. Along with that the degradation of natural environment due to extreme tourism also creates another burden on that coastal belt. The exact impact of tourism development on the coastal belt of Digha cannot be measured by quantity but, the continuing dumping of solid waste and raw sewage in the coastal water, pollution

Plate-2: Beach Protection from Marine Waves

etc. causes an alarming situation which is continuously increasing with every tourist season. It is also to be noted that most of the biota once recorded in Digha coast have disappeared along with the intensification of tourism and resultant increased dumping of untreated solid waste and contaminated water. Moreover, Tourism activity invariably leads to accelerate the development of transport network, hotel business, illegal encroachment and mushrooming of construction by different stakeholders. Each of these activities has a direct impact on both the natural environment and the human being.

Major Findings

Tourism and its Impact on Coastal Ecology

Digha is West Bengal's most popular sea resort. It is located 187 km south-west of Kolkata. Digha has a low gradient with a shallow sand beach extending up to 7 km in length and has gentle rolling waves. The scenic beauty of this place is charming and alluring. It has a number of tourist spots which are rich in respect of both natural resources and scenic beauty. The important viewing point attraction zone are Marine aquarium and research centre, National Cashew Garden, Science Centre, Amravati lake, and Dipak Mitra Snake Farm, this number is enough for the size of the Digha coastal area. The beach is crowded from sunrise to sunset by the peoples for bathing, swimming; about 35,000 people come to Digha per day on average. About 70 per cent of them get bath and the rest obviously use the shore to enjoy the beauty of Digha and use the same place for entertainment purpose like fist, drinking, dancing, playing etc.

These activities also increase day-by-day with the onset of the growth of tourists and the number of hotels and resorts which in turn has a direct impact on both the natural resources and the social environment of Digha.

Ecologically, the coastal region of Digha is very sensitive. Beach is a more dynamic part of this coastal region where hydrology and morphology interact with each other and form beach morphodynamics. In our study area we can find different types of geomorphic features like— Berm, Beach face, Runnel, Ridge Low tide terrace, trough, long shore bar, Ripple, Cusp, Small tidal pool, Crescent mark, Horn, Crabs holes, Mud ball, Small scouring dune etc. and these features help to form a unique combination of coastal ecosystem which include flora, fauna and other related species. But these ecosystems are now remaining in a vulnerable state due to the continuous human interferences. It would be quite clear from the given terrain-wise study (Table 24.1).

Tourism and Its Impact on Landuse Change

If we take a look on the decadal growth of population in Digha (Fig. 24.2), we can see that as well as the interest of people about this tourist place has increased the natural landscape is rapidly converted into cultural landscape. It is true that this kind of change in landuse pattern (Fig. 24.3) mainly happen due to the continuous growth of tourism industry. As tourism is the main economic resource of this region, so to accommodate large amount of people several number of hotels, resorts and guest houses are formed here and there and their number continuously increases day-by-day. Some of them are constructed not only in expense of coastal vegetation, but also violating the rules and laws of Coastal Regulation Zone. Even those regions are covered by indigenous plant species in before several years, now these are transformed into settlement, pasture land, Farm forestry, hotels, resorts etc. This kind of change in land-use pattern possesses an adverse impact on the different parameters of environment of this coastal belt. In Table 24.2 we try to highlight the environment of coastal tourism by dividing the whole area into 3 segments.

Tourism and its Impact on Local Resources

As a profitable land, Digha is most attractive place for both the local dwellers and businessmen. That's why most of the businessmen come here to purchase the land, to construct hotels, resorts, restaurants etc.

Table 24.1: Coastal Ecology of Digha

Terrain Unit	*Morphology*	*Types of Plant*	*Plant Habitat*	*Remark*	*Fauna Species*	*Remarks*
Dune base	Slope 1°50′10″ Height 2-3 m.	Creepers	Lee ward side, sand spray, high temperature, wind stress, seepage water, high nutrients.	Overall open lee ward side, high sand spray, moderate seepage water and nutrients.	Coastal fauna includes mainly on the Digha coast rabbits rats, snake, crabs, starfish, horseshoe crab, limpet, clam, snail, sea urchin and other various types of mammals, reptiles and insects.	Habitat conversion, loss of fauna habitat. Some fauna species are vanished.
Dune crest	Slope 14°5′10″ Height 7-13 m.	Shrubs Small tree Large tree	Exposure to the atmosphere, high wind spit, high soil moisture, decomposition and nutrients.	Moderate soil moisture		
Dune back	Slope 7°37′00″ Height 6-12 m.	Shrubs	Platform surface, sheltered area.	Network, hotel, lodge, settlement, buildup.		
Dune tail	Slope 2°00′00″ Height 2.5-4.5 m.	Large tree	Sheltered zone, sand siding, water table close to the surface.	Salinization, vegetation loss.		

Source: Computed by Authors.

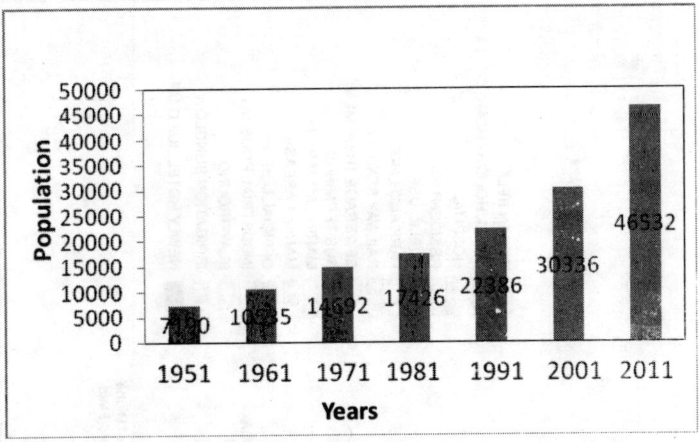

Fig. 24.2: Year-wise Growth of Population (Digha)

Source: Census of India, 2011.

Not only that the local dwellers also involve in different kinds of business and most of them are performing their business in and around the beach area. More than two thousand permanent shops of stationery goods, craft, and restaurants are situated here. Along with that the growth of different kinds of transport network also makes this region more feasible to both the travellers and the businessmen. More than 100 private buses and 50 State government Buses, 3 local trains and 2 express trains regularly serve this region. It is true that a land consists with natural beauties always create a good economically profitable trading situation, but it would always happen in return the exploitation of natural resources. Digha is not out of these situations. Here the growth of urbanisation and tourism industry are basically happen in expense of thousands of coastal vegetations and degradation coastal dunes. As a result of which degradation of coastal land and coastal ecosystem are now become a serious concerns. Most of the flora and fauna species are facing trouble, several species have been vanished. According to some geomorphologists, if this situation persists, it will pose an adverse impact on the ecological balance of coastal landforms.

Tourism and Environmental Pollution

A poor environmental situation has originated as a result of uncontrolled tourism. To maintain the ecological balance, it is very important to organize the whole system of tourism in a sustainable way and this responsible

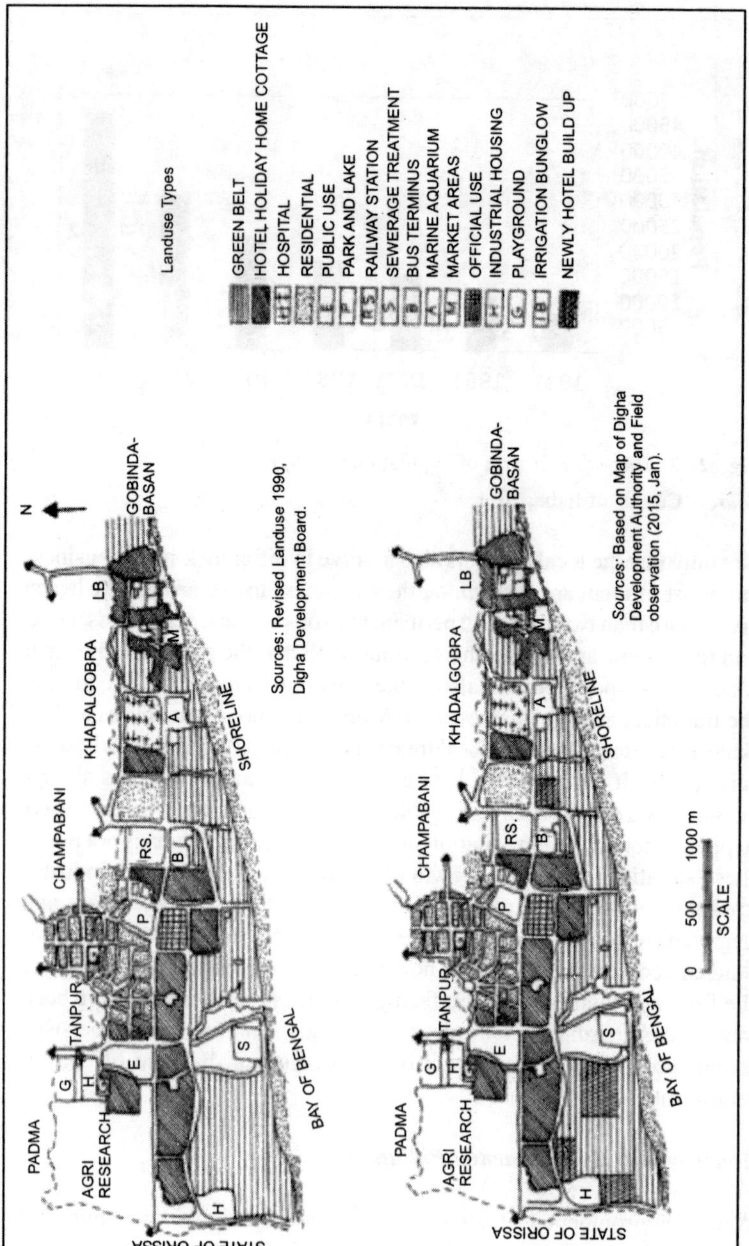

Fig. 24.3: Changing Landuse Pattern of Digha in the Year of 1990 and 2015

(i) **Ecologically Sensitive Zone:** From the ecological point of view this zone is situated in between High Tide Line (HTL) and Low Tide Line (LTL). Most of the ecological functions of different species are done in this part of the coast. So that this zone should remained always undisturbed.

(ii) **CRZ-I:** The zone lying between HTL and LTL and up to 500 m. distance from HTL is called CRZ-I. It is a fragile zone and comprised with full scenic beauty. Any kind of development activity should be prohibited in this zone.

(iii) **CRZ-II**: CRZ mainly comprises the developed parts of the coastal belt. But there should be some limitations on intensive development or new constructions in this zone. This zone should be developed behind CRZ-I.

(iv) **Settlement Sector:** This zone should be developed along the coastal area, i.e. village units. It should be kept free from construction.

(v) **Tourism Sector:** Tourism sector should be developed at the back of CRZ-II and CRZ-III, so that the coastal ecosystems remain undisturbed.

(vi) **Fishing Sector:** The wetlands should be utilized for fishing purpose with more sustainable way and maintain some rules and regulations, so that the hydrological parameters remain unchanged.

Vulnerable Zone Identification: The term zonation simply means categorization of land surface according to the specific characteristics of that particular land. It can be area specific or land specific. Hence, it is the duty of all geographers to specify the land assessing the most vulnerable zone both in ecologically and environmentally. In that case, the position of Digha remains in a most vulnerable state. Thus, the identification of vulnerable zone and its mapping is quite significant in case of Digha coastal belt.

Basically **Vulnerable Zone Mapping** involves a detailed assessment and analysis of land-use and land cover of concerned study area as well as the loss of biodiversity on that particular area. In fact, it is more helpful in preparation of maps of possible hazard zoning. The steps of Vulnerable Zone Mapping are shown in Table 24.3.

From our study it is found that there are two most vulnerable zones in Digha. One is CRZ-I and another is CRZ-II. In one hand, biologically, these zones are quite rich, while in other hand these are the most vulnerable zones especially in case of Old Digha.

Table 24.3: Risk Identification, Estimation, and Evaluation.

Phases of Analysis	*Risk Assessment Processes*	*Risk Perception Process*
Risk identification	Event monitoring, statistical inference of this coastal belt.	Individual intuition, personal awareness.
Risk estimation	Magnitude of biodiversity loss.	Personal experience intangible losses.
Risk evaluation	Cost/ benefit analysis, community policy.	Personality factors individual action.

Source: Compiled by the Authors.

- **Zone-I:** This zone is most vulnerable comprised with ecologically sensitive, biologically rich and productive. Most of the storms hazards occur here with great devastated power. That is why this area should be keet free from any construction, recreation or other economic activities. Regeneration of natural vegetation for attaining the natural stability of this coastal belt is an immediate task to prevent the degradation of this valuable landscape.
- **Zone-II:** Zone-II included the area of economic activities such as fishery, salt processing, tourism or recreation and infrastructure development. Here the land-use activity should be properly planned, so, that it can maintain its present status. But any kind of unplanned construction along the margin of this zone should not be permitted.

As we know that New Digha, an important tourist centre, is a dissipative coast with wide gentle beach and by nature it remains under the CRZ-II, there should be limitations on construction activities and any kind of development.

Conclusion

From the above discussion, it is quite clear that the unscientific construction and the lack of proper knowledge about sustainable tourism continuously help to degrade the natural stability of this concerned study area. Several laws are formulated and implemented to protect this coastal belt, but the application level of these laws are so low than that of the anthropogenic activities. As a result of which several environmental issues are emerged like environmental pollution, loss of biodiversity etc. So, it is the crucial time to take the necessary steps and strategies by the government against such vulnerable condition, otherwise not only the inhabitants of this region will have to pay the penalty of our negligence, we can also lose this valuable tourist spot from the map of India in future.

References

Bera, A., *Impact of Tourism on Coastal Ecology in the Coastal Region of Digha (West Bengal)*.

Carter, R.W.G. (1988) *Coastal Environments*, Academic Press.

Durovic, M., Lovrentjev, S., (2014). Indicators of Sustainability in Cultural Tourism, The Macro-theme Review, *A Micro Disciplinary Journal of Global Macro Trends, 3* (7), 51.

Gunn, Clare, A. (1988) *Tourism Planning*, New York: Taylor and Francis.

Mason, P. (2003), *Tourism Impacts, Planning and Management*. Butterworth Heinemann. London.

Paul, Ashis Kr. (2002): *Coastal Geomorphology and Environment*, ABC Publication, New Delhi.

Pethick, J.S. (1995): *An Introduction To Coastal Geomorphology*, Arnald Publication, London.

25

Scenario of Bankura District, West Bengal

A Geographical Interpretation of Primary Education

Debasis Ghosh, Mrinal Mandal and *Biswajit Ghosh*

1.1 Introduction

Education is the integral part of human-being and the development of society is directly linked with education. John Dewey one of the outstanding philosophers and educationists stated that Education is the development of all those capacities in the individual which will enable him to control of his environment and fulfil his responsibility" (quoted by Roy, 2003 : 14). Primary education is the basic step to fulfil the goal of nation. The free and compulsory education up to the age of 14 is one of the fundamental rights of every citizen of the union as guaranteed by the constitution of India (Mudaliar Commission Report, 1953 : 4). In an article Kingdon, 2007 mentioned that India in compared to other countries of the world, the participation rate in primary school is lesser than youth literacy rate. According to ASER survey (Pratham, 2007), 93.4 per cent of Indian elementary school age children were enrolled in school in 2006. It was also stated, China is more than thirty years ahead of India in terms of proportion of people completed secondary and post-secondary schooling (Kingdon, 2007 : 3). According to the report of UNESCO, 2010, about 124.8 million illiterate people live in the developing countries (99.5% of the world), in which 40.4 million (32.2%) people belong to India. It is known to all that there is a huge gap in terms of income and socio-economic inequality in India and one out of ten children aged 6-10 is out of school (Biswal, 2011 : 3-4). India Human Development

Report 2011: Towards Social Inclusion also argued the same in support of this report that the overall literacy rate of the country has increased and variation among the states in terms of literacy has also decreased in both rural and urban areas of India. The literacy rate is increasing higher in rural areas compared to urban areas. So, the gap between these areas will be reduced soon (Planning Commission, 2011 : 13).

In one study carried out by Mandal and Ganguli in Bankura district, it was found that the status of primary education in the district was in moderate condition based on three basic parameters such as TIR, ISR and TSR (Mandal and Ganguli, 2011 : 178). In another study done in Purulia by Ghosh and Mandal, 2015 stated that the overall condition of all blocks in Purulia is not satisfying in case of higher secondary education (Ghosh and Mandal, 2015 : 93). They also referred that the secondary educational facility of the district Birbhum is found to be moderate (Ghosh and Mandal, 2015 : 85-86).

There are few relevant literatures available on education of Purulia district, which do not try to explore the status of education and how much variation exists in terms of educational facility among the blocks. Beside this, the closeness of the blocks to each other in respect to facility is not identified. In this study, we have set three objectives. Firstly, the study investigates the spatial distribution of educational facilities at primary level. Secondly, from the distribution of individual facility of educational system across the blocks, it is difficult to determine that the relative position of the block in terms of educational status. We have also developed a composite index of educational status of each block. Thirdly, the study assesses the nature of similarity of blocks in terms of the primary educational facility.

1.2 Materials and Methods

Based on secondary data, which have been collected from *District Statistical Handbook Bankura*, 2012, the present work is carried out. The district map of Bankura has been collected from 18th All India Livestock Census, Agriculture Implements and Machinery, Fishery Statistics, West Bengal, 2007. We have adopted three indicators to carry out this study namely: institution, student and teacher of primary school level of Bankura district. All the urban (municipality) primary schools, teachers and students have been added up to their respective administrative blocks, primary schools, teachers and students. The school is termed as institution in this study. Secondary data have been analysed to find out

Teacher Institution Ratio (TIR), Institute Student Ratio (ISR) and Teacher Student Ratio (TSR) using following formulae:

$$\text{TIR} = \frac{\text{Teacher}}{\text{Institution}} \quad \dots (1)$$

$$\text{ISR} = \quad \dots (2)$$

$$\text{TSR} = \frac{\text{Teacher} \times 1000}{\text{Students}} \quad \dots (3)$$

In the second step, we have computed TIR, ISR and TSR indices on the basis of mentioned three indicators namely: TIR, ISR and TSR. The calculated indicators are computed in Table 25.1.

Table 25.1: Indicators of educational facility and their goalposts

Indicators	*Goalpost of Indicators*	
	Maximum Value	*Minimum Value*
TIR	3.888 (Kotulpur)	2.263 (Hirbandh)
ISR	14.601(Chhatna)	10.203 (Patrasayer)
TSR	45.375 (Joypur)	27.293 (Mejia)

Source: Authors' computation.

In order to construct the Primary Educational Facility Index (PEFI), we have computed indicator index for each indicator by the following formula:

$$I_i = \frac{A_i - m_i}{M_i - m_i} \quad \dots (4)$$

Where; I_i = Indicator index of ith indicator, A_i = Actual value of ith indicator, M_i = Maximum value of ith indicator and m_i = Minimum value of ith indicator.

On the basis of the indices of indicators, the actual position of the jth block in the three dimensional Cartesian space may be plotted by the vector (I_{1j}, I_{2j}, I_{3j}). The best situation, which is Primary Educational Facility (PEF), can be found in Cartesian space vector in terms of (1, 1, 1). The worst PEF is denoted by the vector (0, 0, 0). At the end, PEFI has been computed measuring the normalized inverse Euclidian distance of the vector (I_{1j}, I_{2j}, I_{3j}) from the worst condition (0, 0, 0). Therefore, the following formula can be put here as the each indicator/parameter has been given same weightage.

$$\text{PEF I} = \text{I} - \sqrt{\frac{\sum_{i=1}^{3}\left(1-I_i\right)^2}{3}} \qquad \text{... (5)}$$

The normalization of Euclidian distance is done in order to ensure the range of PEFI from '0' to '1'. As the inverse distance has been taken, higher value of PEFI represents good PEF. Thus, the value '0' indicates no PEF and '1' indicates highest PEF. This distance-based approach has an advantage over the UNDP methodology of measuring achievement or deprivation Index. In UNDP methodology, the index presents the arithmetic or geometric average of the standardised indicators. It assumes perfect substitutability across the dimensions or indicators. Under this assumption, a decrease in value of one indicator can be compensated by an increase of equal magnitude in another indicator.

Thus, if all dimensions or indicators are equally important for the all-over index value the perfect substitutability among the indicators is an unrealistic assumption. In the distance based approach, we do not need this unrealistic assumption. Our PEFI formula satisfies the properties of normalisation, symmetry, monotonicity, proximity, uniformity and signalling. But methodology of HDI follows only the properties *viz.* normalisation, symmetry, monotonicity. Thus, our distance based measure of PEFI is superior to the measures based on UNDP methodology. This methodology is also applied in a study by Bagli and Adhikary, 2015 and Ghosh and Mandal, 2015. The PEFI varies from '0' to '1' where; the value '0' and '1' refers to perfect PEF and worst PEF respectively. To have the better understanding of PEFI of each block, the value of PEFI has been divided into five sub-ranges. The very good condition of PEF is represented by 0.8<PEFI=1.0 and good condition of PEF is indicated by 0.6<PEFI=0.8. The range 0.4<PEFI=0.6 indicates the moderate condition of PEF and the poor condition is experienced by those blocks having the PEFI range of 0.2<HPEFI=0.4 and very poor condition is represented by the range of 0=PEFI=0.2.

Ranking of the PEFI has been done (after Kendall's method) to identify the position of each block in the district. In order to investigate which blocks are close to each other based on TIR, ISR and TSR indicators, we have used the tool of cluster analysis (SPSS Software-20) following squared Euclidian distance method. Finally, to show the possible clusters of the blocks we have drawn the Dendrogram adopting average linkage method.

1.3 Study Area at a Glance

The geographical coordinates (*District Statistical Handbook Bankura*, 2007: 1) of Bankura district are 22°38' N latitude 86°36' E longitude to 23°38' N latitude 87°46' E longitude (Fig. 25.1). It has an area of 6,882 km². The population size and density of the district are 35,96,674 (Male 51.11% and Female 48.89%) and 523/km² respectively (Census of India, 2011). Total rural and urban population are 91.67 per cent and 8.33 per cent respectively. The literacy rate of the district is 70.26 per cent in which male is 80.05 per cent and female is 60.05 per cent. Total number of blocks and police stations are 22 and 23 respectively (*District Statistical Handbook Bankura, 2012*).

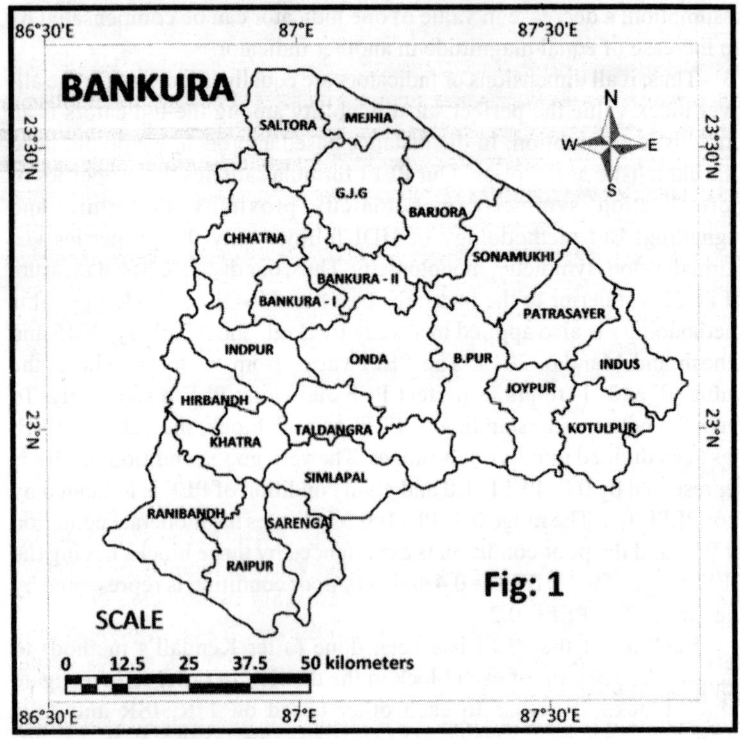

Fig. 25.1 : Map of the study Area
Source: Census of India, 2011.

RESULTS AND DISCUSSION

1.4 Teacher Institution Ratio (TIR)

The Teacher Institution Ratio (TIR) is used to indicate number of teachers available per primary school. Higher the TIR value (Index), higher is the number of teachers available in schools. Based on this parameter, Kotulpur block stands first position having about four teachers per school followed by Bishnupur, Indus, Bankura-I, Joypur and Bankura-II. In contrast, Hirbandh is in the last position where two teachers are available per school and rest of the blocks are in moderate condition.

1.5 Institution Student Ratio (ISR)

The indicator Institution Student Ratio (ISR) refers to number of primary schools available per thousand students. The parameter indicates, Chhatna block enjoys the first position having fourteen institutions per thousand students followed by Ranibandh, Raipur and Joypur. The last rank is experienced by Patrasayer block. Remaining blocks experience the moderate condition.

1.6 Teacher Student Ratio (TSR)

Teacher Student Ratio indicates number of teachers available per thousand students. It is observed that Joypur block enjoys the first position having forty five teachers available per thousand students followed by Kotulpur (43) and Bishnupur (41). The worst condition is experienced by Mejia block where 27 teachers are available per thousand students and rest of the blocks fall in moderate condition.

1.7 Overall Position

The primary educational facility of the district is in moderate condition if we consider all indicators together. Only one block is found to be in very poor and seven in poor condition. Out of twenty two blocks, thirteen blocks enjoy moderate condition and only one block enjoys good condition. It is unfortunate to find that not a single block enjoys very good PEF (Table 25.2).

We observe from Table 25.3 that in an average two teachers available per institution in the district and no such variation of this parameter is

Table 25.2: Primary Educational Facility Index (PEFI) of Bankura district, 2011-2012

C.D. Block	*PEFI*	*Rank*	*Remarks*
Bankura-I	0.426	13	Moderate
Bankura-II	0.421	14	Moderate
Chhatna	0.500	7	Moderate
Saltora	0.242	19	Poor
Mejia	0.117	22	Very Poor
Gangajalghati	0.393	15	Poor
Barjora	0.452	9	Moderate
Onda	0.392	16	Poor
Indpur	0.434	11	Moderate
Khatra	0.323	18	Poor
Hirbandh	0.228	20	Poor
Ranibandh	0.441	10	Moderate
Taldangra	0.568	3	Moderate
Simlapal	0.501	6	Moderate
Raipur	0.376	17	Poor
Sarenga	0.499	8	Moderate
Bishnupur	0.599	2	Moderate
Joypur	0.755	1	Good
Kotulpur	0.559	4	Moderate
Sonamukhi	0.432	12	Moderate
Patrasayer	0.218	21	Poor
Indus	0.552	5	Moderate

Source: Authors' computation.

Table 25.3: Description of the Educational Facility Indicators of Bankura District

Descriptive Statistics	*TIR*	*ISR*	*TSR*	*PEFI*
Mean	2.878	12.610	36.061	0.428
Median	2.779	12.227	35.908	0.433
S.D.	0.401	1.192	4.320	0.144
CV	13.945	9.456	11.980	33.657
Min	2.263	10.203	27.293	0.117
Max	3.888	14.601	45.375	0.755

Source: Authors' computation.

observed in the district. In case of ISR, twelve institutions are available per thousand students in an average, where range is four. In the district, average teachers available per thousand students are thirty six, where maximum and minimum values are 45 and 27 respectively. The actual condition of the district can be understood by the indicator PEFI and we find that the average PEFI is 0.428, which represents moderate condition of PEF. The range of maximum and minimum values of PEFI is 0.638, which indicates the variation of PEF across the blocks of Bankura district. The study also reveals that values of PEFI of ten blocks are less than the average value of the district.

1.8 Cluster Analysis

The similarity among the blocks in terms of the multiple indicators of PEF is not reflected by PEFI. To cope with this problem, we have done cluster analysis for the indicators of PEF following specified methodology. The result of the cluster analysis is represented by the Dendrogram (Fig. 25.2). Here ten possible clusters have been identified from this analysis. The first cluster is made by Kotulpur and Joypur. Second cluster is comprised of Indus and Bishnupur blocks. The third distinct cluster is the result of Mejia. Patrasayer makes fourth cluster. The fifth distinct cluster is made by Hirbandh and Saltora blocks. Taldangra block makes the sixth cluster. In contrast, Chhatna, Ranibandh, Sarenga and Simlapal blocks fall in seventh cluster. The eighth cluster is the result of Indpur,

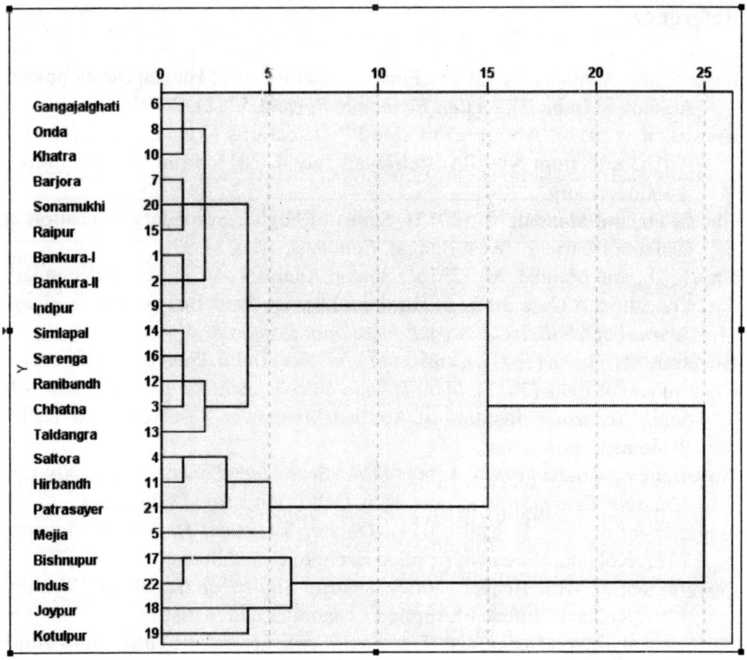

Fig. 25.2: Dendrogram using Average Linkage (Betweeen Groups)

Source: Based on Authors' Computation.

Bankura-I and Bankura-II. The ninth cluster is made by Raipur, Sonamukhi and Barjora blocks. The remaining three blocks fall in tenth cluster. If we consider 10 point scale of dissimilarity, we find all blocks fall in a single cluster.

1.9 Conclusion

We find that the teacher per institution is in moderate condition all-over the district. It is to be noted here, on an average only two teachers, sometimes three teachers in some schools, manage four classes at a time and it is very surprising. This particular portion of education needs attention to improve the quality of education. In case of majority of schools of the district, it is observed that more than hundred students study in a school with limited teachers. The PEF of the district is found to be moderate though there are eight blocks experience below moderate condition.

References

Bagli, S., and Adhikary, M. (2015). Financial Inclusion and Human Development: A Study in India. *The Asian Economic Review, 57* (2), 75-93.

Biswal, K. (2011). About: Download/Publications/Create/PTA%202011/PTA63.pdf. from NUEPA. Retrieved July 4, 2015, from Website: http://www.nuepa.org

Ghosh, D., and Mandal, M. (2015). Status of Higher Secondary Education in Bankura District of West Bengal. *Eduquest, 4*(II), 84-93.

Ghosh, D., and Mandal, M. (2015). Spatial Analysis of Facility of Secondary Education: A Case Study of Birbhum District, West Bengal. *International Journal of Multidisciplinary Educational Research, 4, 9*(3), 79-88.

Government of India (2011). *Census of India.* New Delhi: Directorate of Census.

Government of India (2011). *India Human Development Report 2011: Towards Social Inclusion.* Institute of Applied Manpower Research. New Delhi: Planning Commission.

Government of India (1953). *Report of the Secondary Education Commission, Mudaliar Commission Report.* New Delhi: Ministry of Education.

Government of West Bengal (2014). *District Statistical Handbook, Bankura 2012.* Kolkata: Bureau of Applied Economics and Statistics.

Government of West Bengal (2009). *District Statistical Handbook, Bankura 2007.* Kolkata: Bureau of Applied Economics and Statistics.

Government of West Bengal (2007). *18th All India Livestock Census, Agriculture Implements and Machinery, Fishery Statistics West Bengal, Bankura District.* Kolkata: Directorate of Animal Resources and Animal Health.

Kingdon, G.G. (2007). pubs/workingpapers/pdf/gprg-wps-071-pdf. Retrieved July 5, 2015, from GPRG Website: http://www.gprg.org.

Mandal, M., and Ganguli, M. (2011). Status of Primary Education in Bankura District, West Bengal: A Geographical Interpretation. *Indian Journal of Landscape Systems and Ecological Studies*, *34*(1), 171-182.

Roy, S. (2003). *Sikshaniti.* Kolkata: Soma Book Agency.

26

Community Conservation Initiatives on Open Bill Stork

Rajendra Prasad Mondal, Tapas Kumar Dutta and *Anupam Ghosh*

Introduction

Community-based conservation initiatives (CBCIs) are grassroots level activities that bring individuals and Government or Non-Governmental Organizations to work together to implement a particular conservation strategy. While Organizations set good strategies and prepare plans and policies, their ultimate success in field depends upon the support of people's desire and people's participation. Community-based conservation starts from the most fundamental principle, i.e. individuals will take care of those things in which they have a long-run, sustained interest (Bromley, 1994). The IUCN (1997) has developed a list of ecosystem management principles in which peoples are considered as an integral part of ecosystem and their participation and activity to protect natural resource is considered as a very important aspect under integrated biodiversity management practice.

The Asian Open bill stork, *Anastomus oscitans* (Order *Ciconiiformes*, Family *Ciconiidae*) is a large wading bird in the stork family. They are found mainly in the Indian subcontinent and South-east Asia. They are grayish (non-breeding population) or white (breeding population) with glossy black wings and tail. Young ones have brown tinge to the feathers. Adult birds have a gap between the arched upper mandible and curved lower mandible which is absent in young birds (Robson, 2000). The birds are found mostly in trees near marshes and wetlands. It feeds on mollusks, frogs, crabs and large insects. They are monogamous and highly social and form large nesting colonies in trees. It breeds near inland wetland and builds stick nest in trees laying 2-4 eggs at a time (Vishwakarma, A., 2015). These birds migrate to North India in June and to Southern part of the country in November every year and spent about six months for breeding. The species have been regarded as "Least Concern" by IUCN as (IUCN, 2013).

Avian fauna are the nature's most beautiful creation and bird's habitat, particularly within the aquatic habitat, seems to be strongly influenced by climatic changes and immediate human impact (Bhandarkar and Paliwal, 2014). The objective of the present observation was to study general beliefs present among the villagers associated with inward migration of birds in particular area and the conservation practices initiated by the local people to protect the species.

Study area

Present study was conducted in the 'Barachaka Pakhiralaya' near the Barachaka tribal village (23°19′North latitudes and 87°00′East longitudes) of Bankura District, West Bengal, India. Total area of the village is about 44.22 hector. It is inhabited by about 55 tribal families. The total population of the village is 281, having 139 male and 142 female. The literacy rate is about 61 per cent among males and 39 per cent among females. About 33 per cent of population work as agricultural labour. Non-workers mainly comprises of female and children. Agricultural practices primarily dependent on monsoon rain.

Study Design

The entire study was done by field observation and verbal communication with the villagers. Particular avian species was identified by using the field guide of Ali and Ripley 1987; Grimmett & Inskipp, 2003. The study was done at fortnightly interval between June to November each year during consecutive years between, 2008 to 2012, by visiting the study area at different hours of the day as well as before sunrise and after sunset in different months. All the nest building trees were counted and marked to reduce the probability of duplication of data. The total numbers of individual birds were counted in the middle of September every year because during this time most of the eggs were hatched and chicks were

Table 26.1: Year-wise rainfall and the number of stork population in the study area

Years	*Months of observation*				*Mean Rainfall during study period (mm)*	*Stork population (Number)*
	June	*July*	*August*	*September*		
2008	398.6	438.5	302.8	231.7	342.9	4233
2009	56.8	307.3	325.9	311.7	250.425	4312
2010	188.6	180.7	135.7	199.5	176.125	3987
2011	544.1	183.6	394.3	416.7	384.675	4541
2012	173.2	301.4	345.8	242.7	265.775	4329

Courtesy: Dhua *et al.*, 2013. *International Journal of Advanced Research*.
Source: India Meterological Department, District Bankura West Bengal.

from human habitation. But those conservation initiatives are efficient where human habitat is incorporated with conservation of species. In this way same habitat can be utilized both for human habitation and habitats of some other species. This can be done only by motivating the local communities who can support the conservation. The Government of India may reorient the local tribal communities to restore traditional knowledge through environmental awareness programme.

By following this strategy biodiversity can be conserved to a desired extent. Government and Non-governmental Organizations may provide adequate funding to such tribal villages to encourage them in conservation. At the same time they should be properly trained with the process and ethics of conservation so that the conservation is more fruitful. This will finally help to meet needs of villager and also will improve their living standard.

Although, the bird population is well protected by the villagers but there are some indirect threats that may reduce their population size as mentioned by Vishwakarma, A. (2015). Such as, excessive growth of Invasive weed species can choke wetlands, resulting in reduced water flow and drying of wetland habitat. Large animals such as buffaloes tend to disturb wetland habitats and consume many of their resources. Fishing by the villagers in wetlands can further reduce food sources for Asian open bills. Injudicious application of synthetic, non-biodegradable pesticides used by farmers in agricultural field and their run-off in wetlands can increase mortality among members of this species. In addition use of polythene bags may cause reduction in their population.

Conclusion

So, present study established the Community conservation initiatives of tribal villagers of Barachaka village of Bankura to provide protection and conservation of Multi-species heronry bird especially Asian open bill stork. The visit of these birds is an indicator of onset of monsoon in the village as Open bill stork population concentrated near permanent aquatic habitat of the village in the beginning of monsoon, which can be properly explained with the available rainfall data. Villagers believe the rainfall and availability of food resources is related with the nest formation time and success of reproduction of the particular bird species. This unique co-existence of men and birds in the remote village may become a good conservation model for implementation in different parts of our country in future.

References

Ali, S., and Ripley, S.D., 1987. *Compact Handbook of the Birds of India and Pakistan together with those of Bangladesh, Nepal, Bhutan and Sri Lanka*. 2nd (ed.) New Delhi: Oxford University Press.

Bhandarkar, S.V. and Paliwal, G.T., 2014. Biodiversity and conservation status of water Birds in Shrungarbandh lake district Gondia, Maharashtra, India. *International Journal of Life Sciences*, **2**(3): 239-243.

Bromley, D.W., 1994. Economic dimensions of community-based conservation. In: *Natural Connections Western*, D. Wright, M. (eds.) Island Press, Washington DC.

Dhua, B., Mondal, R.P. and Dutta, T.K., 2013. Study of Anastomusoscitans (Boddaert) population in relation to rainfall and nest formation in Barachaka Village of Bankura District, West Bengal, India. *International Journal of Advanced Research*, **1**(9), 358-363.

Grimmett, R. and Inskipp, T., 2003. *OM Field Guide: Birds of Northern India*. Noida, India: OM Books International.

IUCN 2013. IUCN Red List of Threatened Species. Version 2013.1, www.iucnredlist.org.

Robson, C., 2000. *A Field Guide to the Birds of South-East Asia*. New Holland Publishers Ltd., UK., p. 504.

Vishwakarma, A., 2015. Anonymous bird Asian Open bill stork of Chhattisgarh, India. *International Journal of Multidisciplinary Research and Development*, **2**(2): 618-621.

27

Sustainable Development of Maithon Dam Site Tourism : A SWOT Analysis Approach

Susmita Sengupta and *Manika Saha*

Introduction

Over the years sustainability has been identified as an important 'niche' in the tourism literature with the capability to empower local rural communities to ensure development. This has brought about the term 'community-based tourism' ventures to distinguish those initiatives which are environmentally sensitive and also aim to ensure that members of local communities have a high degree of control over activities taking place and a significant proportion of the benefits accuring to them (Liu, 1996; Ceballos-Lascurain, 1996). Since 1980s, development of tourism has been given a high priority in the economic development of India at regional as well as national level. It bears the immense potential to create earning, generate employment, improving backward regions, minimize regional inequalities and help alleviating poverty in spite of the known adverse environmental, social and economic effects of development of mass tourism (Neto, 2003).

The concept of sustainable tourism development is deeply rooted in the concerns over the environmental consequences of rapid and unplanned mass tourism development (Sharpely, 2009). It revolves around the central issue of how to treat the natural and socio-cultural resources of host communities in order to elevate their economic well-being, sustain their natural and socio-cultural capital, gain intra and inter-generational equity in the distribution of costs and benefits, assure their self-sufficiency and satisfy the needs of the tourists. The principle of sustainable tourism include: minimizing environmental impacts, achieving conservation outcomes, reflecting community values, providing mutual benefits to visitors and hosts and building local capacity among others (Sharpley, 2009).

SWOT is an acronym used to describe the particular strengths, weaknesses, opportunities and threats that are strategic factors for an organization. A SWOT analysis is a simple but widely used tool that helps in understanding the strengths, weaknesses, opportunities and threats of an organization (Robbins and Coulter, 2012). In service quality literature, SWOT analysis appears either as gap analysis or as performance-importance comparison (Grigiriudis and Siskos, 2010). The extreme seasonal character of tourism at Maithon dam on the one hand and lack of proper infrastructural development of the area on the other generate an uncongenial effect on its environment. Hence proper planning and management is a prerequisite for the development of "ecologically and economically viable" tourism at the destination area.

The article is divided into four sections. Section two briefly presents the main objectives as well as the adopted methodology of the present study, section three emphasizes current tourism features in the study area and its main strengths (S), weaknesses (W), opportunities (O) and threats (T). Finally, the last part summarizes with some concluding remarks.

Objectives

The present chapter makes a modest effort in assessing tourism potentiality at Maithon Dam site in order to secure sustainability of tourism and empower local livelihoods economically. It dissects the strengths, weaknesses, opportunities and threats of the Maithon Dam site as a potential and existing tourist destination. The main focus is to highlight the strategic factors of Maithon Dam site as a sustainable tourist spot so that it can enable local people to have better access to tourists so that they can augment their livelihood through employment and small enterprise development

Methods and Data

The methodology employed in the present study is based on primary survey mainly. It was carried out through hotel occupancy survey, tourist questionnaire, observation schedule and field monitoring surrounding the dam site. The study entailed a survey of a purposively selected sample of 15 people from 10 purposively selected tourism-related establishments (hotels, fast food outlets, guest houses, auto drivers, boat operators, bus stands), and 300 visitors randomly selected from the site.

Field monitoring was done at the tourist site during peak tourist season. It includes observation survey as well as questionnaire survey of persons engaged directly or indirectly in tourism activity with particular reference to auto-driver, gateman at park-entrance and ferry-ghat, mobile vendors, small stall owners and local people directly engaged in tourism at the picnic spot. The purpose was to evaluate the level of infrastructural development at the tourism site in terms of attractions, accommodation and infrastructure (Fig. 27.1).

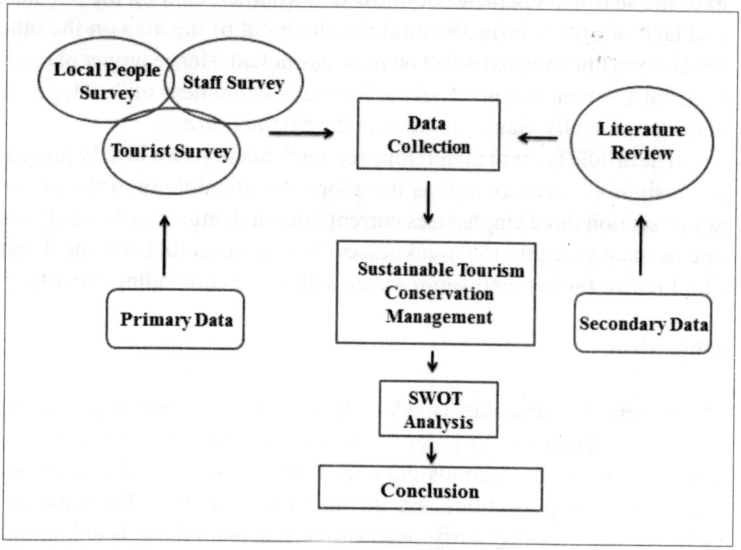

Fig. 27.1: Outline of the research methodology adopted

Secondary data utilized for the analysis included tourist flow at different seasons, revenue generated from ferry ghat services, connectivity through bus services to comprehend the present status of tourism at Maithon Dam site.

Area Identity

The Maithon Dam (Fig. 27.2) is a concrete-cum-earthen dam located in West Bengal and Jharkhand border of India on the Barakar River. The reservoir is spread over an area of 65 km². The dam site is enriched with blessings of nature. The presence of hillocks, dense forests and wildlife add colour to the nature's splendor. The area is connected through road with Asansol, the largest mining town in West Bengal (25 km) and with Dhanbad, largest mining agglomeration in Chhotonagpur plateau in Jharkhand (52 km). All the ingredients make a huge promise and prospects for the development of pleasure tourism around dam area. A few historic temples on the way to Maithon Dam have also aggravated its cultural value. Since, flood control, irrigation and water management being the main thrust area of DVC as well as its inter-state buffer location, dam's recreational importance has been neglected overall. Besides, social capital and human capital have not been utilized properly for integrated regional development in this area. Due to lack of planning and basic infrastructure, the dam site has become a place of seasonal pleasure tourism for picnic purposes mainly posing a threat to the natural environment.

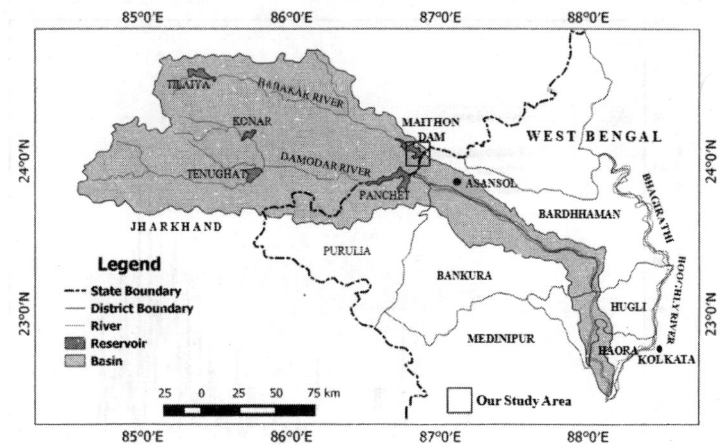

Fig. 27.2: Location Map

Present Status of Maithon Dam Site Tourism

At present, tourist activity developed at Maithon and its surroundings is based on dam, its scenic beauty and religious purposes out of which Maithon Dam is the central attraction. Another important place that attracts considerable number of tourists after Dam is Kalwaneswari Temple where people gather during different festive seasons separately and their main purpose is to visit the temple, dam gets the secondary option. Tourists coming from different parts of West Bengal get the opportunity to visit Ghaghorburi and Chandrachur temple on the transit route. Besides, Millennium Park (Jharkhand state), situated at West Bengal and Jharkhand border and Bhander Pahar are other destinations.

An overwhelming majority of the tourists is of domestic origin. A large segment of domestic tourists are same day visitors (85% to total tourists) who visit the spot for recreational purposes mainly. They are at best 'excursionist'; not 'tourist' because they do not stay 24 hours or more in the destinations. Remaining are night stay tourists coming for religious purposes mainly. Good connectivity from different corners of surrounding districts offers vast potentiality for tourism in the study area. The modes of travel used by the domestic tourists include bus, rented taxi, Tata Sumo, trekker and private car.

The flow of tourists at dam site is largely seasonal in character. Seasonality of ticket selling of a boating site at Maithon Dam proves that huge influx of tourists occurs during winter season mainly (Fig. 27.3).

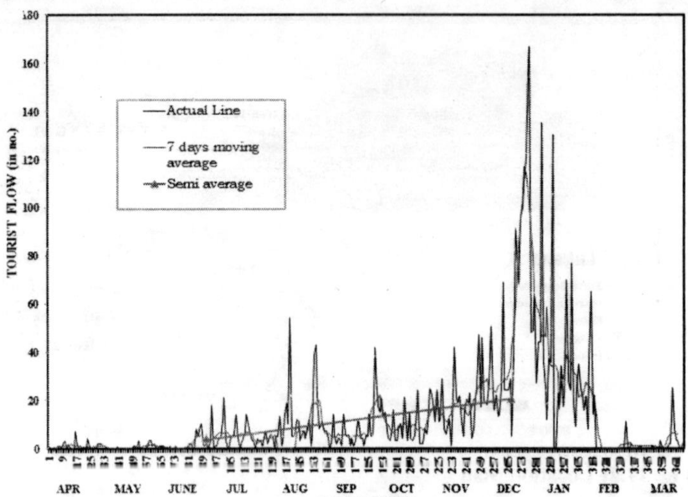

Fig. 27.3: Seasonality of ticket selling of a boating site at Maithon Dam

Source: Based on Field Survey by the Authors.

Monsoon months attract a few tourists to enjoy the beauty of discharge of voluminous water from Maithon Dam. Besides, flow at Christmas holidays, weekend holidays and National Holidays (e.g. Independence Day etc.) highly characterize the seasonality of tourism activity at Maithon Dam site (Fig. 27.4).

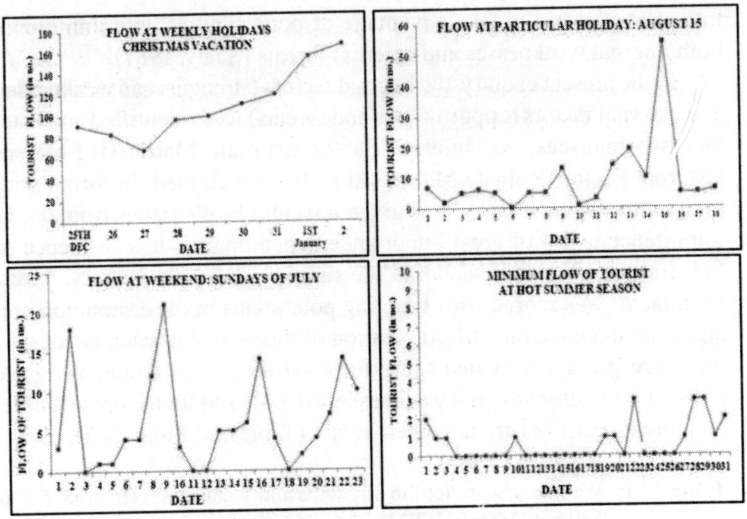

Fig. 27.4: Some instances of seasonality of tourist flow at Maithon Dam
Source: Based on Field Survey by the Authors.

There is little scope for villagers to trade with such visitors. With the increase in demand, a number of hotels and lodges are mushrooming surrounding the Kalyaneswari temple and dam site with its attendant business opportunities. During the peak season, villagers avail themselves of such low-paid opportunities as boat drivers, cooks, drinking water suppliers, sweepers, ticket sellers, street vendors, and as owners of small shops etc. which reflect very marginal in character. Extreme seasonality in tourist arrival throws a very little opportunity for a village household to depend entirely on tourism throughout the year.

SWOT Analysis of Maithon Dam site Tourism

The purpose of the strategic planning is to gather information about the internal and external environment. Internal environment is scanned to identify strengths or weaknesses whereas External environment is scanned to identify possible opportunities and threats. The SWOT analysis helps in analyzing the advantages and disadvantages of the present status of tourism prevailing in the Maithon Dam site and coming out with strategic suggestions for sustainable tourism as well as options for alternate livelihood development. SWOT analysis is intended to maximize strengths and opportunities, minimize external threats, transformation of weaknesses into strengths and to take advantage of opportunities with minimizing both internal weaknesses and external threats (Saaty, 1987).

In the present enquiry, the internal factors (strengths and weaknesses) and external factors (opportunities and threats) were identified and listed and two matrices, *viz.* Internal Factor Estimate Matrix (IFEM) and External Factor Estimate Matrix (EFEM) were formed. In formulating both matrices, each factor was given a weight (with grades from 0 – no importance to 1 – of great importance depending on their influence on the strategic planning) such that the sum in ach matrix is unity. Again, each factor was scored with 1 having poor status in the destination area and 5 having good one. Multiplication of the weight of each factor with the score gives a weighted score for each individual factor. Weighted scores for the strengths and weaknesses (IFEM) and for the opportunities and threats (EFEM) are tabulated below (Tables 27.1 and 27.2).

Table 27.1: Weighted Score for the Strengths and Weaknesses (Internal Factor Estimate Matrix: IFEM)

	Strengths	*Weight*	*Score*	*Weighted Score*
1	Scenic beauty, unique ecosystem, and rich biodiversity along with good weather and climate	0.1456	5	0.728
2	Religious attraction of Kalyaneswari Temple	0.1434	5	0.717
3	Ideal place for recreation, picnic and spending leisure hours	0.0832	4	0.3328
4	Sufficient number of domestic tourists	0.0866	4	0.3464
5	Good connectivity	0.0753	3	0.2259
6	Strategic location	0.0344	2	0.0688
7	Indigenous culture and hospitality of local people	0.0312	1	0.0312
	Weaknesses	*Weight*	*Score*	*Weighted Score*
1	Lack of proper infrastructure and basic facilities	0.0834	4	0.3336
2	Extreme seasonality of recreation tourism	0.1132	5	0.566
3	Poor accessibility (Poor flow of transport)	0.0636	4	0.2544
4	Low involvement of local people	0.0722	3	0.2166
5	Problems of solid waste disposal	0.0438	2	0.0876
6	Lack of strategies ensuring promotion and marketing of tourism	0.0241	3	0.0723
Total		**1.000**	**–**	**3.9806**

Source: Computed by the Authors.

In IFEM the total of weighted scores with a value of more than 2.5 indicate good strengths, similarly in case of EFEM the total weighted scores of more than 2.5 reveal good opportunities (Fig. 27.5).

Table 27.2: Weighted Score for the Opportunities and Threats (External Factor Estimate Matrix: EFEM)

	Opportunities	*Weight*	*Score*	*Weighted Score*
1	Proper tourism package development involving local people in decision-making and planning a possible option for alternate livelihood	0.1532	4	0.6128
2	Conserving natural ecosystem in the form of Eco-park, Butterfly Park, and Medicinal Garden.	0.1437	4	0.5748
3	Feasibility of implementing tourism plans in dam site, considering environmental requirements with emphasis on conserving native culture	0.0936	3	0.2808
4	High international interest for adventure tourism, rural tourism and ecotourism	0.0834	3	0.2502
5	Possibility to attract tourists by exploiting historical, cultural, spiritual and traditional inheritance (Pilgrimage tourism)	0.0734	2	0.1468
	Threats	*Weight*	*Score*	*Weighted Score*
1	Disturbance of the natural environment, pollution of air and water	0.1234	4	0.4936
2	Deforestation and soil erosion	0.1512	3	0.4536
3	Potential negative cultural and environmental impacts	0.0850	2	0.1700
4	Transport infrastructure not up to the standards and emergency medical services are unsatisfactory.	0.0621	3	0.1863
5	Leakage in revenue	0.0310	2	0.0620
Total		**1.000**	**–**	**3.2309**

Source: Computed by the Authors.

Sustainable development of tourism attempts to find a balance between these impacts to create a better quality of life for the host community and destination. Tourism and the environment are linked and interdependent. If tourism continues to grow, ways must be found to improve the relationship between the two, making it more sustainable.

Sustainable tourism and possible alternate livelihood option are the main pivot for Maithon Dam Site and to achieve this pair-wise matching (SO, WO, ST and WT) has been done. The incidence point of the internal and external factors of dam site clearly point towards strong internal factor estimate while high potential of sustainable tourism is suggested from external factor estimate.

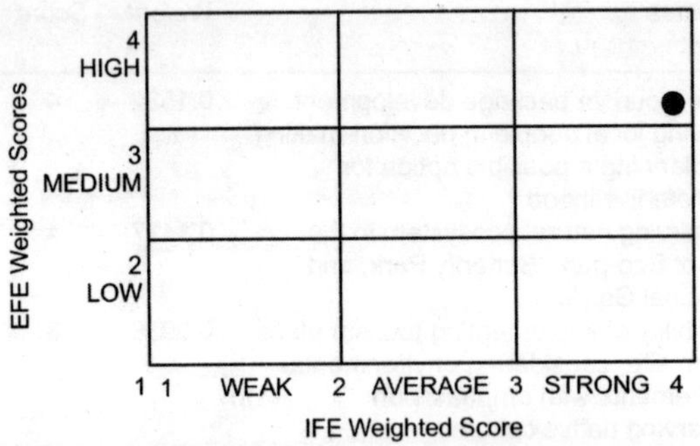

Fig. 27.5: The incidence point of the Internal and External Factors

Thus by comparing internal and external factors, sustainable alternate livelihood strategies through responsible tourism have been formulated as follows:

S-O Strategies: Proposed opportunities that fit with strengths

1 Establishment of welfare places and hotels which will help in creating jobs to the local people.

2 The use of regional potentials for conservation of natural ecosystem.

3 Developing new geographical markets especially attracting sustainable tourism from tourist generating markets.

4 Develop minimal entry fee plan to improve the basic facilities.

S-T Strategies: Use of Strengths to reduce its vulnerability to external threats

1 Sustainable Plan must be developed to avoid negative impacts of tourism on sensitive biodiversity.

2 Establishing facilities required to attract foreign tourists so that the image of the dam site can be improved.

3 Increasing environmental guard stations and patrols to improve conservational capacity.

W-O Strategies: To overcome weaknesses by pursuing opportunities

1. Facilitating the tours operated by tour operators with collaboration of local people.
2. Establishment of well-equipped wild-life watching site in different locations of the park.
3. Integration of solid waste management plan and rules and regulation for visitors.

W-T Strategies: To establish defensive plan to prevent weakness from external threats

1. Infrastructure development harmonized with population increase caused by tourist visits.
2. Environmental education to the people.
3. Investing to improve the quality of infrastructures, such as road transport systems, hospitality and accommodation centres, medical and health services, increasing accss to new technologies in the dam site.

Conclusions and Policy Implications

If tourism development is to be sustainable it must move away from its traditional growth-oriented model to one concerned with a sustainable set of goals and principles. Sustainable tourism must be seen as a goal in tourism development. Achieving such a goal is a difficult task to accomplish. However, developing tourism in a sustainable manner must be an important objective in the developing process.

It may be concluded that the recreational tourism at Maithon Dam site has not reached to its commercial level. The surrounding villages are poverty-stricken and live in a poor quality of life. Keeping this into the mind, proper planning and management must be undertaken for the development of 'responsible' tourism that enables local people to have better access to tourists so that they can improve their livelihood through employment and small enterprise development.

References

Ceballos-Lascurain (1996). *Tourism, Ecotourism and Protected Areas: The State of Nature-based Tourism Around the World and Guidelines for its Development*. IUCN Protected Area Programme Series. Island Press.

Grigiriudis, E. and Y. Siskos, 2010. *Customer Satisfaction Evaluation: Methods* for Measuring and Implementing Service Quality, Springer, New York.

Liu, Z. (2003). Sustainable Tourism Development: A Critique. *Journal of Sustainable Tourism*, 11 (6), pp 459-475.

Neto, F., 2003. A New Approach to Sustainable Tourism Development. ST/ESA/2003/DP/29. DESA Discussion Paper no. 29. Economic and Social Affairs, United Nations, New York.

Robbins, S.P. & Coulter, M. (2012). *Management*. New Jersey: Prentice Hall.

Saaty, R.W. (1987). The Analytic Hierarchy Process: What it is and How it is Used. *Mathematical Modelling*, 9: 161-176.

Sharpley R., 2009. *Tourism Development and the Environment: Beyond Sustainability*? London: Earthscan.

Index